Nietzsche and Kant as Thinkers of Antagonism

Also available from Bloomsbury:

Nietzsche's Engagements with Kant and the Kantian Legacy,
edited by Marco Brusotti, Herman Siemens, João Constâncio and Tom Bailey
Conflict and Contest in Nietzsche's Philosophy,
edited by Herman Siemens and James Pearson
Hope and the Kantian Legacy, edited by Katerina Mihaylova and Anna Ezekiel
'Twilight of the Idols' and Nietzsche's Late Philosophy, by Thomas H. Brobjer
The Parallel Philosophies of Sartre and Nietzsche, by Nik Farrell Fox

Nietzsche and Kant as Thinkers of Antagonism

Towards a Philosophy of Conflict

Herman Siemens

BLOOMSBURY ACADEMIC
LONDON • NEW YORK • OXFORD • NEW DELHI • SYDNEY

BLOOMSBURY ACADEMIC
Bloomsbury Publishing Plc, 50 Bedford Square, London, WC1B 3DP, UK
Bloomsbury Publishing Inc, 1359 Broadway, 12th Floor, New York, NY 10018, USA
Bloomsbury Publishing Ireland, 29 Earlsfort Terrace, Dublin 2, D02 AY28, Ireland

BLOOMSBURY, BLOOMSBURY ACADEMIC and the Diana logo
are trademarks of Bloomsbury Publishing Plc

First published in Great Britain 2024
This paperback edition published 2026

Copyright © Herman Siemens, 2024

Herman Siemens has asserted his right under the Copyright,
Designs and Patents Act, 1988, to be identified as Author of this work.

For legal purposes the Acknowledgements on p. xii constitute an
extension of this copyright page.

Cover illustration based on the painting San Dual by Jordi Gispert Pi

This work is published open access subject to a Creative Commons Attribution-NonCommercial-NoDerivatives 4.0 International licence (CC BY-NC-ND 4.0, https://creativecommons.org/licenses/by-nc-nd/4.0/). You may re-use, distribute, and reproduce this work in any medium for non-commercial purposes, provided you give attribution to the copyright holder and the publisher and provide a link to the Creative Commons licence.

Bloomsbury Publishing Plc does not have any control over, or responsibility for, any third-party websites referred to or in this book. All internet addresses given in this book were correct at the time of going to press. The author and publisher regret any inconvenience caused if addresses have changed or sites have ceased to exist, but can accept no responsibility for any such changes.

A catalogue record for this book is available from the British Library.

A catalog record for this book is available from the Library of Congress.

ISBN: HB: 978-1-3503-4715-1
PB: 978-1-3503-4719-9
ePDF: 978-1-3503-4716-8
eBook: 978-1-3503-4717-5

Typeset by Integra Software Services Pvt. Ltd.

For product safety related questions contact productsafety@bloomsbury.com.

To find out more about our authors and books visit www.bloomsbury.com
and sign up for our newsletters.

For my beloved sisters, Louise, Clara and Julie
in gratitude for their
unwavering love and unstinting support

Uns scheint es so, daß die disharmonische Welt existirt, jene Harmonie im Satz der Identität aber nichts als eine Theorie, eine Vorstellung ist. Kann man sich aber das Sich-Widersprechende als wirklich denken?
Nietzsche, 9[1] 8.136 (1876 commentary on Dühring's 'Der Werth des Lebens')

[T]he question of 'thinking' and the question of 'antagonism' should be treated on their own terms, but, at the same time, cannot be tackled separately.
(Oliver Marchart, Thinking Antagonism)

Wir wenden alle guten und schlechten gewöhnten Triebe gegen uns: das Denken über uns, das Empfinden für und gegen uns, der Kampf in uns – nie behandeln wir uns als Individuum, sondern als Zwei- und Mehrheit [...]
Nietzsche, 6[80] 9.215

Je me souviens de la devise d'un cemitiere, avec ce mot: P a x p e r p e t u a. Car les morts ne se battent point: mais les vivans sont d'une autre humeur: et les plus puissans ne repectent gueres les tribunaux
Leibniz to Jean-Leonor le Gallois de Grimarest, 4. Juni 1712

Contents

Acknowledgements — xii
Abbreviations and references for Kant's and Nietzsche's writings — xiii
Manner of citation — xv
Translations — xvi

Introduction — 1

1 The problem of contradiction and real opposition in Kant and Nietzsche — 17
   I Introduction — 17
      I.1 A short history of 'opposition' (*Gegensatz*) and 'contradiction' (*Widerspruch*) — 20
   II Kant's concept of negative magnitudes: Real vs. logical opposition — 22
      II.1 Kant's ontology of conflict — 25
      II.2 Further applications of real opposition — 27
      II.3 The source or ground of change — 28
      II.4 Kant's ontology of mental life — 29
      II.5 Real opposition between different bodies — 32
      II.6 Critique of logical causation — 33
      II.7 With or without substance? — 34
   III The problem of opposition and contradiction in Nietzsche's thought — 36
      III.1 Introduction — 36
      III.2 Nietzsche's ontology of conflict — 42
      III.3 Nietzsche's genealogy of logic — 46
      III.4 The ontology of mental life — 54
      III.5 From mechanism to physiology and wills to power — 57
      III.6 Nietzsche's critique of mechanism — 68
      III.7 The epistemology of conflict — 75
      III.8 Real opposition in Nietzsche's thought — 77

2 Waging war against war: Nietzsche *contra* Kant on conflict and the question of a living peace — 81
   I Introduction — 81
   II Eternal peace and the peace of the graveyard — 86

	III	Conflict unlimited and limited: Nietzsche's *Vernichtungskampf* and the *Wettkampf*	90
	IV	Kant's philosophical war of extermination against war	92
		IV.1 On the Polemical Use of Reason (KrV B 767 – B 810)	93
		IV.2 Sketch of a sketch: *Zum ewigen Frieden*	103
	V	Rethinking conflict as productive: Nietzsche's affirmative ideal	109
	VI	Nietzsche *contra* Kant, Kant *contra* Nietzsche	114
	VII	Approaching a living peace: A *Rapprochement*?	117
3	Health, sex and sovereignty: Nietzsche *contra* Kant on productive resistance		125
	I	Introduction	125
	II	Resistance in Nietzsche	126
		II.1 Affirmative senses of resistance	127
	III	Nietzsche vs. Kant on productive resistance	131
	IV	Freedom, respect for the law and the physiology of agency	138
4	Towards a new agonism? Nietzsche's 'fine, well-planned, thoughtful egoism' *contra* Kant's 'unsociable sociability'		151
	I	Introduction	151
	II	Kant: *ungesellige Geselligkeit*	153
		II.1 Unsociability and resistance	155
		II.2 Sociability and resistance	159
	III	Nietzsche on fine, well-planned, thoughtful egoism	163
		III.1 Nietzsche's critical diagnosis of the modern subject	166
		III.2 Thoughtful egoism *contra* unsociable sociability	171
		III.3 Thoughtful egoism and sovereignty: *contra* Spinoza	176
		III.4 Thoughtful egoism and our treatment of others	180
		III.5 Translating morality into knowledge	185
	IV	Hostile calm, calm hostility: Towards a new agonism?	190
5	Nietzsche's philosophy of hatred: Against and with Kant		195
	I	Introduction	195
	II	Nietzsche's philosophy of hatred	197
		II.1 Hatred in Nietzsche's ontology of conflict	199
		II.2 Agonal hatred *inter pares*	205
	III	Kant on hatred	210
		III.1 Hatred and ugliness	211
		III.2 Hatred and equality	213
		III.3 Hatred, justice and revenge	216

IV	The hatred of impotence and the spirit of revenge	218
V	Nietzsche's responses to the problem of hatred	225
VI	The slave revolt of morality and the problem of emancipation	231

Epilogue   239

Bibliography   251
Name Index   258
Subject Index   260

Acknowledgements

Much of the work on his book was made possible by the NWO Open Competition grant *Between deliberation and agonism: Rethinking conflict and its relation to law in political philosophy*, and the Internationalization grant *Towards a political ontology of violence: Reality, image and perception*. I also owe a debt of gratitude to Leiden University for the dispensation that allowed me to concentrate on research; I only wish the support had been consistent. To my graduate students for the stimulation provided by their questions and insights on the courses devoted to parts of the book and for forcing me to clarify my thought. And a special thanks to Jamie Pearson, my cum laude PhD student, with and from whom I learned a great deal about Nietzsche's philosophy of conflict.

Parts of Chapter 2 (in section IV and IV.2) draw on articles published in Spanish and Portuguese: 'Haciendo la Guerra a la Guerra: Nietzsche contra Kant a propósito del conflicto' (2014), *Revista Pléyade DOSSIER 'Vida, guerra, ontología: ¿Es posible la política más allá de la soberanía?'* 13: 87–106; 'Travando uma guerra contra a guerra: Nietzsche contra Kant acerca do Conflito' (2013), *Kriterion* 54/128: 419–37. Parts of Chapter 3 and 4 draw on: 'On Productive Resistance' (2019), in *Conflict and Contest in Nietzsche's Philosophy*, 23–43, H. Siemens and J. Pearson (eds), Bloomsbury: New York & London; and on 'Kant's "Respect for the Law" as "Feeling of Power": On (the Illusion of) Sovereignty', in *Nietzsche's Engagements with Kant and the Kantian Legacy*, M. Brusotti, H. Siemens, J. Constâncio and T. Bailey (eds), vol. II, *Nietzsche and Kantian Ethics*, 109–36, J. Constâncio and T. Bailey (eds), London and New York: Bloomsbury. Chapter 5 draws on 'Nietzsche's Philosophy of Hatred' (2015), *Tijdschrift voor Filosofie*, 77/4: 748–84.

On a personal note, I would like to thank my sisters, to whom this book is dedicated, and my beloved children, Zeno, Samu and Alina for the joy, pride and strength they have given me throughout my illness. Everything worthwhile I have done in the past thirteen years I owe to Katia Hay, the love of my life, to her fortitude, intelligence, her thousandfold care and to the influence of our continuous philosophical conversation on my thought … malgré le fin.

Abbreviations and references for Kant's and Nietzsche's writings

References to Kant's texts: follow the standard German abbreviations given in *Kant-Studien* and are listed here. The abbreviations are followed by the page or paragraph number(s) in the 'Akademie Ausgabe' (AA), for example, KU 5.238 (= AA vol. 5, p. 238), Anth 7.315–16 (= AA vol. 7, pp. 315–16).

References to Nietzsche's works follow the standard German abbreviations, as used in the *Kritische Studienausgabe* (= KSA: G. Colli and M. Montinari (eds), Munich and Berlin: DTV and De Gruyter 1980), with section/aphorism numbers and/or names, as appropriate; where necessary, page references are given (e.g. 3.42 = KSA vol. 3, p. 42). References to the *Nachlass*, also from the KSA, follow the notation therein (e.g. 2[13] 7.23 = note 2[13], KSA vol. 7, p. 23). Wherever possible, page numbers are to KSA; otherwise from other editions listed below:

BAW Nietzsche, F. (1933–40), Historisch-kritische Gesamtausgabe, Hans Joachim Mette/Carl Koch/Karl Schlechta (eds), Munich: C.H. Beck'sche Verlags- buchhandlung. Reprinted as: Frühe Schriften 1854–1869, Munich: DTV 1994.

KGW Nietzsche, F. (1967–), Werke. Kritische Gesamtausgabe, established by Giorgio Colli and Mazzino Montinari, continued by Wolfgang Müller-Lauter and Karl Pestalozzi (eds), Berlin/New York: De Gruyter.

KSB Nietzsche, F. (1986), Sämtliche Briefe. Kritische Studienausgabe in 8 Bänden, Giorgio Colli/Mazzino Montinari (eds), Munich/Berlin/ New York: DTV/De Gruyter.

Abbreviations or 'Siglen' for Nietzsche's Writings

AC	Der Antichrist. Fluch auf das Christenthum
EH	Ecce homo. Wie man wird, was man ist
EH (GT)	see GT
EH Schicksal	Warum ich ein Schicksal bin
FW	Die fröhliche Wissenschaft ('la gaya scienza')
GD	Götzen-Dämmerung oder Wie man mit dem Hammer philosophirt
GD Moral	Moral als Widernatur
GD Streifzüge	Streifzüge eines Unzeitgemässen
GM	Zur Genealogie der Moral. Eine Streitschrift
GT	Die Geburt der Tragödie

HW	Homer's Wettkampf
JGB	Jenseits von Gut und Böse. Vorspiel einer Philosophie der Zukunft
M	Morgenröthe. Gedanken über die moralischen Vorurtheile
MA	Menschliches, Allzumenschliches. Ein Buch für freie Geister. Erster Band
VM	(MA II) Erste Abtheilung: Vermischte Meinungen und Sprüche
WS	(MA II) Zweite Abtheilung: Der Wanderer und sein Schatten
Z	Also sprach Zarathustra. Ein Buch für Alle und Keinen

Abbreviations for Kant's Writings with Indication of the Corresponding AA Volume

Anth	Anthropologie in pragmatischer Hinsicht/Anthropology from a Pragmatic Point of View (AA 07)
BDG	Der einzig mögliche Beweisgrund zu einer Demonstration des Daseins Gottes/ The Only Possible Proof of God's Existence (AA 02)
GSE	Beobachtungen über das Gefühl des Schönen und Erhabenen/ Observations on the Feeling of the Beautiful and the Sublime (AA 02)
GSK	Gedanken von der wahren Schätzung der lebendigen Kräfte/ Thoughts on the True Estimation of Living Forces (AA 01)
IaG	Idee zu einer allgemeinen Geschichte in weltbürgerlicher Absicht/ Idea for a Universal History with a Cosmopolitan Aim (AA 08)
KpV	Kritik der praktischen Vernunft/Critique of Practical Reason (AA 05)
KrV	Kritik der reinen Vernunft/Critique of Pure Reason
KU	Kritik der Urteilskraft/Critique of the Power of Judgement (AA 05)
MAN	Metaphysische Anfangsgründe der Naturwissenschaften/ Metaphysical Foundations of Natural Science (AA 04)
MS	Die Metaphysik der Sitten/ Metaphysics of Morals (AA 06)
NG	Versuch, den Begriff der negativen Größen in die Weltweisheit einzuführen/Attempt to Introduce the Concept of Negative Magnitudes into Philosophy (AA 02)
NTH	Allgemeine Naturgeschichte und Theorie des Himmels/ Universal Natural History and Theory of the Heavens (AA 01)
TG	Träume eines Geistersehers, erläutert durch die Träume der Metaphysik/ Dreams of a Spirit-Seer (AA 02)
ZeF	Zum ewigen Frieden/ Towards Perpetual Peace (AA 08)

Manner of citation

As a rule, citations are in English in the main text, with the German in a footnote; only where the German formulations are particularly important are they placed below the English in the main text.

Emphases in English translations for both Nietzsche's and Kant's writings: normal emphases (= 'gesperrt' in KSA) are rendered in *italics*. Further emphases in Nietzsche's *Nachlass* ('halbfett' in KSA) are rendered in ***bold italics***.

Emphases in the original German for both Nietzsche's and Kant's writings: normal emphases (= 'gesperrt' in KSA) are rendered in e x p a n d e d s c r i p t. Further emphases in Nietzsche's *Nachlass* ('halbfett' in KSA) are rendered in **bold**.

Interventions/omissions: any interventions in citations by the author, including insertions of original German words or alternative translations, are indicated by square brackets: []. Any omissions by the author are also inserted in square brackets […] in order to distinguish them from Nietzsche's own ellipses. The same are used where the citation begins or ends in mid-sentence.

Translations

Translations are the author's, although use was also made of existing translations from the following publications:

For Nietzsche: *The Anti-Christ, Ecce Homo, Twilight of Idols* (2005), ed Aaron Ridley, trans Judith Norman, Cambridge: Cambridge University Press; *Writings from Late Notebooks* (2206), ed Rüdiger Bittner, trans Kate Sturge, Cambridge: Cambridge University Press; *On the Genealogy of Morality* (2007), ed Keith Ansell-Pearson, trans Carol Diethe, Cambridge: Cambridge University Press; *Twilight of the Idols/ The Anti-Christ* (1990), trans R. J. Hollingdale, London: Penguin; *Ecce Homo* (1992), trans R. J. Hollingdale, London: Penguin (1992); *Thus Spoke Zarathustra* (2005), trans Graham Parkes, New York: Oxford University Press; *Beyond Good and Evil: Prelude to a Philosophy of the Future* (2002) eds R.-P. Horstmann and J. Norman, trans Judith Norman, Cambridge: Cambridge University Press; *Unpublished Fragments from the Period of Thus Spoke Zarathustra* (Summer 1882–Winter 1883/84) (2019), trans Paul Loeb and David F. Tinslry, Stanford CA: Stanford University Press; Unpublished Fragments (Spring 1885–Spring 1886) (2020), trans Adrian Del Caro, Stanford CA: Stanford University Press.

For Kant: Immanuel Kant (1992), *Theoretical Philosophy 1755–1770*, ed & trans David Walford, Ralf Meerbote, Cambridge: Cambridge University Press; *The Critique of Pure Reason* (1929), trans Norman Kemp Smith, London: Macmillan; *Metaphysical Foundations of Natural Science* (1970), trans James Ellington, Indianapolis, IN: Bobbs-Merril; *Critique of Practical Reason* (2002), trans Werner S. Pluhar, Indianapolis: Hackett Publishing Company; *Anthropology from a Pragmatic Point of View* (2006), trans and ed Robert B. Louden, Cambridge University Press, Cambridge; Kleingeld, P., Waldron, J., Doyle, M.W., Wood, A. (eds) (2006), *Toward Perpetual Peace and Other Writings on Politics, Peace, and History*. New Haven: Yale University Press. *Religion within the Bounds of Bare Reason* (2009), trans Werner S. Pluhar, Indianapolis: Hackett Publishing Company; The Metaphysics of Morals (1991), trans Mary Gregor, Cambridge: Cambridge University Press.

Introduction

I Introducing the philosophy of conflict

This book is an experiment in the philosophy of conflict. By the philosophy of conflict, I mean most broadly a willingness to keep open the question of conflict; not to foreclose it by reducing it to contingent phenomena, disruptions to be resolved or remedied in favour of concord or consensus. In this book I take a primarily ontological approach to the question. An ontology of conflict, as I understand it, is the view that conflict cannot be reduced to local disturbances in otherwise co-operative, peaceful relations; it is ineradicable and all-pervasive, because it is constitutive of relations in all domains of reality, often with destructive, devastating or oppressive consequences, especially for our social and political relations, but also potentially constructive of new capacities, new relations and settlements. With an ontology of this kind in place, I believe we have a viable basis for rethinking and re-evaluating conflict.

The experiment comes out of a dissatisfaction with contemporary democratic theory, in specific, mainstream 'deliberative' theories and 'agonistic' theories that have been marshalled against them in the last twenty years or so. While deliberative theories – as charged by agonists – suppress the ineliminable, constitutive and potentially constructive moment of conflict in democratic relations for fear of its destructive consequences, agonistic theories are marked by weak and problematic notions of conflict. In order to address these shortcomings, and to stimulate more fruitful exchanges between these camps, the experiment is to go back their sources in Kant (for deliberative theories) and Nietzsche (for agonisms), and to rethink them *as philosophers of conflict*. It is striking how deliberative theorists suppress, soften or ignore the tremendous importance given by Kant to conflict on many levels, from 'unsociable sociability' to war, for the advancement of human reason and freedom. It is equally striking how agonists have not felt the need to interrogate the notion of measured, constructive conflict, which they take from Nietzsche's account of the ancient Greek agon, in relation to the unmeasured, destructive potentials of conflict that mark 'the relational character of all occurrence' in his ontology of wills to power. By examining how both philosophers think conflict as part of the 'deep structure' of reality at all levels, my hope is open a space for a genuine engagement (including disagreement!) between deliberative and agonistic theories of democracy. As philosophers of conflict, Kant and Nietzsche raise fundamental questions concerning the constitutive, constructive and destructive potentials of conflict, opposition and contestation, which we can ill afford to ignore in thinking about the state of democracy today, and how best to address it theoretically.

The focus of this book is not, however, democratic theory; its aim, rather, is to lay the groundwork for a renewed discussion of conflict and democracy by considering the questions raised by their philosophies of conflict and comparing their responses. How to think conflict and contradiction as an ineradicable reality without thought being confounded and hollowed out by contradictions? What kinds of negation make for contradiction in thought and in real contradiction? How to understand the passage from senseless, destructive conflict to a constructive order of things? How can the relation between war and peace be thought in a way that makes for a living peace, not the peace of the graveyard? What makes for forms of conflict that break with the logic of destruction and are productive of new orders and settlements? What does it take for resistance to act, not as an inhibitor to be suffered or removed, but as a stimulant, a spur to freedom? Need hatred always be a source of destructive energy in destructive conflict, or can it under certain conditions be a creative and affirmative force? These are just some of the questions to be discussed in the course of the book.

Prima facie, Kant and Nietzsche are implacably opposed, as the celebrated philosopher of 'eternal peace', and the philosopher of conflict *par excellence*, respectively. In this book, however, my contention is that Kant, no less than Nietzsche, engages in a re-evaluation or transvaluation (*Umwerthung*) of conflict grounded in two claims: that conflict is an *ineradicable* dimension of reality at all levels, from ontology to social life, culture, politics and ethics; and that conflict is not merely *destructive* and oppressive in its consequences, but houses prodigious, and immensely valuable *productive* powers. In Nietzsche's philosophy, conflict is not just a recurrent theme, but a dynamic and structural principle that cuts across the different domains of his thought and acts as a moving centre of gravity throughout his philosophical development. He has a highly differentiated understanding of conflict and struggle, and a rich vocabulary to match it (*Agon, Auseinandersetzung, Concurrenz, Dissonanz, Gegensätzlichkeit, Kampf, Konflikt, Krieg, Streit, Wettkampf, Wettspiel, Wettstreit, Widerspruch, Wiederstreit, Zwist, Zwietracht, Zwiespalt*, i.a.). Conflict, struggle and tension are best known for the integral role they play in Nietzsche's dynamic understanding of life or reality in his later thought. In the language of force, life *is* only relations of tension: attraction-repulsion, action-resistance, commanding-obeying among forces without substance; conflict or tension is the manner in which relations are formed and transformed. In the language of will to power, the basic and pervasive character of life at all levels consists of a plurality of life-forms or power-complexes struggling to overcome and extend themselves against the resistance offered by competing forms of life equally bent on self-overcoming and expansion.

What is less well known is how conflict also plays an essential role across the various domains of Kant's thought. This is already evident in his early metaphysics, where Kant develops a dynamic concept of matter as a conflict of forces (*Streit der Kräfte*) around the key concept of real (as distinct from logical) opposition or

'Realrepugnanz',[1] with ramifications in social life (*ungesellige Geselligkeit*),[2] in animal life or health (*continuirliches Spiel des Antagonismus* between the advancement and inhibition of life),[3] in ethics (*Neigung zum Wohlleben und Tugend im Kampfe*; *Tugend* as *die moralische Gesinnung im Kampfe*; as a *Kampf gegen die Einflüsse des bösen Princip im Menschen*),[4] taste (*über den Geschmack läßt sich streiten (obgleich nicht disputiren)*),[5] and Reason (metaphysics as a *Kampfplatz endloser Streitgkeiten*),[6] to name some. In short, Kant has a wide-ranging, differentiated understanding of conflict and, like Nietzsche, a rich vocabulary of conflict to match (*Kampf, Disput, Kontroverse, Gezänk, Ungeselligkeit, Streit, conflictus, Polemik, concordia discors, discordia concors*).[7] He deserves – no less than Nietzsche – to be called a philosopher of conflict.

In broad terms the affirmative and productive senses of conflict in Kant can be placed under four overlapping headings:

1. Conflict as a constitutive principle. This applies to ontological domains (Conflict as constitutive of matter, animal life, social life, etc.), but also to normative ideals (constitutive of humanity, virtue, taste, ideal health);
2. Conflict as a stimulant, motive or driving force: a *Triebfeder der Kultur*, as the key to the development of human capacities;
3. Conflict as an organizing/re-organizing and directive principle, generating both inner organization (e.g. of a people into a state) and outer dynamic order or equilibrium among antagonistic instances or forces;
4. Conflict as a constructive, productive or creative principle: productive of humanity, culture, art, of equality and freedom under the rule of law and even – eternal peace.

All four issues offer rich seams of comparison with Nietzsche's philosophy of conflict; among other things, they reveal Kant to be, like Nietzsche, an analogical thinker by instinct, able to pick out similar antagonistic structures across different domains of reality and thought. My aim in this book is to offer a series of text-based comparative analyses of Kant's and Nietzsche's thought on conflict in these senses, with a view towards addressing my central question:

What does it take to think conflict, real opposition or contradiction as an intrinsic dimension of reality at all levels?

---

[1] *Versuch über den Begriff der negativen Grösse* (= NG) II.198, II.172, 175; BDG II.86.
[2] 'Unsociable sociability'. See TG II.334 and IaG VIII.20.
[3] 'Continuous play of *antagonism*' (Anth VII.231).
[4] 'Inclination to good living and virtue in struggle' (Anth VII.277); 'virtue' as 'moral disposition in struggle' (KprV V.84); as a 'struggle against the evil principle in the human being' (MS VI.440).
[5] 'Of taste there is conflict (although no dispute)' (KdU V.338).
[6] 'battleground of endless disputes' (KrV A VIII).
[7] See Saner (1967 90f., 106f., 118, 121).

Or as Nietzsche puts it:

Kann man sich aber das Sich-Widersprechende als wirklich denken? (9[1] 8.136)

But can one think the self-contradictory as real?

My principal interest, as these questions indicate, is *how to think* conflict, opposition or contradiction as a reality, or rather: how contradiction or opposition in our *manner* of thinking relates to the *matter* of our thought when we try to think reality as contradictory or conflictual. The question of antagonism, posed as an ontological question, implicates the manner of our thinking in the matter of our thinking in a particularly acute way. In Foucault's well-known words, post-Kantian continental philosophy involves 'an ontology of the present, of present reality, an ontology of modernity, an ontology of ourselves' (Foucault 2011 20–1). In refusing to abstract the subject from the object of knowledge for the sake of an 'analytic of truth', thinking comes to be situated in the field of interrogation. This means that our manner of interrogation is implicated in the ontology of conflict and cannot be separated from the question of conflict (Marchart 2018 5). The problem here, as the above question posed by Nietzsche indicates, can be focused on the notion of contradiction, logical opposition or what Kant calls *Repugnanz*: What is the status of logical contradiction or *Repugnanz* in a world structured by real contradiction or *Realrepugnanz*? Is thinking, so to speak, swallowed up by *Realrepugnanz*, so that we cannot think antagonism without contradicting ourselves, i.e. cannot think it at all? Or can, indeed *must* logical contradiction, as a species of negation, be distinguished from the negativity of real contradiction, so that the former can be denied and the latter affirmed? If so, we may be able to think without contradiction – to negate contradiction in thought while affirming it in reality, without falling into contradiction. But does that not imply that thinking, confined to logical contradiction/non-contradiction, will inevitably fall short of real contradiction? We are, it seems, confronted by two alternatives: either thinking is swallowed up by real contradiction, or thinking necessarily falls short of thinking real contradiction. Is this, then, a dead end – or does it describe the extremes *within which* thinking can operate, the extremes that thinking must approximate without ever touching? The first alternative means taking the ontology of conflict seriously at the risk of failure, the second means taking thinking seriously at the risk of it biting its own tail.

As my point of departure for tackling these questions, I take Kant's pre-critical essay *Attempt to Introduce the Concept of Negative Magnitudes into Philosophy* from 1763.[8] In this essay he breaks with the harmonistic tendencies of European rationalism by introducing, for the first time, the notion of radical negativity into philosophy. He does so by distinguishing logical contradiction or opposition from real contradiction or opposition (*Realrepugnanz*) on the basis of two distinct types of negation. The result of Kant's argumentation is of fundamental importance for the philosophy of

---

[8] *Versuch den Begriff der negativen Größen in die Weltweisheit einzuführen.*

conflict and applies no less to Nietzsche than to him. It can be put in the following four propositions or positions, which summarize the problem of thinking reality as intrinsically conflictual or contradictory:

1. If logical contradiction is impossible, and if real contradiction is understood as logical contradiction, it is impossible to think reality as contradictory.
2. If real contradiction is possible and actual, and logical contradiction is thought as real opposition, then it is impossible to think reality as contradictory without contradiction: real contradiction swallows up discourse.
3. So whether we model real contradiction on logical contradiction or logical contradiction on real contradiction: either way it is impossible to think reality as contradictory. For a philosophy of conflict to be possible, therefore, logical contradiction must be distinguished from real contradiction, such that while the first is impossible – making coherent thought possible – the second (real contradiction) is both possible and actual. In this way, our manner of thinking (contradiction is impossible) and the matter of our thinking (contradiction is both possible and actual) do not contradict one another.
4. On the other hand, distinguishing logical from real contradiction and accepting the constraint of non-contradiction in thought has the consequence that we cannot really grasp or describe real contradiction in its concrete facticity: if logical contradiction does not describe real contradiction, this goes even more so for the requirement for non-contradiction in thought. The best we can do is *hinweisen auf*, point towards a reality that resists or withdraws from thought.

Through a comparative study of Kant's *Realrepugnanz* with the notion of opposition (*Gegensatz*) at the centre of Nietzsche's philosophy of power, I argue, in the opening chapter, that, in different ways and for different reasons, both thinkers adhere to these propositions.

I.1 Comparing Nietzsche and Kant

In any worthwhile comparative study, it is essential not to efface fundamental differences for the sake of emphasizing similarities or analogies. In our case, it is indisputable that Kant and Nietzsche take their normative bearings in radically different, not to say opposed ways. For Kant it is well known that philosophy must take its normative principles from pure (practical) reason, understood as an autonomous faculty in all of us with its own constitution, principles and laws. In Nietzsche's case it is much less clear, and there is nothing like a standard or broadly accepted interpretation among scholars. Even if almost everything he writes carries a normative charge, *pro* or *contra*, he rarely issues a direct imperative or 'ought' that is not ironic or paradoxical (provided we do not confuse Nietzsche with Zarathustra). I will therefore set out what I take to be his normative impulses or commitments in this book.

Throughout the book I take Nietzsche's philosophy to be driven by a life-long commitment to the affirmation and enhancement of life. His vocation to be a philosopher of life comes, at least initially, from his negatively derived one-world hypothesis, sparked off by his early engagement with the pre-Socratics, and Heraclitus in particular. With regard to morality and values, around which his thought comes increasingly to gravitate, this means overcoming the self-understanding of morality as sovereign and transcendent by rethinking values from a radically immanent standpoint in nature or life.[9] This project takes ever sharper contours with the critique of Christianity as 'Anti-nature', in favour of a 'naturalism of morality': '[M]y task is to translate the seemingly emancipated moral values that have become *nature-less* back into their nature – i.e., into their natural "immorality"';[10] or more bluntly: 'Fundamental principle: to be like nature.'[11] This involves *first* a *critical-genealogical* project to collapse the normative domain onto the plane of immanence by translating moral concepts and values from the language of reason and morality into of the (physiological, social, political) language of body, the drives, individual and collective conditions for existence.[12] Genealogy, Nietzsche's most sophisticated critical method, deals with really lived or 'grey' values, the life-forms or types (individual and collective) that produce them and which they inform, guide and sustain, as well as the broader (socio-physiological-political) conditions under which they emerge and thrive. In effect, he reorients philosophical reflection on moral values from the autonomous domain claimed by morality and moral philosophy – what he calls '*ignorance* of physics or in *contradiction* with it' (FW 335 3.564) – towards their socio-physiological conditions in the body (politic). But Nietzsche's 'naturalism of morality' also involves *practical-normative project* to reconstruct moral values and modes of practical engagement in terms that acknowledge (*Erkennen und Anerkennen*), affirm and enhance life or nature in its highest forms.

Nietzsche's commitments to life-affirmation and -enhancement articulate, in ethical or normative terms, the aspiration to rethink our values from a radically immanent perspective in life, with its dynamic of intensification, enhancement and overcoming. But no doubt they are also a response to what he learns from his genealogies of European – i.e. Christian-Platonic – values: that they derive from, and sustain, forms of life and willing that are turned against life and specifically: its sources in the body, the drives and the passions. Moreover, two thousand years of life-negation, he contends, have had devastating consequences for those forms life issuing in a pathology designated as 'nihilism', 'degeneration' and 'décadence', and diagnosed variously as: moral bankruptcy; the death of God and the ensuing crisis of authority; the devaluation of our highest values; the loss of 'organizing powers' and its consequences in processes of disgregation, dissolution (*Auflösung*), exhaustion (*Erschöpfung*) and an incapacity to create or 'posit productively a goal for oneself' (9[35], 12.350f.); the depletion of voluntaristic

---

[9] See Herschbell and Nimis (1979); Busch (1989 271ff.); Hölscher (1977).
[10] '[M]eine Aufgabe ist, die scheinbar emancipirten und n a t u r l o s gewordenen Moralwerthe in ihre Natur zurückzuübersetzen – d.h. in ihre natürliche "Immoralität"' (9[86] 12).
[11] 25[309] 11.91.For Christianity as 'Anti-nature': GD Widernatur 4 6.85.
[12] For the body: 7[150] 10.291. For the drives: 7[76] 10.268. For conditions for existence: 10[157] 12.545f.; 14[158] 13.343; 14[105] 13.283. See also: 4[67] 9.115; 25[460] 11.135; 26[38] 11; JGB 188; 9[86] 12.380.

resources; the debilitation and contraction (*Verkleinerung*) of the human being. It is against this background that Nietzsche's project of transvaluation (*Umwertung*) must be understood: as an attempt to raise life as the highest value against life-negating values, to take the side of life, its affirmation and enhancement, so as to question, resist and overcome the forms of life-negation underpinning Christian-Platonic values and their devastating consequences for the value and quality of those life-forms.

Nietzsche's philosophy of conflict is a consequence of his life-long effort to think from a radically immanent standpoint in life, since conflict is the way relations are formed and transformed. But it is also a consequence of an ethical impulse, which in a sense he shares with Kant. If Nietzsche's 'naturalism of morality' gives us a measure of what divides him from Kant, he also shares – in a different shape and form – two impulses with Kant as a philosopher of conflict: *realism* and *perfectionism*. Kant's realism is best known from his historical-political texts, IaG and ZeF, where he takes the view that hatred and antagonism are not to be rooted out of human behaviour and interaction; that our hostile inclinations, ambition, tyranny and greed (*Ehrsucht, Herrschsucht, Habsucht*) drive human behaviour inevitably towards conflict. No doubt Kant has strategic reasons for his Hobbesian presuppositions – to show that even if we assume the worst of humankind, there is still reasonable hope for sustained peace under the banner of 'eternal peace'. Then there are the worldly politicians, the men of experience, addressed in the Preface to ZeF, who must be shown that his idea of peace is not just a 'sweet dream of the philosopher'. But I believe Kant is genuinely troubled, like Nietzsche, by the non-appearance of the idea of freedom in reality. And in response, he formulates the radical thesis that the very capacities and passions that lead to conflict – considered *evil* from the standpoint of pure practical Reason – are the motor of cultural and political development that makes rational insight into the moral law and freedom under the rule of law possible. Our hostile inclinations are prodigiously productive for Kant, and necessary for the *perfectibility* of the species (IaG 4 VIII.21–2); they are what give us reasonable hope that society can be transformed into a 'moral whole' (ibid.).

The hallmark of Nietzsche's philosophy – and one of its most appealing qualities – is the way in which it combines unflinching realism with unremitting perfectionism; the hard, ugly truths of Nietzsche's philosophy of life, truths that he says *cannot be lived with*,[13] with the demand to enhance life, to experiment with ourselves so as to extend the range of human capacities and discover new 'possibilities of life' or arts of living.[14] Ugly truths, truths that cannot be lived with, and new arts of living: this captures the twin impulses, necessary and impossible at once, to which Nietzsche's thought responds. Throughout his writings he attempts time and again to negotiate the conflict

---

[13] On the ugliness of truth, see especially: 16[40] 13.500; 16[30] 13.491; 11[108] 13.51; 41[67] 8.593; GM I 1 5.258 and GT 7 1.56f. on how the Greeks turned the horror and absurdity of existence into the sublime and the comic, as 'representations with which one can live'.

[14] On the pre-Socratic philosophers as discoverers of 'neue Möglichkeiten des Lebens', see 6[48] 8.115–18 and MA 261 2.217. See also 17[44] 8.304 and 6[359] 9.288 on the discovery of new possibilities of life. On Nietzsche as a teacher of the art of living, see: Schmid (2010); Dohmen (2008, 2000). For a sceptical response, see van Tongeren (2012).

or tension between these twin impulses in different ways. Nietzsche's realist impulse first comes to light in his youthful engagement with Schopenhauer and archaic Greek culture, and culminates in his philosophy of conflict. While taking on the ugly truths of Schopenhauer's theoretical pessimism and fusing them with his knowledge of Greek pessimism, he refuses Schopenhauer's practical pessimism of life-negation in favour of the affirmative impulses he discovers in the Greeks. Indeed, it is the Greeks who first show him how the tension between realism and perfectionism can be negotiated. While contending that every Greek was in his heart of hearts a tyrant ('The gods make human beings even more evil; that is human nature': 5[117] 8.71), he advances the contest or 'agon', an archaic Greek institution in which a plurality would-be-tyrants competing creatively for great deeds and works act as a protective measure against the tyranny of one.[15] In the course of this book, we will see how Nietzsche confronts the horrifying, destructive consequences of unmeasured conflict, as a necessary ingredient in life disclosed by his realism, and looks for ways to delimit and describe productive forms of measured conflict that would advance human perfectibility.

I.2 The texts

For Kant, I draw mainly on the 1763 essay NG and other pre-critical texts, as well his historical-political essays, IaG and ZeF, and his *Anthropology*. With this selection of texts, I believe we can see well the formative and enduring influence of his philosophy of conflict on his thought. For Nietzsche, I take my bearings from the philosophy of power, inaugurated by his turn to physiology in the early 1880s, which I argue has nothing to do with scientific realism or biologism, but is an ontology of conflict predicated on a series of negations of the metaphysics of being and substance ontology. These are criticized and rejected by Nietzsche on the grounds that they fail to account for change and spontaneous, creative activity, and he tries his hand at various 'manners of speech' (*Sprecharten*) that would do a better job in line with his anti-metaphysical presuppositions. For this project, he draws extensively on a range of contemporary physiologists, using, combining, adapting their conceptual vocabularies to develop his own physio-ontology of change, which comes into its own with the discourse of will to power. The most important texts in this regard are in Nietzsche's *Nachlass*, on which I draw extensively in this book. The notebooks, on which it is based, contain a hotch-potch of notes on a great variety of subjects, and some scholars question their significance for Nietzsche's philosophical project(s). But I think this is wrong. As I hope to show, the *Nachlass* is a treasure-house of experimental philosophical thought, the laboratory of an extraordinary mind, and while it is hazardous to base an interpretation on a single note, with a thorough study of the notebooks we begin to see patterns in what seems to be haphazard. A single note may be a dead end without any bearing on Nietzsche's cardinal problems, but a series of notes that revolve around the same problem from different perspectives is no accident. It tells us something

---

[15] On the tyrannical desires of the Greeks, see 6[77] 8.99 and MA 261 2.214. Also: 4[301] 9.174; 6[28] 8.109. On the Greek agon, see HW 1.783–92, esp. 789.

important, which may or may not come to light in published works, but deserves in either case to be reconstructed. None of this is to deny conflicting or contradictory positions taken in different notes, or dead ends that did not come to light for good reason, or the element of accident and entropy in the notebooks. But that does not detract from the extraordinary lucidity and directness with which he tackles some of the cardinal problems of his thought in the *Nachlass*. In this book, I have endeavoured to discuss notes, which I take to be part of larger patterns or complexes of thought that Nietzsche is developing in the notebooks at this stage of thought.

I.3 State of the art

While deliberative theorists of democracy tend to pass over Kant's views on the necessity of hostility and danger for human self-realization, important work on his views on war (Saner 1967), resistance (Muthu 2014), unsociable sociability (Schneewind 2015; Wood 2015) and real opposition (van der Kuijlen 2009, 2017; Schnepf 2001; Wolff 2017; Zinkin 2012) has been done by Kant scholars. Saner's book, *Kants Weg vom Krieg zum Frieden*, deserves a special mention for his thorough examination of Kant's vocabulary and changing understandings of conflict. As the title indicates Kant's work is interpreted as a trajectory from conflict to unity free of conflict, as a goal to be approximated but never attained as such. Saner's main aim is to show that Kant's political thought is the moving centre of his entire thought from the very beginning by arguing that key political concepts and forms of thought from his mature thought are prefigured in his early metaphysics. In specific, a series of analogies are drawn, rather ingeniously, between dynamic structures in his early thought and his later political thought: between his monadology and the concept of unsociable sociability; between the commerce of substances and the establishment of civil society; and between real opposition in bodies and the function of war and radical evil in history, among others.[16] To his credit, Saner also points out where these analogies break down, particularly in Kant's philosophy of law, which is grounded in morality and excludes conflict. As a student of Jaspers, Saner criticizes Kant's identification of philosophy as a science (*Wissenschaft*) and argues that he should have transposed the antinomies of aesthetic judgement onto the entire field of philosophy, displacing unity with conflict as the governing principle of non-dogmatic thought (Saner 1967 112). It is, however, questionable whether this would not have imploded the entire critical project. Apart from this attempt to save Kant from himself, much of what follows in this book is broadly in line with Saner's interpretation, especially where Kant's concept of conflict is seen to produce its own negation (Chapter 2), what Saner calls the 'Zerstörung der Zerstörung' (op. cit. 26f.).

In Nietzsche's case, as noted in the Introduction to *Conflict and Contest in Nietzsche's Philosophy* (Bloomsbury 2019), many scholars have pointed to the importance of struggle, war and rivalry in his thought. A systematic study of conflict, as an integral part of his philosophy, especially his philosophy of power, and as a dynamic and structural

---

[16] See Saner (1967 73f.) for a summary.

principle across different domains of his thought, was first made by James Pearson in his 2018 PhD thesis 'Nietzsche's Philosophy of Conflict and the Logic of Organisational Struggle' (revised in Pearson 2022). Regarding comparative research on Nietzsche and Kant, inroads have been made by a few scholars (e.g. Volker Gerhardt 1988, 2005), and a start on more comprehensive approach was made in the three-volume set I co-edited: *Nietzsche's Engagements with Kant and the Kantian Legacy* (Bloomsbury 2017). What has not been done is to read both Nietzsche and Kant as thinkers of conflict and study the astonishing intersections, affinities and analogies between them despite their profound differences. If the diagnosis of the impasse in current democratic theory offered above is correct, the value of this work speaks for itself.

I.4 The book

The **opening chapter** introduces the philosophies of conflict in both thinkers and is consequently the longest. For Kant I concentrate on the ontology of conflict set out in his pre-critical essay *Versuch den Begriff der negativen Größen in die Weltweisheit einzuführen* (1763); for Nietzsche, on the physio-ontology he develops from 1880 on, culminating in the will to power. Both thinkers, I argue, face the difficulty of thinking reality as contradictory or conflictual without falling prey to rampant contradictions in their thought, and they address it by distinguishing the meaning and structure of 'contradiction' in thought and speech (logical contradiction) from real contradiction or opposition. In *negativen Größen* Kant tackles this by distinguishing the kind of negation involved in logical contradiction or *logische Repugnanz* (as impossible or unthinkable), from that involved in real opposition or *Realrepugnanz* (as possible and actual): in the first, negation means 'lack' or 'absence' (*Mangel, Abwesenheit, defectus, absentia*) in line with the tradition, leaving '*nothing at all*': 'g a r n i c h t s (*nihil negativum irrepraesentabile*)'; in the second, negation is thought as *nihil privativum*: as privation or cancellation (*Beraubung, Aufhebung*) of the consequences of what it negates. And it can only do so, according to Kant, as a *positive force that resists its opposite*. Kant goes on to identify the latter, in the form of the conflict between the forces of attraction and repulsion as the principle of reality governing everything: intra- and inter-monadic relations, impenetrability and the interaction of bodies, mental life, the regularity and very perfection of the universe. The notion of real opposition is not, however, restricted to his early metaphysics, but continues to play a key role in his thought, as I show in the course of the book: in the notions of equilibrium (Chapter 2), unpleasure (Chapter 3), unsociable sociability (Chapter 4) and hatred (Chapter 5).

Kant's essay begins with the manifest intention to contribute to rationalist metaphysics by introducing the notion of negation as privation, but it ends by problematizing causation in a way that threatens to undermine metaphysics altogether. At stake in this text is ultimately the same question behind Nietzsche's philosophy of conflict: change, and the cause or 'real ground' of change. And both thinkers share the insight into the *relational sources of change in conflict*. But Nietzsche departs from Kant in rejecting mechanism and the dyadic model of attraction and repulsion in favour of a pluralistic, multi-layered notion of real opposition among entities without substance, informed by physiology and ultimately will to power. His project is further complicated by two factors. While Kant breaks the rationalist equation of logic and reality and restricts logic to thought, Nietzsche develops a full-blown critique of the logical principles of identity and non-contradiction (to which he nonetheless adheres in his thought); and while affirming the reality of contradiction or opposition (*Gegensatz*) in some contexts, in others he denies it in favour of degrees, grades or 'valeurs'.

In order to make sense of Nietzsche's philosophy of conflict, I undertake to distinguish three different senses of the term 'opposition' or 'Gegensatz' in his usage. First there is 'opposition' in the logical and metaphysical sense (Ggz I), in which the terms are mutually exclusive and have nothing in common; they are constructed through the separation and fixing (*Feststellung*) of the terms into self-identical, durable items or entities. Then there is Nietzsche's reinterpretation of Ggz I (Ggz II.1), in which the terms are not mutually exclusive, but genealogically related (*verwandt*), and the higher valued term is derivative of its apparent 'opposite'. Thus, reason (*Vernünftiges*) comes from unreason (*Vernunftlosem*); logic derives from the illogical, and so forth. Through genealogy (GM) and historical philosophizing (MA 2), these relations are exposed, radically transforming the meaning and value of things we value; they cease to have their own origin and are bound up instead with their 'opposites', as their 'sublimations' (MA 1), 'refinements', 'degrees' or later 'stages'. In the third place, Nietzsche takes it upon himself to defend the oppositional or contradictory character of reality against the claims of logic and metaphysics. For this he reinterprets 'opposition' in an ontological register (Ggz II.2) as the antagonism (*Gegeinander*) of a plurality of force quanta or powers without substance in unceasing transformation, whose essence is their relation of overpowering one another. This is Nietzsche's version of *Realrepugnanz* or real opposition, and in order to understand it, it is necessary to reconstruct his critique of logic, metaphysics and substance ontology, and mechanism, issuing in the turn to physiology and the will to power. Through logic (identity and non-contradiction) a simplified world of self-identical things in commerce is constructed by fixing and equalizing (*Festmachen, Gleichmachen*) the complex, dynamic character of reality, a world without cognitive value but one that is life-enabling and therefore binding on us. Metaphysics and substance ontology are criticized and rejected on the grounds that they fail to account for change and spontaneous, creative activity. In response, Nietzsche looks for a 'manner of speech' (*Sprechart*) or 'image language' (*Bilderrede*) that describes better the dynamic, pluralistic, conflictual character of reality; a counter-ontology of becoming, based on a series of negations of metaphysics: process or occurrence (not being); 'originary' plurality (instead of *arche* or first substance); and antagonism, real opposition or contradiction (Ggz II.2) among entities without substance (instead of harmony and consistency). For this project, he draws extensively on a range of contemporary physiologists, using, combining, adapting their conceptual vocabularies to develop his own physio-ontology of change, which comes into its own with the discourse of will to power. In this process, he confronts a psychological constraint, which informs his concept of real opposition: that we can only make sense of change in terms of our self-understanding as agents, which he contends can be reduced to willing power.

In **Chapter 2** I ask how Kant and Nietzsche address the question of war and peace: How do they formulate the problem of conflict? How do they conceptualize the relation between war and peace? And how do they envisage the transformation of, or passage from senseless, destructive conflict (in)to a constructive order of things?

The main thesis of the chapter is that Kant wages a *philosophical war of extermination (Todkrieg, Vernichtungskampf) on all war in the name of eternal peace*. By 'philosophical war of extermination' is meant *Todkrieg*, the term used by Nietzsche in AC to describe a bivalent (*zweiwertig*), oppositional manner of thinking, which makes a total and exclusive claim for its position (*Sich Absolutsetzen*) by eliminating or destroying the opposed position and with it, their relation of opposition. My argument works through an analysis of two texts in which Kant discusses conflict or war and peace: the section on the 'polemical use' of Reason in the latter part of KrV, where he addresses the conflict of Reason with itself; and ZeF, where he discusses warfare among states on the world stage. In both texts, Kant's philosophical war against war *replicates* in thought what he argues for in real terms: the extermination or *Vernichtung* of (the causes of future) conflict in favour of eternal peace. This makes for an utterly barren, destructive notion of conflict and a life-negating idea of peace beyond the reality of conflict. Constructive, autonomous agency requires the *extermination* of conflict under the rule of law. In the end, conflict is productive for Kant, *but only of its own negation*. I then turn to Nietzsche for an alternative manner of thinking conflict and peace, one that overcomes the Kantian oppositions and allows for a genuinely affirmative understanding of conflict and its productive qualities. In the final section I qualify the argument by considering each thinker's position from a perspective in the other's. There is, I conclude, a profound ambiguity in Kant's ideal of peace: on the one hand, it signifies a nihilistic 'peace of the graveyard', but on the other, it stands for a path to a living peace, which can be brought in line with a Nietzschean approach to peace.

In **Chapters 3** and **4** I examine the notion of productive resistance (*Widerstand, Widerstreben*) in Nietzsche and Kant. For both thinkers, I contend, a genuinely constructive concept of conflict requires that resistance work not just as an inhibitor that reduces freedom, creativity and power, but as a stimulant (*Reiz, Stimulus*) to create new orders, new settlements, new possibilities of existence. The main question of these two chapters is, then: *What does it take to think resistance as productive, enabling, empowering – as a stimulant?*

Chapter 3 begins (§I) with an analysis of the meanings of 'resistance' in Nietzsche's ontology of power with a view towards isolating and describing his conception of productive resistance. Drawing on descriptions of the Dionysian and the sexual act, I argue that for resistance to be productive (i.e. a stimulant) the hindrance (*Hindernis, Hemmung*) of my power and the pain it engenders must give me the feeling of power-pleasure. This thought is missing in Kant, because pain is simply equated with the feeling of hindrance and rigidly opposed to pleasure-power. Nietzsche's concept of productive resistance turns on the distinction between *active* and *reactive meanings* of 'resistance': when uttered from an *active position of strength or power*, resistance is sought out as a stimulant or source of power; from a *reactive position of weakness* vis-à-vis an overpowering resistance, by contrast, resistance is experienced and conceived negatively as *disempowering*. In sections II and III this argument is developed through a comparative analysis of resistance: Nietzsche's account of coitus as a 'play of resistance and victory' and Kant's account of health in the *Anthropology* as a 'continual play of *antagonism*' between 'the feeling of advancement' and the 'hindrance of life'. Despite proximities between them, the priority Kant gives to pain and resistance as the 'spur to activity' falls short of a productive notion of resistance, because it is locked in real opposition to the pleasure of empowerment or the feeling of the advancement of life.

In the final section of the chapter I turn to the role of resistance in the context of freedom or sovereignty. For Kant, I focus on the account of 'respect for the law' (*Achtung für's Gesetz*) in the second *Critique*. The 'feeling of elevation', Kant argues, is based on the 'judgement of reason' that the moral law has overcome the resistance of our sensible inclinations, thereby advancing the causality of freedom. This is compared to the figure of the sovereign individual in GM II 2, whose feeling of freedom derives from his judgement that, in redeeming his promise, he has overcome resistances both within and without. In both cases, an equivalence is made *between the overcoming of resistance, and the consciousness or advancement of freedom*. This proximity is, however, complicated in the *Nachlass*, where this judgement is exposed as illusory, a misinterpretation of the body that condenses infinitely complex processes and tensions into a unitary act of will. But Nietzsche's response is not to reject the moral language of law and freedom; instead, he pleads for naturalistic accounts, to make them less illusory through a 'more substantial' interpretation of the physiology of agency. In the next chapter, I consider one such attempt in Nietzsche's socio-physiology of sovereignty.

In **Chapter 4**, the question of productive resistance is approached by comparing Kant's notion of *ungesellige Geselligkeit* or 'unsociable sociability' in the Fourth Proposition his 1784 *History* text with Nietzsche's 'fine, well-planned, thoughtful egoism' from the *Nachlass* of 1881. The argument is that Kant's unsociability involves a very *limited* notion of egoism, derived from Hobbes, in which others are either *obstacles* or *means* to our own selfish ends. On this basis he tries to formulate a productive notion of resistance, as the engine of human – cultural and moral – development, but it remains captive to the reactive notion of power derived from Hobbes. Whereas for Kant sociability (the pursuit of common or other-centred ends) is external and opposed to unsociability or egoism, Nietzsche develops a far richer notion of egoism, in which sociability – specifically: acting for the sake of others' well-being – is central. Drawing largely on Wilhelm Roux, he develops a *socio-physiological prehistory of the individual* and the *emergence of the first individuals*, modelled on his concept of the organism and organismic life-processes. The notion of thoughtful egoism, in which this account culminates, brings a complexity to the question of our treatment of others, which is marked by *reciprocity* and *ambiguity* to the point of undermining Kant's sociability-unsociability opposition. But it also designates a *naturalistic ideal of autonomous self-regulation on the basis of physiological self-knowledge*, i.e. an intelligent, affirmative attention to our needs as unique living beings and the processes of self-regulation that we, and all living creatures, must perform if we are to meet our conditions of existence, thrive and grow. Nietzsche's commitment to life-affirmation and -enhancement leads him to locate the 'quality' or value of actions, not in the universalizability of their maxims à la Kant, but in their capacity to individuate, to actualize the radical particularity of their agents, understood as unique multiplicities. Thoughtful egoism involves *radically individual self-legislation* (as opposed to self-subjection to the universal law) on the part of a *radically socialized and plural subject* or *dividuum* (against the substantive, autonomous subject: *homo noumenon*). As such, it represents an attempt to reconstruct the moral ideal of freedom and the associated feeling of power in a way that is 'less illusory' by giving them a 'more substantial' physiological or socio-physiological interpretation. The chapter ends by considering the potential of Nietzsche's thoughtful egoism for a mode of engagement with others appropriate to agonistic politics. I do so by drawing on his attempt to bypass the false oppositions of morality by displacing the moral discourse of persons with an impersonal, cognitive discourse of things to be known, and by tracking the shift in his later thought from the capacity to resist, to *non*-resistance, or the capacity *not* to resist. In the register of knowledge this involves a practice of possessing and being possessed by others as things to be known (rather than persons) and an episteme of calm hostility or hostile openness, which I propose as a promising basis for an agonistic disposition towards others.

Chapter 5 examines Nietzsche's and Kant's thought on hatred in the light of the realist and perfectionist impulses in both thinkers. The main argument is that Nietzsche performs a *reinterpretation* and *transvaluation* (*Umdeutung, Umwertung*) of the Christian-moral concept of hatred. For his part, Kant's views on hatred are profoundly ambivalent. On one side, he follows the Christian-moral condemnation of hatred in favour of love, reconciliation and peace. But as a philosopher of conflict, he also comes close to Nietzsche and concurs with him on certain aspects of hatred; in a different way Kant too performs a reconceptualization and re-evaluation of hatred.

Most of the chapter is devoted to examining Nietzsche's philosophy of hatred, beginning (§II) with its place in his ontology of conflict. This analysis isolates the familiar, negative sense of hatred as a destructive force, but also unfamiliar senses that disconnect hatred from contempt (*Verachtung*), moral condemnation and subjection, releasing affirmative potentials. Nietzsche's physiology implies that hatred is greatest where struggle and the resistance to assimilation are greatest, that is, among (more or less) equal powers. It is distinguished from revulsion and contempt, since these are attached to the process of excretion, not assimilation. And genuine hatred is bound up with love, understood as attraction and the desire to take on and accept what is hard to assimilate in the other; this is one of several ways in which the opposition between love and hate is broken.

Nietzsche's distinctive claim is that hatred need not be a destructive force, but can take creative forms, and in subsequent sections two very different forms of creative hatred are examined: an active agonal hatred *inter pares* that allows for an affirmative pride in one's enemy (§II.2), and the reactive hatred of the 'spirit of revenge' that gives birth to slave morality (§IV). Thereafter (§V), Nietzsche's philosophical response to the problem of hatred is discussed. Kant's reflections on hatred, revenge and anger are discussed in §III, which I then draw on and develop in the final section (§VI). Here I return to the origins of slave morality for a comparative examination of hatred, revenge and anger, and how each thinker envisions a solution to the pathologies of revenge he diagnoses.

Focussing on the slave revolt in morality allows us to address one of chief problems facing agonistic theories: how emancipation from conditions of radical inequality can avoid replicating *ressentiment* and the zero-sum game of 'imaginary revenge' (self-elevation by degrading the other). Bringing the results of Nietzsche's and Kant's thought to bear on this question yields a number of responses to the problem of emancipation relevant to agonistic theory: to take on from those in power the affective power of *anger* and turn it against them, instead of nurturing a slow-burning, insatiable passion for revenge (Kant); to subvert the morality that legitimates hatred of the powerful by learning to love and affirm their will to power and acknowledging that both weak and strong 'stand on the same ground' with equal standing as forms of will to power (Nietzsche); to exploit the idealizing powers of hatred and turn them *against* its destructive tendencies, in favour of life-affirming and -enhancing ideals; and to see through the errors of hatred through physiological (self-)knowledge and cultivate an *episteme* of indifference 'beyond love and hate'.

The book ends with an **Epilogue**, in which some of the implications for agonistic politics of the two philosophies of conflict explored in the book are drawn and developed with an eye on opening avenues for further research. The topics discussed are the principle of equality; pluralism; freedom; the boundary between non-violent agonism and violent antagonism, and the concept of agonistic respect as a way to secure the boundary. While Nietzsche has little or nothing to contribute to a political analysis of institutions or bureaucracy, I believe that valuable lessons can be learned from his philosophy of conflict for modalities of interaction appropriate to agonistic democracy. They include two affirmative notions of equality touched on in the book; the emphasis on the epistemic difficulties confronting genuine pluralism and the kinds of episteme proposed to address them by Nietzsche; the conjunction of sovereignty and non-sovereignty in the naturalistic account of freedom developed in his sociophysiology; and an attempt on my part to reconceptualize agonistic respect by drawing on his reflections on love and agonal hatred *inter pares*.

1

The problem of contradiction and real opposition in Kant and Nietzsche

I Introduction

Any philosophy of conflict faces the problem of whether reality, conceived as intrinsically conflictual or contradictory, can be thought without falling prey to rampant contradiction. The contradictions or apparent contradictions in Nietzsche's thought have occupied scholars of his work from the beginning, and continue to do so. Without going into this complex issue, I take as my point of departure for this chapter the position, rather obvious to any reader of Nietzsche, that *within* individual texts he tries, like the rest of us, to think consistently and to avoid contradicting himself.[1] And yet the matter of his thought is often characterized by him as contradictory or conflictual. Is this at all possible? Is there not already a contradiction between the *matter* of his thought and the *manner* of his thinking – a contradiction between the affirmation of contradiction at an ontological level and a negation of contradiction in the logic of his thinking? Unless a distinction is made between logical contradiction and real contradiction, it is hard to see how a philosophy of conflict can avoid being infected, not to say swallowed up by the reality of contradiction. What, to use Kant's terms, is the *difference* between the kind of opposition involved in *logical contradiction* and *real opposition*, such that the latter can be affirmed as possible and actual, while maintaining the impossibility of the former? The Kantian notion of real opposition (*Realrepugnanz, reale Entgegensetzung*) may offer a key to this question.

In the 1763 text *Versuch den Begriff der negativen Größen in die Weltweisheit einzuführen* (NG),[2] Kant undertakes to clarify the difference between logical contradiction and real opposition as two different forms of opposition that involve different forms of negation. This text is important not only for the above-mentioned problem, but also because in it Kant sets out the basic terms of his ontology of conflict

---

[1] With Nietzsche's goal in mind to realize a plurality of meanings in his texts, van Tongeren (2000 84) points out that 'his texts will often intentionally be ambiguous and even contradictory or at least full of tension'. But this is not the same as simply disregarding or flouting the principle of non-contradiction. Stegmaier (2008 105f., 110f.), however, has argued that in EH Nietzsche makes logical contradictions fruitful for practical or existential purposes. On Nietzsche's predilection for paradoxes, see also Stegmaier (2004).

[2] *Attempt to introduce the concept of negative magnitudes into philosophy*, in: Kant (1992 203–42).

and how it applies to various domains of philosophy. What is more, it serves him to conduct a fundamental enquiry into the grounds of change, focused on the ontology of mental life. All three issues are of cardinal importance for Nietzsche's philosophy of conflict, and Kant's treatment of them offers valuable points of comparison. This chapter therefore begins with an exposition of NG with an eye on points of comparison with Nietzsche, and then turns to Nietzsche and a comparative enquiry into his treatment of the problem of contradiction and opposition.

The text NG marks an important moment, a turning point in the understanding of reality in modern European philosophy.[3] From the mid-seventeenth to the mid-eighteenth centuries, philosophy in Europe was dominated by rationalist systems with strong harmonistic tendencies (Leibniz, Spinoza, Wolff, Baumgarten i.a.). The conception of reality in these systems was grounded in the equation of perfection, reality (positivity of being) and force. In these terms, there could be no genuine conflict of forces, since force was equated with reality, and reality cannot be opposed to reality. Negativity cannot involve the real opposition of one force by another, but can only be conceived as a diminution or limit (*Schranke*), lack, absence or violation of force or reality. NG introduces a radically new conception of reality grounded in real opposition or the conflict of forces, what Kant calls the 'Conflictus zweier Kräfte' (NG II.180, 183). Conflict is now real, and the real conflict of forces is used by Kant to explain not just the regularity of nature, but the very perfection (*Vollkommenheit*) of the world (NG II.198). Negativity is now a real force, not merely a lack, so that we can speak of evil as a positive force opposed to the good. As Kant writes:

> The error into which many philosophers have fallen as a result of neglecting this truth is obvious. One finds that they generally treat evils as if they were mere negations, even though it is obvious from our explanations that there are evils of lack (*mala defectus*) and evils of deprivation (*mala privationis*). Evils of lack are negations: there is no ground for the positing of what is opposed to them. Evils of deprivation presuppose that there are positive grounds which cancel the good for which there really exists another ground. Such evils of deprivation are a *negative good*. (NG II.182)

As we will see, in NG Kant introduces the notion that negation can signify not just a lack or absence of being, but a positive force that opposes and cancels (*aufhebt*) the effects of an opposed force.

Negative Grössen marks an important moment in the history of modern philosophy in another sense as well.[4] The central assumption of logical rationalism was that logic mirrors and has roots in the structure of nature. In 1755,[5] Kant had subscribed to this assumption, asserting the 'material' validity of the logical principles of identity and

---

[3] I owe this insight and the remarks below on the Seven Years War to Thomas Kisser, who gave a paper on NG at the Leiden Institute for Philosophy in November 2014.
[4] See Schonfeld (2000 231–2).
[5] In: *Principiorum primorum cognitionis metaphysicae nova dilucidatio (New Elucidation of the First Principles of Metaphysical Cognition)* I.385–415.

contradiction as principles of reality. By 1762,[6] the year before NG, he was asserting the non-equivalence of logical difference and physical difference (*Unterscheidung*), with the intention of distinguishing logical distinctions from cognitive discriminations. This assault on the ontological status of logic is also recorded in Herder's notes on Kant's lectures on Metaphysics in the years 1762-4, in which he separates ideal grounds from real grounds (*Idealgrund, Realgrund*), a point to which he returns at the end of NG in order to clarify the difference between his distinction between two grounds from that of Crusius (NG II.203). 'By 1770', Schonfeld (2000 232) tells us, 'Kant would characterize the law of contradiction as a merely subjective condition of judgment.' In this break with the rationalist tradition and the progressive restriction of the laws of logic from principles of reality to subjective principles of thought, NG plays a pivotal role with its central claim that real opposition involves not logical contradiction, but Newton's third Law of action and reaction (NG II.179-80).

In both regards, the change in the understanding of negativity and the caesura between logic and reality, Nietzsche is heir to Kant's NG. Yet in both cases, he radicalizes Kant's moves. As we will see, Kant's restriction of logic to thought is radicalized by Nietzsche into a critique of the principles of identity and non-contradiction. And like Kant, he will posit real opposition or conflict as the dynamic principle of reality, but he will subject mechanism to critique and replace it first with physiological models of conflict and eventually with the will to power. The most fundamental difference is that, from at least FW on, Nietzsche rejects the dualism of the *ordo cognoscendi* and the *ordo essendi*, to which the young Kant was still captive, and the subject-object opposition.[7] At issue for Nietzsche in knowledge is not an adequate account of reality, conceived as an independently existing order of beings, but the construction of a world that is habitable (that can be lived in), against the background of (1) his critique of metaphysics and substance ontology, and (2) his understanding of our psychological limitations.

It is worth remarking that 1763, the year in which Kant wrote NG, was also the end of the Seven Years War waged by Frederick the Great of Prussia in order to strengthen the Protestants' position in the Holy Roman Empire of the German Nation against Catholic Austria.[8] This war marked the transition from the 'Princes' Warfare' (*Kabinettskriege*) waged by the absolute monarchs of the seventeenth and eighteenth centuries in Europe, to the Peoples' Wars (*Volkskriege*) that began with the American and French Revolutions; Frederick's war had characteristics of both. Princes' Warfare often involved strategic manoeuvres by paid armies designed to *minimize* actual conflict, whereas Peoples' Wars involved the mobilization of masses, increasing industrialization of weaponry and became increasingly wars of extermination, which came to a head in 1945. It is against the background of this shift in warfare that Kant introduced conflict as the dynamic principle of reality in NG.

---

[6] *Die falsche Spitzfindigkeit der vier syllogistischen Figuren (The False Subtlety of the Four Syllogistic Figures)* II.45-63, esp. II.59-60.
[7] See FW 354 3.593; also FW 54. This changes of course with the KrV where the subject and object remain distinct, but mutually imply one another (see Gardner 1999 157-60).
[8] See Abbt (1761).

Before moving onto the text itself, some historical background on two key terms, 'Gegensatz' or opposition and 'Widerspruch' or contradiction, is needed in order to understand Kant's and Nietzsche's philosophies of conflict. Both use these terms extensively, but their use and the relations between the terms are far from transparent. The moves they each make and the positions they take are best understood in relation to existing meanings, which will now be sketched in a brief, selective account.

I.1 A short history of 'opposition' (*Gegensatz*) and 'contradiction' (*Widerspruch*)[9]

In Greek pre-Socratic philosophy, *Gegensatz* (ἐναντίον, ἀντικείμενον, ἀντίθεσις; contrarium, contrarietas, oppositum, oppositio) and *Widerspruch* (ἀντίφασις; contradictio), not yet conceptually distinguished, are used to describe (1) the relation of opposition between true being and the sensory world of phenomena (in dualistic philosophers like Parmenides and Anaximander), but also (2) the nature of the phenomenal world itself (Pythagoras, Parmenides, Anaximander, Anaximenes, Heraclitus, Empedocles). In the cosmodicy of Heraclitus, which anticipates certain features of both Nietzsche's and Kant's philosophies of conflict, singular 'things' are displaced by relational complexes, in which relations of attraction and repulsion between opposed qualities (sweet-bitter, light-dark, etc.), vying with each other for pre-eminence, drive processes of transformation (see PHG 5 1.825). Indeed, from the very beginning and throughout the history of Western thought, opposition and contradiction are bound up with the problem of change, and are proposed as an explanation, source or ground of change and transformation in thinkers ranging from Parmenides and Heraclitus to Hegel and Marx. This goes no less for Kant and Nietzsche. For both, the conflict of forces informs their dynamic conceptions of things and is of cardinal importance in accounting for change. The paradoxical-contradictory formulations, for which Heraclitus is renowned, showcase the tremendous difficulty posed for consistent thought and speech by the thought of real opposition or conflict, and the phenomena of change, movement and transformation, with which it has been inextricably linked in the tradition. In other words, it shows the need to distinguish the meaning and structure of 'contradiction' in thought and speech (logical contradiction) from real contradiction or opposition, so as to speak of contradiction (in reality) without falling into (logical) contradiction. As I will argue, this move can be seen in Kant and Nietzsche.

It is Aristotle who first formalized the concept of opposition in order to clarify its bearing on the understanding of beings. Opposition *between concepts* is divided into four types: (a) *relative* opposition, e.g. double/half; (b) *contrary* opposition, which can allow for intermediate terms, e.g. good/bad; (c) *privative* opposition, e.g. blind/sighted; and (d) *contradictory* opposition, e.g. sitting/not sitting (Arist., De cat. 10, 11 b 17–23). This classification was taken up and Latinized by Boethius and has been retained in

---

[9] Based on the article 'Gegensatz' by W. Beierwaltes and A. Menne in HWPh 7623 (= HWPh vol. 3, p. 120 ff.) and the article 'Widerspruch' by E. Angehrn in HWPh 50522 (= HWPh vol. 12, p. 688 ff.).

logic to this day. The same holds for oppositions *between statements*, which Aristotle divides into two kinds, *contrary* and *contradictory* oppositions. But Aristotle's principal interest is ontological, and 'opposition' (ἐναντίωσις, ἐναντιότης) with regard to beings is defined as 'the greatest' or 'complete' difference within a given genus (Met. 1055 a 4. 16.); as such, it can only be opposed to One. The opposition between the One and the Many (ἕν-πολλά) is therefore for Aristotle the fundamental opposition, on which other oppositions are based (Met. 1054 a 30ff. 1061 a 11f.). Beings are themselves constituted by *contrary* – or *relative* – oppositional structures. Within Aristotle's ontological-logical system of relations, these oppositions are what make knowledge possible; they are the presupposition for thinking beings in terms of the logical relations of substance-accident, genus-species, matter-form and possibility-actuality.

The term 'Widerspruch', introduced by Wolff as the German for 'contradictio' or contradiction, is Aristotle's fourth type of conceptual opposition, primarily a logical relation that holds between concepts or statements. It determines the principle of (non-)contradiction, considered by Aristotle to be one of the logical axioms, indeed the first principle and 'principle of all other axioms' (Met. IV, 3, 1005 b 33f.), on which the possibility of thought, speech and demonstration depends. But the concept of contradiction has also been taken as an ontological principle, denoting a relation that holds between things or that governs (specific domains of) reality. This tension between logic and ontology, between an epistemic and a metaphysical problematic, between the impossibility and necessity of contradiction, and between its negative and positive evaluations, runs through the history of the concept – including Kant and Nietzsche. Already in Aristotle's classical formulation of the principle of non-contradiction, logic and ontology are bound up together: 'It is impossible that the same thing belong and not belong to the same thing at the same time and in the same respect' (Met. IV, 3, 1005 b 19–20). According to Aristotle, this ontological definition translates directly into the logical definition: 'The most certain of all basic principles is that contradictory statements are not true simultaneously.' (Met. IV, 6, 1011 b 13–14); or that 'it is impossible to affirm and deny something simultaneously in truth' (Met. IV, 6, 1011 b 13–21). Whoever asserts contradictory statements cancels 'substance (οὐσία) and essence' (Met. X, 4, 1007 a21), and thereby the determinacy to which speaking and signifying necessarily refer. In Kant's terms, such statements cancel the thing to which contradictory predicates are ascribed, leaving '*nothing at all* [g a r n i c h t s] (*nihil negativum irrepraesentabile*)' (NG II.171). It is also worth mentioning Aristotle's third, psychological formulation of the principle of non-contradiction, since it is taken up by both Kant and Nietzsche: 'that it is impossible for someone to believe that the same thing is and is not' (Met. IV, 6, 1005 b 23–24).

The expressions 'Repugnanz'/'Realrepugnanz'[10] occur a number of times in NG, and they are a striking, unusual terminological choice by Kant. They occur only in this text and in BDG (II.79-80) from the same year (1763), in which the notion of real opposition is first thematized. 'Repugnanz' is Stoic in origin (repugnantia, Cicero's translation of μάχη) and serves as a logical term closely related to contradiction. In the Scholastic

---

[10] Based on the article 'Repugnanz' by S. K. Knebel, in HWPh 32802 (= HWPh vol. 8, p. 879 ff.).

tradition, it is an elastic term for incompatibility on various levels: conceptual, logical, ontological, semantic and syntactic. The notion of *Realrepugnanz* first occurs in this tradition with the expression 'repugnantia realis'. In Aquinas 'repugnantia' is a ubiquitous metaphysical term, anchored in the principle of contradiction, and used for dynamic relations between coexistent factors, often with antagonistic connotations: resistance as far as disobedience; sin; (affective) repulsion; reluctance; antagonistic pluralities; conflicting emotions; conflicting wills; excessive dominance of one quality over others; violence of the strong against the weak. Even though Kant's immediate source seems to have been Baumgarten's *Metaphysica*, where it receives only one insignificant mention (Met §66), the dynamic-antagonistic meaning evinced in Aquinas and implied by the term itself is markedly present in Kant's usage and a likely reason for his usage. Although this will not be discussed, it is worth mentioning that the distinction between real and logical opposition is not a one-off or confined to Kant's pre-critical work, but is maintained in KrV, which adds to them a third, 'dialectical' opposition.

II Kant's concept of negative magnitudes: Real vs. logical opposition

In NG Kant proposes to present the 'small beginnings' of an attempt to 'open new perspectives' which may have 'important consequences' for philosophy. The proposal is to introduce the concept of negative quantities or magnitudes from mathematics, an 'unused, although greatly needed' concept,[11] into metaphysics. In Europe, negative numbers were introduced by the German mathematician Michael Stifel (*c.* 1487–1567), but were dubbed *numeri absurdi* by him. The question of whether negative numbers constituted real numbers preoccupied mathematicians from Stifel on (Vieta, Pascal, Cardano, Newton, Arnauld), since they were taken to be less than nothing and hence nothing at all.[12] Nevertheless, in his *Opticks*[13] Newton did use the distinction between 'affirmative Quantities' and 'negative Quantities' to represent relations between opposed forces with mathematical + and − signs. Thus, as noted by Kant in NG (II.69), the transformation of the force of attraction between two bodies into repulsion at a certain point of proximity could be represented as the transition from positive into negative numbers at the point of zero. It is far from obvious that relations between forces in space can be rendered arithmetically in this way, especially given the conceptual difficulties surrounding negative quantities, and Christian Crusius, for one,[14] had

---

[11] The expression borrowed by Willem van der Kuijlen for his PhD thesis, defended at Radboud University Nijmegen in 2009. I owe a great deal to this book and to exchanges with Willem van der Kuijlen for opening up this important dimension of Kant's philosophy of conflict. In the thesis, he argues that this term, which makes only a brief appearance in NG, nonetheless has wide-ranging repercussions for his understanding of contradiction, opposition, tension and conflict in the rest of his work. Next to van der Kuijlen (2009), other useful sources have been Schonfeld (2000), Saner (1967), Wolff (2017), Schnepf (2001), and Zinkin (2012).

[12] Kant (1992 439–40).

[13] Wolff (2017 84–5).

[14] Kant responds to Crusius in NG II.69: Crusius's mistake, as Kant points out, was to confuse negative quantities with logical negation (Schnepf 2001 138; Wolff 2017 85).

rejected Newton's identification of repulsion with negative quantities as absurd. But Kant is undaunted. Drawing on his teacher Kästner's definition,[15] it is clear to him that negative magnitudes are 'something truly positive in itself, only [something] opposed to the other [i.e. positive magnitudes]' (NG II.169).

Kant undertakes to clarify the concept of negative magnitudes by distinguishing real opposition or *Realrepugnanz* from logical contradiction or *logische Repugnanz* as two different forms of opposition distinguished by different forms of negation. In the case of logical contradiction, that is: where 'something is simultaneously affirmed and denied of the very same thing',[16] Kant says it is impossible. Or as he writes elsewhere:

This repugnans I call the formal [principle] of unthinkability or impossibility

Diese Repugnanz nenne ich das Formale der Undenklichkeit oder Unmöglichkeit[17]

The reason logical contradiction is impossible or unthinkable is that A is affirmed and negated of the same thing, where negation here means: 'lack' or 'absence' (*Mangel, Abwesenheit, defectus, absentia*), as it has hitherto been understood in the history of philosophy. In specific, logical opposition or contradiction ascribes a predicate or determination (*Bestimmung*) and the lack or absence of the same predicate to one and the same thing. The determination that ascribes one predicate to the object cancels (*Aufhebung*) the other, such that object itself is cancelled by the contradiction. The consequence of logically contradictory judgements is, then, '*nothing at all*': 'g a r n i c h t s (*nihil negativum irrepraesentabile*)' (NG II.171): there is no thing that can both have and lack the same predicate; or to use Kant's example, a body that is both in motion and not in motion is 'nothing at all': *gar nichts*.

We see here that for Kant, in line with the tradition, the concept of contradiction is not just a logical principle about the predicates of a judgement, but also an ontological principle about real predicates of a thing, which cancel each other and the thing to which they are ascribed.[18] In the case of real opposition, Kant leaves logic altogether behind to write only of real predicates without any relation to logical opposition. In real opposition, the predicates are opposed, yet the result of their opposition is not impossible or unthinkable, but 'something (cogitabile)'. The reason is that the predicates do not stand in a contradictory relation of a and not-a; on the contrary, both terms are positive, such as motive force in one direction and motive force in the opposed direction, or rising and falling. In what sense then are they opposed? Kant's

---

[15] Kästner, *Anfangsgründe der Arithmetik* (1758), emphasizes the relativity of the negative: 'Opposed magnitudes are magnitudes which are such that, when considered under such conditions, the one diminishes the other' (Kant 1992 439).

[16] Cf. BDG II.77 written in the same year, where contradiction is defined as: to negate that which in the selfsame is affirmed (*dasjenige verneinen müsse, was in eben demselben zugleich bejaht ist*), or to conjoin (copula) something that is posited with something through which it is cancelled (*eine Verknüpfung mit Etwas, was gesetzt, und Etwas, wodurch es zugleich aufgehoben wird*).

[17] Ibid.

[18] See Wolff (2017 56) for a helpful explanation of the terminology of 'Prädikate', 'Bestimmung', 'Setzen', 'Aufheben'.

answer is that 'only a certain consequence' of each term is cancelled (*aufgehoben*) by the other, not the terms themselves, which remain positive. The result is what he calls 'a relative nothing', since it bears only on the consequences, which come to nothing, to zero, through real opposition. The result of two equal motive forces acting in real opposition on a body is zero motion or rest, since each cancels the other's consequence, i.e. motion.

The difference between real and logical opposition turns on two different forms of negation, which Kant describes as follows:

> A negation, in so far as it is the consequence of a real opposition, will be designated a *deprivation* [*Beraubung*] (*privatio*). But any negation, in so far as it does not arise from this type of repugnancy, will be called a *lack* [*Mangel*] (defectus, absentia). The latter does not require a positive ground, but merely the lack of such a ground. But the former involves a true ground of the positing and another ground which is opposed to it and which is of the same magnitude. In a body, rest is either merely a lack, that is to say, a negation of motion, in so far as no motive force is present, or alternatively, such rest is a deprivation, in so far as there is, indeed, a motive force present, though its consequence, namely the motion, is cancelled by an opposed force. (NG II.178)

Or, to cite another example:

> Evils of lack are negations: there is no ground for the positing of what is opposed to them. Evils of deprivation presuppose that there are positive grounds which cancel the good for which there really exists another ground. Such evils of deprivation are negative goods. (NG II.182)

In negation as lack, Kant says, there is 'no ground for the opposed position' (so that its absence can simply be posited). In *Realrepugnanz* it is otherwise: here negation requires (presupposes) that there are grounds for cancelling (*Aufheben*) the consequence of the opposed position:

> Real repugnans only occurs in so far as of two things as *positive grounds*, each cancels the consequence of the other. (NG II.175)[19]

Here negation is thought as *nihil privativum*: as privation, *Beraubung* or *Aufhebung*. Negation does not signify mere absence, but the deprivation, robbing (*Beraubung*), cancellation (*Aufhebung*), even annihilation (*Vernichtung*)[20] of the consequences of what it negates. And it can only do so, according to Kant, as a *positive force that resists*

---

[19] 'Die Realrepugnanz findet nur statt, in so fern zwei Dinge als p o s i t i v e G r ü n d e eins die Folge des anderen aufhebt.'

[20] Realrepugnanz occurs 'wenn etwas als ein Grund die Folge von etwas anderm durch eine reale Entgegensetzung vernichtigt' (BDG II.86); cf. van der Kuijlen (2009 47).

its opposite. In effect, we see Kant drawing on the third Aristotelian type of opposition, privative opposition, but reinterpreting it in order to formulate a concept of negation, inspired by Newton's 'negative quantities', that allows him to introduce an entirely new type of opposition into philosophy. With the introduction of radical negativity as privation, we also see *in nuce* the critique of Leibnizian metaphysics that becomes explicit in KrV, that negation need not only signify a limit or lack (*Schranke, Mangel*) of determination or reality, but can also involve privation.[21] What exactly Kant means by real opposition or *Realrepugnanz* can be seen in his discussion of impenetrability.

II.1 Kant's ontology of conflict

Starting out from Newton's force of attraction, Kant argues in NG that we can only explain the impenetrability (i.e. materiality) of a body if we presuppose an inner force of repulsion that resists the force attracting other bodies, so that a body occupies space by virtue of a balance between conflicting forces, or as Kant says: a 'Conflictus zweier Kräfte, die einander entgegengesetzt sind' (NG II.179).[22] Thus, repulsion, although a 'true force' of *Zurückstoßung*, can also be called negative attraction: *negative Anziehung*, to indicate that it is a *positive* ground that resists the force of attraction:

> The cause of impenetrability is consequently a true force, for it does the same as a true force does […] thus impenetrability is a *negative attraction*. In this way it is made clear that it is just as much a positive ground as every other moving force in nature […] (NG II.179)[23]

But it is not clear what exactly Kant means by a 'wahre Kraft' or 'true force' in NG. In the 1740s Kant subscribes to the Leibnizian notion of *vis viva* or *vis activa* for his concept of force against the mechanistic-mathematical notion of force as an impulse of exogenous origin. What Kant calls an essential force or 'innerliche Kraft des Körpers' is an endogenous source of change or motion, a 'Basis der Aktivität'[24] that a body

---

[21] Above all in the 'Amphiboly' chapter of KrV A 260–92 (B 316–49).
[22] The fundamental forces of attraction and repulsion are not original to NG. Kant first introduces them in the *Theory of the Heavens* (1755) as 'both borrowed from the Newtonian philosophy' (NTH I.234). While the former is clearly derived from Newton's universal gravitation, the Newtonian basis for the latter is less clear (see Friedman 2013 131). In the *Physical Monadology* (1756) the two forces recur as phenomenal manifestations of the external, relational determinations of substance, which generate space, understood as the community or co-presence of substances. These external relations are real (contra Leibniz) and are subject to Newton's laws, but Kant also retains a monadological concept of simple substances behind the phenomena, which have a purely internal nature constituted by their internal determinations independently of any other substances. This construction is Kant's attempt to synthesize Leibniz and Newton, which he finally rejects in KrV.
[23] 'Die Ursache der Undurchdringlichkeit ist demnach eine wahre Kraft, denn sie thut dasselbe, was eine wahre Kraft thut. […] so ist die Undurchdringlichkeit eine n e g a t i v e A n z i e h u n g. Dadurch wird alsdann angezeigt, daß sie ein eben so positiver Grund sei als eine jede andere Bewegkraft in der Natur […]'.
[24] GwS (*Gedanken von der wahren Schätzung der lebendigen Kräfte*) I.141; cited in van der Kuijlen (2009 32).

possesses even before it has extension. The 1750s see the replacement or suppression of *vis viva* by the Newtonian *vis attractiva* and *vis repulsiva* and a conversion to Newtonian mechanics. Yet matters are not so clear-cut. In the *Physical Monadology* of 1756, Kant's professorial dissertation, he introduces attraction and repulsion, *vis attractiva* and *vis repulsiva*, as the two immanent moving forces on the ground of all material activity (Schonfeld 2000 168). They govern all intermonadic relations as well as the sphere of each monad: its volume and dynamic extension.[25] And as Schonfeld (2000 172) points out, '[t]he way Kant explicated the relation of force and substance makes one wonder whatever had happened to the living forces. If there was a subject-matter that positively cried out for the reintroduction of *vis viva*, then this was it.' By the time of *negative Grössen*, Kant's Newtonian conversion seems complete when he writes that 'the state of matter can only ever be changed by means of an *external* cause'. Yet he adds immediately:

> '[...] whereas the state of the mind can also be changed by means of an *internal* cause. The necessity of real opposition, however, always remains the same, in spite of the above difference. (NG II.191–2)

Not only does Kant here retain the notion of an inner force or *vis activa* for mental activity; he seems to subordinate both inner and outer causality to the 'necessity of real opposition', as the true ground or source of motion or change in both nature and thought.[26]

The explanation of impenetrability is not an isolated example in NG. The conflict of the forces of attraction and repulsion – the *Conflictus zweier Kräfte* – goes to the very heart of the early Kant's metaphysics: his ontology of conflict. It is enlisted to explain not just impenetrability, but the very perfection (*Vollkommenheit*) of the world and the regularity of the universe as a dynamic-mechanical whole:

> Furthermore, the perfection of the world in general very much consists in this conflict of opposed real grounds, just as the material part of die world is, in

---

[25] In the *Physical Monadology* a monad or substance is an unextended simple point, which fills the space it occupies by the intensive magnitude of its repulsive force: a purely intensive quantum of reality (see Friedman 2013 320).

[26] The inner causality of thought leads Kant to praise Leibniz's doctrine that every monad bears a mirror of the entire universe obscurely within it: 'There is something imposing and, it seems to me, profoundly true in the thought *of Leibniz*: the soul embraces the whole universe with its faculty of representation, though only an infinitesimally tiny part of these representations is clear. It is, indeed, the case that concepts of every kind must have as the foundation on which alone they are based the inner activity of our mind. External things may well contain the condition under which concepts present themselves in one way or another; but external things do not have the power actually to produce those concepts. The power of thought possessed by the soul must contain the real grounds of all concepts, in so far as they are supposed to arise in a natural fashion within the soul. The phenomena of the coming-to-be and passing-away of cognitions are to be attributed, it would seem, simply to the agreement or opposition of all this activity' (NG II.219f.).

the most obvious fashion, maintained in a regular course simply by means of the conflict of forces. (NG II.197)[27]

In this regard, the conflict of forces is a principle of equilibrium. What exactly Kant means by 'perfection' in this text is unclear, but it seems to include order, harmony, fullness of being as well as a moral connotation, goodness.[28] In any case, if the Leibnizian notion of *vis activa* lingers on in Kant's account of mental life, as I have suggested, the identification of perfection with the conflict of opposed grounds marks a radical break with traditional Leibnizian metaphysics, initiated by the inscription of negativity as privation into reality (not just lack or absence of determination). Much later, in 1786, Kant will continue to defend his dynamic theory of matter in the terms of the conflict of attractive and repulsive forces and will dub the third Law of general mechanics the *Gesetz der 'Gegenwirkung der Materien' or lex 'Antagonismi'* (MAN IV.551).

II.2 Further applications of real opposition

The significance of *Realrepugnanz* is not limited to metaphysics, and in the second part of NG Kant goes on to extend it directly to the domains of physics, psychology, ethics, aesthetics and natural science. We have already seen Kant's distinction between evils of lack and evils of privation and his criticism of philosophy for failing to recognize the latter: what in *Religion* he calls 'radical evil'.[29] In the case of psychology, he argues, unpleasure (*Unlust*) is not just the contradictory opposite of pleasure (*contradictorische Gegentheil*), for then it would just be the absence of pleasure (logical negation as lack), which is patently false. As a positive feeling (*positive Empfindung*) it is opposed in reality to pleasure (*real entgegen gesetzt*) and (partially) robs pleasure of its ground, so as to reduce or eliminate it. The difference between the two forms of negation, as lack and as privation, also enables Kant to distinguish indifference (*Gleichgültigkeit*) from equanimity (*Gleichgewicht*):

> The lack of both pleasure and displeasure, in so far as it arises from the absence of their respective grounds, is called indifference (*indifferentia*). The lack of both pleasure and displeasure, in so far as it is a consequence of the real opposition

---

[27] 'Überdem besteht in diesem Conflictus der entgegengesetzten Realgründe gar sehr die Vollkommenheit der Welt überhaupt, gleichwie der materiale Theil derselben ganz offenbar blos durch den Streit der Kräfte in einem regelmäßigen Laufe erhalten wird.'
Or again:
'Allein die Natur hat noch andere Kräfte im Vorrath, welche sich vornehmlich äußern, wenn die Materie in feine Theilchen aufgelöset ist, als wodurch selbige einander zurück stoßen und durch ihren Streit mit der Anziehung diejenige Bewegung hervor bringen, die gleichsam ein dauerhaftes Leben der Natur ist' (NTH I.269).
[28] See Schonfeld (2000 106–10) on the concept of perfection until Kant. This account is indebted to Schonfeld's excellent study.
[29] RGV VI.33–8, 72.

of equal grounds, is called equilibrium (*aequilibrium*). Both indifference and equilibrium are zero, though die former is a negation absolutely, whereas die latter is a deprivation. (NG II. 181)

Kant goes on to apply real opposition to aversion as a 'negative desire', hatred as a 'negative love', ugliness as a 'negative beauty', blame as a 'negative praise'. But as Saner and more recently van der Kuijlen and Zinkin have argued, *Realrepugnanz* also has wide-ranging repercussions outside this text for Kant's understanding of contradiction, opposition, tension and conflict in the rest of his work. We will have occasion to revisit the notions of equilibrium (Chapter 2), unpleasure (Chapter 3) and hatred (Chapter 5) further on. One application of *Realrepugnanz* of particular importance for his political thought is the notion of *ungesellige Geselligkeit* (treated in Chapter 4), understood by Kant as an irreducible dimension of social life and the 'engine of politics' (Saner 1967 21). In *Träume eines Geistersehers* (1766), a few years after NG, he ascribes to us as social beings, by analogy with the conflict of attractive and repulsive forces in nature,

> [...] a conflict of two forces arises, namely of singularity [ownness], which relates everything to itself, and of common interest, through which the soul is driven or drawn towards others outside oneself [...] (TG II.334)

II.3 The source or ground of change

As mentioned, the concepts of opposition and contradiction have been bound up with the problem of change from the beginnings of Western thought. This is also the case for the philosophy of conflict in Nietzsche and Kant and specifically in NG. In the course of the text, it becomes increasingly clear that at stake in the concept of negative magnitudes is ultimately the question of the ground or source of motion and change in reality, the same question motivating Nietzsche's critique of mechanism. As pointed out by Michael Wolff (2017 102–3), the theory of real opposition also enables Kant to criticize mechanistic cosmology for failing to account for change. The mechanistic principles of conservation (the conservation of momentum and the law of inertia (*Trägheit*) are mentioned),[30] while accepted by Kant, cannot explain how 'the state of the world' can change in such a way that 'that which exists should cease to be' or that 'which was not, is posited' (NG II.194, II.190). Negative magnitudes are causes or sources of change and motion insofar as, through their conflict with their opposite, they effect a change in it by cancelling its consequences. Negative magnitudes are not numbers, nor a specific kind of thing; they have nothing to do with inner constitution (*innere Beschaffenheit*) of a thing, but only with a conflictual, reciprocal relation (*Gegenverhältniß*) (NG II.173-75). One term can only be the negative magnitude *of* another, not in itself. A negative magnitude is something that can only exist in a

---

[30] See NG II.195. The conservation of momentum is rendered in Latin in what Friedman (2013 326) sees as a paraphrase of corollary 3 of Newton's third Law of motion.

reciprocal relation with something else, such that when the two are combined, the one necessarily produces changes in the other, and is equally changed by it, where change means: 'each cancels [*aufhebt*] as much in the other as is equal to itself' (NG II.174; see also Zinkin 2012 400f.).

What, then, does this tell us about Kant's view of the source or ground of change? Recall that for Kant, '[t]he necessity of real opposition' cuts across the domains of physical nature (exogenous causality) and mental life (endogenous causality). When understood as a *capacity to produce* an amount, namely, the capacity of something to 'cancel as much in the other as is equal to itself', we can see that negative magnitudes act as 'real grounds' or causal powers that can cause a change in their opposite (see Zinkin 2012 402–4). In this context, then, *change is understood by Kant as a power to cancel (*aufheben*) the power of something else, with its source in a relation of opposition or conflict between two terms*. Change is explained *in relational terms* as the result of conflictual, reciprocal relations between two terms, in which each 'cancels in the other an amount equal to its own worth' (Zinkin 2012 401).

In the second part of this chapter, we will ask how this compares with Nietzsche's understanding of change in his ontology of conflict with its sources in the relational concept of will to power and what he calls 'the relational character of all occurrence' (26[36] 11.157). We will also have occasion to ask how the conception of change, as the power to cancel or annul (*Aufheben*) the power of something else, compares with the notion of fixing or making fast (*Feststellen, Festsetzen*) in Nietzsche's conception of the conflictual nature of reality as 'a fixing [*Feststellen*] of relations of degree and force' (9[91] 12).

II.4 Kant's ontology of mental life

In order to open up the problem of change, Kant makes two moves in Section 3 of NG. The first is a shift to a fundamental enquiry into grounds of change, focused on ontology of mental life; the second, a shift from an enquiry into the real opposition of properties in one and the same subject or thing, to the question of real opposition between different things.

In order to investigate the 'real ground' or cause of change, Kant needs to extend his enquiry to include not just negation: how something is cancelled, but also how something is posited. The question of the ground or cause of change is therefore split into two: how something comes to be and how something ceases to be, with the claim that there must be a positive ground for both events to occur:

> [E]very passing-away is a negative coming-to-be, that is, for something positive which exists to be cancelled, a true real ground is required, just as a true real ground is required in order to bring it forth when it is not. (NG II.190)[31]

---

[31] '[E]in jedes Vergehen ist ein negatives Entstehen, d.i. es wird, um etwas Positives, was da ist, aufzuheben, eben so wohl ein wahrer Realgrund erfordert, als um es hervorzubringen, wenn es nicht ist.'

In the succeeding lines, it becomes clear that for Kant, the basis for this claim is an ontology modelled on motion, according to the principle of inertia:

> A movement never stops, either completely or in part, unless a motive force which is equal to the force which would have been able to bring the lost movement forth is combined with it in a relation of opposition. (NG II.190)[32]

On this basis, Kant asks how a representation ceases to exist. Just as the motion of a body will only stop when it encounters an equal counter-force, so an 'activity' or 'accident of the soul' – whether a representation, thought or desire – only ceases when it encounters real opposition that cancels it (*aufheben*) (just as it only comes to be when there is a 'real ground' or cause). In support of his claim that real opposition governs not just physical nature but also mental life,[33] Kant cites the effort (*Anstrengung*) needed to banish a sorrowful thought, or, on the contrary, an amusing thought when we wish to be serious and concentrate. This effort, as Zinkin (2012 405ff.) rightly notes, is the phenomenal signature of the real opposition needed to eliminate a thought or representation.[34]

Effort is also key to understanding the process of abstraction, in another example Kant gives. Baumgarten had argued that abstraction involves an epistemic loss, because the understanding (*Verstand*) directs our attention (*Aufmerksamkeit*) from one feature (*Merkmal*) of a representation to the next in a successive-discursive sequence. Since our attention is finite, the clarity thereby brought to each feature in succession casts the others in obscurity (*Dunkelheit*) and negates the initial fullness of features and qualitative richness of our sensate representation.[35] Starting out from the finitude of attention, the argument is governed by lack (of attention, of clarity) or *Mangel*, to which Kant responds: lack cannot account for the effort (*Anstrengung der Kraft*) required for abstraction, in contrast with the effortlessness of simply not knowing something. So here again, effort is the epidermal stigma of the real opposition at work in the depths of the soul: the work needed to deprive or rob (privation, *Beraubung*) our attention from

---

[32] 'Eine Bewegung hört niemals gänzlich oder zum Theil auf, ohne daß eine Bewegkraft, welche derjenigen gleich ist, die die verlorene Bewegung hätte hervorbringen können, damit in der Entgegensetzung verbunden wird.'

[33] '[I]n what concerns the cancellation of an existing something, there can be no difference between the accidents of mental natures and the effects of operative forces in the physical world' (NG II.191).

[34] NG II.190: 'In order to banish and eliminate a sorrowful thought a genuine effort, and commonly a large one, is required. And that this is so is something which we experience very distinctly within ourselves. It costs a real effort to eradicate an amusing representation which incites us to laughter, if we wish to concentrate our minds on something serious.' ('Man empfindet es in sich selbst sehr deutlich: daß, um einen Gedanken voll Gram bei sich vergehen zu lassen und aufzuheben, wahrhafte und gemeiniglich große Thätigkeit erfordert wird. Es kostet wirkliche Anstrengung eine zum Lachen reizende lustige Vorstellung zu vertilgen, wenn man sein Gemüth zur Ernsthaftigkeit bringen will.').

[35] See Baumgarten Met 529–31, 625–31; Aesth 557–61.

one feature or representation in order to redirect it to another and render it clearer.³⁶ Kant then proposes the general principle that

> the play of our representations and, in general, of all the activities of our soul, in so far as the consequences which were actual and then cease to exist, presuppose opposed actions of which one is the negative of the other [...] (NG II.191)³⁷

But Kant insists that, even where we cannot detect any effort or striving to cancel a given representation, 'there is no good reason for doubting the occurrence of this activity', and he continues:

> What a marvellous busyness is concealed within the depths of our minds which goes unnoticed even while it is being exercised. And it goes unnoticed because the actions in question are very numerous and because each of them is represented only very obscurely. (NG II.191)³⁸

While referring to Baumgarten's 'field of obscurity' (*Feld der Dunkelheit*) or obscure representations on the 'ground of the soul' (Met 511, 514), Kant cannot resist mentioning another perceptible sign of this imperceptible activity:

> Everybody is familiar with the facts which prove that this is the case. One need only consider, for example, the actions which take place unnoticed within us when we *read*. The phenomenon cannot fail to fill us with astonishment. (NG II.191)

---

³⁶ 'Every abstraction is simply the cancelling of certain clear representations; the purpose of the cancellation is normally to ensure mat what remains is that much more clearly represented. But everybody knows how much effort is needed to attain this purpose. Abstraction can therefore be called negative attention, that is, abstraction a real doing and acting which is opposed to the actions by means of which the representation is rendered clear; the combination of the two yields zero, or the lack of a clear representation. For otherwise, if it were a negation and just a lack, it would not require any more effort of energy than is required not to know something, for not knowing something never needs a ground.'
'Eine jede Abstraction ist nichts anders, als eine Aufhebung gewisser klaren Vorstellungen, welche man gemeiniglich darum anstellt, damit dasjenige, was übrig ist, desto klärer vorgestellt werde. Jedermann weiß aber, wie viel Thätigkeit hiezu erfordert wird, und so kann man die Abstraction eine negative Aufmerksamkeit nennen, das ist, ein wahrhaftes Thun und Handlen, welches derjenigen Handlung, wodurch die Vorstellung klar wird, entgegengesetzt ist und durch die Verknüpfung mit ihr das Zero, oder den Mangel der klaren Vorstellung zu wege bringt. Denn sonst, wenn sie eine Verneinung und Mangel schlechthin wäre, so würde dazu eben so wenig Anstrengung einer Kraft erfordert werden, als dazu, daß ich etwas nicht weiß, weil niemals ein Grund dazu war, Kraft nöthig ist' (NG II.190–91).
³⁷ 'Und so ist zu urtheilen, daß das Spiel der Vorstellungen und überhaupt aller Thätigkeiten unserer Seele, in so fern ihre Folgen, nachdem sie wirklich waren, wieder aufhören, entgegengesetzte Handlungen voraussetzen, davon eine die Negative der andern ist [...]'
³⁸ 'Allein welche bewunderungswürdige Geschäftigkeit ist nicht in den Tiefen unsres Geistes verborgen, die wir mitten in der Ausübung nicht bemerken, darum weil der Handlungen sehr viel sind, jede einzelne aber nur sehr dunkel vorgestellt wird.' See also NG II.199:
'There is no reason to suppose that when we seem to be in a state of complete mental inactivity, the sum of the real grounds of thought and desire is smaller than it is in the state when some degrees of this activity reveal themselves to consciousness.' ('Es ist eben nicht nöthig, daß, wenn wir glauben in einer gänzlichen Unthätigkeit des Geistes zu sein, die Summe der Realgründe des Denkens und Begehrens kleiner sei als in dem Zustande, da sich einige Grade dieser Wirksamkeit dem Bewußtsein offenbaren.').

One cannot help thinking that Nietzsche has the same thing in mind, when he writes that 'today one still hears with one's muscles, one even still reads with one's muscles' (14[119] 13.297). Both thinkers are struck by the 'marvellous busyness' that must be presupposed for conscious thought and perception to be possible. But the context for Nietzsche's remark is his physiology of art, and that alerts us to a crucial difference: his displacement of Kant's 'ground of the soul' by the body, the marvellous intelligence of the body, and complexity of activities which must be presupposed for there to be conscious thought and sensations – albeit for reasons very different from Kant's.

II.5 Real opposition between different bodies

From the outset, Kant announces negative magnitudes, in manifesto-style, as a 'greatly needed' concept for metaphysics, to be borrowed from mathematics, that is, as a contribution to metaphysics. By the end of the text he is professing his bafflement in front of the problem of causation or the ground of change. As seen above, the concept of real opposition has important critical implications for Leibnizian-Wolffian metaphysics and mechanistic cosmology. But in confessing his bafflement before the question of causation at the end, Kant is not just correcting and amending rationalist metaphysics, but putting the very possibility of metaphysics – with causation at its heart – in question.[39]

The first step is to extend the notion of real opposition from the conflict of forces within one subject or body to the relation between different things *(verschiedenen Dingen)*. Drawing again on mathematics, he focuses his philosophy of conflict on real opposition as an *event* (rather than an equilibrium of conflicting forces), as the communication of forces upon the collision of bodies ('actual opposition'), and distinguishes it from 'potential opposition' where two bodies do not actually collide, but are capable of negating one another, that is, 'cancelling the consequences of the other'.[40] The extension of real opposition to the relation between different bodies enables Kant to formulate the fundamental principle of his ontology of conflict:

> if A arises in a natural change occurring in die world, – A must also arise. In other words, no natural ground of a real consequence can exist without its being at the same time the ground of another consequence, which is the negative of it. (NG II.194)[41]

[39] See Schnepf (2001 149ff. 157ff).
[40] 'Dagegen nennt man mit Recht solche Prädicate, die zwar verschiedenen Dingen zukommen und eins die Folge des andern unmittelbar nicht aufheben, dennoch eins die Negative des andern, in so fern ein jedes so beschaffen ist, daß es doch entweder die Folge des andern, oder wenigstens etwas, was eben so bestimmt ist wie diese Folge und ihr gleich ist, aufheben könnte. Diese Entgegensetzung kann die mö gl i c h e heißen (*oppositio potentialis*). Beide sind real, d.i. von der logischen Opposition unterschieden, beide sind in der Mathematik beständig im Gebrauche, und beide verdienen es auch in der Philosophie zu sein.' (NG II.193). The first example Kant gives is of two bodies moving in opposite directions along a straight line, which (counterfactually) would communicate their forces if they moved towards each other.
[41] 'wenn A entspringt, in einer natürlichen Weltveränderung auch – A entspringen müsse, d.i. daß kein natürlicher Grund einer realen Folge sein könne, ohne zugleich ein Grund einer andern Folge zu sein, die die Negative von ihr ist.'

Or, more simply:

that no positive change ever occurs naturally in the world, whose consequence does not consist, as a whole, in an actual or potential opposition, which cancels it. (NG II.194)[42]

It is impossible not to hear an echo of Newton's third Law of action and reaction in this principle, and it is in fact grounded by Kant in a general metaphysical proposition, which, he claims, is also the ultimate ground of the conservation of momentum (Corollary 3 of Newton's third Law: see note 30 above). The general proposition reads:

In all natural changes of the world the sum of the positive [grounds], in so far as it is estimated in such a way that agreeing (not opposed) positings are added and really opposed are subtracted from one another, is neither increased nor decreased. (NG II.194)[43]

But as we know, Kant is keen to apply real opposition to non-mechanical events of the soul as well, and the conflictual character of his ontology is perhaps most striking when he illustrates his basic principle with the way in which the pleasure of one person can actually provoke a destructive displeasure in another: 'for when there is such real conflict (*realen Widerstreit*), one person often destroys (*vernichtigt*) what the other person has taken pleasure in creating' (NG II.194).

II.6 Critique of logical causation

In NG, then, Kant uses negative magnitudes to sketch a general ontology of conflict based on relations of real opposition within and between things or beings, in both physical and mental (non-mechanistic) nature. As a consequence, his ontology invites comparison with Nietzsche's philosophy of conflict, which, in physiological terms and ultimately the language of will to power, is focused on relations of power and interpretation both within and between different life-forms or power-complexes. As we shall see, Kant's fundamental principle that every positive force A must produce a counter-force –A is critically recast by Nietzsche in a physiological register with the claim that 'through every drive a counter-drive is aroused' (6[63] 9). But the immediate consequence of Kant's ontology of conflict is to break and break with Leibniz's account of causation as a logical relation between subject (cause) and predicate (effect), and its location in his ontology of self-unfolding monads (see Schnepf 2001 147, 151). The concept of negative magnitudes brings a level of complexity and a reciprocity to

---

[42] '[...] daß niemals eine positive Veränderung natürlicher Weise in der Welt geschehe, deren Folge nicht im Ganzen in einer wirklichen oder potentialen Entgegensetzung, die sich aufhebt, bestehe.'
[43] 'In allen natürlichen Veränderungen der Welt wird die Summe des Positiven,
insofern sie dadurch geschätzt wird, daß einstimmige (nicht entgegen‐gesetzte) Positionen addirt und realentgegengesetzte voneinander ab‐gezogen werden, weder vermehrt noch vermindert.'

causal relations that cannot be rendered logically in categorical judgements.[44] What is more, causation has now become for Kant a *real relation* between *different entities*. In the condensed formulations of the 'General Remark' at the end of NG, causation boils down to two propositions: '*because something is, something else is*' (NG II.202), or in the case of real opposition: '*because something is, something else is cancelled*' (NG II.203). As a real relation between different entities, causation cannot be expressed as an analytic relation following the principle of identity (or the principle of contradiction, in the case of real opposition).[45] Instead, causation is a synthetic relation, and as such it raises a problem for metaphysics, since it cannot be grounded in logic, but only in experience. This means, for example, that the creation of the world by God – beyond the possibility of experience – cannot be viewed as a case of causality (Schnepf 2001 158), and since the whole of metaphysics is grounded in the relation of God to the world, metaphysics is completely undermined. Indeed, without God the world is reduced to nothing, to zero:

> The totality of the world is in itself nothing, except insofar as it is something through the will of another. Consequently, the sum of existing reality, insofar as it is grounded in the world, if considered for itself, equal to zero = 0. (NG II.197)[46]

II.7 With or without substance?

In the course of NG, we have seen Kant advancing a dynamic, relational ontology of conflict. To name a few instances: impenetrability as the result of a conflict of forces in dynamic equilibrium, not a feature of matter, in some sense given or created; a conflict, which, on a grand scale, is also the signature of the world's perfection and the guarantor of its regularity; the veritable war of real grounds in the obscure depths of the soul presupposed by the dynamics of thought and mental life; and the impulse to destroy another's pleasure when it gives me displeasure. In all these cases, the concept of negative magnitudes allows Kant to address the problem of change in relational terms: to propose relations of real opposition (NG II.191–2) as the 'real ground' or source of change. In line with this, the closing pages (the General Remark) repeatedly draw attention away from the concept of cause, as a power to bring forth or cancel, to the *relation* between real grounds and their consequences, as the 'nexus'[47] of the problem of causation. We see this in his criticism of the proponents of causation as an analytic logical relation:

---

[44] For a detailed account of the logical account of causation in Leibniz-Wolffian metaphysics and in Kant's *Nova Dilucidatio* (1755), see Schnepf (2001 141–5).
[45] In his third dissertation *Nova Dilucidatio* (1755), Kant had still advanced a subject-predicate account of the causal relation.
[46] 'Das Ganze der Welt ist an sich selbst Nichts, außer in so fern es durch den Willen eines andern Etwas ist. Es ist demnach die Summe aller existirenden Realität, in so fern sie in der Welt gegründet ist, für sich selbst betrachtet dem Zero = 0 gleich.'
[47] See Schnepf (2001 148 and 151f.) on causation as the 'nexus' in Herder's transcription of Kant's Metaphysics lectures.

Nor am I willing to be fobbed off by the words 'cause' and 'effect', 'force' and 'action'. For if I already regard something as a cause of something else, or if I attach the concept of force to it, then I am already thinking of the cause as containing the relation of the real ground to its consequence, and then it is easy to understand that the consequence is posited in accordance with the rule of identity. (NG II.203)[48]

But causation is *not* analytic, it is a synthetic relation, a dynamic nexus between different things, which is the real ground or source of change. And 'force' (*Kraft*) is not the predicate of a thing (Crusius), nor that by virtue of which accidents inhere in a substance, much less a substance itself (Baumgarten, Met 197–9). As these lines indicate, 'force' too is a relational concept, just another word for the causal relation, or rather: for the *problem* of causality, in which the text culminates. In the end, Kant despairs even of a form of judgement that would capture it:

[T]he relation of a real ground to something, which is either posited or cancelled by it, cannot be expressed by a judgement; it can only be expressed by a concept. That concept can probably be reduced by means of analysis to simple concepts of real grounds, albeit in such a fashion that in the end all our cognitions of this relation reduce to simple, unanalysable concepts of real grounds, the relation of which to their consequences cannot be rendered distinct at all. (NG II.204)[49]

Does Kant's dynamic, relational ontology mean that he breaks with the metaphysics of being and substance of ontology? Kant's pre-critical efforts to develop a monadology compatible with Newtonian physics have been documented by several scholars (Schonfeld, Friedman, Saner). In the *Physical Monadology* in particular, published some eight years before NG (1756), monads are simple, unextended points, which fill space by virtue of their repulsive force. The forces of attraction and repulsion are phenomenal manifestations of the external, relational determinations of substance, which generate space, understood as the community or co-presence of substances. These external relations are real (*contra* Leibniz) and are subject to Newton's laws. But Kant also retains a monadological concept of simple substances behind the phenomena, which have a purely internal nature constituted by their internal determinations independently of any other substances. For there to be appearances – to paraphrase the second Preface to KrV (B xxvii) – there must be something that appears. Kant's simple substances do the traditional work of substance ontology: to secure the identity

---

[48] 'Ich lasse mich auch durch die Wörter Ursache und Wirkung, Kraft und Handlung nicht abspeisen. Denn wenn ich etwas schon als eine Ursache wovon ansehe, oder ihr den Begriff einer Kraft beilege, so habe ich in ihr schon die Beziehung des Realgrundes zu der Folge gedacht, und dann ist es leicht die Position der Folge nach der Regel der Identität einzusehen.'

[49] 'Aus demselben findet sich, daß die Beziehung eines Realgrundes auf etwas, das dadurch gesetzt oder aufgehoben wird, gar nicht durch ein Urtheil, sondern bloß durch einen Begriff könne ausgedrückt werden, den man wohl durch Auflösung zu einfacheren Begriffen von Realgründen bringen kann, so doch, daß zuletzt alle unsre Erkenntnisse von dieser Beziehung sich in einfachen und unauflöslichen Begriffen der Realgründe endigen, deren Verhältniß zur Folge gar nicht kann deutlich gemacht werden.'

and stability of beings over time, and they do so by virtue of an endogenous force. As Friedman (2013 344) points out:

> [W]hat Kant calls 'innate force [*vis insita*]' in the *New Exposition* and 'force of inertia [*vis inertiae*]' in the *Physical Monadology* is precisely (the phenomenal manifestation of) an internal ground of (unchanging) internal determinations in this sense. It is (the phenomenal manifestation of) an 'internal principle of activity' (1, 408) by which every simple substance or monad, considered independently and on its own, 'strives to persevere' (2, 485) in whatever internal state it finds itself.[50]

In an extraordinary reversal, the *vis viva* of Leibniz and his followers is turned from a principle of *change* into a principle of *stasis* or *inertia*, a kind of active *vis mortua*. Against this background, NG can be viewed as an effort by Kant to confine the principle of change to real external relations, while securing the continuity, stability and identity of substance for beings through an endogenous force of inertia.

And yet, the terms 'substance' and 'monad' do not appear once in NG. The text can certainly be read as presupposing, without naming, Kant's simple substances, as I have just suggested. But could it be that Kant is here experimenting with a dynamic, relational ontology *without substance* – an ontology closer to Nietzsche than to Leibniz? It is worth bearing in mind that NG begins with the manifest(o) intention to draw on the concept of negative magnitudes from mathematics and physics in order to correct and enrich metaphysics, but it ends by problematizing causation in a way that threatens to undermine metaphysics altogether. And perhaps this tension is indicative of an equivocation on Kant's part, which inhibits him from naming substance, without, however, enabling him to reject substance ontology and the metaphysics of being explicitly.

III The problem of opposition and contradiction in Nietzsche's thought

III.1 Introduction

There is no shortage of texts in Nietzsche's oeuvre proclaiming the contradictory character of reality. To take a few examples:

> [...] there is only One world, and it is false, cruel,
> contradictory, seductive, without sense ... A world thus
> composed is the true world ...

---

[50] In note 105 on the same page, Friedman adds: 'It appears, then, that just as *vis viva*, on the Leibnizean–Wolffian conception, is the phenomenal manifestation of the fundamental internal active force of simple substances by which they determine the *changes* of their internal state, Newtonian *vis inertiae*, for the pre-critical Kant, is the phenomenal manifestation of the fundamental internal active force of simple substances by which they rather determine the *preservation* of their internal state.'

[...] es giebt nur Eine Welt, und diese ist falsch, grausam, widersprüchlich, verführerisch, ohne Sinn ... Eine so beschaffene Welt ist die wahre Welt ... [...] (11[415] 13.193)

The principle of contradiction provided the schema: the true world, to which one seeks the way, cannot be in contradiction with itself, cannot change, cannot become, has no origin and no end [...]
    And behold, the world now became false, precisely on account of those qualities that constitute ist reality,
change, becoming, multiplicity, opposition, contradiction, war

Der Satz vom Widerspruch gab das Schema: die wahre Welt, zu der man den Weg sucht, kann nicht mit sich in Widerspruch sein, kann nicht wechseln, kann nicht werden, hat keinen Ursprung und kein Ende.[...]
    Und siehe da: jetzt wurde die Welt falsch, und exakt der Eigenschaften wegen, die ihre Realität ausmachen,
Wechsel, Werden, Vielheit, Gegensatz, Widerspruch, Krieg (14[153] 13.337)

As these texts indicate, 'contradiction' (*Widerspruch*) is closely related to, if not synonymous with terms like 'conflict', 'war', 'falsehood', 'multiplicity', 'cruelty' in Nietzsche's usage. Unlike Kant, he also seems to use it interchangeably with the terms 'opposition', 'opposed', etc. (*Gegensatz, entgegengesetzt*). For Kant, as we have seen, real opposition occurs in conflictual relations that are precisely *non*-contradictory, reflecting his distinction between the two forms of negation, privation and absence. Does this mean that Nietzsche succumbs to the performative contradiction of negating in the logic of his thought what he affirms of reality? Without this distinction, I have suggested, a philosophy of conflict faces intractable problems. How can it avoid being swallowed up by the reality of contradiction? And if, like Nietzsche, one does adhere to the principle of non-contradiction, it is hard to see how one can negate in the manner of one's thought what is affirmed in the matter of one's thought – without committing a blatant performative contradiction. In Nietzsche's case, the problem is aggravated by two further factors. In Kant, as we saw, the rationalist equation of logic and reality is broken and the laws of logic are gradually restricted to subjective conditions of thought. In Nietzsche's thought, this move is radicalized into a critique of the logical principles of identity and non-contradiction, confronting him with a further problem: How can he subject the principle of non-contradiction to critique while adhering to it in the logic of his thinking? Further problems are raised for Nietzsche's philosophy of conflict by a second factor: next to texts like those cited above where the reality of contradiction or opposition is affirmed, there are texts where this is denied in favour of degrees, grades, differences of degree or 'valeurs':

> There are no oppositions: we have the concept of opposition from logical [oppositions] alone – and from these falsely transposed into things. (9[91] 12)[51]

> Through every drive a counter-drive is aroused, and not just this, but like harmonic strings yet others, whose relation cannot be designated with a word as everyday as 'opposition'.

> Durch jede Trieb wird auch sein Gegentrieb erregt, und nicht nur dieser, sondern wie Obertonsaiten [harmonic strings] noch andere, deren Verhältniß nicht in einem so geläufigen Worte zu bezeichnen ist, wie 'Gegensatz'. (6[63] 9)

While it is true that Nietzsche makes little or no effort to control his vocabulary for systematic ends, as Kant does, it will become clear in what follows that he is acutely aware of the differences between logical opposition or contradiction and real opposition, and does not succumb to the contradictions described above. Many of so-called 'contradictions' in Nietzsche's thought arise because we assume that a given term means the same thing in different contexts. This is absolutely not the case for Nietzsche, nor even for Kant,[52] – even if, unlike Nietzsche, he does make the effort to control his vocabulary in a systematic manner. This is why it is so important to ask what a given word means in each specific context where it occurs, and to distinguish the different meanings and connotations of that word *before* launching into philosophical analysis on the assumption that it has the same meaning in different texts – which then contradict one another.[53] In this case, where contradiction is the very issue, the problem of Nietzsche's 'contradictoriness' is particularly virulent. What is more, the issue of opposition/contradiction goes to the very heart of Nietzsche's critique of metaphysics and logic, but also to the core of his ontology of conflict and his critical diagnosis of modernity.

In the case of 'Gegensatz', I propose that three main meanings can be distinguished and that these distinctions enable us to make good sense of Nietzsche's positions. First, there is 'Gegensatz' in the sense of logical contradiction (*Widerspruch*) and, based on it, metaphysical opposition and '*the belief in the oppositions of values* [*Gegensätze der Werthe*]', famously criticized in JGB 2. This belief, he states, 'stands in the background of all their [metaphysicians'] logical procedures'. In Nietzsche's genealogy of logic, as we shall see, logic and the metaphysics of being are complicit and inseparable. Metaphysics involves the projection of logical structures onto reality, conceived as an independently existing order of beings; while logic depends on ontic notions such as that of a 'thing'.

---

[51] 'Es giebt keine Gegensätze: nur von denen der Logik her haben wir den Begriff des Gegensatzes – und von denen aus fälschlich in die Dinge übertragen.'

[52] See Saner (1967 36ff.) on this point.

[53] This is the rationale for the detailed word-studies in the *Nietzsche-Wörterbuch* (Nietzsche Online: http://www.degruyter.com/view/NO/empfindung) in which the different meanings of a given word/word-field are distinguished, described and exemplified with selected quotations. For the methodology, see Siemens and van Tongeren (2012c) and Siemens, van Tongeren, Schank (2000/2001).

This kind of opposition or 'Gegensatz' (henceforth Ggz I) has the following characteristics: the terms are mutually exclusive, they have nothing in common, no inner relation (*Verwandtshaft*), and neither term can be derived from the opposed term; their relation of contradiction or opposition is constructed through the separation and fixing (*Feststellung*) of the terms into self-identical, durable items or entities (which for Nietzsche requires an abstraction from experience of real contradictions) and then (in the case of metaphysics) their projection onto reality.

Nietzsche's critique of logic issues in the claim that oppositions of this kind have zero cognitive value when projected onto reality. On the other hand, what his genealogy shows is that logic, including the principle of non-contradiction, does have value *for life*: it is life-conditioning or life-enabling. For

> without accepting the logical fictions, without measuring reality against the wholly invented world of the unconditioned and self-identical [*Sich-selbst-Gleichen*], without a constant falsification of the world through numbers, the human being [*der Mensch*] could not live (JGB 4.)[54]

The principles of identity and non-contradiction are necessary for thought, where thought is understood to create a world that is habitable for us, that can be lived in, and not to inform us about reality 'in itself'. As Müller-Lauter (1971 13) points out, the falsity of logic 'does not derogate from its usefulness for life. [Nietzsche's] critique is only directed against the fact it later worked *as truth*.' From this, we can understand the rationale for Nietzsche's adherence to the principle of non-contradiction: his thought operates under the constraint of life as the highest value and eschews metaphysical knowledge-claims about an independently existing order of beings in favour of creating a world that can be lived in. At the same time, his critique of logic also highlights the necessity of distinguishing logical opposition from the real oppositions that are the matter of his thought.

This brings us to the meanings of the term 'Gegensatz' that are affirmed by Nietzsche. Both concern his reconceptualization or reinterpretation (*Umdeutung*) of 'opposition' in the logical and metaphysical senses (Ggz I). Once again we can take our cue from JGB 2 when Nietzsche writes

> It could even be possible that *that* which constitutes the value of those good and revered things consists precisely in their being related, linked, bound up in an

---

[54] See also e.g. 9[97] 12.390: 'Logik ist der Versuch, nach einem von uns gesetzten Seins-Schema die wirkliche Welt zu begreifen, richtiger, uns formulirbar, berechenbar zu machen …'; 14[152] 13: 'Die subjektive Nöthigung, hier nicht widersprechen zu können, ist eine biologische Nöthigung […]'; 9[91] 12: 'Logisirung, Rationalisirung, Systematisirung als Hülfsmittel des Lebens.'; 25[427] 11.124: 'NB. – der Kampf als Herkunft der logischen Funktionen. Das Geschöpf, welches sich am stärksten reguliren, discipliniren, urtheilen konnte – mit der größten Erregbarkeit und noch größerer Selbstbeherrschung – ist immer übrig geblieben.'

incriminating manner with those bad, apparently opposed things; perhaps in their even being essentially the same. Perhaps! (JGB 2 5.16)[55]

In Nietzsche's reinterpretation of 'opposition' (henceforth Ggz II.1), the terms that are opposed in logic and metaphysics are not mutually exclusive, but genealogically related (*verwandt*), and the higher-valued term is derivative of its apparent 'opposite': 'linked, bound up in an incriminating manner [...] perhaps even essentially the same'. Thus, reason (*Vernünftiges*) comes from unreason (*Vernunftlosem*) (MA 1 2.23); logic derives from the illogical (FW 111), the will to knowing from the will to not-knowing (JGB 24), the human from the inhuman (HW 1.783), selflessness from egoism (MA 1), Christian love from hatred (GM I 14-16), the good from the evil (1[28] 10.16). Through genealogy (GM) and historical philosophizing (MA 2), Nietzsche's methods for exposing these relations, the meaning and value of things we value are radically transformed: they cease to have their own origin or ground 'in the womb of being', and are bound up instead with their 'opposites', as their 'sublimations' (MA 1), 'refinements', 'degrees' or later 'stages':

> As soon as the refinement is *there*, the *earlier* stage is no longer felt as a stage, but rather as opposite. It is *easier* to think opposites than degrees. (11[115] 9.482)[56]

Clearly, the meaning, structure and constitution of the things we value change when they are viewed as refinements, sublimations or later stages of their so-called 'opposites'. As the lines from JGB 2 cited above make clear, their value can no longer consist in *excluding* their opposites, but lies precisely in their entwinement with their origins in 'those bad, apparently opposed things'. If, as Nietzsche contends, goodwill is 'refined possessiveness, refined sexual pleasure, refined exuberance in security etc.'[57] its value is bound up with the value of the latter for life.

---

[55] 'Es wäre sogar noch möglich, dass was den Werth jener guten und verehrten Dinge ausmacht, gerade darin bestünde, mit jenen schlimmen, scheinbar entgegengesetzten Dingen auf verfängliche Weise verwandt, verknüpft, verhäkelt, vielleicht gar wesensgleich zu sein. Vielleicht!'

[56] In this note 'Gegensatz' means Ggz I:
'Im Wohlwollen ist verfeinerte Besitzlust, verfeinerte
Geschlechtslust, verfeinerte Ausgelassenheit des Sicheren usw.
 Sobald die Verfeinerung d a ist, wird die f r ü h e r e Stufe nicht
mehr als Stufe, sondern als Gegensatz gefühlt. Es ist
l e i c h t e r, Gegensätze zu denken, als Grade.'
See also Nietzsche's use of Ggz I and the notion of sublimation in note 11[105] 9.478f.:
'Liebe und Grausamkeit nicht Gegensätze: sie finden sich bei
den besten und festesten Naturen immer bei einander. (Der
christliche Gott – eine sehr weise und ohne moralische
Vorurtheile ausgedachte Person!)
Die Menschen sehen die kleinen sublimirten Dosen nicht und
leugnen sie: sie leugnen z.B. die Grausamkeit im Denker, die
Liebe im Räuber. Oder sie haben gute Namen für alles, was an
einem Wesen hervortritt, das ihren Geschmack befriedigt.'
[57] 'Im W o h l w o l l e n ist verfeinerte Besitzlust, verfeinerte Geschlechtslust, verfeinerte Ausgelassenheit des Sicheren usw' (11[115] 9.482).

Nietzsche's genealogical notion of opposition (Ggz II.1), in the service of the critique and transvaluation of values, brings a temporal-historical dimension to the notion of opposition entirely absent in Kant. This presupposes an entirely different ontology to the dualisms served by moral and metaphysical oppositions (Ggz I), an ontology of becoming, first limned by the project of 'historical philosophizing' announced in MA 1 and 2 and refined methodologically in Nietzsche's later works (JGB, FW Book V, GM) and notes under the rubric of will to power. The status of Nietzsche's ontology or counter-ontology of becoming will be considered later, but one important affinity between Nietzsche's genealogical sense of opposition and the thought of Heraclitus is worth mentioning. Against the exclusive value placed on the 'good and revered things' by morality and metaphysics, as we have seen in JGB 2, Nietzsche emphasizes their essential sameness ('wesensgleich') with the 'bad, apparently opposed' things. In real life, he writes elsewhere, good and evil are not mutually exclusive, but 'complementary value-concepts' (*complementäre Werthbegriffe*), since life has yes and no 'in all its instincts' and knows not how to separate them (*trennen*).[58] This is one of the insights gained from his genealogies, and it is reminiscent of the way in which opposites are conceived by Heraclitus. Opposites are never really divided for Heraclitus, but are 'the same relatively' and 'complement each other' as a 'unity and a plurality' in tension (Herschbell and Nimis 1979 22). Nietzsche's genealogical notion of opposition (Ggz II.1) can, then, be seen as a temporal-historical reinterpretation of Heraclitus's unity of opposites, when for instance he writes:

> The excess of morality has proven its opposite [*Gegensatz*], evil, as *necessary and useful*, as the source of the good.[59]

> When a human being develops so vigorously and seems to jump from one opposite into the other: upon closer observation, one will uncover *dovetailing*, where the new edifice grows out of the old one.[60]

While Nietzsche usually rejects 'oppositions' (in the sense of Ggz I) in favour of alternatives like 'refinements', 'sublimations', 'stages', etc., there are also occasions – such as the lines just cited – in which 'opposition' or 'opposed' (in the sense of Ggz II.1) is used affirmatively. Both citations perform a reinterpretation of 'Gegensatz' from the moral and metaphysical sense (Ggz I) to the genealogical sense (Ggz II.1). With the distinction between Ggz I and Ggz II.1 in mind, we can, then, begin to make sense of this usage without ascribing spurious contradictions to him.

---

[58] 15[113] 13.473. Earlier in the same note, he writes: 'Man ist gut, um den Preis, daß man auch böse zu sein weiß; man ist böse, weil man sonst nicht gut zu sein verstünde.'
[59] 'Der Exceß der Moral hat ihren Gegensatz, das Böse, als nothwendig und nützlich bewiesen, und als Quelle des Guten' (1[28] 10.16).
[60] 'Wenn der Mensch sich noch so stark fortentwickelt und aus einem Gegensatz in den andern überzuspringen scheint: bei genaueren Beobachtungen wird man doch die V e r z a h n u n g e n auffinden, wo das neue Gebäude aus dem älteren herauswächst' (WS 198).

But as Müller-Lauter (1971 12) points out, Nietzsche also takes it upon himself to defend the oppositional or contradictory character of reality against the claims of logic and metaphysics. For this it is essential to distinguish the kind of opposition involved in the principle of non-contradiction from real opposition. Next to his 'genealogical' reinterpretation of logical/metaphysical opposition (Ggz II.1), he therefore also reinterprets it in an ontological register (Ggz II.2): as the antagonism (*Gegeinander*) of a plurality of force quanta or powers without substance, whose essence is their relation. This takes us to the heart of Nietzsche's ontology of conflict.

III.2 Nietzsche's ontology of conflict

Nietzsche's ontology of conflict was born of his dissatisfaction with the philosophical explanation of reality given by the metaphysics of being (*Seinsmetaphysik*) that has dominated Western philosophy, and the key concept of substance in particular.[61] Substance ontology explains reality as a fixed order of being in which durable things stand in determinate, fixed or at least regular relations to one another. It is the concept of substance that gives things their unity and identity over time by virtue of three features ascribed to it in different ways by different philosophers: substance represents *identity* (durability over time), *unity* and *independence* (self-sufficiency).[62] These qualities define what being, i.e. reality, is. But what of becoming, change and motion? Accounting for change and becoming is one of the central, most intractable problems for substance ontology. Again, there are important differences between the answers given in traditional metaphysics, but again their approaches have something in common. In different ways, substance thinkers have attempted to address this problem on the basis of three shared claims:

1. becoming is opposed to being (substance);
2. becoming is denied reality: it is not real or less real than being; and
3. becoming is denied the independence that belongs properly to being.

By means of these three claims, substance ontology has attempted to explain becoming from fixed, invariable principles. But in doing so, it *negates* becoming and so fails to do justice to the dynamic character of reality – at least according to Nietzsche. His guiding questions from the early 1880s on concern the sources or grounds of change and movement. How can something move itself spontaneously? How can a force spontaneously act in a creative way upon another force?[63] And what concept of force can do justice to movement and change in all domains of reality: physical nature, organic and inorganic, as well as mental life? Nietzsche's 'ontology' is an attempt to

---

[61] For a detailed exposition of the will to power as Nietzsche's response to his critique of substance ontology, see Aydin (2003, 2004).
[62] See Aydin (2003 13–46, 205–6). On Nietzsche's early critique of metaphysics and substance ontology through his epistemological engagement with the pre-Socratics, see Meyer (1998 8–31) and Mattioli (2017) (with reference to Afrikan Spir).
[63] Visser (1989 57–61).

reconfigure the relation of becoming and being in a counter-ontology of becoming that would do justice to the reality of change, movement and spontaneity.

Nietzsche's critique of *Seinsmetaphysik* leads him to reject any underlying unitary ground of beings (arche, first substance, God), and to reject the existence of any substances, that is, self-caused, self-identical, enduring beings. As the negative results of this move he is left with the designation of reality or life as pure process, continuum, occurrence, chaos. These cannot, however, be thought or formulated.[64] Nietzsche therefore takes as the presuppositions for thought, and for his counter-ontology of becoming, a series of negations of *Seinsmetaphysik* and substance ontology. Instead of unitary grounds there is only diversity, difference (*Verschiedenheit*), 'originary' plurality or multiplicity.[65] Against the primacy of being he posits 'the relational character of all occurrence' or the 'in-one-another' (*Ineinander*)[66] of forces or entities without substance (quanta, powers, drives, affects)[67] in unceasing transformation; and instead of harmony, consistency and rational order, there is only opposition (*Gegensatz*), real contradiction (*Widerspruch*), struggle, conflict.[68] These presuppositions are integrated in the thought of will to power as the *Ineinander* of a plurality of force quanta or powers without substance in ever-changing relations of conflict.

It is important to see that these are not positive truth-claims about reality, conceived as an independent order of beings, intended to replace the metaphysics of being and substance ontology with a metaphysics of becoming and flux. Rather, they articulate in positive terms the *negative* results of his critique of *Seinsmetaphyik* and substance ontology in the attempt to develop a language that operates within the constraints of language and thought but does a better job of describing, or at least pointing towards, the reality of change and spontaneity. By 'reality' is meant, not a 'true world', an underlying ground of appearances or an objective 'in itself' opposed

---

[64] 'Der Charakter der werdenden Welt als unformulirbar, als "falsch", als "sich-widersprechend"'(9[89] 12.382); '[…] der Gegensatz dieser Phänomenal-Welt ist nicht "die wahre Welt", sondern die formlos-unformulirbare Welt des Sensationen-Chaos, – also eine andere Art Phänomenal-Welt, eine für uns "unerkennbare"'. (9[106] 12.396).

[65] E.g. 7[110] 7.163: 'In logic the principle of contradiction rules, which perhaps is not valid for things, which are different, opposed [*Verschiedenes, Entgegengesetztes*]'; 25[427] 11.124: '– Preservation of the individual: i.e. to assume that a multiplicity [*Vielheit*] with the most manifold [*mannichfaltigsten*] activities wants to "preserve" itself, not as identical-with-itself, but "living" – ruling – obeying – nourishing itself – growing – […]'; 1[58] 12.25: 'The human as a multiplicity of "wills to power" […]'.

[66] 'The unchanging sequence of certain appearances does not demonstrate a "law," but rather a power relation between two or more forces. To say "But exactly this relation remains the same!" means nothing other than "One and the same force cannot also be another force." – It is not about a *sequence* [lit. after-one-another: *Nacheinander*], – but rather an *interconnectedness* [lit. in-one-another: *Ineinander*], a process in which the single moments that follow one another condition one another *not* as causes and effects …' (2[139] 12.135f.).

[67] On drives, see 7[25] 10.250: '"drive [*Trieb*]" is only a translation into the language of feeling from non-feeling [*aus dem Nichtfühlendem*] […]'. On force: 2[159] 12.143: 'Has a force [*Kraft*] ever been detected yet? No, rather effects, translated into an entirely alien language.'

[68] 26[276] 11.222: 'There must be struggle [*Kampf*] for the sake of struggle: and *mastering* [Herrschen] is to bear the counter-weight of the weaker force, so a kind of *continuation* of the struggle. *Obeying* equally a *struggle*: precisely as much force as *remains* to [be able to] resist.' On consistency as a feature of the world in the rationalist tradition, see Schonfeld (2000 136–8).

to a knowing subject, but what Nietzsche calls *Schein* (GS 54): what is alive for us as sentient beings, the phenomenal world of appearance (*Erscheinung*) stripped of any reference to its opposite outside it (*Sein, Wesen*, essence, substance). He writes of the 'fluid, ungraspable proteus-nature' of our *Schein*-world, as 'the actual and only reality of things […] best signified with opposed predicates', but which can also be signified 'from the inside' as '"the will to power"' (40[53] 11.654).[69]

It is indisputable that Nietzsche's presuppositions depend on what they negate for their meaning, and that he can only resist metaphysics in the discourse of metaphysics. But everything depends on how we take this discourse. We need to distinguish logical presuppositions (what must be presupposed in order to think) and grammatical presuppositions (what must be presupposed in order to speak) from ontological presuppositions (what must be presupposed as existing, as real). While it is clear that Nietzsche can only think and speak in ways that presuppose and depend on the metaphysics he criticizes, it does not follow that he subscribes to a positive ontology that remains captive to the metaphysical structures he is contesting. Nietzsche tries to think *within and against* the presuppositions of thought, to speak *with and against* subject-predicate grammar, but his 'ontology' is a stand-in discourse. As we shall see, it is what he calls a 'manner of speaking' (*Sprechart*) that negates metaphysics and describes better the dynamic, pluralistic, conflictual character of reality.

---

[69] 'gegen das Wort "E r s c h e i n u n g e n".
NB. S c h e i n wie ich es verstehe, ist die wirkliche und einzige Realität der Dinge, – das, dem alle vorhandenen Prädikate erst zukommen und welches verhältnißmäßig am besten noch mit allen, also auch den entgegengesetzten Prädikaten zu bezeichnen ist. Mit dem Worte ist aber nichts weiter ausgedrückt als seine U n z u g ä n g l i c h k e i t für die logischen Prozeduren und Distinktionen: also "Schein" im Verhältniß zur "logischen Wahrheit" – welche aber selber nur an einer imaginären Welt möglich ist. Ich setze also nicht "Schein" in Gegensatz zur "Realität" sondern nehme umgekehrt Schein als die Realität, welche sich der Verwandlung in eine imaginative "Wahrheits-Welt" widersetzt. Ein bestimmter Name für diese Realität wäre "der Wille zur Macht", nämlich von Innen her bezeichnet und nicht von seiner unfaßbaren flüssigen Proteus-Natur aus.'

'against the word *"appearances" ['Erscheinungen']*
N.B. Semblance [*Schein*] as I understand it, is the actual and sole reality of things – that to which all present predicates belong and which can best be signified by all predicates, even the opposed ones. With the word, however, nothing more is expressed than its *inaccessibility* to logical procedure and distinctions: thus "semblance" ['Schein'] in relation to "logical truth" – which, however, itself is only possible in an imaginary world. I thus place "*Schein*" not in opposition to "reality" but rather on the contrary accept semblance as the reality which resists transformation into an imaginative "true world". A more determinate name for this reality would be "the will to power", that is, signified from the inside and not from its ungraspable, fluid Protean nature.'

The centrality of conflict in Nietzsche's ontology of becoming is most succinctly expressed in the following lines from the last *Nachlass*:

All occurrence, all movement, all becoming as
a fixing [making fast] of relations of degree and power, as a
struggle ...[70]

Here we can make out the three key moments of Nietzsche's ontology: *dynamism* (*Geschehen, Bewegung, Werden*), *pluralism* or relations of difference (*Grad- und Kraftverhältnissen*) and *struggle* or *conflict* (*Kampf*). Against the ontological priority and greater reality given to being over becoming in traditional metaphysics and substance ontology, Nietzsche posits the primacy of occurrence, movement, becoming. The reality of occurrence consists not of beings or substances (self-supporting, unified and enduring entities) interacting causally, but of relations of difference among a plurality of forces or powers without substance. Yet being does not simply disappear. Rather, it is *integrated* into becoming – thereby overcoming their opposition in metaphysics – with the claim that reality as becoming has the character of an incessant *Feststellen*, a multiple fixing (*Fest-setzen*) or positing (*Setzen*) of being[71] within an ongoing struggle or conflict of forces; being is hereby dynamized and pluralized. At the heart of Nietzsche's ontology of conflict is a *relational* concept of power, or rather powers; that is, (1.) power as activity, the activity of increasing power, which can only be an overpowering, because (2.) power-as-activity can only act in relation to the resistance offered by other counter-powers.[72] Since power can only act (increase power) in relation to the resistance of other powers, these relations are relations of struggle, conflict, tension (*Kampf, Streit, Krieg, Spannung*), of reciprocal action-reaction or overpowering-and-resisting. As Nietzsche writes in note 14[153] 13.337: reality is 'Wechsel, Werden, Vielheit, Gegensatz, Widerspruch, Krieg' – change, becoming, multiplicity, opposition, contradiction, war.

At the centre of Nietzsche's ontology of conflict is his version of *Realrepugnanz* or real opposition. Here 'Gegensatz' (Ggz II.2) signifies the antagonism (*Krieg, Gegeneinander*) of a plurality (*Vielheit*) of force quanta or powers without substance in unceasing transformation (*Wechsel*), whose essence is their relation of exercising power over one another through the activity of fixing or *Feststellen*. Further on in this chapter we will ask how these antagonistic relations, in which each term (force quantum or power-complex) seeks to fix others, compare with Kant's account of the source of change in relations of real opposition in which each term cancels the effects of the other.

Nietzsche's ontological concept of opposition (Ggz II.2) is intended to do more justice to the reality of change and becoming than the metaphysics of being. But it is

---

[70] 'Alles Geschehen, alle Bewegung, alles Werden als
ein Feststellen von Grad- und Kraftverhältnissen, als ein
K a m p f ...' (9[91] 12.385).
[71] See also: 34[88][89] 11.449; 26[359] 11.244; 39[13] 11.623; 2[139] 12.135f.; UB III 3 1.360; FW 370 3.622; AC 58 6.245.
[72] On Nietzsche's dynamic, relational concept of force (*Kraft*) and its sources, see: Abel (1998 6–27); Mittasch (1952 102–13). On Nietzsche's concept of power (*Macht*), see also Gerhardt (1996 155–61, 203–45, 285–309).

also meant to displace the qualitative oppositions (Ggz I) projected by metaphysics onto reality (good vs. evil, right vs. wrong, true vs. false, real vs. illusion, beautiful vs. ugly, etc.; see JGB 2). Indeed it is part of a broader initiative to *de-anthropomorphize* reality by stripping it of all human qualities and values, including 'laws of nature' (cf. FW 109; JGB 22). As we shall see, however, this move is complicated by Nietzsche's realization that there is one anthropomorphic quality that we need in order to make sense of change: the activity of willing more power. In order to see how Nietzsche reaches this conclusion and what it means for his concept of opposition, we will need to examine his critique of mechanism in favour of physiological models of conflict and eventually the will to power. But first, we need to ask what exactly Nietzsche's critique of logical contradiction is.

III.3 Nietzsche's genealogy of logic

In line with Nietzsche's genealogical reinterpretation of 'opposition' (Ggz II.1), he argues that logic derives from its 'apparent opposite', the illogical (*Unlogic*). What he means by this is that judgement, in which logic operates, presupposes a process by which what is not the same is made the same: 'das Gleichsetzen des Nicht-gleichen' as Nietzsche already puts it in WL (1.880). What is different (*verschieden*) but similar (*ähnlich*) is treated as the same (*gleich*), thereby effacing difference. Here lies the 'illogical,' as he explains in FW 111:

> But the overwhelming tendency to treat that which is similar as the same, an illogical tendency – for there is in itself nothing the same –, first created the basis for logic. (FW 111 3.471f.)[73]

According to Nietzsche, logic also presupposes that the items that have been made the same (*das Gleichgesetzte*) remain the same and identical with themselves, i.e. that there are substances[74] and 'things', for it is on this basis that the principle of identity (A = A) was constructed.

> The 'thing' – that is the actual substrate of A: our belief in things is the presupposition for the belief in logic. The A of logic is like the atom a derivative re-construction of the 'thing' ... (9[97] 12.389)[75]

---

[73] 'Der überwiegende Hang aber, das Aehnliche als gleich zu behandeln, ein unlogischer Hang – denn es giebt an sich nichts Gleiches –, hat erst alle Grundlage der Logik geschaffen.' For the young Nietzsche's reflections on the illogical sources of knowledge, philosophy and language under the spell of the metaphorical drive, see: 19[216, 236, 242, 321] 7, and PHG 3 1.814; PHG 11 1.847.

[74] FW 111 goes on to claim that 'the concept of substance [is] indispensable for logic, even if in the strictest sense nothing actual [*nichts Wirkliches*] corresponds to it.' In MA 18 he quotes Afrikan Spir on substance: '"Das ursprüngliche allgemeine Gesetz des erkennenden Subjects besteht in der inneren Nothwendigkeit, jeden Gegenstand an sich, in seinem eigenen Wesen als einen mit sich selbst identischen, also selbstexistirenden und im Grunde stets gleichbleibenden und unwandelbaren, kurz als eine Substanz zu erkennen"' (MA 18 2.38f.). He goes on to argue that the belief that there are 'the same things' (*gleiche Dinge*) has been inherited from 'the period of lowly organisms'.

[75] 'Das "Ding" – das ist das eigentliche Substrat zu A: unser Glaube an Dinge ist die Voraussetzung für den Glauben an die Logik. Das A der Logik ist wie das Atom eine Nachconstruktion des "Dings" ...'

It is through processes of *Festsetzen* or *Fest-machen*, fixing or making-fast, that the dynamic character of reality is effaced in favour of things with enduring identity or 'beings'.[76] According to Nietzsche, then, logic presupposes processes of equalization or making-the-same and making-fast, *Gleichmachen* and *Festmachen*. Things go wrong when we neglect to see this and project the principle of identity onto reality:

> Insofar as we do not grasp that, and make of logic a criterion of *true being*, we are well on the way to positing all those hypostases – substance, predicate, object, subject, action, etc. – as realities: i.e., to conceiving a metaphysical world, i.e., a 'true world' (- *but this is the apparent world once again* …) (ibid.)[77]

To the question: why should we believe in a world of self-identical things if there are no such things? Nietzsche's answer is that we do so 'under the impact of endless empirical experience [*der unendlichen Empirie*], which seems to *confirm* it continuously' (ibid.). This is not because empirical experience tells us how things really are, but because empirical experience, indeed sensation (*Empfindung*) at the most basic level,[78] is already complicit in the sameness of things and their identity. For it was the capacity to see sameness among phenomena, to overlook change in things, and to subsume quickly that gave organisms a competitive advantage in the struggle for existence (FW 111). And the struggle of the organisms, he argues, dictates that whatever has been preserved – including intellectual activities – has been preserved because it has life-enabling value:

> It is only all the functions which bring with them the preservation of the organism that have been able to preserve and propagate themselves.
>
> The intellectual activities have been able to preserve themselves, which preserved the organism; and in the struggle of the organisms these intellectual activities have become strengthened and refined, i.e. – – –
>
> NB. – struggle as the provenance of the logical functions. The creature which could regulate, discipline, judge itself the strongest – with the greatest excitability [*Erregbakeit*] and even greater self-control – has always prevailed. (25[427] 11.124)

---

[76] In 9[91] 12 he describes *Fest-machen* as a 'making-true-enduring, a putting-out-of-sight' ('Wahr-Dauerhaft-Machen, ein Aus-dem-Auge-schaffen') of becoming, 'that false character, a reinterpretation of it into beings' ('Umdeutung desselben ins Seiende').

[77] 'Indem wir das nicht begreifen, und aus der Logik ein Kriterium des w a h r e n S e i n s machen, sind wir bereits auf dem Wege, alle jene Hypostasen, Substanz Prädicat Object Subject Action usw., als Realitäten zu setzen: d.h. eine metaphysische Welt zu concipiren, d.h. "wahre Welt" (– d i e s e ist a b e r d i e s c h e i n b a r e W e l t n o c h e i n m a l …).'

[78] In note 40[15] 11.634f, Nietzsche argues that judgement presupposes identical cases, and argues that these identities must be created at the level of sensation (*Empfindung*):
'– Es könnte gar keine Urtheile geben, wenn nicht erst innerhalb der Empfindungen eine Art Ausgleichung geübt wäre: Gedächtniß ist nur möglich mit einem beständigen Unterstreichen des schon Gewohnten, Erlebten
– – Bevor geurtheilt wird, muß der Prozeß der Assimilation schon gethan sein: also liegt auch hier eine intellektuelle Thätigkeit vor, die nicht in's Bewußtsein fällt […]'

On this basis, Nietzsche states:

> Life is founded on the presupposition of a belief in things that endure and recur regularly; the more powerful the life, the broader must be the divinable world – the world, so to speak, that is *made* to be. Logicising, rationalising, systematising as life's resources. (9[91] 12)[79]

Given the sources of logic in the illogical procedures of making what is different the same and making fast (*Fest-setzen*) what is changeable, its cognitive value is zero:

> Supposing there were no A identical with itself, as is presupposed by every proposition of logic (as also of mathematics), supposing A were already a *semblance* [or *illusion*], then logic would have as its presupposition a merely *illusory* world. (9[97] 12.389)[80]

Yet it is precisely in the illogical sources of logic that its value for life lies:

> But our *false*, contracted, *logicised* world of causes ist he world in which we can live. We can 'know' to the extent that we can satisfy our needs. (34[46] 11.434)[81]

These lines remind us that what we consider to be knowledge is subject to the constraints of life and life-needs.[82] All forms of thought and 'knowledge' – including Nietzsche's – must operate with self-identical terms, since we are all living beings. But it makes a world of difference, whether these are taken to represent or to 'grasp' (*fassen*: 9[97] 12) an independent order of beings that are fixed and determinate, or whether we are reflectively aware that our thought is constrained by our needs as living beings to construct or create self-identical terms through processes of *Gleichmachen* and *Festmachen*. In adhering to the logical principle of non-contradiction in the manner of his thinking, Nietzsche operates under the constraint of life as the highest value. But in the matter of his thought, I argued in the previous section, he also operates under the constraints of his critique of metaphysics and substance ontology, taking as his presuppositions a series of negations of the latter. Of course, these presuppositions are posited as self-identical terms and depend for their meaning on

---

[79] 'Das Leben ist auf die Voraussetzung eines Glaubens an Dauerndes und Regulär-Wiederkehrendes gegründet; je mächtiger das Leben, um so breiter muß die errathbare, gleichsam seiend g e m a c h t e Welt sein. Logisirung, Rationalisirung, Systematisirung als Hülfsmittel des Lebens.'

[80] 'Gesetzt, es gäbe ein solches Sich-selbst-identisches A gar nicht, wie es jeder Satz der Logik (auch der Mathematik) voraussetzt, das A wäre bereits eine S c h e i n b a r k e i t, so hätte die Logik eine bloß s c h e i n b a r e Welt zur Voraussetzung.'

[81] 'Unsere f a l s c h e, verkleinerte, l o g i s i r t e Welt der Ursachen ist aber die Welt, in welcher wir leben können. Wir sind soweit "erkennend", daß wir unsere Bedürfnisse befriedigen können.'

[82] 'There would be nothing that could be called knowledge, if thought did not first refashion the world for itself in such a way into "things", identical with themselves.' ('Es gäbe nichts, was Erkenntniß zu nennen wäre, wenn nicht erst das Denken sich die Welt dergestalt umschüfe zu "Dingen", Sich-selbst-Gleichem.') 8[25] 10.342.

the negation of their 'opposites'. But as positive formulations of the *negative* results of his critique of metaphysics and substance ontology, they allow Nietzsche to point to the cognitive insufficiency of the simplified, logicized world we construct out of life-needs and the delusions of metaphysics – of taking it to represent a ready-made and independent order of self-identical determinate beings – by confronting them with his presuppositions: the primacy of occurrence, originary plurality, the *Ineinander* of entities without substance, and real contradiction or antagonism (Ggz II.2).

Logical contradiction

With this in mind, we can turn to logical contradiction and an early note from 1870 to 1871, where Nietzsche first expresses his suspicion towards the principle of non-contradiction:

> I have the suspicion that things and thinking are not adequate to one another. For in logic the principle of contradiction rules, which *perhaps* is not valid for things, which *are* different, opposed [to one another].

> Ich habe den Verdacht, daß die Dinge und das Denken mit
> einander nicht adäquat sind. In der Logik nämlich herrscht der
> Satz des Widerspruches, der v i e l l e i c h t nicht bei den
> Dingen gilt, die Verschiedenes, Entgegengesetztes s i n d. (7[110] 7.163)

From this note it is evident that Nietzsche sees a close relation between logical contradiction and real opposition, or in Kant's terms: that they are both forms of opposition (*Entgegensetzung*); for otherwise the principle of non-contradiction would not make thought fall short of the oppositions among things. At the same time, the verbal distinction between *Widerspruch* and *Entgegensetzung* indicates Nietzsche's awareness of the difference between them and the need to clarify it. This was, of course, Kant's task in NG, only Nietzsche gives it a non-Kantian twist that will culminate in a critique of logical contradiction. The problem lies not in two different forms of negation, and the inadequacy of logical negation (qua absence) to represent real negation (qua privation); the problem is that logical (non-)contradiction falls radically short of difference, diversity (*Verschiedenes*) or plurality among things. Nietzsche's critical task will be to show that logical contradiction simplifies and impoverishes the complex, pluralistic structure of real opposition.

We see Nietzsche tackling this task in the late *Nachlass*. In a note from 1887 he engages in a critique of logical contradiction and reformulates his earlier suspicion as an 'open' question:

> [A]re the axioms of logic adequate to the real, or are they standards and means to *create* for us the real, the concept 'reality'?... But to be able to affirm the former one would [...] already need to be acquainted with what is; which is simply not the

case. The principle thus contains not a *criterion of truth*, but rather an *imperative* about *what **ought to** count as true*. (9[97] 12.389)[83]

In a quite typical line of argumentation, repeated in the *Nachlass*, Nietzsche here criticizes the traditional conception of knowledge as *adequatio* for helping itself to a standpoint beyond the subject-object opposition in order to secure its knowledge-claims. The deployment of the principle of non-contradiction in our cognitive truth-claims presupposes that we already know, prior to making or proving these claims, that objects cannot be ascribed opposed predicates. Since we do not, the only alternative, Nietzsche claims, is that the principle of non-contradiction is a *norm* that we posit in order to create a world that meets our life-needs. As such, this principle expresses not a 'necessity' or 'truth', but our incapacity (*Nicht-vermögen, Unvermögen*) to affirm and negate the same thing:

> The subjective constraint not to be able to contradict is a biological constraint: the instinct of utility to infer the way we infer is embedded in our body, we *are* almost this instinct ... But what a naivity to conclude from this a proof that we hereby possessed a 'truth in itself' ...
>
> Not-being-able-to-contradict demonstrates an incapacity, not a 'truth'. (14[152] 13.334)[84]

Not only is Aristotle's psychological definition of the principle of non-contradiction hereby disparaged; the impossibility or unthinkability of logical contradiction in Kant is reinterpreted by Nietzsche as our incapacity to contradict; the lack expressed by logical negation in Kant becomes for Nietzsche a lack of power on our part that has its sources in experience. It is this experience, Nietzsche argues, that warrants the belief, presupposed by our cognitive truth-claims, that reality cannot be ascribed opposed predicates.

> Here the course, sensualist prejudice *reigns* that sensations teach us *truths* about things – that I cannot say at the same time of one and the

---

[83] '[S]ind die logischen Axiome dem Wirklichen adäquat, oder sind sie Maaßstäbe und Mittel, um Wirkliches den Begriff "Wirklichkeit" für uns erst zu s c h a f f e n? ... Um das Erste bejahen zu können, müßte man aber [...] das Seiende bereits kennen; was schlechterdings nicht der Fall ist. Der Satz enthält also kein K r i t e r i u m   d e r   W a h r h e i t, sondern einen I m p e r a t i v über das, was a l s w a h r g e l t e n **s o l l**.'

[84] 'Die subjektive Nöthigung, hier nicht widersprechen zu können, ist eine biologische Nöthigung: der Instinkt der Nützlichkeit, so zu schließen wie wir schließen, steckt uns im Leibe, wir s i n d beinahe dieser Instinkt ... Welche Naivetät aber, daraus einen Beweis zu ziehen, daß wir damit eine "Wahrheit an sich" besäßen ....
Das Nicht-Widersprechen-können beweist ein Unvermögen,
nicht eine "Wahrheit".'
Note 9[97] 12.389 begins: 'Ein und dasselbe zu bejahen und zu verneinen mißlingt uns: das ist ein subjektiver Erfahrungssatz, darin drückt sich keine "Nothwendigkeit" aus, sondern nur ein Nicht-vermögen.'

same thing that it is *hard* and it is *soft* (the instinctive proof 'I cannot have 2 opposed sensations at the same time' – *quite course and false*). (9[97] 12)[85]

Earlier we saw that the struggle between organisms means that empirical experience all the way down to sensation (*Empfindung*) is complicit in the sameness of things and their identity. Here Nietzsche seems to be saying that the same goes for the principle of non-contradiction. Kant, it seems, disagrees with Nietzsche on this point when he writes that we can 'simultaneously feel pleasure and displeasure [*Lust und Unlust zugleich empfinden*] in relation to one and the same object', reflecting a real opposition between desire and aversion (NG II.196). But perhaps Nietzsche has only sensations (*sinnliche Empfindungen, Sinnesempfindungen*) in mind, such as hardness and softness, when he writes that '"I cannot have 2 opposed sensations [*Empfindungen*] simultaneously."'[86] In this case, it is hard to object to the 'instinctive proof' of non-contradiction. What exactly is 'course and false' about saying that we cannot sense hardness and softness simultaneously?

There are two texts that explain what Nietzsche means here. Both texts berate the projection of logical opposition (Ggz I) onto reality and seek to expunge it as a crude simplification of the complexity of real opposition or antagonism (Ggz II.2), sufficient for life needs, but false. In the first text, Nietzsche plays the subject-object opposition off against his counter-ontology of conflict:

> Duration, identity with itself, being, inhere neither in what is called subject nor in what is called object. They are complexes of occurrence which appear to have duration in relation to other complexes – for example due to a difference in the tempo of what occurs (rest-motion, fixed-loose: all oppositions which do not exist in themselves and with which in fact only *differences of degree* are expressed, which only look like oppositions for a certain perceptual measure.
>
> There are no oppositions: we have only acquired the concept of opposition from those of logic, and from there wrongly transferred it to things. (9[91] 12.384)[87]

---

[85] 'Hier r e g i e r t das sensualistische grobe Vorurtheil, daß die Empfindungen uns W a h r h e i t e n über die Dinge lehren, – daß ich nicht zu gleicher Zeit von ein und demselben Ding sagen kann, es ist h a r t und es ist w e i c h (der instinktive Beweis "ich kann nicht 2 entgegengesetzte Empfindungen zugleich haben" – g a n z g r o b u n d f a l s c h).'

[86] The term 'Empfindung' in German has an inner, emotive meaning (*Lust, Hass empfinden*) and a perceptual meaning, often combined in Nietzsche's usage. See the article 'Empfindung' in the *Nietzsche-Wörterbuch* (Nietzsche Online: http://www.degruyter.com/view/NO/empfindung).

[87] 'Die Dauer, die Gleichheit mit sich selbst, das Sein inhärirt weder dem, was Subjekt, noch dem, was Objekt genannt wird: es sind Complexe des Geschehens, in Hinsicht auf andere Complexe scheinbar dauerhaft – also z.B. durch eine Verschiedenheit im tempo des Geschehens (Ruhe-Bewegung, fest-locker: alles Gegensätze, die nicht an sich existiren und mit denen thatsächlich nur G r a d v e r s c h i e d e n h e i t e n ausgedrückt werden, die für ein gewisses Maaß von Optik sich als Gegensätze ausnehmen.'

Es giebt keine Gegensätze: nur von denen der Logik her haben wir den Begriff des Gegensatzes – und von denen aus fälschlich in die Dinge übertragen.'

The concept of substance derives from the moments of relative duration that emerge in the opposition or antagonism (Ggz II.2) of power-complexes without substance, all engaged in a struggle of reciprocal fixing or *Fest-setzen*. In effect, it is reduced to a misperception on the part of power-complexes, a crude simplification of the fine differences of degree and tempo between power-complexes into mutually exclusive, logical opposites (Ggz I): stasis-motion, firm-loose. Nietzsche's radical move here is to derive the concept of substance (self-identity and duration) from real opposition (Ggz II.2) – as one term in the logical oppositions (Ggz I) projected onto reality by power-complexes engaged in real opposition or struggle (Ggz II.2). Subjectivity is reduced to the feeling of power: 'what arouses feeling the strongest ("I")'; and objectivity, to the feeling of resistance in the struggle of complexes:

> The feeling of power [strength], of struggle, of resistance persuades that there *is* something, which is resisted here. (9[91] 12.387)[88]

While the concept of substance is derivative of real opposition (Ggz II.2) in this sense, logical contradiction (Ggz I) relies on and presupposes substance. As Müller-Lauter (1971 12-14) points out, Nietzsche's objection to logical contradiction is that it falsifies real opposition by positing self-identical, enduring entities and placing them into mutually exclusive opposition. And as promised in the early *Nachlass* note, Nietzsche takes up the cause of 'originary' plurality and the complexity of real opposition against logical contradiction, as the second text shows:

> Judgement is very slow in comparison with the eternal, endlessly small activity of our drives – the drives are thus always there much more rapidly, and judgement is only ever in place after a fait accompli: either as an effect and consequence of drive-stimulation or as the effect of *the opposed drive stimulated with it*. Memory is aroused by the drives to deliver its material. – Through every drive its counter-drive is aroused, and not just this one, but rather also others like upper harmonic chords, whose relation is not to be signified by such an everyday day word like 'opposition'. (6[63] 9.210)[89]

Earlier we saw that Nietzsche refers our incapacity to contradict to a 'biological constraint', almost an 'instinct', embedded in our body (14[152] 13), and it is not unusual for him to speak of the logical as a 'drive'.[90] In the above text, Nietzsche takes

---

[88] 'Das Gefühl der Kraft, des Kampfes, des Widerstandes überredet [es] dazu, daß es etwas g i e b t, dem hier widerstanden wird.'

[89] 'Das Urtheil ist etwas sehr Langsames im Vergleich zu der ewigen unendlich kleinen Thätigkeit der Triebe – die Triebe sind also immer viel schneller da, und das Urtheil ist immer nach einem fait accompli erst am Platze: entweder als Wirkung und Folge der Triebregung oder als Wirkung des m i t e r r e g t e n e n t g e g e n g e s e t z t e n T r i e b e s. Das Gedächtniß wird durch die Triebe erregt, seinen Stoff abzuliefern. – Durch jeden Trieb wird auch sein Gegentrieb erregt, und nicht nur dieser, sondern wie Obertonsaiten noch andere, deren Verhältniß nicht in einem so geläufigen Worte zu bezeichnen ist, wie "Gegensatz".'

[90] E.g. 'Das Logische ist der Trieb selber, welcher macht, daß die Welt logisch, unserem Urtheilen gemäß verläuft' (25[333] 11.97).

up the relation of logic to the body again, but in a very different sense: as a plural, multi-layered complex of relations governed by real opposition (Ggz II.2). At issue is the relation of judgement – and, we can add, the logical functions therein, such as non-contradiction (Ggz I) – to real contradiction or opposition (Ggz II.2), as the dynamic principle of the body. Judgement, Nietzsche argues, is the product ('effect and consequence') of the infinitely small, much faster, immensely complex, plural and multi-layered activities of the drives[91] acting in relations of opposition (*Entgegesetzung*: Ggz II.2). The emphasis is on the coarseness, slowness and simplistic nature of the logical functions of judgement, such as contradiction ('"Gegensatz"' = Ggz I), in comparison with the complexity of the body and the dynamics of real opposition therein. From this it follows that the term 'contradiction' ('"Gegensatz"' = Ggz I) is completely insufficient to signify (*bezeichnen*) the complexity of real contradiction in the body, let alone to grasp it (*fassen*). Yet it also follows from the necessity of logic for life that real oppositions are ungraspable in their concrete facticity and unknowable in their complexity, for thought is constrained by the principle of non-contradiction. This, of course, goes for Nietzsche too, whose thought operates under the constraint of life. What is more, he seems to acknowledge this clearly when he writes:

> Thinking is *underivable*, just like *sensations* [and/or *feelings*]: but this does *not* in the least demonstrate it to be originary or 'being in itself'! rather, [it] only establishes that we cannot get *behind it*, because we *have* nothing but thinking and sensing [and/or feeling]. (8[25] 343)[92]

But if thinking is 'underivable', since thinking and sensing/feeling are all we have, how then can Nietzsche derive judgement (and its logical functions) from the body as the 'effect and consequence' of the drives in real opposition? Nietzsche cannot 'get behind' thought and 'grasp' what lies beyond it any more than we can, but he can remain open to it, confront thought with the negative results of his critique of substance, and point towards it (*hinweisen auf*) by drawing on a series of negations of substance ontology as his presuppositions. The challenge for thought is to think both *within and against* the constraints of thought, to acknowledge and confront the 'fluid, ungraspable proteus-nature' of 'semblance,' where 'semblance is the actual and only reality of things [...] best signified with opposed predicates' (40[53] 11.654). For there is 'no good reason for doubting' the tremendous complexity and 'busyness' of the body, even if we cannot know it ...

---

[91] Recall that the term 'Trieb' does not signify anything substantive, but is just a 'placeholder' in the familiar language of feelings for further complexes and processes: '"drive [*Trieb*]" is only a translation into the language of feeling from non-feeling [*aus dem Nichtfühlendem*] [...]' (7[25] 10.250).

[92] 'Das Denken ist u n a b l e i t b a r, ebenso die E m p f i n d u n g e n: aber damit ist es noch lange n i c h t als ursprünglich oder 'an sich seiend' bewiesen! sondern nur festgestellt, daß wir nicht d a h i n t e r können, weil wir nichts als Denken und Empfinden h a b e n.'

III.4 The ontology of mental life

Nietzsche's reflections on the relation of thought to real opposition invite comparison with Kant, for whom, as we saw, 'there is no good reason for doubting' the activity of real opposition in mental life, 'even if we do not clearly notice it within us'. And like Nietzsche he marvels at the complexity of the numerous activities involved:

> But what a marvellous busyness is concealed within the depths of our minds which goes unnoticed even while it is being exercised. And it goes unnoticed because the actions in question are very numerous and because each of them is represented only very obscurely. (NG II.191)[93]

For Kant, of course, Nietzsche's hidden drives are not in the body, but 'concealed within the depths of our minds [*Geist*]', yet both thinkers see the necessity to posit the activity of real opposition in the background of mental life and thought. However, they do so for very different reasons. As we saw, Kant is after the grounds or sources of change in mental life, which he breaks down into two questions: why does a representation come into existence? And why does it cease to exist and come to be replaced by another? On the presupposition that there must be a 'positive real ground' or cause for both to happen, Kant models existence in general and the ontology of mental life in specific on motion, more precisely: on exogenous causation and the principle of inertia or Newton's first Law:

> A movement never stops, either completely or in part, unless a motive force which is equal to the force which would have been able to generate the lost movement is combined with it in a relation of opposition. (NG II.190)[94]

Yet, as we also saw, Kant's ontology of mental life is more complicated than this. While it is true that quasi-mechanistic forces act as the exogenous causes of change among our representations, Kant also reserves an inner causality for mental life, a *vis activa* that secures the autonomy and internal coherence of thought. In the end, however, both thought and nature (inner and outer causality) are subordinated to a *relational source of change*: 'the necessity of real opposition' (NG II.191–2). What exactly Kant means by real opposition in connection with the inner causality of thought is unclear, and he does not, to my knowledge, discuss the relation between real opposition and the mental operation of logical contradiction.

For Nietzsche the explanandum is quite different. Since substance ontology – to which Kant is presumably attached in NG – is incapable of accounting for change, he rejects substances and all unitary grounds of existence. The problem is then to explain

---

[93] 'Allein welche bewunderungswürdige Geschäftigkeit ist nicht in den Tiefen unsres Geistes verborgen, die wir mitten in der Ausübung nicht bemerken, darum weil der Handlungen sehr viel sind, jede einzelne aber nur sehr dunkel vorgestellt wird.'

[94] 'Eine Bewegung hört niemals gänzlich oder zum Theil auf, ohne daß eine Bewegkraft, welche derjenigen gleich ist, die die verlorene Bewegung hätte hervorbringen können, damit in der Entgegensetzung verbunden wird.'

how objects of thought and judgement as identical with themselves come to exist in the absence of any real grounds of identity – out of an 'originary' plurality of entities without substance, out of process or occurrence, and out of real contradiction or antagonism (Ggz II.2). This is but one instance of the fundamental problem generated by Nietzsche's critique of substance ontology: how to account for the formation of the (apparently) stable unities and identities we experience out of multiplicities without presupposing unitary grounds of any kind, a problem which he tackles repeatedly throughout his work at various levels: sensation and feeling, thought, forms of life or organisms, persons or individuals, social groups or associations, unified cultures, works of art, states. The answer he will try to develop in the context of the will to power revolves around self-organizing multiplicities (Aydin 2007).

We have seen how, according to Nietzsche, identity derives from the concept of substance, constructed through processes of *Gleichmachen and Festmachen*. The question is how these processes can generate unity and identity out of an 'originary' multiplicity, and how these processes can be explained without smuggling a unitary ground or 'agent' into the explanans. Nietzsche addresses these questions at two levels. The first is that of sensation/feeling: *Empfindung*; that is, the 'input' of our mental life or consciousness. The second is that of the body, understood as an organism or form of life able to sustain itself and grow by meeting its conditions of existence.

1. Drawing on biologists and other scientists of his time, and especially Lange's account of the physiology of sensation,[95] he argues that the 'apparently simplest conscious sensations' ('scheinbar einfachste bewusste Empfindungen') presuppose complex, unconscious processes of synthesis, discrimination and selection.[96] 'Complexes' are 'sensed as unities', which come to mind isolated from one another (MA 14, 18; 25[336] 11; cf. DAR KGW II/4.425). Our sensations are thus 'something extremely scant and seldom in relation to the countless occurrences [*zahllosen Geschehn*] in every instant' (24[16] 10; cf. 11[93] 9). The act of judgement presupposes that there are identical cases, as we have seen, and it is in our sensations that the processes of *Festmachen* and *Gleichsetzen* are performed: 'There could be no judgements if a kind of making-the-same [*Ausgleichung*] were not first performed within sensations [*innerhalb Empfindungen*]' (40[15] 11.635).

2. But for Nietzsche there can be no disembodied mental life or thought, and the processes of selection and synthesis that generate the identities of mental life out of countless sensations and memories are directed by the life-needs of the conscious being. With Kant, he agrees that 'the true world of causes [of mental life-HS] is

---

[95] Lange 1866. First read by Nietzsche in 1866 (see letter of 8/1866 to v. Gersdorff: KSB 2.159f.). As Crawford notes (1988 73f.), Lange's chapter on 'Die Physiologie der Sinnesorgane und die Welt als Vorstellung' (Buch 2, 3. Abschn. Kap. IV) provoked a turn from metaphysical (especially Schopenhauerian) to physicalist (mechanistic/materialistic) accounts of perception. Cf. Schlechta and Anders (1962 50ff.); Stack (1983 20, 127). On the theme of 'einfache Empfindungen' in nineteenth-century psychology, see the article 'Empfindung' in HWPh (Piepmeier 1992 468f.).

[96] The 'simplest' sensation, Nietzsche argues repeatedly, is 'no primal phenomenon' (*Urphänomen*) (with reference to Lange: 21[17] 7; cf. 19[217] 7; also with reference to Spir: 40[41] 11), but the result of simplifying processes ('simplificatio' or 'Zurechtmachung'), which distort and limit our sensations.

concealed from us: it is unspeakably more complicated'. Yet he draws very non-Kantian consequences from this. The first is that it is 'the study of the body [that] gives us an idea of this unspeakable complication'. In comparison, 'the intellect and senses are above all a simplifying apparatus' that create a world that is false but meets our life-needs:

> But our *false*, contracted, *logicised* world of causes is the world in which we can live. We can 'know' to the extent that we can satisfy our needs. (34[46] 11)[97]

But perhaps Nietzsche differs from Kant most sharply when he argues that, as 'end-phenomena' of hidden causes, our feeling, willing and thinking lack the inner causality for mental life claimed by Kant:

> The course of logical thoughts and inferences in our brains today corresponds to a process and struggle of drives, which, taken separately are all very illogical and unjust; we usually experience only the outcome of the struggle: that is how quickly and covertly this ancient mechanism runs its course in us. (FW 111; cf. 34[46] 11)

Or as Nietzsche famously asks in M 119 (3.113), could it be that 'all our so-called consciousness is a more or less phantastic commentary on an unknown, perhaps unknowable, but felt text?'

This position has two consequences. In the first place, it *displaces* the question of unity from (self-)consciousness – what Nietzsche variously calls *Das Ichgefühl, Das Ich-bewusstsein, Einheits-Gefühl des Bewußtseins*[98] – towards the body, and *decentres* it from the conscious 'I' or 'I think' towards the self-regulating plurality of drives, functions or life-processes; what Nietzsche calls 'the really inborn incorporated working unity of all functions' ('der wirklich eingeborenen einverleibten arbeitenden Einheit aller Funktionen': 11[316] 9.563). In the second place, this position throws the internal coherence of thought into question in a quite radical way, to which Nietzsche can only respond that 'thinking and sensing/feeling is all we have' (8[25] 10.342), but that we can and should turn our attention to 'the study of the body' in its 'unspeakable complication'.[99] Both consequences signal a shift from mechanism to physiology in Nietzsche that divides him further from Kant, who remains committed to Newtonian science. This divide is most clearly inscribed in a passage cited above, which paradoxically also signals a profound affinity between Nietzsche and Kant. It concerns the dynamic of drives underpinning thought:

---

[97] 'Unsere f a l s c h e, verkleinerte, l o g i s i r t e Welt der Ursachen ist aber die Welt, in welcher wir leben können. Wir sind soweit "erkennend", daß wir unsere Bedürfnisse befriedigen können.'

[98] 11[316] 9.563; 11[21] 9.450.

[99] The problem for Nietzsche is not how the internal coherence of thought can be maintained if thinking is epiphenomenal to blind drives. As several scholars have noted, the body, its processes and drives are themselves intentional and cognitive. On this topic see Mattioli (2017 91ff.); Luca Lupo (2006 49) on 'primary consciousness' (the cognitive-intentional structure on the subpersonal level) and 'secondary consciousness' (intentional contents in reflexive awareness). Also: Lupo (2006 85–132); Abel (2001 9); Schlimgen (1999 49–54).

- Through every drive its counter-drive is aroused, and not just this one, but rather also others like upper harmonic chords, whose relation is not to be signified by such an everyday day word like 'opposition'.
- Durch jeden Trieb wird auch sein Gegentrieb erregt, und nicht nur dieser, sondern wie Obertonsaiten noch andere, deren Verhältniß nicht in einem so geläufigen Worte zu bezeichnen ist, wie 'Gegensatz'. (6[63] 9.210)

Reading this together with Newton's third Law, 'To every action there is always opposed an equal reaction',[100] brings Nietzsche in the region of Kant's thought. For Kant, as we saw, real opposition is a metaphysical formulation of the law of action and reaction (as distinct from logical contradiction), or as he puts it, 'the rule the equality of effect and counter-effect' (NG II.179), and he goes on to argue that the principle of real opposition implies that

> if A arises in a natural change occurring in die world, -A must also arise. In other words, no natural ground of a real consequence can exist without its being at the same time the ground of another consequence, which is the negative of the first [...] It follows from these considerations that a positive change only ever occurs naturally in the world, if its consequence consists, as a whole, in a real or potential opposition, which cancels itself. (NG II.194-5)

What divides Nietzsche's opposition of drives (Ggz II.2) from Kant's real opposition is its pluralistic, multi-layered structure, as distinct from the latter's dyadic structure. But what they share is a relational concept of force or power as the source or ground of change. Nowhere is this expressed more clearly than in Newton's third Law, unmistakably present in both passages above, which locates forces in the *interactions between* different bodies, and effectively states that there is no such thing as a force that is not accompanied by an equal and opposite force. For Nietzsche, however, the problem of change must be tackled without substances or unitary grounds, on the basis of plurality, the primacy of occurrence or process and real opposition or antagonism, and he comes to reject mechanism in favour of physiological models of opposition and ultimately the will to power. To see why and what this implies for his understanding of real opposition, we must turn to his critique of mechanism.

III.5 From mechanism to physiology and wills to power

Like Kant, Nietzsche works with the necessary relation between attraction and repulsion across all domains of reality (Kant's *Conflictus zweier Kräfte*). But from the early 1880s on he rejects this mechanistic model of conflict in favour of physiological models and wills to power for several reasons. They have to do with the constraints imposed by his

---

[100] The third Law reads: 'To every action there is always opposed an equal reaction: or the mutual actions of two bodies upon each other are always equal, and directed to contrary parts' (Frautschi 2007).

critique of substance ontology, but also with what he sees as a psychological constraint on our capacity to make sense of change.

In this period, Nietzsche is in search of a unified concept of force or power that is capable of accounting for spontaneous activity/interaction and change across all domains of reality: physical nature, inorganic and organic, as well as mental life. As we have seen, his critique of *Seinsmetaphysik* and substance ontology means that he must take as his starting points 'originary' plurality, the primacy of occurrence or process, and real opposition or antagonism. At the same time, these presuppositions confront him with the problem of accounting for the creation of the (apparently) stable unities and identities in the world we inhabit and experience out of multiplicities, without presupposing unitary grounds of any kind. We have already encountered this with regard to the identity of objects of thought and sensation. The early 1880s mark Nietzsche's turn to the body, motivated by the insight that the language of physiology developed by contemporary biologists such as Wilhelm Roux[101] offers models of conflict that are in line with his presuppositions. They prioritize *processes* of self-regulation and self-organization that account for the formation of *living unities* or organisms out of the *struggle* of *multiplicities* at all levels: molecules, cells, tissues and organs. In the context of human existence, his reflections are focused on the body, but the organismic model is extended well beyond the human body. In what follows, some key texts will be used to reconstruct aspects of this thought-process with an eye on the value Nietzsche invests in the discourse of physiology.

Nietzsche's quest for a unified concept of force is evident in a note in which he reflects on the relation between the organic and the inorganic world:

> The drive to draw near – and the drive to repulse
> are in the inorganic as in the organic world the
> link. The entire separation is prejudice.
>
>   Der Trieb, sich anzunähern – und der Trieb, etwas
>   zurückzustoßen, sind in der unorganischen wie organischen Welt das
>   Band. Die ganze Scheidung ist ein Vorurtheil. (36[21] 11.560)

The 'link' (*Band*) in question refers both to the linkage between attraction/drawing near and repulsion/exclusion, and to the linkage between the organic and inorganic worlds: what they share is the mechanistic dynamics of attraction-repulsion, translated here into the physiological register of drives. Of importance for Nietzsche is that these forces or drives are processual and non-substantial: the note ends with the remark 'NB. D i e P r o z e s s e a l s "W e s e n", and in the same note he offers two further translations of these processes. The first is strictly physiological:

> The weaker pushes its way to the stronger, out of a lack of food; it wants
> to take shelter, if possible to become *one* with it. Conversely, the stronger

---

[101] Müller-Lauter (1999a 163) (also Müller-Lauter 1978 189–235) and Pearson (2018 306–42).

repulses the weaker, it doesn't want to perish this way; instead, as it grows it splits into two and more. The greater the urge to unity, the more one may infer weakness; the more there is an urge to variety, difference, inner disaggregation, the more force there is.

> Das Schwächere drängt sich zum Stärkeren, aus Nahrungsnoth; es will unterschlüpfen, mit ihm womöglich E i n s werden. Der Stärkere wehrt umgekehrt ab von sich, er will nicht in dieser Weise zu Grunde gehen; vielmehr, im Wachsen, spaltet er sich zu Zweien und Mehreren. Je größer der Drang ist zur Einheit, um so mehr darf man auf Schwäche schließen; je mehr der Drang nach Varietät, Differenz, innerlichem Zerfall, um so mehr Kraft ist da. (36[21] 11.560)

Nietzsche recasts the mechanistic *vis attractiva* as the urge on the part of weaker entities to unite with stronger ones for the sake of nutrition, while the *vis repulsiva* becomes the urge of the stronger to defend themselves by warding off the weaker for the sake of growth, internal differentiation and (asexual) reproduction. However, this interpretation seems to break the linkage between attraction and repulsion by associating the first with weaker, the second with stronger entities. It also predicates the whole dynamic on lack (of nutrition) and the urge on both sides, the weak and the strong, not to go to ground, that is, to preserve themselves.[102] Both points are then corrected further on in the note, where the forces of attraction and repulsion are reinterpreted in terms of the will to power:

The will to power in every combination of forces – *resisting what 's stronger, pouncing on what is weaker* – is more correct. NB. Processes as 'essence'.

> Der Wille zur Macht in jeder Kraft-Combination, s i c h w e h r e n d g e g e n d a s S t ä r k e r e, l o s s t ü r z e n d a u f d a s S c h w ä c h e r e ist richtiger. NB. D i e P r o z e s s e als 'W e s e n'. (ibid.)

Here both forces are ascribed to one and the same power-complex, restoring their linkage. Attraction is now interpreted as 'pouncing on' or overpowering the weaker power-complex, repulsion as defending itself against the stronger, whereby both processes are at work in every 'combination of forces'. This dynamic is predicated not on lack, but on the kind of excess that makes overpowering possible, what Nietzsche

---

[102] As Pearson (2018 321, 339) points out, these lines are based on Wilhelm Rolph's account of isophagy, said by the latter to occur under conditions of scarcity. With Rolph, Nietzsche rejects self-preservation and the struggle for scarce resources – which he associates with Darwin and Roux – as fundamental to organic life in favour of growth and reproduction under conditions of plenitude and excess. For Rolph, the fundamental drive is nutrition, an insatiable drive to acquire (*Mehrerwerb*) or assimilate, modelled on the negative concept of desire as lack and pain (like Schopenhauer's will), which Nietzsche rejects in favour of the exercise and demonstration of power, based on excess. See Pearson (2018 325 and 319 note 97) for further sources on Nietzsche and Rolph.

elsewhere describes as the 'insatiable demand for the demonstration of power; or the use, exercise of power, as creative drive etc.' ('unersättliches Verlangen nach Bezeigung der Macht; oder Verwendung, Ausübung der Macht, als schöpferischen Trieb usw.' 36[21] 11.563).

The succeeding note in the same notebook reiterates this line of thought in ways that further divide Nietzsche from Kantian real opposition. The emphasis here is on 'the repulsive force, which every force-atom exercises' as the link between inorganic and organic nature, and Nietzsche goes on to define life in processual terms:

> Life would be defined as an enduring form of the *process of fastening force*, where the different combatants grow unequally. In how far obeying also involves resisting; the obeyer by no means gives up its own power. Likewise, in commanding there is a concession that the opponent's absolute power has not been vanquished, not incorporated, dissolved. 'Obeying' and 'commanding' are forms of combative play. (36[22] 11.560)[103]

The relative stability or duration of living unities is achieved by processes of (relatively stable) fastening or fixing (*Kraftfeststellungen*) of relations across power-differentials among entities or complexes of *unequal* power. These relations are described, not in mechanistic terms, but in anthropomorphic or political terms as relations of command-and-obeying, whereby *both* are taken as activities from within (*Eigenmacht*), as the exercise of power, rather than active domination versus passive submission. On this basis, Nietzsche is able at the end of the note to reaffirm conflict (*Kampf*) as the dynamic principle in both organic and inorganic nature, where conflict is understood as a form of play (*Spiel*) that allows for endless repeatability without an external telos (such as nutrition) and for positional shifts and reversals among the players.

In the physiological model we first encountered (p. 59), power was associated with *processes* of differentiation and *pluralization* ('the urge to variety, difference, inner disaggregation' 36[21] 11.560), in contrast with Kant's dyadic relations between unitary monads. With the language of commanding and obeying Nietzsche presents a further permutation of Kant's *Conflictus zweier Kräfte*, whereby obeying includes a repulsive activity of resistance (*Widerstreben*), and attraction is recast as an attempt to vanquish (*besiegen*) the resistance of the other and incorporate (*einverleiben*) it, which succeeds only in establishing command over it.

We will return to Nietzsche's choice of the language of commanding and obeying in the context of his critique of mechanism. For now, it is important to note two further differences it brings to Nietzsche's concept of real opposition or conflict (Ggz II.2)

---

[103] 'Leben wäre zu definiren als eine dauernde Form v o n P r o z e ß
d e r K r a f t f e s t s t e l l u n g e n, wo die verschiedenen Kämpfenden
ihrerseits ungleich wachsen. In wie fern auch im Gehorchen
ein Widerstreben liegt; es ist die Eigenmacht durchaus
nicht aufgegeben. Ebenso ist im Befehlen ein Zugestehen, daß
die absolute Macht des Gegners nicht besiegt ist, nicht einverleibt,
aufgelöst. "Gehorchen" und "Befehlen" sind Formen des
Kampfspiels.'

over and against Kant's. The first is the claim that unity and (relative) stability are not the result of an equilibrium between two equal forces of attraction and repulsion cancelling one another's effects through real opposition, but of a complex and dynamic regime of power-differentials – what Nietzsche will come to call hierarchy or *Rangordnung* – among *unequal* forces or power-complexes engaged in an open-ended struggle of incorporation-and-resistance. The second difference concerns Nietzsche's notion of *Eigenmacht*; that is, his firm commitment to a concept of force or power as an endogenous source of change and spontaneous motion from within, over and against the mechanistic-mathematical notion of force as an impulse of exogenous origin, to which Kant is committed in NG, at least with regard to physical nature. In this regard Nietzsche is heir to Leibniz's *vis viva* or *vis activa* – with important qualifications: there can be no 'metaphysical points' or windowless monads for Nietzsche, for these are just another attempt to subordinate becoming to being through the 'doer'-'deed' schema.

We now need to ask what the benefits of these translations are for Nietzsche. We have already noted the displacement of substance or essence (*Wesen*) by physiological processes and the formation of relatively stable living unities out of processes of fixation among a plurality of forces. Both are in line with Nietzsche's anti-metaphysical presuppositions. But how exactly this works, and what is needed for Nietzsche's *vis activa* to be a *vis creativa*, a 'creative drive' (36[21] 11.563) capable of forming a viable whole, is far from clear.

One important indication comes in a note where Nietzsche reflects on the creation of the simplified, logicized, life-enabling world that we inhabit:

> All organic [life], which 'judges', *acts like the artist:*
> it creates out of single excitations stimuli a whole,
> it leaves many single [stimuli] aside and creates a simplification, it
> makes the same and affirms its creation as *being. The logical
> is itself the drive that makes it so that the world runs logically, in line
> with our judging.*
>   The creative – 1) appropriative 2) selective 3)
> transformative element – 4) the self-regulating element – 5)
> the exclusionary. (25[333] 11.97)[104]

The processes required for the creation of this world as a unity or whole (*Ganzes*) are modelled by Nietzsche on the processes and capacities needed for an organism to regulate itself, so as to maintain its unity in the struggle with other organisms and

---

[104] 'Alles Organische, das "urtheilt", handelt w i e d e r K ü n s t l e r:
es schafft aus einzelnen Anregungen Reizen ein Ganzes,
es läßt Vieles Einzelne bei Seite und schafft eine simplificatio, es
setzt gleich und bejaht sein Geschöpf als s e i e n d. D a s L o g i s c h e
i s t d e r T r i e b s e l b e r, w e l c h e r m a c h t, d a ß d i e W e l t l o g i s c h, u n s e r e m
U r t h e i l e n g e m ä ß v e r l ä u f t.
  Das Schöpferische – 1) Aneignende 2) Auswählende 3)
Umbildende Element – 4) das Selbst-Regulirende Element – 5)
das Ausscheidende.'

live. The processes listed here, gleaned from Nietzsche's readings of Wilhelm Roux and others, recur in variations across the *Nachlass* from the early 1880s on. In this note, they enable him to analyse the elements that go into the creation of our common empirical world that is false, but life-enabling. This requires (a) taking on stimuli on the basis of (b) a strict selection, to be combined with (c) the transformation of the 'chaos' or 'jumble of sensations'[105] into the same (simplificatio through *Gleichmachung*), the (d) extrusion of this picture as a whole and (e) its affirmation as an independent order of beings. Each element (a, b, c, d) is modelled on a physiological process or capacity listed by Nietzsche: (a) appropriation, (b) selection, (c) transformation, (d) exclusion/ excretion on the part of a self-sustaining, self-regulating[106] whole.

On the basis of the above-cited notes, Nietzsche's reinterpretations of Kantian real opposition can be schematized as follows:

MECHANISM	PHYSIOLOGY	WILL TO POWER
Attraction/ Vis attractiva	weaker seeks to unite with stronger	stronger pounces on weaker/overpowers it
Repulsion/ Vis repulsiva	stronger defends itself/ wards off weaker	weaker defends itself against stronger OR
Attraction	incorporation, assimilation appropriation	commanding (qua attempt to incorporate)
Repulsion	secretion/excretion	obeying (qua resisting)

Of particular importance for the problem of real opposition is the opposition in a range of *Nachlass* notes between appropriation, assimilation, incorporation on one side, and excretion, secretion, exclusion, on the other. This is perhaps the most frequently used physiological translation of the mechanistic opposition between attraction and repulsion in Nietzsche's vocabulary, and it does work for him that Kant's *Conflictus zweier Kräfte* cannot do. Conceptually they are opposed (as input and output), but in a complex of powers they combine as the two fundamental processes needed for it to sustain itself as a stable whole. As Pearson (2018 279–341) has argued at length, the linkage between assimilation and excretion is key to Nietzsche's understanding

---

[105] See 9[106] 12.396: 'der Gegensatz dieser Phänomen-Welt ist n i c h t "die wahre Welt", sondern die formlos-unformulirbare Welt des Sensationen-Chaos, – also e i n e a n d e r e Art Phänomenal-Welt, eine für uns "unerkennbare". Also 19[91] 12.383: 'Wir haben nur nach dem Vorbilde des Subjektes die D i n g l i c h k e i t erfunden und in den Sensationen-Wirrwarr hineininterpretirt.' ('the opposite of this phenomenal world is *not* "the true world" but the formless, unformulatable world of the chaos of sensations – thus, *a different* kind of phenomenal world, an "unknowable" one for us.' And: 'We have only invented *thingness* on the model of the subject and interpreted it into the jumble of sensations.')

[106] This could also refer to the processes in the organism that regulate the appropriation and selection of stimuli, their fixation, equalization and excretion as a world of beings, enabling the organism to overpower other items and meet its conditions of existence.

of the organizational struggle and self-regulation needed to maintain viable unities. This goes especially – but not exclusively – for living organisms, and it can be seen in connection with several issues we have already touched on. Thus, where Nietzsche seeks to displace the question of unity from (self-)consciousness to the body, the dynamics of appropriation and excretion play a crucial role:

> If *I* have something of a unity in me then it certainly does not
> lie in the conscious I and in feeling, willing, thinking, but
> somewhere else: in the preserving, appropriating, excluding,
> surveying prudence of my entire organism, of which my
> conscious I is only a tool. – (34[46] 11.434)[107]

The dynamics of assimilation and excretion are again central to the text in which Nietzsche situates the processes of *Gleichmachung* and *Festmachung*, presupposed by judgement, within sensations (*innerhalb Empfindung*):

> – – *Before* there is judging the *process of assimilation must already have*
> *been done*: so here, too, an intellectual activity is there, that does not fall under
> consciousness, as with pain resulting from a wounding. Probably
> there is an inner event corresponding to all organic functions,
> hence an assimilating, secreting, growing etc. (40[15] 11.635)[108]

Organic functions, and the lessons from morphology, have the further benefit in Nietzsche's eyes of enabling us to account for the possibility of novelty. In a note that reflects again on the conditions under which the unity of consciousness can arise out of multiplicity, he writes:

> It comes down to designating the unity in the right way, in
> which thinking willing and feeling and all affects are combined:
> evidently the intellect is only a *tool*, but in whose hands?
> Certainly the affects: and these are a multiplicity behind which

---

[107] 'Wenn i c h etwas von einer Einheit in mir habe, so liegt sie
gewiß nicht in dem bewußten Ich und dem Fühlen Wollen Denken,
sondern wo anders: in der erhaltenden aneignenden
ausscheidenden überwachenden Klugheit meines ganzen Organismus,
von dem mein bewußtes Ich nur ein Werkzeug ist. –'
In a Rolphian vein, Nietzsche writes that 'the human being, as an organic being, has drives of nutrition (acquisitiveness)': 'Triebe der Ernährung (Habsucht)', but also 'drives of excretion (love) (to which regeneration belongs)': 'Triebe der Ausscheidung (Liebe) (wozu auch die Regeneration gehört)'. This note associates conscious thought or the intellect with 'the assimilation of nutrition' ('die Assimilation der Nahrung') and reduces it to an instrument or 'apparatus of self-regulation': 'Apparat der Selbstregulirung' in the service of drives (25[179] 11.62).

[108] '– – B e v o r geurtheilt wird, m u ß d e r P r o z e ß d e r A s s i m i l a t i o n s c h o n g e t h a n s e i n: also liegt auch hier eine intellektuelle Thätigkeit vor, die nicht in's Bewußtsein fällt, wie beim Schmerz infolge einer Verwundung. Wahrscheinlich entspricht allen organischen Funktionen ein inneres Geschehen, also ein Assimiliren, Ausscheiden, Wachsen usw.'

it is not necessary to posit a unity: it suffices to construe it as a regency. (40[38] 11.647)[109]

The morphological development of organs, he continues, offers a good metaphor or analogy (*Gleichniß*) for understanding how something 'new', something that breaks the rule of identity in thought, can be formed out of the multiplicity of affects: it is a matter of excretion (*Ausscheidung*), that is, the physiological analogue of Kant's *vis repulsiva*. Just as new organs are formed (*sich herasugebildet*) out of the synthetic interactions of existing organs, so in thought, 'something "new" can only ever be grasped through the excretion (Ausscheidung) of a single force out of a synthetic force'. By '"new"' Nietzsche means something original that cannot be understood in terms of its causal antecedents: 'not to be understood from the conditions of emergence – or [...] included within them'.[110] At stake in novelty in this sense is something fundamental that is lost in logic and quantitative science: '*quality*' in the sense of the unicity or 'the intrinsic, special character of every course of events' ('der eigentliche spezielle C h a r a k t e r jedes Vorgangs'), which is effaced or thought away (*weggedacht*) under the rule of *Gleichmachung* and *Festmachung*. Or to put it positively: at stake is the question of how to break through identitarian logic and thinking and open thought up to genuine diversity. The question for Nietzsche is how to avoid tearing reality apart into quantifiable units in commerce[111] and attend instead to how genuine multiplicities can organize themselves into synthetic unities.

At times, Nietzsche takes the analogy between mental processes and organic processes very far, as when he reflects on the temporal structures involved in both. In the following note he speculates on the 'complete analogy' or 'parallelism' between the thought-processes involved in abstraction and in the development of a work of art out of an initial idea, and the way in which sperm cells and organisms carry in condensed

---

[109] 'Es kommt darauf an, die Einheit richtig zu bezeichnen, in
der Denken Wollen und Fühlen und alle Affekte zusammengefaßt sind: ersichtlich ist der Intellekt nur ein Werkzeug,
aber in wessen Händen? Sicherlich der Affekte: und diese sind eine Vielheit, hinter der es nicht nöthig ist eine Einheit anzusetzen:
es genügt sie als eine Regentschaft zu fassen.'

[110] 40[37] 11.646:
'Das "Zählen" ist nur eine Vereinfachung, wie alle Begriffe. Nämlich: überall wo etwas rein arithmetisch gedacht werden soll, wird die Q u a l i t ä t weggerechnet. Ebenso in allem Logischen, wo die I d e n t i t ä t d e r F ä l l e die Voraussetzung ist, also der eigentliche spez<ielle> C h a r a k t e r jedes Vorgangs einmal weggedacht ist (das N e u e, nicht aus den Bedingungen des Entstehens Zu-Begreifende – r<espektive> Inbegriffene).'
'"Counting" is only a simplification, like all concepts. Namely: wherever something should be thought purely arithmetically, *quality* is calculated away. Likewise in everything logical, where the *identity of cases* is the assumption, therefore the actual spec<ial> *character* of each event is simply thought away (the *new*, not to be understood from the conditions of emergence – or r<espectively> included).'

[111] The note ends: 'Das Denken selber ist eine solche Handlung, welche auseinanderlegt, was eigentlich Eins ist. Überall ist die Scheinbarkeit da, daß es zählbare Vielheiten giebt, auch im Denken schon. Es giebt nichts "Addirtes" in der Wirklichkeit, nichts "Dividirtes", ein Ding halb und halb ist nicht gleich dem Ganzen' (40[38] 11.647).

form (what we today call DNA) immense amounts of information from the past with them in their developmental processes:

> A perfect analogy can be drawn between the simplifying
> and compressing of countless experiences to general principles
> *and* the becoming of the sperm cell, which bears within it the
> entire abbreviated past: and likewise in the artistic forming
> from fertile basic thoughts up to a 'system' *and* the becoming
> of an organism as a thinking-through and thinking-forth, as a
> *remembering-back* of an entire previous life, of bringing-back to present, embodiment.
> In brief: *visible* organic life and *invisible* creative psychic
> overseeing and thinking contain a parallelism: in the 'artwork'
> one can demonstrate these two sides most clearly as
> parallel. – To what extent thinking, inferring and everything
> logical can be seen as *exterior*: as symptom of a much
> more inner and more fundamental occurrence? (2[146] 12.139)[112]

Nietzsche's speculations on the analogies and parallels between mental and physical life are reminiscent of Kant's remarks that '[t]he necessity of real opposition' is the same in mental life and physical nature, even if they follow different laws (NG II.191-2), and that 'there can be no difference between the accidents of mental natures and the effects of operative forces in the physical world', where it concerns the cancellation of existents through real opposition (NG II.191). Of course, Nietzsche's presuppositions are not shared by Kant and his recourse to physiological models complexifies and pluralizes the strictly dyadic structure of Kantian real opposition. This enables Nietzsche to make stronger and more precise connections between specific thought-processes and physical processes than Kant, whose ontology of mental life in NG is limited to the grounds for representations to come into existence and to cease existing, and his correction of Baumgarten's account of abstraction. More importantly, his aim in NG is to argue that there is a *dis*-analogy between real opposition and logical contradiction. But both Kant and Nietzsche are after a unified account of the sources of change across

---

[112] 'Es läßt sich eine vollkommene Analogie führen zwischen dem Vereinfachen und Zusammendrängen zahlloser Erfahrungen auf General-Sätze u n d dem Werden der Samenzelle, welche die ganze Vergangenheit verkürzt in sich trägt: und ebenso zwischen dem künstlerischen Herausbilden aus zeugenden Grundgedanken bis zum "System" u n d dem Werden des Organismus als einem Aus- und Fortdenken, als einer R ü c k e r i n n e r u n g des ganzen vorherigen Lebens, der Rück-Vergegenwärtigung, Verleiblichung. Kurz: das s i c h t b a r e organische Leben und das u n s i c h t b a r e schöpferische seelische Walten und Denken enthalten einen Parallelismus: am "Kunstwerk" kann man diese zwei Seiten am deutlichsten als Parallel demonstriren. – In wiefern Denken, Schließen und alles Logische als A u ß e n s e i t e angesehen werden kann: als Symptom viel innerlicheren und gründlicheren Geschehens?'

different domains of reality, and in a sense Nietzsche's position is somewhat weaker than Kant's. So far, his reflections bear on mental life and organic nature, leaving the question of inorganic nature open. And he writes, not of one and the same principle in both domains, but of 'analogy', 'metaphor' (*Gleichniß*), 'parallelism' and 'symptoms'. This will change when he comes to clarify what he means by 'a more inner and more fundamental occurrence': this concerns his quest for a unified concept of force or power and real opposition that cuts across all domains of reality, including inorganic nature. We will approach this by way of Nietzsche's thoughts on the unity of the body and the critique of mechanism it implies.

Nietzsche's most sophisticated accounts of the generation of unity out of diversity are to be found in his reflections on the body. It is here, above all, that the shortcomings of mechanism and logic come to light in consideration of the complex processes of self-organization and self-regulation needed for a living whole to sustain itself. Nowhere is Nietzsche's starting point in an originary multiplicity clearer than in this context. Given that, in the light of Nietzsche's critique of substance, there is no such thing as an individual, the burning question is how an 'individual' (qua dividuum) can be composed and preserved as a living whole:

> – Preservation of the individual: that is, to assume that a
> multiplicity with the most manifold activities wants to 'preserve'
> itself, *not* as identical with itself, but rather 'living' –
> ruling – obeying – nourishing itself – growing – (25[427] 11.125)[113]

This telegraphic list of words – a curious mixture of the organismic terms with the moral/political language of command and obedience – makes it clear that for Nietzsche mechanism is of no use for understanding the dynamics of a living whole. Indeed his point here is to contrast the unity of the '"living"' whole with the logical concept of identity ('identical with itself') and by implication, *not* to ground the former on the latter. He does, however, concede life-enabling value to the presuppositions of mechanism: 'the synthesis "thing"' and cause-and-effect.[114] But in doing so, he effectively subordinates mechanism to physiology: the success of mechanism is given a physiological explanation on the principle that whatever has been preserved – including intellectual activities – has been preserved because it has life-enabling value.

---

[113] '– Erhaltung des Individuums: d.h. voraussetzen, daß eine
Vielheit mit den mannichfaltigsten Thätigkeiten sich 'erhalten'
will, nicht als sich-selber-gleich, sondern "lebendig" –
herrschend – gehorchend – sich ernährend – wachsend –'

[114] The note continues:
'Die Synthese "Ding" stammt von u n s: alle Eigenschaften
des Dinges von u n s. "Wirkung und Ursache", ist eine
Verallgemeinerung unseres Gefühls und Urtheils.
  Alle die Funktionen, welche die Erhaltung des Organismus
mit sich bringen, haben sich allein erhalten und fortpflanzen
können.
  Die intellektuellen Thätigkeiten haben sich allein erhalten
können, welche den Organismus erhielten; und im Kampfe der
Organismen haben sich diese intellektuellen Thätigkeiten immer
v e r s t ä r k t und v e r f e i n e r t, d.h. - - -'.

The shortcomings of mechanism are again evident in one of Nietzsche's longest and most detailed notes on the body in the late *Nachlass* (37[4] 11.576f., 1885). Here again, consciousness is reduced to an organ akin to the stomach. The '"wonder of wonders"' in need of explanation is instead the astonishing act of synthesis that constitutes the body out of multiplicities:

> [H]ow such a tremendous unity of living beings can live as a whole, grow and for a time exist, each one dependent and subservient and yet in a certain sense in turn commanding and acting from its own will – [...] (37[4] 11.576)[115]

Indeed, Nietzsche goes so far as to call the body (in quotation marks) only the best analogy or simile (*Gleichniß*) for the collaboration of the 'smallest living beings that constitute the body: (more accurately: for whose working-together the best metaphor [*Gleichniß*] is that which we call "body" –)' (ibid.). At issue for Nietzsche are processes of self-organization on the part of an indeterminate living multiplicity, which he begins to describe as follows:

> The marvellous binding together of the most manifold life, the order and integration of the higher and lower activities, the thousand-fold obedience which is not a blind, even less a mechanistic but rather a selecting, circumspect, considerate, even resisting obedience [...] (ibid.)[116]

In order to account for the processes of self-organization that constitute the '"body"' Nietzsche recurs to the language of obedience and combines it with a notion of intelligence: the complexity of these organizing processes requires relations of unequal power between (indeterminate) living beings that command (attempted incorporation) and those that obey, that is, resist or repulse (*widerstreben*) their incorporation by those in command. To be effective, however, such obeying/resisting cannot be understood in mechanistic terms as a 'blind' *vis repulsiva*, Nietzsche argues, since it requires discrimination and selection, as well as prudence or thought, in short: intellect. The argument turns on the need for communication among the body's constituents for the purposes of agency. The 'enormous synthesis' that we call 'human being' can only live

> if that subtle connecting- and mediating-system, and through it lightning-fast communication among all these higher and lower beings is created – and moreover exclusively by living mediators: but this is a moral and not a mechanistic problem! (ibid.)[117]

---

[115] '[W]ie eine solche ungeheure Vereinigung von lebenden Wesen, jedes abhängig und unterthänig und doch in gewissem Sinne wiederum befehlend und aus eignem Willen handelnd, als Ganzes leben, wachsen und eine Zeit lang bestehen kann – [...]'.

[116] 'Die prachtvolle Zusammenbindung des vielfachsten Lebens, die Anordnung und Einordnung der höheren und niederen Thätigkeiten, der tausendfältige Gehorsam welcher kein blinder, noch weniger ein mechanischer sondern ein wählender, kluger, rücksichtsvoller, selbst widerstrebender Gehorsam ist [...]'.

[117] '[...] wenn jenes feine Verbindungs- und Vermittlungs-System und dadurch eine blitzartig schnelle Verständigung aller dieser höheren und niederen Wesen geschaffen ist – und zwar durch lauter lebendige Vermittler: dies aber ist ein moralisches, und nicht ein mechanistisches Problem!'

For those in command to be able to act, they must be supplied with a stringent selection of data or experiences (*Erlebnisse*), experiences that must already be 'simplified, made overseeable and graspable [*übersichtlich und faßlich*], thus *falsified* experiences' (ibid.). This operation of 'abstracting and condensing' ('Abstrahiren und Zusammendenken'), in short: *Gleichmachung* is what the intellect of the obeying instance performs, and it enables the commanding instance to formulate a resolution or 'act of will' (*Willensakt*), which Nietzsche also describes as a simplification, vague and indeterminate: a 'thin and extremely imprecise value- and power-representation [*Werth- und Kraft-Vorstellung*]'. In order to be executed, this command must then be communicated back to the obeying instances, which means: translated into the thousand-fold operations that must be performed in the body for it to act.

Clearly, what Nietzsche is describing are relations of mutual dependency: the (obeying) multiplicities are dependent on a single resolution or 'act of will' formed by the commanding instances for the body to act on their behalf; the commanding instances are dependent on multiplicities to execute it, that is: to translate a vague decision into thousands of specific actions. Ultimately, it is the first dependency that makes consciousness, as the locus of highest instance of command at a given moment, an 'organ' of the body and explains the need for unity and specifically: consciousness of self as a unitary will. At the same time, all these instances are in relations of opposition or antagonism, (attempted) incorporation-and-resistance, since they are not beings or substances, but only 'something growing, struggling, extending itself and dying off again' (*etwas Wachsendes, Kämpfendes, Sich-Vermehrendes und Wieder-Absterbendes*) in unceasing change. But what is most pronounced and puzzling in this account is its profoundly *anthropomorphic* character. Nietzsche's anti-mechanistic thesis is that the complexity of the body as self-organizing multiplicity is a 'moral', not a mechanistic problem, requiring 'lightning-fast' understanding (*blitzartig schnelle Verständigung*) between all instances as 'living communicators' (*lebendige Vermittler*). This is puzzling because, as we have seen, Nietzsche's key move against metaphysics is to strip reality of all human qualities, including qualitative oppositions (Ggz I), in favour of relations of opposition or antagonism among entities without substance (Ggz II.2). We therefore need to ask why he seems willing to re-anthropomorphize reality in this way and whether it undermines his entire project.

III.6 Nietzsche's critique of mechanism

We have already seen that mechanism effaces (*Wegdenken*) novelty or the unicity of every occurrence under the rule of *Gleichmachung* and *Festmachung* (p. 64), and that it is incapable of accounting for the intellectual and communicative processes needed for the complex self-organization that we call the 'body.' In this connection, Nietzsche also objects that the concepts of pressure and thrust (*Druck und Stoß*), upon which mechanistic causality depends, are 'non-originary': they presuppose processes of self-organization that first form the entities (atoms, things, bodies, etc.) that can thrust – processes that cannot be explained mechanistically because mechanism always presupposes entities that can thrust, raising again the question of how these entities are formed, and so on:

Pressure and thrust as something unutterably late, derived, non-originary. For it presupposes something that *holds together* and *can* press and thrust! But how would it come to hold together? (2[105] 12.112)[118]

But Nietzsche's main objection to mechanism is that it cannot account for the reality of change and transformation. This can be seen in a text on the physicists' 'victorious concept "force"':

The physicists cannot rid the 'effect at a distance' from their principles: just as little as a repelling force (or attracting one) There is no helping it: one must grasp all movements, all 'appearances', all 'laws' only as symptoms of an inner occurrence and use the analogy of the human being all the way to the end. (36[31] 11.563)[119]

But why should this reference to an 'inner occurrence' – which we have already come across (2[146] 12.139; p. 65) – be linked to anthropomorphization ('the analogy of the human')? A pointer is given in the following note:

'Attracting' and 'repelling' in a purely mechanical sense is a complete fiction. We cannot think an attraction without a purpose. – The will to get something into one's power or to defend oneself against its power and to repel it – *that* 'we understand': that would be an interpretation we could use.

In short: the psychological need for a belief in causality lies in the *unrepresentability [U n v o r s t e l l b a r k e i t] of an occurrence without purposes* […] (2[83] 12.102f.)[120]

The key claim here is that we cannot think, represent or make sense of any occurrence – and this includes attraction and repulsion – without a purpose (*Absicht*). Nietzsche then translates mechanistic attraction-repulsion into the language of will to power as purposive agency: attraction as overpowering/getting something in one's power, and repulsion as self-defence/warding off. The important, somewhat obvious point being made here is that this translation involves a *re-anthropomorphization* of reality. Indeed, as a somewhat later note makes clear, it involves the reintroduction of one quality back

---

[118] 'Druck und Stoß etwas unsäglich Spätes, Abgeleitetes,
Unursprüngliches. Es setzt ja schon etwas voraus, das z u s a m m e n h ä l t und drücken und stoßen k a n n ! Aber woher hielte es zusammen?'

[119] 'Die Physiker werden die "Wirkung in die Ferne" aus ihren Principien nicht los: ebensowenig eine abstoßende Kraft (oder anziehende) Es hilft nichts: man muß alle Bewegungen, alle "Erscheinungen", alle "Gesetze" nur als Symptome eines innerlichen Geschehens fassen und sich der Analogie des Menschen zu Ende bedienen.'

[120] '"Anziehen" und "Abstoßen" in rein mechanischem Sinne ist eine vollständige Fiktion: ein Wort. Wir können uns ohne eine Absicht ein Anziehen nicht denken. – Den Willen sich einer Sache zu bemächtigen oder gegen ihre Macht sich zu wehren und sie zurückzustoßen – d a s "verstehen wir": das wäre eine Interpretation, die wir brauchen könnten.
Kurz: die psychologische Nöthigung zu einem Glauben an Causalität liegt in der U n v o r s t e l l - b a r k e i t   e i n e s   G e s c h e h e n s   o h n e   A b s i c h t e n […]'.

into reality: activity as willing more power. For all human motivations and affects can in Nietzsche's view be reduced to 'the purpose of increasing power':

> A force that we cannot represent to ourselves (like the so-called purely mechanical force of attraction and repulsion) is an empty word and should not have any rights of citizenship in *science*: which wants to make the world *representable* [*intelligible*] to us, nothing more!
> All occurrence from purposes is reducible to the *purpose of increasing power*. (2[88] 12.105)[121]

But why should Nietzsche insist that we can only make sense of occurrences in terms of anthropomorphic purposes? In the previous note he writes of a 'psychological need' or constraint: we believe in causality because we cannot represent an occurrence without purposes to ourselves. Clearly, he has a specific notion of causality in mind. The claim is that 'we have formed the idea [*Vorstellung*] of cause and effect on the model [*Vorbild*] of our will' (40[37] 11.646), or as he puts it elsewhere:

> We have believed the will to be a cause to the extent that in general we have placed a cause in that what which occurs following our personal experience (i.e. purpose as cause of occurrence –) [...] (14[152] 13.335)[122]

Nietzsche's claim is, then, that we can only make sense of change (occurrence) in terms of causality, and we can only make sense of causality in terms of our personal self-understanding as willing, purposive agents. That, of course, does not make our practical self-understanding true; on the contrary, in several texts on the physiology of agency Nietzsche seeks to expose it as an illusion and a misunderstanding of the body.[123] Nonetheless, our self-understanding as agents acts as an *unbreakable psychological*

---

[121] 'Eine Kraft, die wir uns nicht vorstellen können (wie die sogenannte rein mechanische Anziehungs- und Abstoßungskraft) ist ein leeres Wort und darf kein Bürgerrecht in der W i s s e n s c h a f t haben: welche uns die Welt v o r s t e l l b a r machen will, nichts weiter!
Alles Geschehen aus Absichten ist reduzirbar auf die A b s i c h t d e r M e h r u n g v o n M a c h t.'

[122] 'Wir haben den Willen als Ursache geglaubt, bis zu dem Maße, daß wir nach unserer Personal-Erfahrung überhaupt eine Ursache in das Geschehen hineingelegt haben (d.h. Absicht als Ursache von Geschehen –) [...]'

[123] On our self-understanding as a misunderstanding of the body, see Chapter 3 pp. 144–6. See also 24[9] 10.647:
　　　　'Psychology of Error'
Whenever we do something, a *feeling of force* emerges, often preceding what is done, in envisioning what is to be done (as when we catch sight of an enemy, an obstacle that we believe we are *equal to*): always accompanying this feeling. We instinctively think that this feeling of force ought to be the cause of the action, that it ought to be "the force". Our belief in causality is the belief in force and its effect; a transference of our experience; whereby we identify force with the feeling of force. – Yet nowhere does the force move things, the force that is felt "does not set the muscles in motion". "We have no idea, no experience, of such a process." – "We experience just as little of the

constraint on our capacity to make sense of change. This point is made clearly in a note in which Nietzsche compares our self-understanding with the efforts of scientists of his time to explain action in mechanistic terms without regard for conscious motives:

Thus: either no will – the hypothesis of science – or free will. Latter assumption the prevailing feeling that we cannot rid ourselves of, even if the hypothesis were *proved*.

The popular belief in cause and effect rests on the presupposition *that free will is the cause of every effect*: it is only [OR in the first place] from here that we have the feeling of causality. Thus it is also therein that the feeling lies that every cause is *not* an effect but rather in the first place always a cause – if the will is cause. (24[15] 10.651)[124]

The fact that we cannot free ourselves from our self-understanding as agents with free will means that the scientific alternative is no real alternative. The real alternative is to give up on making sense of change altogether, as Nietzsche makes clear elsewhere:

Either one must take all effects as an illusion (for we have formed our representation [*Vorstellung*] of cause and effect on the model of our will as cause!) and then nothing at all is comprehensible: *or* one must attempt to think all effects as being of the same kind, as act of will, thus make the hypothesis as to whether all

necessity of a movement as of the force as something that makes things move." Force ought to be that which compels! "We only experience that one thing follows another – we experience neither the compulsion, nor the choice, that one thing follows another." Causality is first created through the projection of compulsion into the process of following. A certain "comprehension" emerges thereby, i.e., we have anthropomorphized the process for ourselves, made it "more familiar": that which is familiar is the habitual familiarity of a *feeling of force that is conjoined to human compelling*.'

    'Psychologie des Irrthums
Wenn wir etwas thun, so entsteht ein K r a f t g e f ü h l, oft schon vor dem Thun, bei der Vorstellung des zu Thuenden (wie beim Anblick eines Feindes, eines Hemmnisses, dem wir uns g e w a c h s e n glauben): immer begleitend. Wir meinen instinktiv, dies Kraftgefühl sei Ursache der Handlung, es sei "die Kraft". Unser Glaube an Kausalität ist der Glaube an Kraft und deren Wirkung; eine Übertragung unsres Erlebnisses; wobei wir Kraft und Kraftgefühl identificiren. – Nirgends aber bewegt die Kraft die Dinge, die empfundene Kraft "setzt nicht die Muskeln in Bewegung". "Wir haben von einem solchen Prozeß keine Vorstellung, keine Erfahrung." – "Wir erfahren ebensowenig, wie die Kraft als Bewegendes, die N o t h w e n d i g k e i t einer Bewegung." Die Kraft soll das Zwingende sein! "Wir erfahren nur, daß eins auf das andere folgt – weder Zwang erfahren wir, noch Willkür, daß eins auf das andere folgt." Die Kausalität wird erst durch die Hineindenkung des Zwangs in den Folgevorgang geschaffen. Ein gewisses "Begreifen" entsteht dadurch d.h. wir haben uns den Vorgang angemenschlicht, "bekannter" gemacht: das Bekannte ist das Gewohnheitsbekannte des mit K r a f t g e f ü h l v e r b u n d e n e n m e n s c h l i c h e n E r z w i n g e n s.'

[124] 'Also: entweder kein Wille – die Hypothese der Wissenschaft – oder freier Wille. Letztere Annahme das herrschende Gefühl, von dem wir uns nicht losmachen können, auch wenn die Hypothese b e w i e s e n wäre.'
    Der populäre Glaube an Ursache und Wirkung ist auf die Voraussetzung gebaut, daß d e r f r e i e W i l l e U r s a c h e i s t v o n j e d e r W i r k u n g: erst hierher haben wir das Gefühl der Causalität. Also darin liegt auch das Gefühl, daß jede Ursache nicht Wirkung ist, sondern immer erst Ursache – wenn der Wille die Ursache ist.'

mechanical occurrence, insofar as there is a force in it, is not simply force of will. – (40[37] 11.647)[125]

From this point of view, the mistake has been to strip causation of purposes, as recommended by Spinoza, and treat the understanding of reality 'in a geometrical way' with the help of 'mathematics', which is 'concerned not with ends but solely with the essences and properties of figures' as the 'standard of truth' (Ethics I Appendix).[126] For according to Nietzsche, 'the belief in causae falls with the belief in τέλη (against Spinoza and his causalism)' (2[83] 12.103). We need instead to translate mechanistic (exogenous, efficient) causality back into the sphere from which we first took it, and make the hypothesis 'as to whether all mechanical occurrence, insofar as there is a force in it, is not simply force of will [*ob nicht alles mechanische Geschehen, insofern eine Kraft darin ist, eben Willenskraft ist*]' (40[37] 11.647):

> [...] let us [OR if we] translate the concept 'cause' back into the only sphere we are familiar with, from which we took it: then we cannot represent a *change* to ourselves in which there is not a will to power. We do not know how to infer a change, unless an encroaching of power over other power takes place. (14[81] 13.260)[127]

So far I have argued that Nietzsche's thought operates under two constraints: in adhering to the logical principle of non-contradiction, he operates under the constraint of life as the highest value. But he does not simply repeat the life-enabling errors he exposes. Under the constraint of his critique of metaphysics and substance ontology, he takes as his presuppositions a series of negations of the latter, including real contradiction or antagonism. We can now see that in seeking to describe change and becoming, he operates under a further constraint, an unbreakable psychological constraint on our capacity to make sense of change, proposing that we address all change in terms of our self-understanding as agents, that is, in terms of the causality of willing (*Willenskraft*) as a matter of purposive overpowering. This does not, however, amount to a new 'standard of truth' to compete with Spinoza's *more geometrico*. Indeed, it cannot, given Nietzsche's own critiques of our practical self-understanding. Instead, it amounts to giving up on truth-claims for the kind of discourse that best enables us to make sense of the reality of change. This is made clear by Nietzsche at the end of the note on our psychological constraint cited earlier:

---

[125] 'E n t w e d e r muß man alle Wirkung als Illusion auffassen (denn wir haben uns die Vorstellung von Ursache und Wirkung nur nach dem Vorbilde unseres Willens als Ursache gebildet!) und dann ist gar nichts begreiflich: o d e r man muß versuchen, sich alle Wirkungen als gleicher Art, wie Willensakte zu denken, also die Hypothese machen, ob nicht alles mechanische Geschehen, insofern eine Kraft darin ist, eben Willenskraft ist. – [...]'.
[126] Spinoza (2000 108).
[127] '[...] übersetzen wir den Begriff "Ursache" wieder zurück in die uns einzig bekannte Sphäre, woraus wir ihn genommen haben: so ist uns keine Veränderung vorstellbar, bei der es nicht einen Willen zur Macht giebt. Wir wissen eine Veränderung nicht abzuleiten, wenn nicht ein Übergreifen von Macht über andere Macht statt hat.'

In short: the psychological necessity for a belief in causality lies in the *unrepresentability of an occurrence without intentions*: which naturally says nothing about truth or untruth (justification of such a belief). The belief in causae falls with the belief in τέλη (against Spinoza and his causalism). (2[83] 12.103)[128]

It is important to see that this does not mean that the question of truth is somehow overcome by Nietzsche, as some commentators have it. For Nietzsche there can be no philosophical thinking without the will to truth in one form or another.[129] But it does not follow from this that truth value must be attached to one's philosophical discourse. These notes show clearly that Nietzsche detaches the will to truth, necessary for philosophy, from truth-claims for philosophical discourse. This, of course, raises the question of the epistemic status of Nietzsche's philosophical discourse (to be addressed in the next section).

The broader context for these reflections is Nietzsche's quest for a unified concept of force or power and real opposition that cuts across all domains of reality, including inorganic nature. It is worth noting, to begin with, that the concept of 'force' (*Kraft*) is thoroughly problematic for Nietzsche. For Kant, as we saw, we can sense the forces at work in mental life in the effort it sometimes requires to banish certain thoughts from our mind (see pp. 30–1). In this regard Nietzsche agrees with Hume against Kant,[130] when he asks: 'Has a force ever been detected [*constatirt*]? No, only effects, translated into a thoroughly alien language' (2[159] 12.143). The 'thoroughly alien language' Nietzsche has in mind is of course the thoroughly anthropomorphic language of our self-experience as agents. Any action, Nietzsche argues, is accompanied by a 'feeling of force' (*Kraftgefühl*), or even preceded by it 'with the representation of what is to be done (as in in the sight of an enemy, a hindrance, to which we believe we are equal)' (24[9] 10.647).

Our belief in causality is the belief in force and its effect; a transference [OR metaphor] of our lived experience; whereby we identify force with the feeling of force. (ibid.)[131]

We falsely identify our feeling of force with real force as the cause of our action, whereas we have in fact worked backwards from the effects to putative cause by inserting

---

[128] 'Kurz: die psychologische Nöthigung zu einem Glauben an Causalität liegt in der U n v o r s t e l l - b a r k e i t e i n e s G e s c h e h e n s o h n e A b s i c h t e n: womit natürlich über Wahrheit oder Unwahrheit (Berechtigung eines solchen Glaubens) nichts gesagt ist. Der Glaube an causae fällt mit dem Glauben an τέλη (gegen Spinoza und dessen Causalismus).'

[129] Even the 'philosophers of the future' projected in JGB are driven by the will to truth (JGB 211). Similarly, the end of GM III 27 (5.410) on the 'coming to consciousness of the will to truth' as a problem, often misread as an overcoming of the will to truth, is driven by the will to truth.

[130] See Zinkin (2012 399) on this point.

[131] 'Unser Glaube an Kausalität ist der Glaube an Kraft und deren Wirkung; eine Übertragung unsres Erlebnisses; wobei wir Kraft und Kraftgefühl identificiren.'

coercion or compulsion (*Zwang*), making force the coercive instance from which the effects 'follow'. In the light of this critical genealogy, the word 'force' for Nietzsche is but a placeholder for the source or ground of change that we cannot experience but posit. Nietzsche's question is whether 'force' can be conceived in a way that cuts across inorganic and organic nature, as well as mental life.

This task is tackled in a *Nachlass* note from 1885, which eventually sees light as JGB 36. Both texts pose the question of whether the world can be constructed from what is strictly '"given" as real' (JGB 36) or 'given as "real"' (40[37] 11) to consciousness:

> In the end, nothing is given as 'real' other than thinking and sensing [AND/OR feeling] and drives: is it not permitted to make the attempt whether this given is not *sufficient* to construct the world? (40[37] 11.646)[132]

From the preceding, we know that this must be a world we can live in (1st constraint), but one that is stripped of substance(s), unitary grounds or any originary concept of being in favour of plurality, process and real contradiction (2nd constraint), and one that enables us to make sense of the reality of change in anthropomorphic terms: as the causality of willing (*Willenskraft*), reduced to purposive overpowering (3rd constraint). Nietzsche's thought here is perhaps best reconstructed backwards, as a two-step genealogy: what is strictly '"given"' to consciousness consists of three distinct operations – thinking, sensing/feeling and drives. They have their genealogy in the organic processes or functions that are distinguishable but operate together to sustain the living unity of the organism. In their differentiated unity, organisms thus represent the first steps or initiatives towards the separation of the conscious operations of thinking, sensing/feeling and drives:

> [T]he organic beings as approaches towards separation, so that all the organic functions are still together in that unity, thus self-regulation, assimilation, nourishment, excretion, metabolism […] (ibid.)[133]

The differentiated unity of organic functions in turn has its genealogy in '"force,"' understood as 'a unity […] in which willing, feeling and thinking are mixed and unseparated' ('"Kraft" [als] eine Einheit […], in der Wollen Fühlen und Denken noch gemischt und ungeschieden sind'). The effect of this genealogy is to reinterpret the mechanistic concept of force non-mechanistically, as a '*precursor* [*Vorform*] of life' (i.e. the organism) and a 'more primitive form of the world of affects' (JGB 36 5.54f.;

---

[132] 'Zuletzt ist als "real" nichts gegeben als Denken und Empfinden und Triebe: ist es nicht erlaubt zu versuchen, ob dies Gegebene nicht a u s r e i c h t, die Welt zu construiren?' In the context of his 'Phänomenalismus' (15[90] 13.459), Nietzsche often posits as 'given': *Empfindung* (sensation/feeling) and thinking/representation (26[11] 7; 7[64], 12[25] 10); 'and drives' (40[37] 11; cf. JGB 36: 'desires and passions', 'drives', 'affects'); or physiological stimuli (*Reize*) (19[209] 7; 10[F100] 9, 11[270] 9; 25[313] 11, 38[10] 11).

[133] '[…] die organischen Wesen als Ansätze zur Trennung, so daß die organischen Funktionen sämmtlich noch in jener Einheit beieinander sind, also Selbst-regulirung, Assimilation, Ernährung, Ausscheidung, Stoffwechsel […]'.

cf. 40[37] 11.647). The implication of Nietzsche's unified concept of 'force' is that action, interaction and change in the inorganic world can no longer be conceived mechanistically – as a matter of attraction and repulsion, thrust and exogenous causality – but only anthropomorphically, in terms of our self-understanding as agents:

> In the end the question is this: whether we acknowledge the will really as effecting? If we do this, then naturally it can only have effect on something that is of its kind: and not on 'materials'. *Either* one must interpret all effect as illusion (for we have formed our idea of cause and effect only according to the model of our will as cause!) and then nothing at all is comprehensible: *or* one must attempt to think all effects as being of the same kind, like acts of will, hence make the hypothesis as to whether all mechanical events, insofar as there is a force in them, are not simply force of will. – (ibid.)[134]

And yet, as we have seen, Nietzsche considers our self-understanding as agents to be false. So how exactly are we to take this anthropomorphic language? I will approach this question by addressing the epistemology of Nietzsche's physiological discourse. At issue in these questions is the status of Nietzsche's concept of real opposition as conflict or antagonism (Ggz II.2).

III.7 The epistemology of conflict

It is important to be clear on the epistemology of Nietzsche's recourse to physiology. It has nothing to do with scientific realism, as mainstream naturalistic readers believe, or biologism in Heidegger's sense. It is characteristic of Nietzsche's style of thought to subject concepts or approaches that he is at that moment using extensively to intensive critique; a kind of auto-critique in which he homes in on their first presuppositions and their ultimate consequences. This goes in particular for his use of scientific concepts and approaches,[135] and is no less true of his physiological writings in notebook 11 (KSA 9). In note 11[128] Nietzsche takes issue with the physiologist Roux, Mayer and other scientists on whom he is drawing elsewhere in that same notebook:

---

[134] 'Die Frage ist zuletzt: ob wir den Willen wirklich als wirkend anerkennen? Thun wir das, so kann er natürlich nur auf etwas wirken, was seiner Art ist: und nicht auf "Stoffe". E n t w e d e r muß man alle Wirkung als Illusion auffassen (denn wir haben uns die Vorstellung von Ursache und Wirkung nur nach dem Vorbilde unseres Willens als Ursache gebildet!) und dann ist gar nichts begreiflich: o d e r man muß versuchen, sich alle Wirkungen als gleicher Art, wie Willensakte zu denken, also die Hypothese machen, ob nicht alles mechanische Geschehen, insofern eine Kraft darin ist, eben Willenskraft ist. –'.

[135] This is well illustrated by Nietzsche's engagement with the scientific conceptions of 'sensation' (*Empfindung*) and 'laws of nature'. See the article 'Empfindung' in the *Nietzsche-Wörterbuch* (Nietzsche Online: http://www.degruyter.com/view/NO/empfindung); and Siemens 2014 82–102).

> Nowadays *struggle* has once again been discovered everywhere and one speaks of the struggle of the cells, tissues, organs, organisms. But in them one *can* recognise various of our conscious affects – and then, when this has occurred, *we turn the matter around* and say: what really happens in the arousal of our human affects are those physiological movements, and the affects (struggles etc.) are only intellectual interpretations in areas where the intellect knows absolutely nothing, and yet *believes* itself to know everything. With the word 'anger' 'love' 'hatred' it believes it has designated the Why?, the *ground* of movement; just so with the word 'will' etc. – Our natural science is now on the way to elucidate the smallest occurrences through our acquired affect-feelings, in short to create a *way of speaking* about those occurrences: very well! But it remains an image-language.[136]

These lines pinpoint the circularity of the physiologists' scientific discourse. On the one hand, they purport to explain our first person affects in terms of impersonal physiological processes or movements (*de-anthropomorphization*); on the other, our first person affective dispositions and modes of engagement – '"ärger" "Liebe" "Haß"' and 'Kämpfe' – are used to elucidate (*verdeutlichen*) or make sense of those processes (*re-anthropomorphization*). We can recognize in this the double-movement we have traced in Nietzsche's thought: on the one hand, to de-anthropomorphize and demoralize reality by stripping it of all human qualities and qualitative oppositions (Ggz I): good vs evil, being vs becoming, altruism vs egoism, etc.; on the other, to re-anthropomorphize reality in order to make sense of self-motion and change: as causality of the will, purposive overpowering, struggle/antagonism (Ggz II.2). But for Nietzsche, this circularity is not sterile. Since he rejects the claim of scientific discourse to speak of a reality outside discourse, we can only speak of speech (*Rede*), and the key question is not: Which discourse explains 'what really happens'? but rather: Which discourse best addresses the burning question of spontaneous movement and change falsified by substance ontology and *Seinsmetaphysik*? In this regard we have seen (2nd constraint) that he displaces the mechanistic conflict of attraction-repulsion with organismic models of conflict and why (plurality of processes, organizational struggle, derivative unity, novelty, 'quality' as unicity); but also why, given our psychological limitations (3rd constraint), any kind of speech (*Sprechart*) that enables us to make sense of spontaneous self-movement must do so in terms of our self-experience as agents and our 'acquired affect-feelings' – love, hate, anger, willing more power, and ultimately: struggle or antagonism (*Kampf*).

---

[136] 'Jetzt hat man den K a m p f überall wieder entdeckt und redet vom Kampfe der Zellen, Gewebe, Organe, Organismen. Aber man k a n n sämmtliche uns bewußte Affekte in ihnen wiederfinden – zuletzt, wenn dies geschehen ist, d r e h e n w i r d i e S a c h e u m und sagen: das was wirklich vor sich geht bei der Regsamkeit unserer menschlichen Affekte sind jene physiologischen Bewegungen, und die Affekte (Kämpfe usw.) sind nur intellektuelle Ausdeutungen, dort wo der Intellekt gar nichts weiß, aber doch alles zu wissen m e i n t. Mit dem Wort "ärger" "Liebe" "Haß" meint er das Warum? bezeichnet zu haben, den G r u n d der Bewegung; ebenso mit dem Worte "Wille" usw. – Unsere Naturwissenschaft ist jetzt auf dem Wege, sich die kleinsten Vorgänge zu verdeutlichen durch unsere angelernten Affekt-Gefühle, kurz eine S p r e c h a r t zu schaffen für jene Vorgänge: sehr gut! Aber es bleibt eine Bilderrede' (11[128] 9.487).

So the discourse of physiology and physiological models of conflict are taken and taken on by Nietzsche, not as a set of empirical truth-claims about extra-discursive reality, but as fictional devices (*Bilder*), heuristic fictions devised to address the dynamic principle or *Grund der Bewegung* of life-processes. They enable him to 'translate' our life-world of stable objects in regular relations, that is: our life-enabling world of *Festsetzen* and *Gleichsetzen*, back into multiplicities of processes in complex, multi-layered relations of real opposition (Ggz II.2), forming unities at various levels through processes of self-organization. But in order to make sense of these processes, and to elucidate (*verdeutlichen*) their dynamic qualities, he 'makes use of the human analogy all the way', drawing on the concept of struggle and our practical experience of ourselves as will-power (*Willenskraft*), purposive overpowering, commanding and obeying. This double-movement allows for a unified conception of force without substance that overcomes metaphysical dualisms and substance ontology and gives him a 'manner of speaking' that enables us to make sense of the dynamic character of reality (unlike metaphysics) in a way that acknowledges the psychological limitations of human knowledge. At the same time, we have also seen that the language of physiology and organizational struggle does work for Nietzsche that Kant's mechanistic *Conflictus zweier Kräfte* cannot do: accounting for the creation of (relatively) stable living unities (our common life-world, the body, unitary self-consciousness) and even thought-processes, on the model of organismic processes; accounting for the possibility of novelty; and breaking through identitarian thinking so as to open thought up to genuine diversity.

III.8 Real opposition in Nietzsche's thought

We now have the relevant philosophical contexts needed for a better understanding of the third ontological meaning of the term 'Gegensatz' (Ggz II.2) in Nietzsche's vocabulary. Like Kant, he distinguishes sharply between logical opposition or contradiction (Ggz I) and real opposition (Ggz II.2), but he also takes it upon himself to 'save the phenomena': to defend the oppositional or contradictory character of reality against the claims of logic. At issue in real opposition, for Nietzsche as for Kant, is the dynamic principle of reality rooted in relations of conflict. While adhering to the principle of non-contradiction in his thinking, Nietzsche looks for a manner of speaking (*Sprechart*) or metaphorical language (*Bilderrede*) that can 'overcome' substance ontology and metaphysics by addressing the dynamic character of reality, which they fail to describe. Here he deviates sharply from Kant, in developing a counter-ontology of becoming based on a series of negations of substance ontology: process, 'originary' multiplicity/diversity, and antagonism or conflict. This is essentially an ontology of conflict with the concept of real opposition at its centre. Here 'Gegensatz' (Ggz II.2) signifies the antagonism (*Krieg, Gegeneinander*) of a plurality (*Vielheit*) of force quanta, powers or power-complexes without substance in unceasing transformation (*Wechsel*), whose essence is their relation: to exercise power over one another through the activity of fixing or *Feststellen*.

Nietzsche also deviates from Kant by rejecting the forces of attraction and repulsion (Kant's *Conflictus zweier Kräfte*) for failing to make change and self-motion intelligible, and by recurring to organismic models of interaction and conflict (especially assimilation-excretion) instead, in line with the presuppositions of his counter-ontology. The effect of this language is to de-anthropomorphize and demoralize reality by stripping it of all human qualities and qualitative oppositions (Ggz I). Yet according to Nietzsche, there is one anthropomorphic quality that we need in order to make sense of change: the purposive activity of willing more power. As Müller-Lauter (1971 30) notes, this is no metaphysical quality, since willing more power can only be actual or effective in the radically immanent context of an antagonism (*Gegeneinander*) of powers. It is not the underlying unity behind the multiplicity of appearances, but the shared quality of all differential power relations, which can only exist across different degrees of power in antagonism (Ggz II.2). In this regard, real opposition or antagonism is key to Nietzsche's overcoming of metaphysics.

The features of 'Gegensatz' as ontologeme can therefore be summarized as follows:

- Real opposition, contradiction (*Widerspruch*), antagonism (*Gegeneinander*), struggle (*Kampf*), war (*Krieg*) in various forms: attacking/pouncing/overpowering – self-defence/warding off/resisting; incorporation/assimilation – secretion/excretion; fixing/making fast; active commanding – active obeying.
- Force-quanta, forces, powers, power-complexes, organisms without substance: as endogenous sources of (inter)action and change.
- Plurality, diversity, difference.
- Differences of degree or grade, inequality of power.
- Shared quality: activity as the causality of willing (*Willenskraft*), reduced to willing more power or purposive overpowering.

In all these respects, Nietzschean real opposition differs from Kant's concept, despite their shared insight into the relational sources of change in conflict. But perhaps there is one point on which, in different ways, they do come closer. For Kant, as we saw, real opposition robs (privatio) each entity of its effects (such as motion in a specific direction) to a degree equal to its value, through an act of cancellation (*Aufhebung*). For Nietzsche, the conflict of powers takes the form of reciprocal (attempts at) fixing or *Festsetzen*. Prima facie, *Festsetzen* has nothing to do with Kantian *Aufhebung*. It names a *Setzen* or positing, which can take a great many different forms and meanings, but they are all so many attempts to arrest or fix the flow of events and ever-changing relations of power – even if only momentarily.

In the first instance *Festsetzen* designates relations of power between unequal opponents.[137] For Nietzsche, equilibrium is the exception, not the rule as it is for Kant, and it never involves strict quantitative equality as it does for Kant, but only an

---

[137] See 9[91] 12.384. In note 40[55] 11.655, Nietzsche distinguishes the 'absolute fixing [*Feststellung*] of power relations', 'the absolute momentariness [*Augenblicklichkeit*] of the will to power' in inorganic nature from the intelligence (*Geist*) and anticipation of *Feststellung* in human beings (and already in the cell), as a 'process which continually displaces itself with the growth of all constituents – a struggle [*Kampf*] [...]'.

approximate equality, since equilibrium involves complex intelligent, communicative and evaluative interactions, as do commanding and obeying.[138] These relations can take various forms, but for Nietzsche the act of *Festsetzen* has a particular affinity with the act of legislation and the concept of law,[139] and with the will to truth and the concept of truth:

> The will to truth is a *making* fixed, a *making* true and enduring, a putting out of sight of that *false* character, its reinterpretation into something that *is*. (9[91] 12.384)[140]

Here *Fest-setzen* or *Fest-machen* designates the process of hypostasization through which the 'false' world of becoming and occurrence is reinterpreted in life-enabling terms of self-identical beings in commerce. In this regard Kant's reliance on substance in his early metaphysics could be viewed as just another case of metaphysical *Festsetzen*, despite the dynamic concept of conflict of forces or real opposition as its centre. But for Nietzsche, *Festsetzen* is part of a process of overpowering, 'a will of overpowering' (*einen Willen der Überwältigung*: ibid.), which can only act in relation to an opposing 'will of overpowering'. And as such it bears a certain affinity with Kant's real opposition, despite all the differences catalogued above. For they do in a sense have the same effect, namely, to cancel the effects, or the capacity to have effects of that to which they stand in real opposition. If Kantian *Aufhebung* robs (privation, *Beraubung*) the other of its power to act against us, Nietzschean *Festsetzen* arrests the other's power to overpower us, separating it from what it can do.

In more systematic terms, the results of our analysis can be summarized in a number of key positions or propositions common to Kant and Nietzsche as philosophers of conflict:

1. If logical contradiction is impossible, and if real contradiction is understood as logical contradiction, it is impossible to think reality as contradictory.
2. If real contradiction is possible and actual, and logical contradiction is thought as real opposition, then it is impossible to think reality as contradictory without contradiction: real contradiction swallows up discourse.
3. So whether we model real contradiction on logical contradiction or logical contradiction on real contradiction: either way it is impossible to think reality

---

[138] On Nietzsche's concept of approximate equilibrium and approximate equality, see Gerhardt (1983, discussed in Chapter 2, p. 119). On the communicative acts in commanding and obeying, see 37[4] 11, discussed above on pp. 67–8.

[139] In connection with the act of (*Fest-*)*Setzen*, law (*Gesetz*) is thematized in a wide variety of contexts in different senses, e.g. the 'Wille zum Schein' as 'Setzen des Unwahren als wahr' (26[359] 11.244); das 'Gesetz der Uebereinstimmung' as the basis for '"Vernünftigkeit"' (FW 76 3.431); and philosophical legislation (*Gesetzgebung*) as 'einen Begriff fest zu setzen' (34[88] 11.449).

[140] 'Der Wille zur Wahrheit ist ein Fest-m a c h e n, ein Wahr-Dauerhaft-M a c h e n, ein Aus-dem-Auge-schaffen enes f a l s c h e n Charakters, eine Umdeutung desselben ins S e i e n d e.'

as contradictory. For a philosophy of conflict to be possible, therefore, logical contradiction must be distinguished from real contradiction, such that while the first is impossible – making coherent thought possible – the second (real contradiction) is both possible and actual. In this way, our manner of thinking (contradiction is impossible) and the matter of our thinking (contradiction is both possible and actual) do not contradict one another.

4. On the other hand, distinguishing logical from real contradiction and accepting the constraint of non-contradiction in thought have the consequence that we cannot really grasp or describe real contradiction in its concrete facticity: if logical contradiction does not describe real contradiction, this goes even more so under the requirement of non-contradiction in thought. The best we can do is *hinweisen auf*, point towards a reality that resists or withdraws from thought.

2

Waging war against war: Nietzsche *contra* Kant on conflict and the question of a living peace

I Introduction

At first sight, Kant and Nietzsche stand at opposite ends of the spectrum as philosophers of conflict. For good measure, one need only juxtapose the title of Kant's famous philosophical sketch (*philosophischer Entwurf*): *Zum ewigen Frieden* (ZeF) with Nietzsche's infamous extra-moral imperative in *Der Antichrist*:

> *Not* contentment, but more power; *not* peace at all, but war; *not* virtue, but proficiency (virtue in the Renaissance style, virtù, virtue free of moralism)

> N i c h t Zufriedenheit, sondern mehr Macht; n i c h t Friede überhaupt, sondern Krieg; n i c h t Tugend, sondern Tüchtigkeit (Tugend im Renaissance-Stile, virtù, moralinfreie Tugend) (AC 2)

Or the even more pointedly anti-Kantian imperative of Zarathustra:

> You ought to love peace as the means to new wars. And the short peace more than the long one.

> Ihr sollt den Frieden lieben als Mittel zu neuen Kriegen. Und den kurzen Frieden mehr, als den langen. (Z I War 4.58)

Nietzsche's anti-Christian opposition to the Christian tradition of the *Friedensrufe* opened by Erasmus and invoked by Kant's *Zum ewigen Frieden*[1] remains implacable, but the matter does not end there. At times, Nietzsche does advocate mortal or military war, specifically in his early and middle period, either as a periodic, cathartic discharge of destructive drives (CV3), or (in MA) as a cultural stimulant and energizing force (although not without qualifications).[2] In a series of texts from 1875, Nietzsche laments

---

[1] Gerhardt (1995 8, 24). The version known to Kant was by the Abbé de Saint-Pierre *Projet pour rendre la paix perpétuelle en Europe* (1713). See also von Raumer (1953).
[2] Pearson (2018 31–80) (chapter 1).

the '*Fatum tristissimum generis humani!*' taught us by history, that violence, abuse and '*wild forces*' ignite the energy needed for the cultivation of intelligence.³ But there are also pacifist texts, like WS 284, where, like Kant (ZeF VIII.345), he argues against standing armies.⁴ For his part, Kant writes of the sublimity of war, when conducted with 'a sacred respect for the rights of civilians', and in the same breath decries 'the predominance of a mere commercial spirit', the 'debasing self-interest, cowardice, and weakness' favoured by a prolonged peace (KU §28 V.263).⁵ Like Nietzsche, he also views war as a 'spur for developing to the highest pitch all talents that minister to culture', while lamenting with Nietzsche, 'the terrible calamities which it inflicts on the human race, and the hardships, perhaps even greater, imposed by the constant preparation for it in time of peace' (KU §83 V.433). In ZeF, as is well known, Kantian Reason⁶ acknowledges that the general will grounded in Reason is impotent in practice (Zef II.307); since it cannot improve humans morally, Reason, in its cunning, looks instead to make use (*benutzen, gebrauchen*) of the conflict of their hostile inclinations (*Widerstreit ihrer unfriedlichen Gesinnungen*) as a means to secure its own end of eternal peace through the rule of law (ZeF II.307–8; 366–7). The underlying thought here is that our hostile and destructive *ends* in conflict have unintended consequences, which can be used by Reason as *means* towards its own end of peace and freedom. In this regard war is a force for the good, generating pluralization, organization and ultimately concord and freedom under the rule of law. As a 'mechanism of nature' grounded in human fear, antagonism and will to power, it turns destructive ends into a means to produce ends that coincide with Reason's ends.

These brief remarks suffice to dispel any simple opposition between the two thinkers on the question of war and peace. In this chapter I ask how Kant and Nietzsche address this question: How do they formulate the problem of conflict? How do they conceptualize the relation between war and peace? And how do they envisage the transformation of, or passage from senseless, destructive conflict (in)to a constructive order of things? My questions concern the relation between the *manner* and the *matter* of their thought as philosophers of conflict, more than their theories of peace or political theories.⁷ As a way into these questions, it is helpful to compare Kant and Nietzsche against Hobbes on three distinct issues:

1. The necessity (vs contingency) of conflict as a constitutive and ineradicable element of human agency and interaction.
2. The positive value to be given to conflict.
3. And the desirability of peace without conflict (as a norm, value, ideal, or duty).

---

³ For unlimited conflict as the necessary source of energy, see MA 233, MA 235 and the notes 5[180, 178, 185, 188] 8.
⁴ See also MA 481, VM 320 and WS 284.
⁵ In ZeF, by contrast, Kant argues in favour of commerce as propitiating peace (ZeF VIII.364, 368).
⁶ In this chapter, Kant's notion of reason will be specified with a capital R.
⁷ For Kant's theory of peace, see Kleingeld (2006). For ZeF as a political theory, see Gerhardt (1995).

Clearly, the positions taken on these issues depend on the exact nature and level of conflict in question. In political matters, Hobbes can be said to favour 3: the extirpation of conflict within and between states, to negate 2 (even if he favours economic competition), and to negate 1 (despite his insistence on human unsociability). Hobbes is a philosopher of peace, not of war, as Foucault (2003 78ff.) rightly notes. At the other extreme, Nietzsche unequivocally rejects 3: the ideal of peace to the exclusion of conflict, while affirming against Hobbes 2 and 1: that positive value can be ascribed to conflict, understood as constitutive of human agency and interaction, ineradicable and potentially productive. With Hobbes, Kant can be said to favour 3: the idea or ideal of eternal peace within and between states. Despite his call for eternal peace, however, Kant seems to share with Nietzsche 1: the realist view that conflict is deeply and ineradicably rooted in human action and interaction, and 2: the view that conflict can have valuable constructive or productive qualities.

This schema offers a first approximation to the problem of conflict for the three thinkers. For Hobbes the problem is simply how to put an end to conflict. For Nietzsche, given his commitment to 1 above, an end to conflict signifies a negation of life or reality: death or non-being. In Nietzsche's philosophy of life there can be no 'peace', 'harmony' or 'consensus' in a sense that is opposed to and excludes conflict or tension. To posit such an idea or ideal is to act against the character of life, to negate life in thought. For in Nietzsche's relational ontology of life, life *is* only relations of tension, attraction-repulsion, action-resistance, commanding-obeying among forces without substance; tension is the way in which relations are formed and transformed. Peace, understood as the absence of tension and antagonism, signifies not an actual or possible state of affairs, but simply: the absence of life or reality, non-being or nothing. To posit peace in a way that is not only opposed to conflict but eliminates conflict altogether, is therefore to make an absolute claim for nothingness, for non-being rather than being.

From this point of view, the problem is how to secure a living or life-affirmative peace, i.e. one that includes conflictual relations and the benefits they provide. This may sound incoherent, but as we will see it is not, since it turns on a form of conflict that admits limits or a degree of measure. But for Kant, both of these options are problematic. The Nietzschean option is complicated, if not foreclosed by his claim (in Zef and IaG) that the very same conditions, passions or 'mechanism' that make conflict evil and destructive are what make conflict productive of Reason, freedom and peace, a force for the good. And the Hobbesian option is complicated by Kant's commitment to 1 and 2 above; for how can he advocate an ideal of eternal peace exclusive of conflict while maintaining the ineradicability of conflict in reality and reaping the benefits of conflict? For Kant only peace can secure the conditions for freedom by transforming society into 'a moral whole' (IaG VIII.21). And as Wood (2015 120–3) points out, the content of the moral law of Reason is in direct opposition to the natural tendencies that make for hostility and conflict, yet it is through these tendencies that our faculties are developed, above all Reason, and our capacity to understand the moral law.

The three-fold schema also gives us a first approximation of what peace means for Kant and Nietzsche, or rather: what peace does *not* mean. The thought experiment is to ask what kind of peace is implied if we reduce conflict or even subtract it from agency and relations. The view that conflict is a necessary, constitutive and ineradicable dimension of human agency and interaction, to which both thinkers subscribe, and the value they give to conflict despite lamenting the horrors of war (points 1. and 2. in the schema) mean that reducing or seeking to minimize conflict can only lead to a *debilitation* of human beings and a loss of human potential, with capacities undeveloped or dormant. For Kant, this is a false sense of peace, the stuff of dreams,[8] but also a hypothetical state of nature, posited and repudiated by him in IaG, Anth and elsewhere.[9] It signifies a primordial inactivity or indolence, a herd-like tranquillity 'of perfect concord, contentment and mutual love', in which human capacities would lie fallow and 'human beings, as good-natured as the sheep they tended, would give their existence hardly any greater worth than that of their domesticated beasts' (IaG VIII.21).

For Nietzsche, the problem is far more acute, since what Kant describes is not a hypothetical state of nature, but the human condition in modernity, the debilitation of the human into a 'tame and civilized animal, a *household pet*' (GM I 11).[10] Nietzsche's starting point is not the threat of war, given the fragility of ceasefires during the French Revolutionary Wars of Europe, as it is for Kant; it is the false peace and tranquillity[11] of the modern European herd-animal of the mid- and late 1800s, and the contraction of human powers under the rule of the 'autonomous herd' (JGB 202). The arcadian dream of indolent tranquillity and contentment repudiated by Kant is recast by Nietzsche as the slavish ideal of happiness incorporated by Christianity: the longing for 'a narcotic, an anaesthetic, rest, peace, "sabbath", relaxation of the mind and stretching of the limbs, in short [...] something *passive*' (GM I 10). And like Kant, Nietzsche repudiates this dream of false peace. But to posit indolence, inactivity, passivity as hypothetical primordial state or slumber, from which we were awakened by conflict, as does Kant, is suspect for Nietzsche. Is it any different from the approach of the 'English psychologists', berated in GM for presupposing passivity in their genealogies of moral sentiments; in, 'for example, the *vis inertiae* of habit, or in forgetfulness, or in a blind and random coupling and mechanism of ideas, or in something purely passive, automatic, reflexive, molecular and thoroughly stupid –' (GM I 1). In the *Physical Monadology*,

---

[8] MAM VIII.114–15; 120–22.
[9] 'See: IaG VIII.21' cf. II.26; MAM VIII.114–15, 120–22; KU V.429–31; Anth VII.324–25, 327–28; RezHerder VIII.65.
[10] Kant's progressive view of civilization, spurred on by conflict, is of course diametrically opposed to Nietzsche's equation of the civilizational process with domestication, but he does agree that domestication is a weakening: 'Domestic animals are more useful to the human being than wild animals only because of *weakening*' (Anth VII.327).
[11] See also GD Moral 3 on the 'one-time desideratum of "peacefulness of the soul", the Christian desideratum; there is nothing we envy less than the moral cow and the fat happiness of good conscience.' ('Nichts ist uns fremder geworden als jene Wünschbarkeit von Ehedem, die vom "Frieden der Seele", die christliche Wünschbarkeit; Nichts macht uns weniger Neid als die Moral-Kuh und das fette Glück des guten Gewissens.') – to which Nietzsche opposes the spiritualization of enmity (*Vergeistigung der Feindschaft*). The quoted passage continues: 'One has renounced on greatness in life, if one renounces war ....' ('Man hat auf das grosse Leben verzichtet, wenn man auf den Krieg verzichtet ...').

as we saw (p. 36), the very same expression, *vis inertiae* ('force of inertia'), is used by Kant for his remarkable reversal of Leibniz's *vis viva* from an active endogenous source change into a principle of stasis or inertia. Nietzsche, of course, is closer to Leibniz's *vis viva* with his principle of 'Aktivität' (activity) from within as an endogenous source of change – the primacy of the 'spontaneous, aggressive, expansive, re-interpreting, re-directing and formative forces' (GM II 12 5.316) *against* passivity and merely 'reactive' adaptation.[12] Could Kant, in positing the primacy of human indolence, be a reactive thinker of conflict?

At the limit, conflict can be reduced from indolence and inactivity to the point of zero in a frictionless ideal of peace. For Nietzsche, as pointed out, this is a nihilistic ideal of peace that negates life from a transcendent standpoint in negating conflict; not a living peace, but non-being, a will to nothing. According to Nietzsche, this has been the dominant tendency not only in philosophy, but in European civilization, with devastating effects: impoverishing, reducing, weakening the forms of life that have posited nothingness as their ideal, resulting in the modern European herd-animal. Instead, he asks: What does it take to enrich, empower, extend and affirm life? What kind of ideals or idealization can articulate a striving for being, rather than non-being or nothingness?

In this chapter I ask whether Kant's idea of eternal peace is complicit in the history of life-negation, a nihilistic rejection of reality, or whether it stands for a living peace. The main thesis of the chapter (set out in §IV) is that Kant wages a *philosophical war of extermination (Todkrieg, Vernichtungskampf) on all war in the name of eternal peace*. By 'philosophical war of extermination' is meant *Todkrieg*, the term used by Nietzsche in AC to describe a bivalent (*zweiwertig*), oppositional manner of thinking, which makes a total and exclusive claim for its position (*Sich Absolutsetzen*) by eliminating or destroying the opposed position and with it, their relation of opposition. Kant's philosophical war against war, I argue, *replicates* in thought what he argues for in real terms: the extermination or *Vernichtung* of conflict in favour of eternal peace. This makes for an utterly barren, destructive notion of conflict and a life-negating idea of peace beyond the reality of conflict. I then turn (§V) to Nietzsche for an alternative manner of thinking conflict and peace, one that overcomes the Kantian oppositions and allows for a genuinely affirmative understanding of conflict and its productive qualities. In the final section I qualify the argument by considering each thinker's position from a perspective of the others. There is, I conclude, a profound ambiguity in Kant's ideal of peace: on the one hand, it signifies a nihilistic 'peace of the graveyard', on the other, it stands for a path to a living peace, which can be brought in line with a Nietzschean approach to peace. The first step is to ask how Kant formulates the problem of conflict and its relation to peace.

---

[12] According to Nietzsche, the English psychologists lack historical depth because they are caught up in 'merely "modern" experience' (GM II 4) and project it onto their histories of morality. And it is because they are reactive, passive herd-beings that they presuppose reactivity, instead of activity.

II Eternal peace and the peace of the graveyard

Kant knows several different senses of 'peace'. There is first the *empirical* concept of peace, that is, actual or *empirical peace* in the sense of the absence of war, known through experience. As a matter of empirical knowledge, it is contingent, potentially unstable and therefore unreliable – it could be a mere ceasefire, a prelude to future wars or a stable peace supported by guarantees. Then there is the *dream of peace* described above, the human longing for a false, sub-human, arcadian peace of indolence and passivity, posited by Kant as a hypothetical primordial state. But Kant's principal philosophical concern is with neither of these. It is rather with the *idea* of peace, what he calls 'perpetual' or 'eternal peace' (*ewige Frieden*) in ZeF, KrV and elsewhere.[13] For Kant it signifies an idea and a normative ideal: the highest political good (MS VI.355) and the condition for freedom; as such, it cannot be a matter of determining judgement. What exactly he means and does not mean by this idea(l) is far from clear, but a start can be made by examining the so-called satirical foreword to ZeF, where he formulates the problem of conflict with great perspicacity:

Towards Perpetual Peace

We can leave open the question whether this satirical caption to the picture of a graveyard, which was painted on the sign of a Dutch innkeeper, applies to *human beings* in general, or specifically to the heads of state, who can never get enough of war, or even just to philosophers who dream the sweet dream of perpetual peace. The author of this essay shall, however, stipulate one condition: since the practical politician tends to look disdainfully upon the political theorist as a mere academic, whose impractical ideas present no danger to the state (since, in the eyes of the politician, the state must be based on principles derived from experience), and who may show his hand without the *worldly* statesman needing to pay it any heed; then, in case of a conflict with the theorist, the statesman should deal with him consistently and refrain from any allegations of perceived threat to the state in whatever views that the theorist might dare set forth and publicly express. With this *clausula salvatoria* the author of this essay is hereby invoking the proper form to protect himself from any malicious interpretation.[14]

---

[13] KrV B 750, B 805; RGV VI.34, 124, MS VI.350, 354–5; VNAEF VIII.412, 416, 419, 421–2.
[14] Z u m   e w i g e n   F r i e d e n
Ob diese satirische Überschrift auf dem Schilde jenes holländischen Gastwirths, worauf ein Kirchhof gemalt war, die M e n s c h e n überhaupt oder besonders die Staatsoberhäupter, die des Krieges nie satt werden können, oder wohl gar nur die Philosophen gelte, die jenen süßen Traum träumen, mag dahin gestellt sein. Das bedingt sich aber der Verfasser des Gegenwärtigen aus, daß, da der praktische Politiker mit dem theoretischen auf dem Fuß steht, mit großer Selbstgefälligkeit auf ihn als einen Schulweisen herabzusehen, der dem Staat, welcher von Erfahrungsgrundsätzen ausgehen müsse, mit seinen sachleeren Ideen keine Gefahr bringe, und den man immer seine eilf Kegel auf einmal werfen lassen kann, ohne daß sich der w e l t k u n d i g e Staatsmann daran kehren darf, dieser auch im Fall eines Streits mit jenem sofern consequent verfahren müsse, hinter seinen auf gut Glück gewagten und öffentlich geäußerten Meinungen nicht Gefahr für den Staat zu wittern; – durch welche Clausula salvatoria der Verfasser dieses sich dann hiemit in der besten Form wider alle bösliche Auslegung ausdrücklich verwahrt wissen will (Zef VIII.343).

By drawing on the satirical caption 'Zum ewigen Frieden' on the Dutch innkeeper's sign depicting a graveyard,[15] Kant poses the problem of conflict as one of death and destruction, what Nietzsche calls the *Vernichtungskampf, Vernichtungskrieg* or *Todkrieg* (struggle for annihilation, war of annihilation, war-to-the-death). Kant poses the problem by opening or leaving open the question whether it is a problem at the level of human nature, or only a problem at the level of international politics: Is destructive conflict deeply and ineradicably rooted in human nature and interaction? Or is it a specifically political problem created by heads of state and their insatiable thirst for warfare? Kant may or may not be inviting us to laugh at death with the Dutch innkeeper, but by invoking the innkeeper's sign in the opening lines he does invite us to consider what he does *not* mean by 'eternal peace' in these two cases. The image of the graveyard comes back twice, haunting Kant's text like a ghost or shadow of the idea of peace he is trying to advance. So what is the peace of the graveyard?

1. The graveyard first returns in the 6th preliminary article, which forbids all the 'hellish arts' of warfare, such as assassination, poisoning, espionage. By undermining trust in the enemy they make eventual peace impossible, leading inexorably to a war of extermination or *Ausrottungskrieg,*

> in which both parties and, moreover, all right can be eradicated simultaneously, [and which] could bring about perpetual peace only over the great graveyard of humanity. Such a war, therefore, and hence the use of the means which would lead to it, must be utterly forbidden. (ZeF VIII.347)

By *Ausrottungskrieg* Kant means a lawless war of annihilation in the arena of international politics. In the absence of law, neither side can be declared to be unjust (*einen ungerechten Feind*), so that violence (*Gewalt*) takes the place of right (*Recht*). Only the outcome (*Ausschlag*) of violent combat is decisive – and the only decisive outcome of violent combat is the extermination or annihilation of the opponent. Here, the peace of the graveyard signifies the *victor's peace*, the despotic peace imposed upon the vanquished (or what is left of them) in the wake of an absolute victory. Or, in the extreme case imagined by Kant, the peace of the graveyard is the annihilation of *both* sides and with them, the annihilation of all right; that is, the graveyard of peace. In international politics, then, Kant's 'eternal peace' does *not* signify the victor's peace, much less the eradication of all right.

2. The second mention of the graveyard takes us straight to Kant's core concern: human freedom. The context is the 'First Supplement' on the 'Guarantee of Perpetual

---

[15] Kant's source seems to have been Leibniz's 1693 Foreword to his *Codex Juris Gentium Diplomaticus*: 'Itaque elegans nugator in Bataviscum more gentis signum pro domo suspendisset, pacis perpetuae, pulchro titulo figuram coemeterii subjecerat. Ibi scilicet mors quietem fecit.' ('And so, in the manner of the Dutch nation, the elegant man had hung up a sign before his house, and with the beautiful title of perpetual peace, he had hung the figure of the cemetery. There, of course, death made rest.') (Leibniz 2004 51).

Peace', where Kant tries to show what nature does[16] to establish the conditions for freedom, whether we like it or not; in this case, by pluralizing peoples and states through the reciprocal hatred and war[17] provoked by the 'diversity of *languages* and *religions*'. Kant's background worry is that the fusion (*Zusammenschmelzung, Vermischung*) of peoples through the establishment of a 'universal monarchy' or global empire absorbing all peoples will overstretch the reach of laws, leading to a 'soulless despotism', which is 'the graveyard of freedom' (*Kirchhofe der Freiheit*). It is unclear whether Kant means inner (moral) freedom or external (political) freedom here; in any case, the two are interconnected.[18] For Kant, the realization of inner freedom depends upon external freedom, which can only be secured by the rule of law at three interdependent levels: a republican state, in which citizens are free and equal as co-legislators who enact their own laws through their representative,[19] international law between states, and cosmopolitan law. But what *is* clear, is that 'graveyard of freedom' under despotism is the same as the victor's despotic peace, only from the position of those vanquished or subjugated.

Of importance for Kant's philosophy of conflict is that he goes on to associate peace with an 'equilibrium' of all powers 'in the liveliest competition', as against the 'weakening of all powers' in the despotic graveyard of freedom.[20] Again, the text is unclear: what kind(s) of competition and what 'powers' or 'forces' (*Kräfte*) Kant has in mind, who or what is to regulate it and on which principles are a matter of conjecture. But it is clear that Kant has *a living peace* in mind, not a peace of the graveyard, one which allows for the kind(s) of conflict that exclude(s) destruction, death (the *Vernichtungskampf*) and the graveyard of freedom in favour of the 'liveliest competition' (*Wetteifer*) combined with freedom.

---

[16] 'Wenn ich von der Natur sage: sie w i l l, daß dieses oder jenes geschehe, so heißt das nicht soviel als: sie legt uns eine P f l i c h t auf, es zu thun (denn das kann nur die zwangsfreie praktische Vernunft), sondern sie t h u t es selbst, wir mögen wollen oder nicht (fata volentem ducunt, nolentem trahunt)' (ZeF VIII.365).

[17] 'Verschiedenheit der S p r a c h e n und der R e l i g i o n e n, die zwar den Hang zum wechselseitigen Hasse und Vorwand zum Kriege bei sich führt […]' (ZeF VIII.367).

[18] 'A firmly established peace, combined with the greater interaction among people [*Menschen*] is the idea through which alone is made possible the transition from the duties of right to the duties of virtue. Since when the laws secure freedom externally, the maxims to also govern oneself internally in accordance with laws can liven up; and conversely, the latter in turn make it easier through their dispositions for lawful coercion to have an influence, so that peaceable behavior [*friedliches Verhalten*] under public laws and pacific dispositions [*friedfertige Gesinnungen*] (to also end the inner war between principles and inclinations), i.e., legality and morality find in the concept of peace the point of support for the transition from the Doctrine of Right to the Doctrine of Virtue' (VAMS XXIII.54–5, quoted in Kleingeld 2004 317).

[19] See Kleingeld (2006 480) and Airaksinen and Siitonen (2004 320f.) on Kant's maxim: 'Whatever a people cannot impose upon itself cannot be imposed upon it by the legislator either (Theory and Practice, 85)'.

[20] '[…] ein[.] Frieden […], der nicht wie jener Despotism (auf dem Kirchhofe der Freiheit) durch Schwächung aller Kräfte, sondern durch ihr Gleichgewicht im lebhaftesten Wetteifer derselben hervorgebracht und gesichert wird' (Zef VIII.367).

In the preface, however, Kant casts suspicion on his philosophic idea of eternal peace as yet another version of the peace of the graveyard. This time it means that the idea is just a 'sweet dream' of philosophers, an utterly unrealistic ideal dreamed up by philosophers, which belongs – like Saint Augustine's pax aeterna[21] – in the afterlife. This suspicion is spoken by the 'practical politician' or 'worldly statesman', a man of experience, who enters the preface to challenge the a priori, empty ideas of the philosopher. Here Kant is bringing conflict into the text in a *self-referential, performative* register, for he goes on to envisage 'the case of a conflict' (*im Fall eines Streits*) with politicians, and requests to be treated with their usual contempt, and not as a threat, if they disagree with his proposal. Kant's defensive anticipation of conflict, his performative 'Clausula salvatoria', shows us another aspect of his philosophy of conflict. It is, no doubt, with the politician's realist-empirical suspicion in mind that he will go on to argue for eternal peace on the basis of realist, not to say deeply pessimistic assumptions about the conflictual proclivities of human nature.

This suspicion regarding Kant's idea of eternal peace can be sharpened by asking how Nietzsche might have read the preface. At issue is the question of life-affirmation and life-negation that Nietzsche brings to philosophy. In *The Birth of Tragedy* he rehearses Plato's account of Socrates' final hours in the *Phaedo*, the story of the 'dying Socrates', who, as the one 'who through knowledge and reasons was delivered of the fear of death', became 'the new hitherto unknown ideal of the noble Greek youth' (GT 15 1.99, GT 13 1.91). At the centre of this dialogue is the question of the best life, and Socrates argues – while demonstrating – that it is the life of philosophy, understood as 'the practice of dying' (Ph. 12, 81) or the 'preparation for death' (Ph. 40). What he means is a life devoted to intellectual activity, eschewing as much as possible knowledge and pleasures deriving from the body, so that upon death the soul is prepared to be released from 'the prison-house of the body' (Ph. 82) and to unite with the forms. The desire for wisdom is the soul's longing for the death of the body, and the question is whether Kant's eternal peace is heir to the complicity of philosophy and philosophical ideals in death, inaugurated by Plato's dialogue. In the preface to ZeF, we saw that Kant leaves open the question as to whether conflict is a problem endemic to human nature, as it is for Nietzsche. If it is, an idea of peace that excludes or extirpates conflict would just be one in a long line of life-negating philosophical ideals since Plato. Indeed, in spite of Kant's rejection of wars of annihilation and the victor's peace, we could ask whether his philosophical idea of peace is any different – whether it offers anything other than a cessation of hostilities through death.

---

[21] Augustine de civitate dei book XIX [xx]. In IaG (VIII.30), Kant confronts this problem when he asks whether the history of humankind is an objection to divine providence, 'the sight of which requires us to turn our eyes away from it in disgust and, in despair of ever encountering a completed rational aim in it, to hope for the latter only in another world?' ('dessen Anblick uns nöthigt unsere Augen von ihm mit Unwillen wegzuwenden und, indem wir verzweifeln jemals darin eine vollendete vernünftige Absicht anzutreffen, uns dahin bringt, sie nur in einer andern Welt zu hoffen?')

III Conflict unlimited and limited: Nietzsche's *Vernichtungskampf* and the *Wettkampf*

Thus, the preface brings us back to the main question of the chapter: whether Kant's idea of eternal peace signifies a living, life-affirmative peace or a nihilistic rejection of reality. At the same time, the preface indicates that the answer may not be at all straightforward. As we saw, Kant's rejection of the victor's despotic peace, and its correlate in the 'graveyard of freedom', is coupled with the desideratum of the 'the liveliest competition' (*Wetteifer*) of all powers (*Kräfte*), a living peace that would exclude destruction but not conflict altogether. This thought brings to mind the distinction between the *Vernichtungskampf* and the *Wettkampf*, the struggle-for-annihilation and the contest or agon, in Nietzsche's short but influential essay *Homer's Wettkampf*.[22] In Nietzsche's philosophy of conflict, the *Vernichtungskampf*, like Kant's *Ausrottungskrieg*, designates a limit-concept of conflict, marked by excess (*Übermaass*) or the absence of measure, and the absence of law (for Kant: the eradication (*Vertilgung*) of all right in wars of extermination: ZeF VII.347). In dynamic terms, it can be described as the *absolute* (i.e. unmeasured) self-assertion of A (for Kant: the 'universal monarchy' or global empire coveted by every statesman) through *unmeasured* antagonism with B, which undergoes *absolute* disempowerment, that is: annihilation (*Vernichtung*) or death (*Todkrieg*). This is Nietzsche's version of the victor's peace of the graveyard. But for Nietzsche conflict also operates in the symbolic register of words, thoughts and interpretations, where the *Vernichtungskampf* signifies the absolute negation or exclusion of B in a move that empties it of value (*Entwertung*) by designating it as evil, false, illusory, mendacious, etc. In the symbolic register, A's absolute self-assertion takes the form of totalizing claims to goodness (to the exclusion of B as evil), or absolute truth concerning what really is (*das wahrhaft Seiende*) to the exclusion of B (as lie, error, illusion, etc.).

Over and against the extreme or limit case of the *Vernichtungskampf*, Nietzsche addresses a variety of conflict-types which admit limits or a degree of measure lacking in the struggle for annihilation. In broad terms, these types of conflict involve the *relative* self-assertion or empowerment of A through *measured* antagonism (*mässige Gegnerschaft*) with B, which undergoes *relative* disempowerment. The relative self-assertion or empowerment of A can take the forms of strengthening,[23] healing (*Heilung*), intensification (*Steigerung*), while the relative disempowerment of B involves its containment within boundaries (*in der Grenze des Maaßes*), limitation or restraint (*Bändigung*),[24] not its annihilation.

---

[22] In this text, the all-pervasive war of annihilation or *Vernichtungskampf* stands as a shorthand for a pessimistic view of life, both ancient and modern: Schopenhauer's 'self-lacerating will'; Darwin's 'struggle for existence'; Heraclitus's 'father of all things'; and Hesiod's 'evil Eris' and the 'Children of the Night' described in *Works and Days*. See Siemens (2021 52 n.37).

[23] See, e.g., UB III 3 1.359 on Schopenhauer.

[24] See 16[22] 7.402: 'The contest unleashes [*entfesselt*] the individual: and at the same time restrains [*bändigt*] it according to eternal laws.' 'The love for the maternal city encloses and restrains [*umschließt und bändigt*] the agonal drive' (21[14] 7.526). But also, e.g., 'Restraint [*Bändigung*] of the knowledge drive through art' (19[72] 7.443).

Nietzsche's 'ideal type' of measured conflict is the agon or *Wettkampf*, which stands for a type of conflict that is supremely creative, life-affirmative and life-enhancing. In *Homer's Wettkampf* he draws on the signature institution of the agon in archaic Greek culture to describe a 'competitive play of forces' (*Wettspiel der Kräfte*) set in motion by a plurality of forces or geniuses playing at war.[25] In dynamic terms the agon involves relations of reciprocal stimulation and reciprocal limitation: 'sich gegenseitig zur That reizen, wie sie sich auch gegenseitig in der Grenze des Maaßes halten' (HW 1.789). Agonal relations effect an affirmative displacement (*Übertragung*) or transformation of unmeasured, destructive impulses into measured, constructive cultural forces. Agonal struggle (*Wett-kampf*) is thus inseparable from the struggle for annihilation (*Vernichtungs-kampf*) as a form of *Kampf*, but also distinguished from it, as a regime of limited hostility that allows for temporary, inconclusive victory or mastery, not the absolute victory of annihilation. Unlike the *Vernichtungskampf*, with its radical disequilibrium of forces, Nietzsche's competitive play of forces (*Wettspiel der Kräfte*), like Kant's competition of all forces (*Wetteifer aller Kräfte*), is contingent on an equilibrium (*Gleichgewicht*) of more-or-less equal forces.[26] But the crucial difference between the *Vernichtungskampf* and the *Wettkampf*, and the key to the creative potential of the latter, lies in the concept of resistance. In the *Vernichtungskampf*, the resistance offered by antagonist B acts as an obstacle that inhibits or limits what A can do and must therefore be weakened or destroyed. In the *Wettkampf*, by contrast, the principles of equilibrium and equality mean that resistance takes on a dual significance as both a *stimulant* and *limit*: in the first instance, it acts as a positive stimulant (*Reiz*) that empowers A to overcome it by surpassing or bettering B's deed; in the second instance, it acts as a limit on what A can do, constraining (but not destroying) it. Presumably Kant has the creative dynamic of reciprocal stimulation or empowerment in mind when he writes of 'the liveliest [*lebhaftesten*] competition' in Zef, and the dynamic reciprocal limitation when he writes in IaG (VIII.26) of the 'reciprocal *effect and counter-effect*' of equal powers (*Kräfte*) in equilibrium under cosmopolitan law, 'so that they may not destroy each other'.

In reality, Nietzsche's *Vernichtungskampf* and Kant's *Ausrottungskrieg* are extreme or limit cases because the norm in conflict, even in military combat, involves limits of some

---

[25] HW 1.789. See also 16[26] 7.404: 'The contest emerges from war? As an artistic game and mimesis [*künstlerisches Spiel und Nachahmung*]?'

[26] Nietzsche's concept of equilibrium/equality will be discussed below. ZeF does not mention equality in relation to the equilibrium of forces, but in IaG, Kant does, writing that '[...] the ills that arise out of this necessitate our species to devise to the in itself salutary resistance of many states to one another arising from their freedom to devise a law of equilibrium and to introduce a united power giving emphasis to that law, hence to introduce a cosmopolitan condition of public state security, which is not wholly without *danger* so that the powers of humanity may not fall asleep, but it is at least not without a principle of *equality* between its reciprocal *effect and counter-effect*, so that they may not destroy each other' (IaG VIII.26). ('[...] die Übel, die daraus entspringen, unsere Gattung nöthigen, zu dem an sich heilsamen Widerstande vieler Staaten neben einander, der aus ihrer Freiheit entspringt, ein Gesetz des Gleichgewichts auszufinden und eine vereinigte Gewalt, die demselben Nachdruck giebt, mithin einen weltbürgerlichen Zustand der öffentlichen Staatssicherheit einzuführen, der nicht ohne alle G e f a h r sei, damit die Kräfte der Menschheit nicht einschlafen, aber doch auch nicht ohne ein Princip der G l e i c h h e i t ihrer wechselseitigen W i r k u n g und G e g e n w i r k u n g, damit sie einander nicht zerstören.').

kind designed to avoid mutual extermination. In the symbolic register, however, it is otherwise. In the register of language and thought, the norm is the *Vernichtungskampf* in the form of bivalent, oppositional thinking; for as we saw in Chapter 1, '[i]t is *easier* to think opposites [*Gegensätze*] than degrees' (11[115] 9.482). What was called Ggz I, typical of metaphysical and moral thought, involves mutually exclusive terms and is constructed through the separation and fixing (*Feststellung*) of the terms into self-identical, durable items or entities. Over against this, Nietzsche marshals forms of thinking in which the terms opposed in Ggz I are related (*verwandt*) as 'complementary value-concepts' (*complementäre Werthbegriffe*), 'perhaps even essentially the same' (Ggz II.1). Whereas the former (Ggz I) are constructed by abstracting from the complexity real oppositions (Ggz II.2), the latter are intended to do them greater justice.

IV Kant's philosophical war of extermination against war

With this distinction between unlimited and limited conflict in mind, we can now turn to the questions of how exactly Kant conceptualizes the relation between war and peace, and how he explains the transformation of, or passage from, senseless, destructive conflict (in)to a constructive order of things. Kant's writings are teeming with insights into the benefits of conflict. But if we ask how Kant, as a philosopher of conflict, *conceptualizes* conflict in relation to peace, his thought falls short of the wealth of insights and remarks in his work. This, I contend, is because he fails to formulate a *genuinely affirmative concept of conflict*, one that is able to do justice to the prodigious creative powers of conflict that he describes. My thesis in this section is that *Kant wages a philosophical war of extermination (Todkrieg, Vernichtungskampf) on all war in the name of eternal peace*. By 'philosophical war of extermination' I mean *Todkrieg*, the term used by Nietzsche in AC to describe *Idealism*, which then serves as the umbrella term in EH for what he has fought against in his philosophical life-work.[27] For Nietzsche, 'Idealismus' names a bivalent, oppositional manner of thinking along the lines of the *Vernichtungskampf* described above: absolute self-assertion in the form of totalizing claims to goodness, to the exclusion of the opposed term as 'evil'. Following the analysis of the term 'gegen' in EH by Gerd Schank (1993), idealism's *Todkrieg* can be described as a bivalent (*zweiwertig*), oppositional manner of thinking, which makes a total and exclusive claim for its position (*Sich Absolutsetzen*) by

1. positing value-oppositions (good/evil, true/false, beautiful/ugly), oppositions that
2. *separate* or *isolate* positively valued terms (own position) from negatively valued terms (antagonistic position), in order to
3. *eliminate* or *destroy*[28] the negatively valued terms (in thought as 'evil') and thereby,

---

[27] See, e.g., EH klug 2 6.283; EH klug 2 6.283; EH klug 10 6.297; EH (MA) 6.326; EH (MA) 6.324 (cf. Schank 1993, 110, 114, 100f.); EH Schicksal 1 6.365 and Siemens (2021 258–66) for further references.
[28] Cf. 11[138] 13.64: 'das w i d e r n a t ü r l i c h e I d e a l / – m a n   n e g i r t, man   v e r n i c h t e t –'. 'the *antinatural ideal* / – one negates, one destroys –'.

4. *eliminate* opposition or war altogether, making space for an absolute and exclusive claim for its own positive terms ('eternal peace').

My argument works through an analysis of two texts in which Kant discusses conflict or war and peace: the section on the 'polemical use' of Reason in the latter part of KrV, where he addresses the conflict of Reason with itself; and ZeF, where he discusses warfare among states on the world stage. As in Chapter 1, attention will be paid to the relation between *matter* of his thought as a philosopher of conflict and the *manner* of his thought, that is: the prospect of 'eternal peace', given the ineradicable reality of conflict, and the conceptual schema or model used to construct the idea of peace in relation to conflict in each text. In Chapter 1, we saw that Kant argues for the *difference* between real opposition and logical opposition, as a precondition for thinking the reality of conflict and change. In the present context, I argue that Kant *replicates* in thought what he argues for in real terms: the extermination or *Vernichtung* of conflict in favour of eternal peace. In both texts, I will try to show, Kant succumbs to a Hobbesian logic that has the effect of impoverishing the concept of war and depriving it of all constructive potential. On this model, conflict is neither irreducible nor genuinely constructive. Constructive, autonomous agency requires rather the *extermination* of conflict under the rule of law. In the end, conflict is productive for Kant, *but only of its own negation* in a life-negating ideal of eternal peace. In the next section (V) I then turn to Nietzsche for an alternative way of thinking conflict and peace, one that draws on the model of limited conflict or *Wettkampf* and allows for a genuinely affirmative understanding of conflict and its creative or productive powers. In the final section of the chapter, I consider each thinker's position from a perspective in the other's and qualify the argument. While each opens critical perspectives on the other, there are also ways in which they can be combined in an approach to an affirmative or 'living peace'.

IV.1 On the polemical use of reason (KrV B 767 – B 810)

> *There is something worrisome and depressing that there should be an antithetic of pure reason at all and that pure reason, though it represents the supreme court of for all disputes, should still come into conflict with itself.*
>
> *Es ist etwas Bekümmerndes und Niederschlagendes, daß es überhaupt eine Antithetik der reinen Vernunft geben und diese, die doch den obersten Gerichtshof über alle Streitigkeiten vorstellt, mit sich selbst in Streit gerathen soll.* (B 768)

This is how Kant puts the worry he will address in the section on the 'polemical use' of Reason. In a sense, the problem is straight-forward: what is pure Reason – having gone through the rigours of critique set out in the previous parts of the book and attained self-knowledge – to do in the face of pre-critical, dogmatic claims? But the problem runs deeper. On the one hand, critical Reason, through its insight into the constitutive principles of Reason, has jurisdiction over the whole of reason and is co-extensive with the entire field of reason, including dogmatic claims. In adjudicating conflicting dogmatic claims, it is above the fray. On the other hand, critical Reason is party to the conflict of Reason: in its 'polemical use' it must attack or at least resist dogmatic metaphysics. Reason is therefore divided against itself in three ways: the quarrel or 'polemic' of dogmatic claims of reason against each other; the 'polemical use' of Reason against dogmatic claims; and the conflict between critical Reason as the entire field of reason and critical Reason as a domain within this field pitted against dogmatic reason. The stakes in this section, then, could not be higher: the unity of Reason upon which the entire Enlightenment project depends. Kant will want to argue that these conflicts are not real or at least not a serious threat to Reason, so as to make place for 'eternal peace' (B 779). The question is to what extent he can succeed, given the three-way divisions in play.

Much of the argumentation turns on how Kant construes the kinds of conflict he addresses. Since dogmatic metaphysical claims misapply the categories beyond possible experience, they cannot be grounded, so their proponents concentrate instead on negating (*Verneinen*) or refuting the claims of their dogmatic opponents. This is Nietzsche's *Vernichtungskampf* or idealist *Todkrieg*: absolute self-assertion through totalizing claims that exclude the opposed position as 'false', 'evil', etc. It is therefore with dogmatic claims, understood as *negations* (*Verneinungen*), that critical Reason must take issue in its polemical use:

> Under the polemical use of pure reason I understand the defence of its propositions against dogmatic negations of them. Here the issue is not whether its own assertions might perhaps also be false, but rather that no one can ever assert the opposite with apodictic certainty (or even only greater appeal).

> Unter dem polemischen Gebrauche der reinen Vernunft verstehe ich nun die Vertheidigung ihrer Sätze gegen die dogmatischen Verneinungen derselben. Hier kommt es nun nicht darauf an, ob ihre Behauptungen nicht vielleicht auch falsch sein möchten, sondern nur, daß niemand das Gegentheil jemals mit apodiktischer Gewißheit (ja auch nur mit größerem Scheine) behaupten könne. (B 768)

The polemical use of Reason takes place in the real world, where the very existence of Reason depends on the freedom of critical thought, and its claims are no more than the 'consensus of free citizens'.[29] And yet, as we shall see, the real world is the world of dogmatic reason, in which Reason is 'as it were, in the state of nature' (B 779). So what is critical Reason to do, when it 'does not have to do with censure of a judge, but with claims of its fellow citizens' (B 767) in a state of nature? Critical Reason can certainly expose and diagnose the errors of metaphysics, but it cannot engage in direct combat or 'polemic' with dogmatic claims of pre-critical reason. In any case, as Saner (1967 99, 102) points out, conflict would be pointless: right, victory and the standard

---

[29] 'The very existence of reason depends upon this freedom, which has no dictatorial authority, but whose claim is never anything more than the agreement of free citizens, each of whom must be able to express his reservations, indeed even his *veto*, without holding back' (B 766–7).

of victory are already on the side of critical Reason. There could be no real conflict; the antagonists are unequal and there is nothing at stake, since Reason has already decided in favour of the critical thinker. The 'polemical use' of Reason thus signifies an anti-polemical form of polemic, a merely 'defensive' strategy to resist dogmatic negations of the propositions of Reason, which limits itself to showing that they cannot be opposed with certainty (B 768, quoted above).[30] It is, in other words, a minimal form of antagonism into which critical Reason is drawn by dogmatic reason, but one designed to put an end to conflict. For as Kant twice asserts, there is 'no real polemic' and 'there must not be any polemic of pure Reason':

> There must not be any polemic of pure reason. For how can two people conduct a dispute about a matter the reality of which neither of them can exhibit in an actual or even in a merely possible experience, about the idea of which he broods in order to bring forth from it something more than an idea, namely the actuality of the object itself? (B 778)

> There is accordingly no real polemic in the field of pure reason. Both parties fence in the air and wrestle with their shadows, for they go beyond nature, where there is nothing that their dogmatic grasp can seize and hold. Fight as they may, the shadows that they cleave apart grow back together in an instant, like the heroes of Valhalla, to amuse themselves anew in bloodless battles. (B 784)

Indeed, the squabbles of dogmatic reason are so remote from posing a serious threat for Kant that he recommends them as entertainment from the safe seat of critical Reason:

> Thus, instead of charging in a sword, you should instead watch this conflict peaceably from the safe seat of critique, a conflict which must be exhausting for the combatants but entertaining for you, with an outcome that will certainly be bloodless and advantageous for your insight. For it is quite absurd to expect enlightenment from reason and yet to prescribe to it in advance on which side it must come out [...] In this dialectic there is no victory about which you would have cause to worry. (B 775)

But is this just bravado? Is Kant's defensive conflict to end conflict really enough? Kant, I believe, equivocates. The conflict in question in this section cannot be exposed as pseudo- or non-conflict due to a misapplication of the categories, as in the third Antinomy. Kant has in mind two key issues of *metaphysica specialis*: the immortality of the soul and the existence of God. The conflict of opposed dogmatic positions on these issues (God does/does not exist, the soul is/is not immortal) in the form of reciprocal negations (*Verneinungen*) or Nietzsche's *Vernichtungskampf* cannot

---

[30] Or, as Kant puts it in B 804: a strategy to foil or block (*Vereitlung*) the dogmatic opponent's pseudo-insights that would demolish (*Abbruch tun*) our assertion.

be defused as a non-conflict, a mere 'misunderstanding', since God and the soul are ideas completely beyond the bounds of experience and the categories.[31] But this is also where critical Reason is most vulnerable, so it cannot afford to sit above the fray in the seat of judgement; it must do something. For Kant cannot agree with Sulzer that God's existence and the immortality of the soul will someday admit of a satisfactory proof (B 769), nor with the empiricist Priestley (B 773), who denies the possibility. The existence of God and immortality of the soul are strictly beyond the bounds of reason and can only be postulated as articles of rational faith (*Vernunftglaube*) (B 772f.). With this in mind, Kant advocates a number of active measures to defend these postulates. He enters the fray.

Kant's views on scepticism are instructive in this regard. To adopt a position of 'neutrality' (B 784) on the polemics in metaphysics is insufficient both for critical Reason and for putting an end to the conflict of Reason with itself and securing a lasting or 'eternal peace'.[32] Kant does permit a transitional function for the 'sceptical use' of Reason (B 784) as a tool to unsettle dogmatic convictions and prepare the mind for critique. But under duress, Reason is compelled to abandon its sceptical 'neutrality' and offer real resistance to dogmatic negations in defence of its articles rational faith. In the face of the 'invincible bragging and posturing of the speculators, who will not be moderated by any critique,'

> there is really no other recourse than to set the boasting of one side against another, which stands on the same rights, in order at least to shock reason, by means of the resistance of an enemy, into raising some doubts about its pretensions and giving a hearing to the critique. (B 784–5)[33]

For Kant's shock tactic to work, critical Reason must abandon not just the 'neutrality' of the sceptic, but also the proper response of critical Reason to its opponents: 'non liquet' or non-decidability of matters beyond Reason (B 770). It is to 'fight [the opponent] solely with weapons of reason' (B 772),[34] but to do so at the level of dogmatic reason.

Apart from 'sceptical polemicising' (B 791), there is also the 'hypothetical' method for the polemical use of Reason. By 'hypotheses' here Kant means (non-contradictory)

---

[31] B 781: 'This proposition lies outside the field of possible experience, therefore also the boundaries of all human insight.'

[32] 'But for reason to leave just these doubts standing, and to set out to recommend the conviction and confession of its ignorance, not merely as a cure for dogmatic self-conceit but also as the way in which to end the conflict of reason with itself, is an entirely vain attempt, by no means suitable for arranging a peaceful retirement for reason; rather it is at best only a means for awaking it from its sweet dogmatic dreams in order to undertake a more careful examination of its condition' (B 785).

[33] 'Wenn man indessen die unbezwingliche Verblendung und das Großthun der Vernünftler, die sich durch keine Kritik will mäßigen lassen, ansieht, so ist doch wirklich kein anderer Rath, als der Großsprecherei auf einer Seite eine andere, welche auf eben dieselben Rechte fußt, entgegen zu setzen, damit die Vernunft durch den Widerstand eines Feindes wenigstens nur stutzig gemacht werde, um in ihre Anmaßungen einigen Zweifel zu setzen und der Kritik Gehör zu geben.'

[34] 'Lasset demnach euren Gegner nur Vernunft zeigen, und bekämpfet ihn bloß mit Waffen der Vernunft.'

claims that transgress the limits of experience, to be used 'only as weapons of war, not for grounding a right but for defending it' (B 805). Kant allows the critic the freedom 'to use, as it were in an emergency, the very same means for his good cause as his opponent would use against it', not for purposes of proof, but only 'to show that the opponent understands far too little about the object of the dispute to be able to flatter himself with an advantage in speculative insight over us' (B 805). Once again, critical Reason is drawn irresistibly into the fray in defence of its postulates. At this point in the text, however, when the matter of eternal peace comes into the picture, the language of defence slides into violent assault: the critic must hunt down (*hervorsuchen*) the negations of dogmatic reason in himself, 'in order to ground an eternal peace on their destruction [*Vernichtigung*]':

> The seed of the attacks, which lies in the nature of reason, must be exterminated [*ausgerottet*]; but how can we exterminate it if we do not give it freedom, indeed even nourishment, to send out shoots, so as thereby to expose itself, so we can afterwards eradicate [*vertilgen*] it with the roots? (B 805–6)[35]

With the language of destruction, extermination, eradication, focused on the root causes of conflict, Kant has clearly entered the sphere of the idealist *Todkrieg* denounced by Nietzsche. Nowhere is the equivocation between critical Reason as the seat of judgement above all conflict and its engagement in conflict more clearly expressed than in a central passage of this section, where Kant discusses the relation between the conflict of Reason and 'eternal peace', and the passage from the former to the latter.

> One can regard the <u>critique</u> of pure reason as the true <u>court of law for all</u> controversies of pure reason; for critique is not involved in these disputes, which pertain immediately to objects, but is rather set the task of determining and judging <u>what is lawful</u> in reason in general in accordance with the principles of its primary institution.
>
> Without this, reason is as it were in the **state of nature**, and it cannot make its assertions and claims valid or secure them except through **war**. Critique, on the contrary, which derives all decisions from the ground-rules of its own institution, whose authority no one can doubt, grants us the <u>peace of a state of law</u>, in which we ought not to conduct our controversy except by due <u>process</u>. What brings the quarrel in the state of nature to an end is a **victory**, of which sides boast, although for the most part there follows only an **insecure peace**, arranged by an authority in

---

[35] 'Wir müssen sie gleich alten, aber niemals verjährenden Ansprüchen hervorsuchen, um einen ewigen Frieden auf deren Vernichtigung zu gründen. Äußere Ruhe ist nur scheinbar. Der Keim der Anfechtungen, der in der Natur der Menschenvernunft liegt, muß ausgerottet werden; wie können wir ihn aber ausrotten, wenn wir ihn nicht Freiheit, ja selbst Nahrung geben, Kraut auszuschießen, um sich dadurch zu entdecken, und es nachher mit der Wurzel zu vertilgen?' The expression 'sich entdecken' is used by Kant with the eighteenth-century meaning of 'uncover' or 'expose', not the current meaning of 'discover'.

the middle; but in the state of law it is the <u>verdict</u>, which, since it goes to the source of the controversies themselves, must secure a <u>perpetual peace</u>. And the **endless controversies of a merely dogmatic reason** finally make it necessary to seek peace in some sort of critique of this reason itself, and in a <u>legislation</u> grounded upon it; just as Hobbes asserted, the **state of nature** is a state of **injustice** [without right] and **violence**, and one must necessarily leave it in order to submit oneself to the <u>lawful</u> **coercion** which alone <u>limits our freedom</u> in such a way that it can be consistent with the <u>freedom of everyone else</u> and thereby with <u>the common good</u>. (**BOLD** AND <u>UNDERLINING</u> ADDED)

Man kann die <u>Kritik</u> der reinen Vernunft als den wahren <u>Gerichtshof für alle Streitigkeiten</u> derselben ansehen; denn sie ist in die letzteren, als welche auf Objecte unmittelbar gehen, nicht mit verwickelt, sondern ist dazu gesetzt, die <u>Rechtsame</u> der Vernunft überhaupt nach den Grundsätzen ihrer ersten Institution zu bestimmen und zu beurtheilen.

Ohne dieselbe ist die Vernunft gleichsam im **Stande der Natur** und kann ihre Behauptungen und Ansprüche nicht anders geltend machen oder sichern, als durch **K r i e g**. Die Kritik dagegen, welche alle Entscheidungen aus den Grundregeln ihrer eigenen Einsetzung hernimmt, deren Ansehen keiner bezweifeln kann, verschafft uns die <u>Ruhe eines gesetzlichen Zustandes</u>, in welchem wir unsere Streitigkeit nicht anders führen sollen, als durch <u>P r o c e ß</u>. Was die Händel in dem ersten Zustande endigt, ist ein **Sieg**, dessen sich beide Theile rühmen, auf den mehrentheils ein nur **unsicherer Friede** folgt, den die Obrigkeit stiftet, welche sich ins Mittel legt, im zweiten aber die <u>S e n t e n z</u>, die, weil sie hier die Quelle der Streitigkeiten selbst trifft, einen <u>ewigen Frieden</u> gewähren muß. Auch nöthigen die **endlosen Streitigkeiten einer bloß dogmatischen Vernunft**, endlich in irgend einer Kritik dieser Vernunft selbst und in einer <u>Gesetzgebung</u>, die sich auf sie gründet, Ruhe zu suchen; so wie Hobbes behauptet: der **Stand der Natur** sei ein Stand des **Unrechts** und der **Gewaltthätigkeit**, und man müsse ihn nothwendig verlassen, um sich dem <u>gesetzlichen</u> **Zwange** zu unterwerfen, der allein unsere <u>Freiheit dahin einschränkt</u>, daß sie mit <u>jedes anderen Freiheit</u> und eben dadurch mit dem <u>gemeinen Besten</u> zusammen bestehen könne. (B 778–9) (**BOLD** AND <u>UNDERLINING</u> ADDED)

How, on this account, does critical Reason resolve the conflict of Reason with itself? And what is the relation between conflict and peace underpinning Kant's argument?

The argument in this passage turns on a conceptual model that opposes *eternal peace* on one side to *endless conflict* on the other. This can be seen by considering first the terms associated with the conflict of reason with itself [**BOLD**], and then those associated with Reason after Critique or Critical Reason [<u>UNDERLINING</u>]:

BOLD:
DOGMATIC/PRE-CRITICAL REASON
STATE OF NATURE

ENDLESS CONFLICTS/WAR
NO LAW/RIGHT
VIOLENCE
VICTORY (FORCE WITHOUT RIGHT)
AT BEST: INSECURE PEACE

Dogmatic reason is inscribed within the *state of nature*, a domain characterized by *war*: a war between absolute claims or a war of absolute self-assertion (*Sich Absolutsetzen*) between conflicting claims (Nietzsche's *Vernichtungskampf*). Following Hobbes, it is a domain defined by the *absence of law* and normative right or rightness. As a consequence, claims can only be pursued through *violence*: brute force or might, and claims can only be asserted against others in the form of *victory* through brute force or might without right. Yet there can be no conclusive victory, since each side claims absolute victory without right for themselves. The war is therefore endless, and the best we can hope for is an *insecure peace* or ceasefire instituted by a third party between two opponents. Since dogmatic or pre-critical reason is reason without right, or reason that violates the laws of Reason, it is an irrational reason, or reason as *Unreason*.

This characterization of dogmatic reason is opposed to Reason by way of critique, or critical Reason. Because it operates in line with the statutes of Reason itself (*nach den Grundsätzen ihrer ersten Institution, aus den Grundregeln ihrer eigenen Einsetzung*), critical Reason is Reason proper. On the side of critical Reason or Reason proper, we have:

UNDERLINING

CRITIQUE/(CRITICAL) REASON
LAW COURT OF LAW/LEGAL STATE/LEGISLATION: NORMATIVE
    RIGHT(NESS)
LEGAL PROCESS (instead of WAR)
PEACE/CALM (*RUHE*) (instead of VIOLENCE)
VERDICT/JUDICIAL SENTENCE (NORMATIVE RIGHTNESS instead of
    VICTORY by FORCE)
ETERNAL PEACE

Combining the two, we have:

DOGMATIC/PRE-CRITICAL REASON	CRITICAL REASON
STATE OF NATURE	COURT OF LAW/LEGAL STATE/LEGISLATION: NORMATIVE RIGHT(NESS)
NO LAW/RIGHT	
ENDLESS CONFLICTS/WAR	LEGAL PROCESS
VIOLENCE	PEACE/CALM (*RUHE*)

VICTORY (FORCE WITHOUT RIGHT)	VERDICT/JUDICIAL SENTENCE (NORMATIVE RIGHTNESS)
AT BEST: INSECURE PEACE[36]	ETERNAL PEACE

Critical Reason is inscribed within a *legal state (gesetzlicher Zustand)*, and *founds a new normative domain,* a domain of *normative right(ness)*. Law transforms conflicts into *legal process* and replaces violence with *calm*. Instead of victory by force a *judicial sentence* is passed, whose claim rests not on force without right or victory, but on its normative rightness. Normative rightness in the absence of force or violence makes possible *eternal peace.*

DOMAIN OF
On this model: WAR = UNREASON = LAWLESS VIOLENCE {DESTRUCTIVE}

PEACE = REASON (BY WAY OF CRITIQUE) = COURT of LAW: founds
= (NOT-WAR) DOMAIN OF NORMATIVE
RIGHT {= CONSTRUCTIVE}

From this analysis one can see that Kant's critical project is to establish (critical) Reason, conceived as peace under the rule of law, by eliminating conflict, conceived as force and unreason. Conflict is violent, senseless and destructive; only law can establish the conditions for constructive agency (knowledge and freedom), and it does so by transforming conflicts into judicial process. Reason and the rule of law establish a constructive order by instituting a normative order of right that excludes force, violence and conflict.

We can now begin to see how Kant's thought instantiates what Nietzsche calls idealist warfare: eternal peace is *separated* from endless conflict and *isolated* in the domain of law, *opposed* to the domain of nature, which is assigned a purely negative value: war is senseless and destructive. Only the exclusion of conflict makes secure peace and constructive orders possible. The consequence of Kant's idealist war against war is that war is negated and emptied of any constructive value. And because it is robbed of all constructive potential, conflict is endless and can only be ended by the

---

[36] See the schema by Airaksinen and Siitonen (2004 327) on the Hobbesian elements in Kant's account of dogmatic reason in this passage:

'The following table summarizes how Kant applies Hobbes's ideas in this rhetorical context of the enlightened values:

Hobbes	Kant
State of nature	Dogmatic reason (reason in the state of nature)
Injustice	Endless disputes (quarrel)
Violence	Polemical employment of reason (war)
Constrain of law (sic.)	Critique of reason (legislation)
Freedom	Open discussion (social life)
Sovereign	Universal human reason (ruler)
Rule of law	Enlightenment (progress of science)'.

institution of a normative-legal order. Only the rule of law can effect the passage from senseless, destructive conflict (in)to a constructive order by instituting a normative-legal domain that excludes force and transforms conflict into due process. Constructive order is identified exclusively with the normative domain founded by Reason.

Now this account raises two questions. The first is how Reason via legal process and judicial sentence excludes conflict once and for all in favour of eternal peace. In the above passage, Kant's answer is: By going to the origin or source (*Quelle*) of the conflicts. But what does he mean by this? On the one hand, in cases where dogmatic Reason is misapplying categories on both sides of the dispute, critical Reason can expose the 'source' of the conflict in error and issue a verdict from its seat of judgement with reference to the laws and limits of Reason. In these cases (such as the second *Antinomy*) what Kant means by going to the 'source' is that *there is no real conflict* of Reason with itself: the disputes are pseudo-conflicts with their sources in misunderstandings. On the other hand, there are cases where the conflict cannot be dismissed in this way (such as God's existence and the immortality of the soul) and where the 'sources' are rooted deeply in the nature of Reason and the natural 'dialectic' and *metaphysica naturalis* in all of us. In these cases, Kant's talk of the 'source' of conflict in the above passage mirrors his concern with the root causes of conflict, the 'seeds' and 'roots' (B 805-6) of dogmatic negations in the 'hypothetical' use of Reason. Yet as we saw, when 'eternal peace' comes into Kant's text, the limited, defensive war against dogmatic Reason turns into violent assault: conflict must be rooted out. Only by exterminating (*ausrotten*) 'the seeds' of dogmatic negations and eradicating (*vertilgen*) them 'with the roots' can eternal peace be grounded on their destruction (*Vernichtigung*) (ibid.). In either case, to posit eternal peace requires not just the *exclusion* of conflict from the domain of normative right; it requires the *extermination* of conflict in thought, as a presupposition for positing peace as absolute. The conflict of Reason with itself, it turns out, is either a non-conflict rooted in misunderstandings, or it must be rooted out by exterminating the seeds of dogmatic claims. In the end, eternal peace can only be thought by *denying conflict altogether*. Kant's eternal peace depends upon a philosophical war of extermination against war.

The second question concerns the institution of a new normative order, as the basis for constructive agency: How is the claim of Reason to establish normative right justified? By what right does Reason claim to establish right, such that conflicts can be resolved without violence? I propose that the normative force of critical Reason rests on two claims. The first concerns:

1. The autonomy of Reason: Kant's account presupposes that Reason is a domain constituted by fundamental laws or rules (*Grundsätzen, Grundregeln*) intrinsic to its institution. The decisions and sentences through which Critical Reason resolves conflicts derive from a process of legislation (*Gesetzgebung*) grounded in fundamental laws that constitute the domain of Reason. Their normative force derives from the fact that these self-given norms are *all-inclusive*: not only do all antagonistic positions, as dogmatic claims of reason, belong to its domain; even the state of nature and conflict, as a conflict of Reason with itself, falls within the

domain of Reason. *To posit a domain of normative rightness that would resolve all conflict requires, as a presupposition of thought, the extension of that normative domain to include all conflicting parties and the domain of conflict itself.* The problem, then, is not one of exclusion; rather, it is one of non-recognition on the part of dogmatic claims, which brings us to Kant's second claim: namely that

2. Conflict arises from a claim to *limitless freedom* on the part of all antagonists: Hobbes's right to everything, or Nietzsche's absolute self-assertion (*sich Absolutsetzen*). The legal domain of normative right, by contrast, is grounded in a will or willingness to *limit one's freedom* by *acknowledging the freedom of others* for the sake of the common good (*dem gemeinen Besten*). Acknowledgement of the other is the key to right over force.

It is, however, important to see that acknowledgement on its own cannot effect the transition from violent conflict to a constructive order of normative right that calmly puts an end to conflict. On Kant's own presuppositions, conflict is identified with (reason as) unreason in the sense of lawless force or violence, while (critical) Reason is identified with law and normative right to the exclusion of violence. But in order to *establish* the rule of law and normative validity, reason is drawn into conflict: it must cross over to the domain of force and perform an act of violence (against itself), by applying coercive force (*Zwange*) against the conflict of forces. In Kant's words, the establishment of right requires 'subjecting oneself to the legal coercion' (*sich dem gesetzlichen* **Zwange** *zu unterwerfen*) on the part of antagonistic parties. It follows that the entire conceptual construction collapses, since Reason can no longer be identified with normative rightness to the exclusion of violence.

This analysis brings the fatal discord or equivocation of critical Reason into sharp relief – between the seat of adjudication in the calm and autonomous domain of normative right extending over the entire field of Reason, and a specific domain of critical Reason drawn into conflict with dogmatic reason. In terms of Nietzsche's concept of opposition or *Gegensatz*, and the different meanings he gives the terms as set out in Chapter 1 §III we can say that in the key passage from the 'polemical use' of Reason, war and peace are opposed by Kant in the logical and metaphysical sense of Ggz I. According to Nietzsche, there are no such oppositions in reality. They are fictions with highly questionable motivations and consequences, and he re-interprets them genealogically as Ggz II.1. In Nietzsche's genealogical opposition-type, the terms are 'related' (*verwandt*), and '*that* which constitutes the value of those good and revered things consists precisely in their being related, linked, bound up in an incriminating manner with those bad, apparently opposed things; perhaps in their even being essentially the same' (JGB 2). On this interpretation, peace under the rule of law is to be understood, not as opposed to lawless conflict, but as inseparably bound up with conflict, as its *sublimation* (MA 1) or *refinement* (*Verfeinerung*). In reality, peace and conflict are 'complementary value-concepts' (*complementäre Werthbegriffe*), so that the value of peace under the rule of law is to be sought in its *relation* to conflict, or rather: in the ways in which it is related to conflict in ever-changing, concrete situations.

From a perspective in the philosophy of conflict, it is hardly surprising that critical Reason is drawn into battle and resorts to force. Given the ineradicable reality of conflict (which includes the natural dialectic of Reason), war and peace are indeed 'essentially the same', and the value we give to peace requires that we find ways to affirm conflict as its 'complementary value-concept'. There is, then, a need to rethink the relation between conflict and peace, one that crosses or crosses out the mutually exclusive oppositions of destruction/construction, Unreason/Reason, might without right/right without might, such that conflict, however destructive, contains genuine constructive potential and can be affirmed as such. This will be taken up in section V below.

IV.2 Sketch of a sketch: *Zum ewigen Frieden*

If the difficulties of the passage we looked at are tied up with Kant's reliance on Hobbes, this is even more so in the second text I will consider. In what follows I will offer a sketch of Kant's philosophical sketch *Zum ewigen Frieden*, with the purpose of showing that it too fails on his own presuppositions.

Kant's ZeF is dedicated to the establishment of peace, a *Friedenszustand* that is final, that excludes war because it destroys (*vernichtet*) all causes for future war.[37] In the first Preliminary Article, he distinguishes a genuine peace accord from 'a mere ceasefire or postponement of hostilities'.

> For peace signifies the end to all hostilities, and even merely adding the adjective *eternal* [OR *perpetual*: e w i g] to the term renders it a suspicious-looking pleonasm. The existing causes of a future war, even if perhaps not yet known to the parties themselves, are destroyed [*vernichtet*] without exception by a peace settlement [...] (ZeF VIII.343-44)

Eternal Peace is a suspect pleonasm because peace *means* the annihilation (*Vernichtung*) of all causes of future war. In Nietzschean terms, we can say that Kant opens the text by declaring a *philosophical war of annihilation against all (future) war, a Vernichtungskrieg gegen den Krieg*. The text can be read as an argument that a lasting 'final' peace can and should be realized, even if we assume, as undeniable, a deeply pessimistic-realist Hobbesian view of human nature: 'the evil principle in him (which he cannot deny) [*das böse Prinzip in ihm (was er nicht ableugnen kann)*]' (ZeF VIII.355). No doubt with the suspicions of the 'worldly statesmen' in mind, Kant punctuates his argument with realist moments throughout. Reason acknowledges its practical impotence and that it cannot improve humans morally (*realism*), but it can and should make use of our hostile inclinations to secure its own end of final peace.[38] So what is final peace and how can it be realized? Final peace is the negation, exclusion or extermination

---

[37] ZeF VIII.343: 'Die vorhandene, obgleich jetzt vielleicht den Paciscirenden selbst noch nicht bekannten, Ursachen zum künftigen Kriege sind durch den Friedensschluß insgesammt **vernichtet**' (HS).

[38] ZeF VIII.366: 'Denn es ist nicht die moralische Besserung der Menschen, sondern nur der Mechanism der Natur, von dem die Aufgabe zu wissen verlangt, wie man ihn an Menschen benutzen könne, um den Widerstreit ihrer unfriedlichen Gesinnungen in einem Volk so zu richten, daß sie sich unter Zwangsgesetze zu begeben einander selbst nöthigen und so den Friedenszustand, in welchem Gesetze Kraft haben, herbeiführen müssen [...]'. ZeF VIII.367: 'mithin der Mechanism der Natur durch selbstsüchtige Neigungen, die natürlicherweise einander auch äußerlich entgegen wirken, von der Vernunft zu einem Mittel gebraucht werden kann, dieser |ihrem eigenen Zweck, der rechtlichen Vorschrift, Raum zu machen und hiemit auch, soviel an dem Staat selbst liegt, den inneren sowohl als äußeren Frieden zu befördern und zu sichern.'

of all war. But what is war? Kant, following Hobbes, has a broad concept of war: war is not just actual battle, but the constant threat of conflict, a condition (*Zustand*) of radical insecurity.[39] This broad concept of war makes exceedingly strong demands on the concept of peace: peace can only be the complete negation or extermination of insecurity – a condition of total security. Peace requires the guarantee of security; if it falls short of a guarantee, it is already a condition of war. So what makes for insecurity, and how to exclude it in a condition of security? The condition of radical insecurity has its sources in human nature, in Kant's extraordinary claim (*realism*) that (where there is no explicit guarantee or security of peace) for a human being (or people), the mere proximity (*Nebeneinander*) of another constitutes an injury (*lädirt*) that invites hostility:

> Peoples, as states, can be judged as individual human beings who, when in the state of nature (that is, when they are independent from external laws), bring harm to each other already through their proximity to one another [...](ZeF VIII.354)

> – But a person (or a people) in a mere state of nature deprives me of this security and harms me through this very state by existing next to me, although not actively (*facto*), nonetheless through the lawlessness of his state (*statu iniusto*), by means of which he represents a constant threat to me. (ZeF VIII.348 note)[40]

Underpinning this claim is the essentially *reactive* concept of power that Kant takes from Hobbes: power as oriented towards self-preservation in the face of an external threat.[41] How then can the threat be taken out of the other's proximity? Kant's best answer is: the rule of law. Law *cannot* actually take the threat out of the other's proximity,[42] but it can give us rights, and administer justice with reference to law as

---

[39] ZeF VIII.348: 'Der Friedenszustand unter Menschen, die neben einander leben, ist kein Naturstand (*status naturalis*), der vielmehr ein Zustand des Krieges ist, d.i. wenn gleich nicht immer ein Ausbruch der Feindseligkeiten, doch immerwährende Bedrohung mit denselben.'

[40] ZeF VIII.354: 'Völker als Staaten können wie einzelne Menschen beurtheilt werden, die sich in ihrem Naturzustande (d.i. in der Unabhängigkeit von äußern Gesetzen) schon durch ihr Nebeneinandersein lädiren [...]'
ZeF VIII.348 note: '– Der Mensch aber (oder das Volk) im bloßen Naturstande benimmt mir diese Sicherheit und lädirt mich schon durch eben diesen Zustand, indem er neben mir ist, obgleich nicht thätig (*facto*), doch durch die Gesetzlosigkeit seines Zustandes (*statu iniusto*), wodurch ich beständig von ihm bedroht werde.'

[41] Hobbesian power is exercised from a position of weakness or lack (of security, of a future good) in relation or reaction to something external. See Patton (2001 153 and p. 159 below).

[42] I would argue that this is because it is built into the very notion of power à la Hobbes. See also ZeF VIII.355: 'Bei der Bösartigkeit der menschlichen Natur, die sich im freien Verhältniß der Völker unverhohlen blicken läßt (indessen daß sie im bürgerlich-gesetzlichen Zustande **durch den Zwang der Regierung sich sehr verschleiert**) [...]' (**HS**): the depravity of human nature is veiled by law, not eliminated or transformed.

peaceful mediation (*Ausgleich*) of conflicts, instead of law determined by the outcome of conflict (*Ausschlag*): the victor's law.[43]

But on its own, law can only state, not secure rights. As for Hobbes, law must be backed up by overwhelming coercive force (*realism*), understood in Hobbesian terms as 'a power able to over-awe them all' (Lev 13).[44] The opposition between war and peace, then, is that between a lawless state of nature (*gesetzlose Zustand*) and coercive law/legal coercion ('Zwangsgesetzen'/'gesetzliche Zwang').[45] Final peace can only be secured through the establishment of an *overarching power over all parties* capable of enforcing the law when necessary. Anything short of this cannot secure our rights and is therefore a condition of war. On these assumptions, however, Kant's argument fails. Reason cannot make use of our hostile inclinations to secure its own end of final peace, because an overarching power over all parties cannot be established where the parties are nation-states. This is because, as Kant says (*realism*), nation-states will not sign away their sovereignty.[46] On this basis, Kant can only argue in favour of a league or federation of states rather than a world republic:

- As concerns the relations among states, according to reason there can be no other way for them to emerge from the **lawless condition**, which contains only war, than

---

[43] On the notion of outcome (*Ausschlag*):
ZeF VIII.347: 'da der Krieg doch nur das traurige Nothmittel im Naturzustande ist (wo kein Gerichtshof vorhanden ist, der rechtskräftig urtheilen könnte), durch Gewalt sein Recht zu behaupten; wo keiner von beiden Theilen für einen ungerechten Feind erklärt werden kann (weil das schon einen Richterausspruch voraussetzt), sondern der **Ausschlag** desselben (gleich als vor einem |so genannten Gottesgerichte) entscheidet, auf wessen Seite das Recht ist [...]' (**HS**). At ZeF VIII.355 he goes on (like Rousseau) to make a disjunction between victory (*Sieg*) or might and right (*Recht*): 'durch diesen [Krieg] aber und seinen günstigen Ausschlag, den Sieg, das Recht nicht entschieden wird [...].' It is Reason which damns war as a legal process and makes peace an immediate duty (ZeF VIII.356).

On *Ausgleich*:
ZeF VIII.356: A people says: 'Es soll unter uns kein Krieg sein; denn wir wollen uns in einen Staat formiren, d.i. uns selbst eine oberste gesetzgebende, regierende und richtende Gewalt setzen, die unsere Streitigkeiten friedlich ausgleicht.'

[44] ZeF VIII.348 note: 'Gemeiniglich nimmt man an, daß man gegen Niemand feindlich verfahren dürfe, als nur wenn er mich schon thätig lädirt hat, und das ist auch ganz richtig, wenn beide im bürgerlich-gesetzlichen Zustande sind. Denn dadurch, daß dieser in denselben getreten ist, leistet er jenem (vermittelst der Obrigkeit), **welche über Beide Gewalt hat**) die erforderliche Sicherheit' (**HS**).

[45] See Kant's talk of *Zwang* throughout essay, e.g., ZeF VIII.354: 'Gleichwie wir nun die Anhänglichkeit der Wilden an ihre gesetzlose Freiheit, sich lieber unaufhörlich zu balgen, als **sich einem gesetzlichen, von ihnen selbst zu constituirenden Zwange zu unterwerfen** [...]' (**HS**).

[46] The above passage continues: '[...] so, sollte man denken, müßten gesittete Völker (jedes für sich zu einem Staat vereinigt) eilen, aus einem so verworfenen Zustande je eher desto lieber herauszukommen: statt dessen aber **setzt vielmehr jeder Staat seine Majestät** (denn Volksmajestät ist ein ungereimter Ausdruck) gerade darin, **gar keinem äußeren gesetzlichen Zwange unterworfen zu sein** [...]' (**HS**).
Also Zef VIII.356: 'Wenn aber dieser Staat sagt: »Es soll kein Krieg zwischen mir und andern Staaten sein, **obgleich ich keine oberste gesetzgebende Gewalt erkenne**, die mir mein und der ich ihr Recht sichere,« so ist es gar nicht zu verstehen, worauf ich dann das Vertrauen zu meinem Rechte gründen wolle, wenn es nicht das Surrogat des bürgerlichen Gesellschaftbundes, nämlich der freie Föderalism, ist, den die Vernunft mit dem Begriffe | des Völkerrechts nothwendig verbinden muß, wenn überall etwas dabei zu denken übrig bleiben soll' (**HS**).
Everything before the 'wenn es.' makes sense on Kant's assumptions, everything after does not: the federation lacks the overarching power of the world republic, which is the only security, i.e., ground for trust in rights.
See the other argument at ZeF VIII.354 on *Völkerstaat*: 'Darin aber wäre ein Widerspruch: weil ein jeder Staat das Verhältniß eines **Oberen** (Gesetzgebenden) zu einem Unteren (Gehorchenden), nämlich dem Volk) enthält, **viele Völker aber in einem Staate nur ein Volk ausmachen würden**, welches (da wir hier das Recht der Völker gegen einander zu | erwägen haben, so fern sie so viel verschiedene Staaten ausmachen und nicht in einem Staat zusammenschmelzen sollen) der Voraussetzung widerspricht' (**HS**).

for them to relinquish, just as do individual human beings, their wild (lawless) freedom, to accustom themselves to **public coercive laws**, and to thereby form a *state of peoples* (*civitas gentium*), which, continually expanding, would ultimately comprise all of the peoples of the world. But since, according to their conception of international right, they **do not want** the positive idea of a *world republic* at all (thus rejecting *in hypothesi* what is right *in thesi*), only the *negative* surrogate of a lasting and continually expanding *league* that prevents war can curb the inclination to hostility and defiance of the law, though there is the constant threat of its breaking loose again (*Furor impius intus – fremit horridus ore cruento.* Virgil). (**HS**)[47]

But a league lacks the *overarching power* to enforce cosmopolitan law on all parties (nation states), and cannot therefore exterminate insecurity and guarantee final peace. On Kant's Hobbesian assumption, the 'constant danger of war' *is* war; anything short of the guarantee of security is already a condition of war. Reason cannot therefore make use of our hostile inclinations to secure its own end of final peace under the rule of law, after all. And if it cannot, there is no ground for arguing that it *should*.

By focusing on the Hobbesian logic and presuppositions in Kant's argumentation, we can see how ZeF repeats some of the patterns noted above in the polemical use of Reason in KrV. From the very start, in the first Preliminary Article of Kant's sketch or draft-treaty (*Entwurf*), he homes in on the root causes of conflict: Just as critical Reason is to eradicate the 'seeds', 'roots' or 'source' of conflict and build eternal peace on the destruction (*Vernichtigung*) of dogmatic negations (KrV B 805–6, p. 97), so '[t]he existing causes of a future war' are to be 'destroyed [*vernichtet*] without exception' by a peace treaty that would make for eternal peace (ZeF VIII.343–4). As in the first text, Kant rehearses the first two steps of idealist warfare or *Todkrieg* (see pp. 92–3): eternal peace is *separated* from war and *isolated* in the domain of law *opposed* to the domain of nature characterized by war.[48] Following Hobbes the relation between war and peace is

---

[47] '– Für Staaten im Verhältnisse unter einander kann es nach der Vernunft keine andere Art geben, aus dem **gesetzlosen Zustande**, der lauter Krieg enthält, herauszukommen, als daß sie eben so wie einzelne Menschen ihre wilde (gesetzlose) Freiheit aufgeben, sich **zu öffentlichen Zwangsgesetzen** bequemen und so einen (freilich immer wachsenden) **V ö l k e r s t a a t** (*civitas gentium*), der zuletzt alle Völker der Erde befassen würde, bilden. Da sie dieses aber nach ihrer Idee vom Völkerrecht durchaus **nicht wollen**, mithin, was *in thesi* richtig ist, *in hypothesi* verwerfen, so kann an die Stelle der positiven Idee einer **W e l t r e p u b l i k** (wenn nicht alles verloren werden soll) nur das n e g a t i v e Surrogat eines den Krieg abwehrenden, bestehenden und sich immer ausbreitenden B u n d e s den Strom der rechtscheuenden, feindseligen Neigung aufhalten, doch mit beständiger Gefahr ihres Ausbruchs (*Furor impius intus – fremit horridus ore cruento.* Virgil)' (ZeF VIII.357; **HS**).

[48] The inverse of this move can be seen in the 6th Preliminary Article considered above (p. 87), where Kant seeks to *separate* and *isolate* war against peace. His concern is that the 'hellish arts' of warfare (espionage, assassination, etc.) undermine all trust between the enemies, making future peace impossible. So by forbidding them, Kant builds the minimal condition for future peace into his concept of permissable war. For the worry is that these malicious practices 'would not long hold themselves within the boundaries of war [...] but would carry over into peacetime and thus destroy

conceived as an opposition between a lawless and destructive state of nature and a state of security guaranteed by coercive law, which alone allows for constructive agency and freedom. War is stripped of constructive or productive powers à la Hobbes, and Kant rightly draws the conclusion that eternal peace under the rule of law must 'annihilate' the grounds for future war. The underlying problem with the argument is that it involves too broad a notion of war, grounded in a reactive concept of power, such that in the absence of coercive law, the mere proximity of another (*Nebeneinander*) constitutes a threat that invites, even justifies[49] hostility.

Yet in ZeF, Kant's idealist war on war takes a different, more nuanced form from what we saw in the first text. Unlike the latter, war, conflict and hostility are not simply 'destroyed' – negated and emptied of constructive value – in order to make an absolute and exclusive claim for 'eternal peace' (steps 3 and 4 of idealist warfare). This is partly because of the *realist* moments in Kant's political thought, and partly because he works with a layered understanding of conflict (between states, between individuals, between powers or *Kräfte*). On the one hand, eternal peace under the rule of law must 'annihilate' the grounds for future war: to posit eternal peace requires the *annihilation* of war in thought, as the presupposition for positing peace as absolute. On the other hand, the 'wickedness [*Bösartigkeit*] of human nature' can only be veiled (*verschleiert*) by the coercive force of law (*Zwang der Regierung*). Hostility and conflict are rooted deep in human nature and interaction, and the rule of law cannot altogether exclude or exterminate them; nor does eternal peace require it. While our hostile ends and inclinations are *evil* from the point of view of Reason's end, Reason can also see their instrumental value for the realization of its end. For in ZeF, conflict is both an irreducible feature of human nature and interaction and prodigiously productive: as a mechanism of nature, it has the unintended consequences of populating the earth and pluralizing peoples;[50] of nobilifying humanity;[51] of organizing states into republics;[52] and developing culture and human capacities, especially Reason, to the point of recognizing our duty to seek peace under the rule of law for sake of freedom.[53]

The *locus classiscus* for the productive power of conflict is of course where Kant writes that the artist Nature herself is able 'through discord among people, to create

---

its purpose altogether.' ('[...] daß jene höllische Künste, da sie an sich selbst niederträchtig sind, wenn sie in Gebrauch gekommen, sich nicht lange innerhalb der Grenze des Krieges halten [...] sondern auch in den Friedenszustand übergehen und so die Absicht desselben gänzlich vernichten würden.') Just as peace must be separated and isolated from war within the bounds of law, so war too must be isolated and separated from peace, so that it does not overrun its boundary and destroy peace and law altogether ('all right') in a war of extermination or *Ausrottungskrieg*.

[49] In Hobbes it is clear that any defensive move in the state of nature is justified; in ZeF, it is unclear.
[50] ZeF VIII.363–5. At ZeF VIII.367f. writes of the diversity of languages and religions as Nature's means to separate and differentiate peoples (*Völker*), since it brings with it the tendency to mutual hatred and the pretext for war.
[51] ZeF VIII.365: 'Veredelung der Menschheit'. This position is at least ascribed to unnamed philosophers. It is hard not to think anachronistically of Nietzsche in this connection.
[52] At ZeF VIII.365-6 Kant argues that a people is compelled to organize itself into a state by the pressure exerted by a neighbouring people, so that it can arm itself as a power against its neighbour.
[53] ZeF VIII.362, 356, 365, 368.

harmony, even against their own will [*durch die Zwietracht der Menschen Eintracht selbst wider ihren Willen emporkommen zu lassen*]' (ZeF VIII.361). But this line also encapsulates the problem with Kant's concept of conflict: conflict is productive, but only of its own negation in harmony and consensus (*Eintracht, Einhelligkeit*). Nor is this an isolated case: there are several places where Kant describes a dynamic of *Selbst-Aufhebung* as intrinsic to conflict.[54] The most striking example is in ZeF, when Kant imagines a 'republic of devils'. Against those who dismiss a republican constitution as unrealistic, given our selfish inclinations, Kant draws on the notion of real opposition to argue that a republican state can be organized, such that it

> directs the forces within it against each other in such a way that the one hinders or nullifies the destructive effects of the other. Thus, the result for reason turns out as if neither existed and the human being, if not exactly a morally good person, is nonetheless forced to be a good citizen. (ZeF VIII.366)[55]

– as if the web of conflicting wills were like bodies moving towards one another in a straight line. This, in any case, is one of the forms taken in ZeF by Kant's anti-polemical 'polemic use' of Reason in KrV. In the end Kant is unable to match his insights into the constructive powers of conflict with a genuinely productive concept of conflict in ZeF, and eternal peace is possible only because conflict, although irreducible, produces its own negation. In line with idealist warfare, the concept of eternal peace depends upon the negation, exclusion and annihilation or self-annihilation of conflict. Thus Kant replicates, in his way of thinking, what he argues for in real terms: the extermination or *Vernichtung* of conflict in favour of eternal peace.

---

[54] While the diversity of languages and religions, as pointed out above, separates and disperses peoples through mutual hatred and war, Kant goes on to write that with increasing culture and ever greater contact among the dispersed peoples it ultimately leads to greater consensus in principles and peace ('bei anwachsender Cultur und der allmähligen Annäherung der Menschen zu größerer Einstimmung in Principien zum Einverständnisse in einem Frieden': ZeF VIII.367). In KU §83 he writes of war: 'der, so wie er ein unabsichtlicher (durch zügellose Leidenschaften angeregter) Versuch der Menschen, doch tief verborgener, vielleicht absichtlicher der obersten Weisheit ist, Gesetzmäßigkeit mit der Freiheit der Staaten und dadurch Einheit eines moralisch begründeten Systems derselben, wo nicht zu stiften, dennoch vorzubereiten' (V.433). And in the discussion of taste in KU §56, he writes: 'Denn Streiten und Disputiren sind zwar darin einerlei, daß sie durch wechselseitigen Widerstand der Urtheile Einhelligkeit derselben hervorzubringen suchen [...] Denn worüber es erlaubt sein soll zu streiten, da muß Hoffnung sein unter einander überein zu kommen [...]' (V.339).

[55] Further on he writes of arranging a constitution for rational beings in such a way that, '"[...] although they strive against each other in their private intentions, the latter check each other [*aufhalten*] in such a way that the result in their public conduct is just as if they had no such evil intentions." It must be possible to *solve* such a problem. For it is not precisely how to attain the moral improvement of the human being that we must know, but rather only how to use the mechanism of nature on human beings in order to direct the conflict between their hostile intentions in a people in such a way that they compel each other to submit themselves to coercive laws and thereby bring about the condition of peace in which laws are in force.' The idea is that if evil intentions cancel each other out, the forces of the good, however weak they are, can prevail among rational beings. See Saner (1967 54f.).

V Rethinking conflict as productive: Nietzsche's affirmative ideal

As a consequence of his idealist war against war, it looks like Kant is unable to formulate a living, affirmative notion of peace in ZeF. His idea of 'eternal peace' is a peace of the graveyard in Nietzsche's sense (pp. 83–5, 89); one that, in negating or 'destroying' war, effectively condemns the conflictual character of reality from a transcendent standpoint in a nihilistic 'ideal' of frictionless peace opposed to reality.

In the next section I will consider some objections to this conclusion and some alternatives to the Hobbesian reading proposed by Kant scholars. But first I turn to Nietzsche for an alternative model for thinking conflict and peace, one that crosses out the oppositions (might without right/right without might, lawless destruction/lawful order, good/evil, etc.) that militate against an affirmative, genuinely productive notion of conflict in Kant.

Nietzsche's philosophy of conflict is a consequence of his life-long effort to think from a radically immanent standpoint in life. As argued in Chapter 1, he develops a relational ontology or 'counter-ontology' of life, in which life *is* only antagonistic relations of attraction-repulsion, action-resistance, commanding-obeying among forces, powers or power-complexes without substance; antagonism is the way in which relations are formed and transformed.

> We are haunted by a false concept of concord and peace as the most *useful* condition. In truth a strong *antagonism* belongs to everything, to marriage friendship state league of states corporation scholarly associations religions, for something worthwhile [OR right: *etwas Rechtes*] to grow. Resisting is the form of power [*Kraft*]– in peace as in war [...] (11[303] 9.558)
>
> Es spukt ein falscher Begriff von Eintracht und Frieden, als dem n ü t z l i c h s t e n Zustande. In Wahrheit gehört überall ein starker A n t a g o n i s m u s hinein, in Ehe Freundschaft Staat Staatenbund Körperschaft gelehrten Vereinen Religionen, damit etwas Rechtes wachse. Das Widerstreben ist die Form der K r a f t - im Frieden wie im Kriege [...]

From this standpoint, an idea or ideal of peace that negates antagonism and resistance negates life in thought, and Nietzsche asks instead what it takes to enrich, empower, enhance and affirm life. What kind of ideals or idealization can articulate an affirmative striving for life, rather than non-being or nothingness? It is tempting – and not uncommon – to think that the Nietzschean project of life-affirmation and -enhancement issues in an affirmation of domination, violence and aggression. This is confirmed, it seems, by all those texts where he insists on the ineradicability of hatred, cruelty, tyrannical impulses, on the logic of subjection, domination, etc. But I believe this is wrong, and in this section I argue that his ontology of conflict culminates in affirmative ideals that *exclude* domination and devastation.

Let me begin by recalling a late note that expresses in a highly condensed form the key features of Nietzsche's philosophy of life – dynamism, pluralism/difference and conflict or struggle:

[…] All occurrence, all movement, all becoming as
a fixing [making fast] of relations of degree and power, as a
struggle … (9[91] 12.385)

[…] Alles Geschehen, alle Bewegung, alles Werden als
ein Feststellen von Grad- und Kraftverhältnissen, als ein
Kampf … (9[91] 12.385)

Against the ontological priority and greater reality given to being over becoming in traditional metaphysics and substance ontology, Nietzsche posits the primacy of occurrence, movement, becoming. The reality of occurrence consists not of beings or substances (self-supporting, unified and enduring entities) interacting causally, but of relations of difference among a plurality of forces or powers without substance; he writes of the '*relational character* of all occurrence [*R e l a t i o n s c h a r a k t e r alles Geschehens*]': 26[36] 11.157. Yet being does not simply disappear. Rather, it is *integrated* into becoming – thereby overcoming their opposition in metaphysics – with the claim that reality as becoming has the character of an incessant *Feststellen*, a multiple fixing (*Fest-setzen*) or positing (*Setzen*) of being[56] within an ongoing struggle or conflict of forces. Thus being, while derivative of becoming, is not opposed to it, but is dynamized and pluralized as that which emerges from the essential or characteristic tendency of becoming. This move has important implications for the ideal of affirmation that issues from his ontology of conflict.

If there is no such thing as peace to the exclusion of conflict, there are at least two ways in which it can be approximated.

1. The first involves the attempt to *totalize being to the virtual exclusion or suppression of becoming*. If the characteristic tendency of becoming is to be a multiple fixing or positing of being: *Fest-Setzen*, then there are, it seems, two ways in which this can go wrong. At one extreme, the processes of fixing or *Fest-setzen* can be reduced to a minimum, so that becoming descends into a formless, disorganized and unlimited conflict of forces, what Nietzsche sometimes calls the lawless 'war of annihilation' (*Vernichtungskrieg*).[57] At the other extreme, peace can be imposed – a 'victor's peace' – through an excessive fixing of becoming that subjugates, assimilates and reduces all

---

[56] See also: 34[88][89] 11.449; 26[359] 11.244; 39[13] 11.623; 2[139] 12.135f.; UB III 3 1.360; FW 370 3.622; AC 58 6.245.

[57] See Nietzsche's diagnoses of the present as a pervasive conflict of forces: Compare 30[8] 7.733 (1873–4): '[…] Jetzt fehlt das, was alle partiellen Kräfte bindet: und so sehen wir alles feindselig gegen einander und alle edlen Kräfte in gegenseitigem aufreibendem Vernichtungskrieg' and 9[35] 12.351: '[…] daß die Synthese der Werthe und Ziele (auf der jede stärke Cultur beruht) sich löst, so daß die einzelnen Werthe sich Krieg machen: Zersetzung'.

'external' difference to the same. At both extremes, the *pluralistic* character of life is negated and lost, in the first through a lack of form-giving force, in the latter through overwhelming force, an excess of unity and order. As an example of the latter, Nietzsche cites law or any legal order, when it is 'thought as sovereign and universal' (GM II 11 5.313). Similarly, the attitude or ethos presupposed by law – 'to withhold reciprocally from injury, violence, exploitation, to posit one's will as equal to the other's' (JGB 259) – becomes problematic when it is universalized: made into a 'fundamental principle of society' (*Grundprinzip der Gesellschaft*) (JGB 259). It is in the *totalizing universal* claims made for any given legal order – and this would include Kant's ideal of cosmopolitan law – that the problem lies: for in excluding anything external or irreducible to the claims of law, they do not just 'displace' difference, but negate it, and so negate life in its pluralistic and dynamic character.

In these senses the ideal of eternal peace under the rule of cosmopolitan law is *inconsistent* with a commitment to life-affirmation and -enhancement. But it does not follow that Nietzsche advocates the other extreme of lawless violence or the 'war of annihilation'; for this too involves a negation of life's pluralism (presupposing as it does a *Fest-setzen* or fixing of diverse forms of life). Even if the unifying, eternalizing, universalizing functions of law contradict the dynamic and pluralistic character of life, Nietzsche does not simply negate law. Rather, from a radically immanent standpoint in life as will to power, a given legal order can be affirmed, *not* in universal terms, but in *local* terms, as a 'state of exception' (*Ausnahmezustand*), a kind of damming up and 'partial restricting' of power in the service of a power-complex bent on extending or expanding its power. It is, then, not as end in itself, as something 'sovereign and universal' that a legal order enhances life and can be affirmed; but as 'a *means*' by which a given power complex can extend itself within a dynamic struggle with other complexes of power all bent on expansion (GM II 11 5.313).

Nietzsche thus performs a *reversal* of Kant's thought that completely undermines the cunning of Kantian Reason: if Kantian Reason values conflict instrumentally for its own end of establishing a universal legal order, Nietzsche's standpoint in life values particular legal orders instrumentally as means for the expansion of will to power complexes.

2. Given that there is no such thing as peace, a second way in which it can be approximated is by *reducing* antagonism to a minimum. Nietzsche writes:

> Whoever has the capacity for deep feelings must also suffer the vehement struggle between them and their opposites. One can, in order to be perfectly calm and without inner suffering, just wean oneself from deep feelings, so that in their weakness they arouse only weak counter-forces: they can then, in their sublimated rarity, *not be heard* [überhört] and give human beings the impression that they are quite in harmony with themselves. – [...] (6[58] 9.207f.)

In reducing to a minimum the vehement discord of our feelings towards their opposites, we can *miss hearing* (*überhören*) the inner antagonism and mistake it for peace, harmony or agreement with ourselves. This is a clear reference to the Socratic ideal of agreement with oneself (also evinced by Kant)[58] and the eudemonistic tendency Socrates introduced into philosophy.[59] Nietzsche goes to spell out the political correlate of this individual, moral strategy:

> *Just so* in social life: if everything is to work in an altruistic fashion, the oppositions among individuals must be reduced to a sublime minimum: so that all inimical tendencies and tensions, through which the individual maintains itself as individual [*durch welche das Individuum sich als Individuum erhält*] can barely be perceived; that is: the individuals must be reduced to the palest tonality of individuality! Thus equality [or uniformity: *Gleichheit*] prevailing by far. That is euthanasia, entirely unproductive! (6[58] 9.208)

[58] Plato Gorgias 482c: 'It would be better for me [...] that multitudes of men should disagree with me rather than that I, being one, should be out of harmony with myself.' In 'Philosophy and Politics' Hannah Arendt's version is: 'it is much better to be in disagreement with the whole world than *being one*, to be in disagreement with myself' (Arendt 1990 87). In this essay, she defends this position against the divisiveness of the agonal spirit in Greece and denies that Socratic oneness or harmony with oneself excludes pluralism. Nietzsche's position is that disagreement or a measure of conflict is necessary for genuine pluralism.

For Kant, see RGV VI.58: 'Natural inclinations, *considered in themselves*, are *good*, i.e., irreprehensible; and not only is it futile, but it would also be harmful and censurable, to want to exterminate them. Rather, one must only tame them, so that they do not themselves wear one another out but instead can be brought to harmony in a whole called happiness. The reason, however, that accomplishes this is called *prudence*.' However, where inclinations violate the moral law, they must be exterminated (*ausgerottet*), a strategy Nietzsche calls 'castratism' (GD Moral 1 and 2). Kant's text continues: 'Only what is morally unlawful is in itself evil, absolutely reprehensible, and must be exterminated; but the reason that teaches this, and even more so if it also puts it into practice, alone deserves the name of *wisdom*, in comparison with which vice may indeed also be called *folly*, but only when reason feels within itself sufficient strength in order to *despise* it (and all inducements to it), not merely to *hate* it as an entity to be feared, and to arm itself against it.' ('Natürliche Neigungen sind, a n   s i c h   s e l b s t   b e t r a c h t e t,   g u t, d.i. unverwerflich, und es ist nicht allein vergeblich, sondern es wäre auch schädlich und tadelhaft, sie ausrotten zu wollen; man muß sie vielmehr nur bezähmen, damit sie sich untereinander nicht selbst aufreiben, sondern zur Zusammenstimmung in einem Ganzen, Glückseligkeit genannt, gebracht werden können. Die Vernunft aber, die dieses ausrichtet, heißt K l u g h e i t. Nur das Moralisch-Gesetzwidrige ist an sich selbst böse, schlechterdings verwerflich, und muß ausgerottet werden; die Vernunft aber, die das lehrt, noch mehr aber, wenn sie es auch ins Werk richtet, verdient allein den Namen der W e i s h e i t, in Vergleichung mit welcher das Laster zwar auch T h o r h e i t genannt werden kann, aber nur alsdann, wenn die Vernunft gnugsam Stärke in sich fühlt, um es (und alle Anreize dazu) z u   v e r a c h t e n, und nicht bloß als ein zu fürchtendes Wesen zu h a s s e n, und sich dagegen zu bewaffnen'.)

[59] See 19[20] 7.422: 'Nach Sokrates ist das allgemeine Wohl nicht mehr zu retten, darum die individualisirende Ethik, die die Einzelnen retten will.' But already in 1869 Nietzsche writes: 'Euripides hat von Sokrates die Vereinzelung des Individuums gelernt' (1[106] 7.41). See also 23[35] 7.555: 'Sokrates bricht mit der bisherigen Wissenschaft und Kultur, er will zurück zur alten Bürgertugend und zum Staate.' See also the notes on 'Wissenschaft und Weisheit und im Kampfe' from KSA 8 (1875): 6[13] 8.102 'Von Sokrates an: das Individuum nahm sich zu wichtig mit einem Male'; 6[15] 8.103 on the pre-Socratic philosophers: 'Bei ihnen hat man nicht "die garstige Pretension auf Glück", wie von Sokrates ab. Es dreht sich doch nicht alles um den Zustand ihrer Seele: denn über den denkt man nicht ohne Gefahr nach'; and equally 6[15] 8.103 'sie [die ältere Philosophie – HS] ist n i c h t s o   i n d i v i d u e l l - e u d ä m o n o l o g i s c h, ohne die garstige Pretension auf Glück'. In 6[26] 8 he accuses Socrates of tearing the individual out of his historical context and in 6[21] 8 he characterizes Socrates' position with the words: 'da bleibt mir nichts als ich mir selbst; Angst um sich selbst wird die Seele der Philosophie.'

The advantage of this strategy, as Socrates saw (cf. 11[182] 9.512), is to save the individual, or rather: the 'dividuum' (MA 57) from suffering. However, eudaimonia or happiness in this sense comes at a high cost: with the reduction of tension goes *first* a loss of *diversity*, so that 'equality or uniformity prevails by far'. And with the reduction of tension goes *secondly* the loss of *creative or productive power*: it is a kind 'euthanasia, entirely unproductive'. As the ultimate consequence of the Socratic ideal of inner harmony, Nietzsche presents us with the herd-animal that has come to dominate in modernity, with its 'insufficient strength to posit productively a goal for itself anew, a Wherefore? a belief' under nihilistic conditions.[60]

At stake in *creative* or *productive power* is not just an aestheticist preference for creative individuality. Rather, as the reference to 'euthanasia' makes clear, it is life itself, in its character as an incessant and multiple positing (i.e. producing, creating) of being, that is negated and impoverished by the *living death* or euthanasia of unproductive individuality; just as it is life in its *pluralism* that is negated and impoverished through the rule of uniformity that follows upon the reduction of tension and antagonism. What then does it take to enhance and affirm life or reality at the level of individual lives and their interactions? What affirmative alternative is there to reducing tension, one that would advance and enhance life in its productive and pluralistic character as an incessant and multiple *Fest-setzen*? What, in other words, does it take to *maximize*, rather than minimize tension?

An answer to this question can be found in the *theory of creativity* underpinning the above analysis of the loss of productive power. According to Nietzsche, a certain level or measure of tension or antagonism among a multiplicity of drives or impulses is the *sine qua non* for creative power

> One is *fruitful* at the price of being rich in oppositions; one can only remain *young* on the assumption that the soul does not stretch out, does not long for peace … (GD Moral 3 6.84)[61]

Now if we ask, what the conditions for tension are, what it takes for a dividuum to become 'rich in oppositions', Nietzsche's answer is one that *excludes* relations of domination, subjection, incorporation or destruction: it takes a kind of *equilibrium*

---

[60] In *Nachlass* note 9[35] 12.350, Nietzsche describes nihilism as a 'Zeichen von nicht genügender Stärke, um produktiv sich nun auch wieder ein Ziel, ein Warum? einen Glauben zu setzen'.

[61] On the importance of inner contradictions for human greatness, see Müller-Lauter (1971 10): '"Um Classiker zu sein", müsse man "alle starken, anscheinend widerspruchsvollen Gaben und Begierden haben". An Händel, Leibniz, Goethe und Bismarck – die "für die deutsche starke Art charakteristisch" seien – bewundert er die Unbedenklichkeit des Lebens "zwischen Gegensätzen …, voll jener geschmeidigen Stärke, welche sich vor Überzeugungen und Doktrinen hütet, indem sie eine gegen die andere benutzt und sich selber die Freiheit vorbehält". Es ist Nietzsches grundsätzliche "Einsich", "dass mit jedem Wachsthum des Menschen auch seine Kehrseite wachsen muss". Sucht man die Kehrseite abzuschaffen, so schwindet auch das Ideal der Vorderseite hin, das man doch gerade erhalten sehen möchte. Die Gegensätze gehören komplementär zueinander. Daher gilt es, die Gegensatz-Spannungen zu fördern in Richtung auf das Entstehen des höchsten Menschen. Er könnte "den Gegensatz-Charakter des Daseins am stärksten" darstellen. Und dieses soll in ihm seine "Glorie und einzige Rechtfertigung" finden.' (References to pre-critical editions omitted.)

among a multiplicity of *more-or-less equal forces*, impulses or power-complexes, all bent on extending their power. Only if these impulses or 'feelings' are of 'similar power' can they resist succumbing to subjection, assimilation or domination by their antagonists and hold one another in a certain equilibrium, such that tension is *maximized*.

Nietzsche's life-affirmative and life-enhancing alternative to the Socratic ideal of peace or agreement with ourselves through the reduction of tension is, then, an ideal of *equilibrium among more-or-less equal antagonistic forces* that allows for the maximum of inner tension, the vehement antagonism between our feelings and their opposites. But the problem now arises: How can this productive and dynamic equilibrium within individuals/dividua be sustained, *without* the complete loss of unity, the complete dis-integration of individuals under the pressure of an unmeasured conflict of more-or-less equal drives? What level or measure of conflict within the dividua enables them to persist as living unities?

If the problem is how to avoid the dis-integration or explosion of individuals under the (outward) pressure of an unmeasured conflict of more-or-less equal drives, the solution would seem to involve the exercise of *inward pressures* from the outside, pressures that neither overpower and absorb the individual, nor are overpowered by it, but would be more-or-less equal to the outward expansionist pressure exerted by the individual. In other words, the measure or degree of tension that allows for a maximization of inner tension consistent with the unity of the individual is given by social, inter-subjective or *political relations of approximate equality*. In the text we have been considering, Nietzsche himself draws this consequence and offers a social or rather *political* answer to the question, when he writes of the 'inimical tendencies and tensions, through which the individual maintains itself as individual [*durch welche das Individuum sich als Individuum erhält*]'. Here, strong inner tension is connected with outer, interpersonal tension as its condition: it is through relations of tension and antagonism with others that the antagonism of inner drives is best contained, so that the dividuum can attain unity, or maintain itself as an individual with a maximum of inner tension. The level or measure of maximal inner antagonism consistent with unified, individual existence is determined by relations of tension *between* individuals. Equality in the sense of an *equilibrium among more-or-less equal antagonistic forces* is the *sine qua non* for tension or antagonism to persist, whether within or between individuals. In this regard, we can say that Nietzsche's project of life-affirmation or -enhancement implies a politics of equality, not in the sense of universal equal rights that protect us from conflict and incursion, but a politics of enmity among more-or-less equal powers that allows individuals to be productive dividua while maintaining their unity as individuals.

VI Nietzsche *contra* Kant, Kant *contra* Nietzsche

Nietzsche's ontology of conflict, I have argued, culminates in the affirmative ideal of *maximizing tension on the basis of an equilibrium of powers*. This affirmative ideal is at the same time the presupposition for productivity or creativity, so that Nietzsche is able to formulate an affirmative concept of conflict that is genuinely productive. In giving us a way to think conflict in relation to peace that crosses out the mutually exclusive opposition of destruction versus construction, he offers an alternative to Kant's Hobbesian concept of conflict, which is at worst purely destructive, at best productive of its own negation. The key question for both thinkers is how destructive and futile conflict can be transformed into constructive order. Since for Nietzsche conflict is ontologically irreducible and essential for creativity, it cannot be a matter of repressing or resolving conflict altogether through the rule of law backed up by overwhelming coercive force, as implied by the Hobbesian logic in Kant's argumentation. Rather, the destructive potential of hostile inclinations or impulses is best contained by plurality of more-or-less equal powers able to limit each other, while stimulating each other. Destruction and domination are not to be avoided through legal coercion, but through the reciprocal resistance offered by diverse but equal powers, powers that at the same time stimulate or provoke one another to create new orders within an incessant struggle of powers. Nietzschean life-affirmation commits us to a middle position between the lawless war of annihilation and the excess of being represented by law, understood as sovereign and universal; between Kant's Hobbesian war and cosmopolitan law. Both of these negate the pluralistic character of life, and Nietzsche himself seems to articulate a third position that would affirm any local legal order that serves as a *means* for a given power-complex to extend and expand its power over others. This looks like the promotion of expansionist, imperialistic orders, so often associated with Nietzsche. But on its own, it falls short of his commitment to life-affirmation and -enhancement as the maximization of creative tension, since this is realized *not* under conditions of expansion and subjugation, but where an equilibrium of more-or-less equal forces holds the expansionist dynamic of the each in check. A commitment to life-affirmation and -enhancement seems to imply that we give up Reason's dream of an all-inclusive, cosmopolitan rule of law in favour of antagonistic relations within and between a plurality of local legal orders, all bent on extending their jurisdiction.

Nietzsche's affirmative ideal raises, without answering, fundamental questions: How to ensure that antagonistic relations within and between a plurality of local legal orders, all bent on extending their jurisdiction, are constructive and do not descend into destructive conflict? And what kinds of political settlements, institutions and legal frameworks would make for an approximate equality of power among constituents? When set against the republican principles and the three interdependent levels of law (republican state law, international law and cosmopolitan law) sketched in ZeF, Nietzsche's affirmative ideal looks remote from political reality next to Kant's theory of peace. But Kant's account of peace is also problematic when placed under a Nietzschean perspective. As we have seen, the idea of eternal peace is a life-negating peace of the graveyard in Nietzsche's eyes, since it depends on the negation, exclusion and annihilation or self-annihilation of conflict, and can only be realized through the actual annihilation or *Vernichtung* of (the causes of future) conflict. And yet, it is far from clear how exactly Kant's *manner* of thinking war and peace relates to the *matter* of his thinking in the prospect of actual peace. The Hobbesian reading of ZeF sketched is well supported by the text, as I have tried to show in section IV.2. But it singles out one strand in a complex and ambiguous text comprising many argumentative strands,[62] which still divides scholars. They are divided on Kant's ideal in ZeF – whether a voluntary 'league' of states (*Bund*), or a '*state of peoples* (*civitas gentium*)' (*Völkerstaat*), a '*world republic*' (*Weltrepublik*) with coercive powers, or something like the 'league of nations' (*Völkerbund*) in IaG, with 'united might' and laws based on a 'united will'.[63] Where an entity with coercive powers is seen to follow from the logic of the state of nature (as argued above), scholars disagree on what moves Kant to advocate the '*negative* surrogate' of a voluntary league instead. We have already seen his concern with a world republic leading to 'soulless despotism' (p. 88). There is also his argument for the indivisibility of state sovereignty (ZeF VIII.354), and his concern that the non-voluntary imposition of coercive power over a state will violate its citizens' autonomy (Kleingeld 2007 485f.). For some, the view that Kant's negative surrogate is a realist concession to the fact that sovereigns will not renounce their power (as argued above) is anathema, and they point to his repeated position that normative demands should not be grounded on empirical or pragmatic considerations. Some scholars then argue *contra* ZeF for a federation with coercive powers.[64]

Perhaps the strongest interpretation of Kant's argument, addressing this problem and giving due weight to his concerns about coercing unwilling states into a federation of state of states, his arguments in favour of voluntary accession to a league of states, and the disanalogies (not just analogies) between individuals and states in the state of nature, is one in which the voluntary league of states is a necessary step on the way towards an international federation or state of states with the authority to coercively enforce a common federal law.[65] On this reading, Kant's emphasis falls not on the realization of the latter as the condition for perpetual peace, but on *striving towards* it on the basis of our moral and political duty to continually *approximate* the idea of a single state of states. As Kleingeld (2007 493-4) notes, this position finds support in the *Nachlass* to MS (XXIII.353-4). It also finds support in the closing lines of ZeF:

> If it is a duty to realize a condition of public right, and if there is well-founded hope that this can be attained, even if only in the form of an endlessly progressing approximation of it, then the *perpetual peace* that follows the peace treaties that have been concluded up to now (although they have wrongly been designated so, since they actually are mere ceasefires) is not an empty idea, but rather a task which, carried out gradually, steadily moves toward its goal (since the periods in which equal advances are made will hopefully grow shorter and shorter).

---

[62] Pogge (1988 esp. 427-33) emphasizes the multiplicity of unsuccessful argumentative strands in ZeF.

[63] In IaG (VIII.23-4), Kant argues that nature drives states 'to go beyond a lawless condition of savages and enter into a league of nations [*Völkerbund*], where every state, even the smallest, could expect its security and rights not from its own might, or its own juridical judgment, but only from this great league of nations (Foedus Amphictyonum), from a united might and from the decision in accordance with laws of its united will.'

[64] See, e.g., Dodson (1993); Habermas (1997); Höffe (1995); Höffe (1998). See Kleingeld (2007) for further references.

[65] See Kleingeld (2004 and 2007).

> Wenn es Pflicht, wenn zugleich gegründete Hoffnung da ist, den Zustand eines öffentlichen Rechts, obgleich nur in einer ins Unendliche fortschreitenden Annäherung wirklich zu machen, so ist der ewige Friede, der auf die bisher fälschlich so genannte Friedensschlüsse (eigentlich Waffenstillstände) folgt, keine leere Idee, sondern eine Aufgabe, die, nach und nach aufgelöst, ihrem Ziele (weil die Zeiten, in denen gleiche Fortschritte geschehen, hoffentlich immer kürzer werden) beständig näher kommt. (ZeF VIII.386)

Of importance for the philosophy of conflict is that an argument that there is well-grounded hope that eternal peace under public law can be asymptotically approximated *without being fully realized*, leaves open the prospect of future conflicts and acknowledges that conflict cannot be eradicated from political reality. In this case, Kant's idea of eternal peace, even if it negates conflict as an irreducible dimension of reality, need not signify a life-negating peace of the graveyard, but could work instead as a guide for us to strive for a living peace that excludes the victor's peace of despotism and the 'graveyard of freedom'. Support for this interpretation comes from the 'liveliest competition' of forces in equilibrium, which Kant associates with peace, as we have seen (pp. 88, 90–1); a thought that approaches Nietzsche's ideal of peace, in excluding destruction, but not conflict altogether.

VII Approaching a living peace: A *Rapprochement*?

The two readings presented above point towards a profound ambiguity in of Kant's ideal of peace in ZeF. On the Hobbesian reading sketched in section IV.2, it signifies a nihilistic 'peace of the graveyard'. On the 'approximative' reading, however, the idea of eternal peace serves as a guide for an asymptotic approximation to the goal of a moral and political whole, leaving open the question of conflict. Not only does this suggest a rapprochement with Nietzsche's ideal of a living peace by including 'liveliest competition' of powers in equilibrium; an 'approximative' interpretation of ZeF also brings Kant closer to Nietzsche's pluralistic model of local legal orders in limited conflict by emphasizing a voluntary league of states, understood as a transitional stage within an 'endlessly progressing approximation' to a cosmopolitan legal order with coercive authority.

In concluding this chapter, I will suggest some ways in which each thinker's position can be thought from the perspective of the other, or one that approximates it; not in order to deny their differences as philosophers of conflict, but in order to use each to throw light on the other, both critical and constructive. I do so by considering two points made in the *Nachlass* note cited in part at the beginning of section V (p. 109):

> Richness of individuals is richness of those who are no longer ashamed of what is their own and deviant. When a people becomes proud and seeks out opponents, it grows in strength and goodness [...] *Equality* counts as binding and worth striving for! We are haunted by a false concept of concord and peace as the most *useful* condition. In truth a strong *antagonism* belongs intrinsically [*hinein*] to

everything, to marriage friendship state league of states corporation scholarly associations religions, for something worthwhile [OR right: *etwas Rechtes*] to grow. Resisting is the form of *power* [*Kraft*] – in peace as in war, consequently there be diverse forces and not the same, for these would hold one another in equilibrium! (11[303] 9.557–8)[66]

For the present argument, Nietzsche makes two important points in this note:

1. That an idea of 'concord and peace' that excludes antagonism, like Kant's idea of eternal peace, is life-negating and has (had) a negative, debilitating effect on human existence at large by reducing diversity and promoting a universal aspiration for equality.
2. That a diversity of forces, and *not* an equilibrium, is needed for the kinds of productive antagonism that enhance and empower life-forms at all levels. To begin with this point:

2. Prima facie, this note problematizes the idea of an equilibrium among more-or-less equal forces as a Nietzschean ideal, reminding us instead of his anti-egalitarian pathos and his increasing emphasis on hierarchy or *Rangordnung* in later years. But I think this is wrong. The adjective 'gleich' can mean 'equal' or 'the same', and when Nietzsche writes of 'verschiedene Kräfte und nicht gleiche' he means 'different and not the same'; for the concern in the note is with the loss of human diversity or 'richness' (of individuals, of peoples) that has accompanied the universal aspiration to equality as a moral and political value.[67] What is clear is that he associates diversity with 'a strong *antagonism*' – what I have called a 'maximization of tension' – and equilibrium (*Gleichgewicht*) with sameness among its constituents (*gleiche Kräfte*).

---

[66] The full note (to which we will return in Chapter 4) reads:
'Der E g o i s m ist verketzert worden, von denen die ihn übten (Gemeinden Fürsten Parteiführern Religionsstiftern Philosophen wie Plato); sie brauchten die entgegengesetzte Gesinnung bei den Menschen, die ihnen F u n k t i o n leisten sollten. – Wo eine Zeit ein Volk eine Stadt hervorragt, ist es immer, daß der E g o i s m u s derselben sich bewußt wird und kein Mittel mehr scheut (sich n i c h t m e h r seiner selber s c h ä m t). Reichthum an Individuen ist Reichthum an solchen, die sich ihres Eigenen und Abweichenden nicht mehr schämen. Wenn ein Volk stolz wird und Gegner sucht, wächst es an Kraft und Güte. – Dagegen die Selbstlosigkeit verherrlichen! und zugeben, wie Kant, daß wahrscheinlich nie eine That derselben gethan worden sei! Also nur, um das entgegengesetzte Princip herabzusetzen, seinen Werth zu drücken, die Menschen kalt und verächtlich, folglich g e d a n k e n f a u l gegen den Egoismus stimmen! – Denn bisher ist es der M a n g e l an feinem planmäßigen gedankenreichen Egoismus gewesen, was die Menschen im Ganzen auf einer so niedrigen Stufe erhält! G l e i c h h e i t gilt als verbindend und erstrebenswerth! Es spukt ein falscher Begriff von Eintracht und Frieden, als dem n ü t z l i c h s t e n Zustande. In Wahrheit gehört überall ein starker A n t a g o n i s m u s hinein, in Ehe Freundschaft Staat Staatenbund Körperschaft gelehrten Vereinen Religionen, damit etwas Rechtes wachse. Das Widerstreben ist die Form der K r a f t – im Frieden wie im Kriege,, folglich müssen verschiedene Kräfte und nicht gleiche dasein, denn diese würden sich das Gleichgewicht halten!'.
[67] One of Nietzsche's main criticisms of democracy from the early 1880s on is that the rule of equality as the supreme political value has had the effect of excluding difference and reducing diversity, culminating in the rule of the herd animal. See Siemens (2009a).

The term 'Gleichgewicht' is not a stable signifier in Nietzsche's vocabulary; while he tends to oppose it in later writings, it is of crucial importance in his thought on law and justice. In MA and WS,[68] he argues that 'the principle of equilibrium' is profoundly productive and of cardinal importance for the establishment of social life, since, as a 'settlement between approximately equal powers [*Ausgleich[.] zwischen ungefähr Gleich-Mächtigen*]', it is the basis of law and justice; a claim repeated in M 112 (3.102) and GM (Vorrede 4 5.251). As Gerhardt (1983) has pointed out, it is important to understand the term 'equal' here in Nietzsche's sense. The qualification *ungefähr*, 'approximately' or 'more-or-less', indicates that 'equality' does not denote a quantitative measure of objective magnitudes, but 'a correspondence of real social factors, between which there can never be a quantitative equality in the strict sense' (Gerhardt 1983 116). Equality is not determined from an external, neutral standpoint, but by the antagonistic powers themselves, each of which judges itself in relation to the other(s). As 'the expression of an estimated correspondence between the powers themselves', it involves perception, anticipation and evaluation, announcement and symbolic understanding. Equality in this sense is perfectly consistent with *qualitative difference* or *diversity* and the richness of human life-forms of concern to Nietzsche in the above note. It is also consistent with *relative differences in power*, such that the weakest power in a given equilibrium is equal to challenging or pressuring the strongest. This is best seen in Nietzsche's concept of the agon, which only takes off when there is a current victor who is challenged by (a) weaker power(s), and which breaks down when there is an absolute victor to whom none are equal.[69]

The notion of approximately equal power in Nietzsche's dynamic concept of equilibrium is not, then, the concept of equality criticized by the later Nietzsche as the tendency for democracy to promote uniformity or sameness (*Gleichheit* as *Gleichmachung*). Instead, it designates a relational or relative notion of power which is *inclusive* of the qualitative diversity lost under modern democratic values, and *includes* relative differences of power.

[68] See MA 92, 93, WS 22, 26, 28, 29, 32, 39, 57. Also Gerhardt (1983).
[69] By banishing the towering individual to whom none are equal, Nietzsche argues, the Greek institution of ostracism secured a dynamic plurality of more-or-less equal forces or geniuses, and under these conditions a form of interaction unique to the agon comes into play: what Nietzsche calls the 'competitive play of forces' or *Wettspiel der Kräfte*, consisting of relations of reciprocal stimulation or provocation (*zur That reizen*) on one side, and reciprocal limitation within the bounds of measure (*in der Grenze des Maaßes halten*) on the other:
'The original sense of this peculiar institution [ostracism – HS] is not, however, that of a vent [escape-valve], but rather that of a stimulant: one removes the outstanding individual so that the competitive play of forces [*Wettspiel der Kräfte*] may reawaken: a thought that is inimical to the "exclusivity" of genius in the modern sense, but presupposes that in a natural order of things there are always several geniuses who rouse [stimulate] one another to action [lit. deed], as they also hold one another within the bounds of measure. That is the crux of the Hellenic notion of contest: it loathes one-man rule [*Alleinherrschaft*] and fears its dangers; it desires, as a protection against genius – a second genius' (HW 1.789). From his reading of Roux's *Der Kampf der Theile im Organismus* in 1881, Nietzsche will have encountered a physiological analogue of these notions of approximate equality and equilibrium. Roux argues that the life of organisms depends on an equilibrium among their parts (organs, tissues, cells) engaged in a struggle for nutrition and space. It is a conflict *inter pares*, driven by the fact that the parts are not completely or absolutely equal, but approximately equal, whose equilibrium is fragile and subject to disruption. See Pearson (2018 308ff.).

Although it goes beyond the scope of this chapter, I would argue that the notion of hierarchy or *Rangordnung* promoted by the later Nietzsche is no less dynamic and designates differences that are consistent with this notion of equality, but was emphasized by him instead because of his preoccupation with democratic equality. This preoccupation may also have blinded him to the more nuanced attitudes to equality and the aspiration to equality he took earlier in WS. In this book, first published in 1880, Nietzsche develops a social theory of the first human communities as grounded 'when human beings posited themselves as *equal* to one another for the sake of security [*Da die Menschen ihrer Sicherheit wegen sich selber als einander g l e i c h gesetzt haben, zur Gründung der Gemeinde*]', in contrast with the 'unconcerned, ruthless inequality' of the state of nature (WS 31).⁷⁰ Against this background, he distinguishes two different attitudes to equality, and two different modes of action, within a social order in which 'equality has really prevailed and been solidly grounded' (WS 29). In one case, whenever someone else rises above the level of equality or the 'common measure' (*gemeinsame Maass*) and stands out, envy leads to the wish to push him back down to that level (*ihn bis dahin herabdrücken*). In the other case, which Nietzsche associates with, 'the good Eris', goddess of the *agon*, envy works as a positive stimulant 'to raise oneself' to equal standing with the outstanding one (*sich bis dorthin erheben*). This attitude, Nietzsche continues, also gives rise to indignation at the injustice of someone who suffers misfortune falling below the level of equality, while another fares better due to good fortune. The first case, as a disposition to 'level down', encapsulates what Nietzsche comes to criticize as the uniformity engendered by the democratic value of equality, motivated by 'misarchism' or hatred of rule (GM II 12 5.315) and ressentiment. But the second case describes an entirely different attitude to equality, an aspirational 'levelling up' coupled with a sensitivity to undeserved injustices, which gets lost in Nietzsche anti-democratic polemics of later years. With this qualitative distinction in mind, we can think with Nietzsche against Nietzsche's one-sided condemnation of the universal aspiration to equality in note 11[303] above, and argue that this need not signify a levelling down to the 'autonomous herd' (JGB 202), but can also point to an aspiration to level up akin to the noble form of envy described in WS 29. What is more, the association of this aspirational attitude to equality with the good Eris of the agon there suggests its consonance with Nietzsche's affirmative ideal of a dynamic equilibrium of approximately equal powers in tension. This brings us to the first point in note 11[303] concerning the status of Kant's ideal of peace (p. 118).

1. Here again we can think with Nietzsche against Nietzsche's one-sided condemnation of the Kantian idea of peace without antagonism as a life-negating, debilitating ideal complicit in the 'levelling down' aspiration to equality. A more

---

[70] Similarly, in WS 27 Nietzsche equates 'the grounding of society' (*Begründung der Gesellschaft*) with the moment in which 'the human being first learned to see its equal in other humans' (*in anderen Menschen seines Gleichen zu sehen*). In WS 31, Nietzsche goes on to argue that, after having left this state of nature, the human desire to dominate gives rise to vanity in people. Vanity in its turn leads to social inequalities within the bounds of communal life, thereby creating the preconditions for the envious feelings described in WS 29. With gratitude to Wouter Veldman for pointing this out.

nuanced or ambiguous interpretation is suggested by an important *Nachlass* note from 1887, which is also a key text for Nietzsche's critique of idealism as warfare.

Note 10[194] (12.572) takes issue with eminently modern forms of idealism embodied in the autonomous ideals of '"morality for morality's sake"', '"art for art's sake"' and knowledge for knowledge's sake. Each of them is out to 'slander reality' (*Realitäts-Verleumdung*) by reading a 'false opposition into things' (*falschen Gegensatz*), which allows an 'ideal to be separated from the actual' (*ein Ideal ablöst vom Wirklichen*). To separate the ideal and place it in opposition to life is to impoverish (*verarmt*) life and make it ugly ('*Idealisirung*' *ins Häßliche*), instead of recognizing art, knowledge and morality as ways to intensify and propel life towards new possibilities:

> '*Morality for morality's sake*' – an important stage in its denaturalization: it appears as the ultimate value itself. In this phase it has permeated religion: e.g. in Judaism. There is also a phase when it *severs religion from itself* again, and no God is 'moral' enough for it: then it prefers the impersonal ideal ... That is the case today.
>
> '*Art for art's sake*' – this is an equally dangerous principle: it brings a false opposition into things – it amounts to slandering reality ('idealization' *into the ugly*). When one separates an ideal from what's real, one casts down the real, impoverishes it, slanders it. '*Beauty for beauty's sake*', '*Truth for truth's sake*', '*Good for the sake of the good*' – these are three forms of the *evil eye* for the real. 10[194] (12.572)[71]

In the last paragraph of the note, Nietzsche then switches perspective. The false oppositions are situated on the plane of immanence in relation to the complexes of (will to) power that posit them. The separation they effect in the domain of values serves idealist warfare as a means to separate and secure idealist power-complexes from their adversaries.

> – '*beautiful* and *ugly*', '*true* and *false*', '*good* and *evil*' – these *separations* and *antagonisms* betray conditions of existence and enhancement, not of man in general, but of various fixed and lasting complexes which sever their adversaries

---

[71] '"Die Moral um der Moral willen!" – eine wichtige Stufe in ihrer Entnaturalisirung: sie erscheint selbst als letzter Werth. In dieser Phase hat sie die Religion mit sich durchdrungen: im Judenthum z.B. Und ebenso giebt es eine Phase, wo sie die Religion wieder v o n s i c h a b t r e n n t, und wo ihr kein Gott "moralisch" genug ist: dann zieht sie das unpersönliche Ideal vor ... Das ist jetzt der Fall.
"D i e K u n s t u m d e r K u n s t w i l l e n"– das ist ein gleichgefährlihes Princip: damit bringt man einen falschen Gegensatz in die Dinge, – es läuft auf eine Realitäts-Verleumdung ("Idealisirung" i n s H ä ß l i c h e) hinaus. Wenn man ein Ideal ablöst vom Wirklichen, so stößt man das Wirkliche hinab, man verarmt es, man verleumdet es. "D a s S c h ö n e u m d e s S c h ö n e n w i l l e n", "d a s W a h r e u m d e s W a h r e n w i l l e n", "d a s G u t e u m d e s G u t e n w i l l e n" – das sind drei Formen des b ö s e n B l i c k s für das Wirkliche' (10[194] 12.572 f.).

from themselves. The *war* thus produced is what is essential: as a *means of separating* that *strengthens* the isolation ... (ibid.)[72]

By separating positive from negative values through false value-oppositions, the idealist power-complex seeks to separate itself from antagonistic complexes (*Widersacher*), and identifying with the former, strengthen itself in isolation.

> – *Art, knowledge, morality* are means: instead of recognising in them the purpose to enhance life, one has placed them in *opposition to life* [...] (ibid.)[73]

With regard to Kant's idea of eternal peace, this is the decisive point. *On the one hand*, Kant's idea is a perfect example of life-negating idealist warfare: through the (self-) annihilation of (the causes of future) war as the opposite of peace, an absolute claim is made for peace, whereby its very relation of opposition or antagonism with its opposite, war, is annihilated.[74] When viewed on the plane of immanence, the opposition 'war – peace' would then be in the service of a power-complex in decline: one reduced to self-preservation through defensive isolation. Nietzsche could well have the 'autonomous herd' in mind, and the modern democratic state, which he identifies with weakness (the inability to command) and 'the declining form of the state'.[75] In this case, Kant's ideal would be complicit for Nietzsche in the movement to secure modern democratic states in the face of their inevitable decline. *On the other hand*, the approximative reading of Kant's argument in ZeF suggests a completely different interpretation of the power-complex in question. In this case, Kant's idea of eternal peace – despite its exclusive opposition to war – would be a 'means' (*Mittel*) for 'the purpose to enhance life' (*die Absicht auf Steigerung des Lebens*) by acting as guide for a 'lasting and continually expanding league of states' (*sich immer ausbreitende Bund*: Zef VIII.357),

---

[72] '– "s c h ö n und h ä ß l i c h", "w a h r und f a l s c h", "g u t und b ö s e" – diese S c h e i d u n g – e n und A n t a g o n i s m e n verrathen Daseins – und Steigerungs-Bedingungen, nicht vom Menschen überhaupt, sondern von irgendwelchen festen und dauerhaften Complexen, welche ihre Widersacher von sich abtrennen. Der K r i e g, der damit geschaffen wird, ist das Wesentliche daran: als M i t t e l d e r A b s o n d e r u n g, die die Isolation v e r s t ä r k t ...' (10[194] 12.572 f.).

[73] '– K u n s t, E r k e n n t n i ß, M o r a l sind Mittel: statt die Absicht auf Steigerung des Lebens in ihnen zu erkennen, hat man sie zu einem G e g e n s a t z d e s L e b e n s in Bezug gebracht [...]' (10[194] 12.572 f.).

[74] 'In the case of "idealist oppositions" an "idealist war" is in play: Any given plus value aims at the elimination or "usurpation" of the minus value: the "evil ones" ought to disappear, the "good ones" alone ought to remain. The intention is, then, the quasi-amputation of the opposed pair: only the plus part ought to be left over, whereby of course the opposition as such is completely removed: in favour of the plus halves that alone remain' (Schank 1993 145).

[75] Already in MA 472 Nietzsche calls modern democracy 'the historical form of the decline [*Verfall*] of the state': 'The disdain, the decline [*Verfall*] and the death of the state, the unleashing of the private person (I avoid saying: of the individual) is the consequence of the democratic concept of the state; herein lies its mission.' This is repeated later in the *Nachlass* of 1884: 'Europe is a declining world. Democracy is the *decaying form* [*Verfalls-Form*] of the state' (26[434] 11.267) and the late preface to GT: 'Could it be that – in spite of all "modern ideas" and the prejudices of democratic taste – the victory of *optimism*, the now dominant *rationality*, the practical and theoretical *utilitarianism*, together with democracy itself, with which it coincides, – are a symptom of declining force, of approaching senescence, of physiological fatigue?' GT Versuch 4 (1.16 f.): Cf. JGB 203; GD Streifzüge 39; 9[29] 10.354; 34[146] 11.469; and Siemens (2009a 33).

to which individual states accede voluntarily. Of course, Kant would never accept that the idea of a moral and political whole, which pure practical Reason requires us to strive for as a duty, could be a mere means for the enhancement of a form of life. And for Nietzsche, an expanding power-complex under the sign of Kantian eternal peace would always need the resistance of (an)other complex(es), conceived as its opposite, and to cultivate belief in itself as a 'means of aggression' (*Aggressiv-Mittel*) by making exclusive claims to reason, virtue, 'the good cause' and 'victory for the sake of victory' against its opponent(s).[76]

With these caveats in mind, a final approximation can be hazarded to close the chapter. There is no reason why Nietzsche's life-affirmative and life-enhancing ideal of a multiplicity of diverse, more-or-less equal legal orders in equilibrium could not take the form of a 'continually expanding league of states', provided it was characterized not by concord, but by Kant's 'liveliest competition' of powers in equilibrium. For as we saw, Nietzsche writes:

> In truth a strong *antagonism* belongs to everything, to marriage friendship state **league of states** corporation scholarly associations religions, for something worthwhile [OR right: *etwas Rechtes*] to grow. Resisting is the form of *power* [*Kraft*]– in peace as in war [...] (11[303] 9.558; **HS**)

In favour of such an approximation, we should bear in mind that the equilibrium of more-or-less equal forces is the origin of law and justice for Nietzsche, so that the limited conflict of states would be productive of new legal orders (*etwas Rechtes*) to incorporate the voluntary accession of new states. And while Nietzsche's ideal would exclude equal rights as a protection against conflict and incursion, it would not exclude the aspirational attitude to equality opened in WS 29, coupled with a sensitivity to the injustice of those who fare worse or better than the standard of equality set by those with the highest standing. The limit of such an approximation does, however, remain: to give up on Reason's dream of an all-inclusive cosmopolitan legal order.

---

[76] The succeeding note to 10[194] on idealist warfare makes these points:
'*Consequence of struggle*: the one struggling seeks to
transform its opponent into its *opposite* [*Gegensatz*], – in
representation naturally
– it seeks to believe in itself to the degree that
it can have the courage of the "good cause" (as if it
were the *good cause*): as if reason, taste, virtue is being
fought by its opponent ...
– the belief that it needs, as the strongest
means of defence and aggression is a *belief in itself*,
which is capable of misunderstanding itself as belief in God
– never to think of the advantages and uses of victory,
but only ever victory for the sake of victory,
as "God's victory"-
– Every small community that finds itself in struggle (even
individuals) seeks to persuade itself: "*we have
good taste, good judgement and
virtue for us* ... Struggle forces this kind
of *exaggeration* in self-*assessment* ...' (10[195] 12.573).

3

Health, sex and sovereignty:
Nietzsche *contra* Kant on productive resistance

I Introduction

In this and the next chapter, I examine the notion of productive resistance (*Widerstand, Widerstreben*) in Nietzsche and Kant. An important element of Nietzsche's philosophy of conflict is to contest the Christian and post-Christian condemnation of conflict in favour of love, concord and (eternal) peace by exploring the productive potentials of conflict. That resistance plays an important role in his 'transvaluation' (*Umwertung*) of conflict and concord was already clear in the last chapter, when he writes: 'Resisting [*Das Widerstreben*] is the form of force – in peace as in war [...]' (11[303] 9.557). In a more polemical vein, he writes in AC 2:

> What is happiness? – The feeling that power *grows*, that a resistance is overcome. *Not* contentment, but more power; *not* peace at all, but war [...]

> Was ist Glück? – Das Gefühl davon, dass die Macht w ä c h s t, dass ein Widerstand überwunden wird.
> N i c h t Zufriedenheit, sondern mehr Macht; n i c h t Friede überhaupt, sondern Krieg [...]

Kant's motivations could not, of course, be further from Nietzsche's, yet the constructive potentials of conflict are no less important for his philosophy of conflict. For both thinkers, I contend, a genuinely constructive concept of conflict requires that resistance work not just as an inhibitor that reduces freedom, creativity and power, but as a stimulant (*Reiz, Stimulus*) for a given activity, capacity or potential to create new orders, new settlements, new possibilities of existence. The main question of these two chapters is, then: *What does it take to think resistance as productive, enabling, empowering – as a stimulant?*

The chapter begins (§II) with an analysis of the meanings of 'resistance' in Nietzsche's ontology of power with a view towards isolating and describing his conception of productive resistance. Drawing on descriptions of the Dionysian and the sexual act, I argue that Nietzsche formulates an *active concept of resistance* as the thought that the *hindrance (Hemmnis) of my power by a resistance and the pain it engenders can give me the feeling (not of obstruction or oppression, but) of power-pleasure.* With this notion in mind, I turn in Sections III and IV to comparative analyses of resistance in Nietzsche and Kant. Nietzsche's account of coitus as a 'play of resistance and victory' invites comparison with Kant's account of health in the *Anthropology* as a 'continual play of *antagonism*' between 'the feeling of advancement' and the 'hindrance of life'. Despite proximities between them, I argue that Kant's claim that the pain of resistance acts as the 'spur to activity' falls short of a productive notion of resistance, because it is locked in real opposition to the pleasure of empowerment or the feeling of the advancement of life. In Section IV, turn to the role of resistance in the context of freedom or sovereignty. For Kant, I focus on the account of 'respect for the law' (*Achtung für's Gesetz*) in the second *Critique* and the 'feeling of elevation' that motivates moral action, based on the 'judgement of reason' that the moral law has overcome the resistance of our sensible inclinations and thereby advanced the causality of freedom. This is compared to the figure of the sovereign individual in GM II 2, whose feeling of freedom derives from his judgement that, in redeeming his promise, he has overcome resistances both within and without. In both cases, an equivalence is made *between the overcoming of resistance, and the consciousness or advancement of freedom*. This proximity is, however, complicated in the *Nachlass*, where this judgement is exposed as illusory, a misinterpretation of the body that condenses infinitely complex processes and tensions into a unitary act of will. But Nietzsche's response is not to reject the moral language of law and freedom; instead, he pleads for naturalistic accounts, to make them less illusory through a 'more substantial' interpretation of the physiology of agency (4[216] 9). In the next chapter, I consider one such attempt in Nietzsche's socio-physiology of sovereignty.

II Resistance in Nietzsche

Like so many of key terms in Nietzsche's vocabulary, 'resistance' (*Widerstand* and related terms[1]) has a range of different meanings and uses. The basic and recurrent meaning of 'resistance' (its 'Grundbedeutung'), following normal usage, is: as an obstacle, impediment, hindrance (*Hemmung, Hemmniss, Hindernis*) to something, usually an activity or impulse. But this can carry positive-normative or negative-critical connotations for Nietzsche, depending on the conditions under which resistance is encountered or exercised, and/or on the consequences it has for the activity or initiative in question. From the early 1880s, when he begins to develop his ontology of power (often under the rubric of will to power), resistance is an indispensable descriptive (relational) term, but is also used affirmatively: to affirm power entails that one affirms (the) resistance (upon which power-relations depend). Somewhat more surprising are his critical uses of 'resistance'.[2] For the argument of this chapter, only one

---

[1] 'Widerstehen', 'Widerstandskraft', 'Widerstandsgefühl', 'Widerstands-Unfähigkeit', 'Widerstreben', 'Widersacher' among others.
[2] For a survey of his critical uses and more detailed account of Nietzsche's use of 'resistance', see Siemens (2019b).

is important: resistance is part of the false phenomenology of 'free will' that trades on a misinterpretation of the actual physiology of human agency.

II.1 Affirmative senses of resistance

In the late *Nachlass* (1888) there is a note, which, in reflecting on the 'artist's metaphysics' of his first work, *Die Geburt der Tragödie*, describes some key aspects of his late ontology of power:

> [A] Here the will to semblance, to illusion, to deception, to becoming and change counts as deeper and more originary, more 'metaphysical' than the will to truth, to reality, to being: – the latter is itself just a form of the will to illusion. [B] Likewise pleasure counts as more originary that pain: pain is just conditioned as a consequence of the will to pleasure (of the will to becoming, growth, form-giving, consequently to overpowering, to resistance, to war, to destruction) [C] A highest state of the affirmation of existence is conceived, in which even pain, every kind of pain is eternally included as a means of intensification: the *tragic-Dionysian* state. (14[24] 13.229)[3]

In these lines, three senses of resistance can be distinguished.

1. The first line [A] reiterates in the idiom of willing the three moves against the metaphysics of being and substance ontology that inform Nietzsche's counter-ontology of becoming (see pp. 42–4). Being is neither presupposed (as more real) by becoming, nor is it opposed to becoming, as it is in traditional metaphysics. Instead, Nietzsche asserts the primacy of becoming over being – of 'the will to semblance, to illusion, to deception, to becoming and change' over 'the will to truth, to reality, to being' – and the derivative, lesser reality of being – as 'just a form of the will to illusion'. In Nietzsche's ontology, being is dynamized and pluralized as that which emerges from the essential or characteristic tendency of becoming, as an incessant, multiple fixing or positing (*Feststellen, Fest-setzen*) of being. The reality of becoming or occurrence consists not of beings or substances (self-supporting, unified and enduring entities), but of *relations among forces or powers without substance*. In Nietzsche's relational concept power, activity is the only quality of power, the activity of increasing power. But this only

---

[3] '[A] Der Wille zum Schein, zur Illusion, zur Täuschung, zum Werden und Wechseln gilt hier als tiefer und ursprünglicher "metaphysischer" als der Wille zur Wahrheit, zur Wirklichkeit zum Sein: – letzterer ist selbst bloß eine Form des Willens zur Illusion. [B] Ebenso gilt die Lust als ursprünglicher als der Schmerz: der Schmerz ist nur bedingt als eine Folge des Willens zur Lust (des Willens zum Werden, Wachsen, Gestalten, folglich zur Überwältigung, zum Widerstand, zum Krieg, zur Zerstörung) [C] Es wird ein höchster Zustand der Daseins-Bejahung concipirt, in dem sogar der Schmerz, jede Art von Schmerz als Mittel der Steigerung ewig einbegriffen ist: der t r a g i s c h - d i o n y s i s c h e Zustand' (14[24], 13.229).

becomes actual or effective as an overpowering in relation to the resistance of counter-powers:

> The degree of resistance and the degree of power-over – that is what it is about in all occurrence
>
> Der Grad von Widerstand und der Grad von Übermacht – darum handelt <es> sich bei allem Geschehen (14[79] 13.257)

This gives us the *first meaning of resistance* in Nietzsche's philosophy of conflict: resistance or *Widerstand* is the correlate of his relational concept of power or force. It is implied in the analytic structure of Nietzsche's concept of power or force, so that he can write: 'Resisting is the form of force – in peace as in war […]' (*Das Widerstreben ist die Form der Kraft – im Frieden wie im Kriege*: 11[303] 9.557)

2. But if power as the activity of overpowering can only be exercised in relation to resistance, then overpowering must itself involve resistance: resisting the resistance it encounters so as to overpower it. In the second line of the note [B], resistance appears as the will 'to overpowering, to resistance, to war, to destruction', and Nietzsche derives the will to resistance and the pain of resisting from the primary principle of reality: 'the will to becoming, to growth, to pleasure' ('Wille zum Werden, zum Wachsen, zur Lust'): because becoming (*Werden*), in the form of growth (*Wachsen*) necessarily encounters (cannot be conceived without) resistance, the will to growth implies – 'as its consequence' (*folglich*) – the will to resistance needed to overcome these resistances. In this thought, resistance occurs in two forms: (1) as the correlate of Nietzsche's dynamic-relational concept of power: the activity of increasing power (*Wachsen*) can only be exercised (and thought) in relation to resistance(s). But resistance also occurs as (2) the will to resist the resistance of the counter-power(s), to react so as to overcome them for the sake of growth and intensification (*Wachsen, Steigerung*). This is the *second meaning of resistance*: the resistance (2) needed to overpower the resistance (1) encountered by power as activity, where the will to resistance (2) is linked with *pain* and is *derivative* of the primary will to becoming, to growth to pleasure, as its consequence. Conflict and resistance are indeed necessary, but only 'as a consequence' of the primary principle of occurrence or becoming, and their derivative, conditioned status in this line intimates Nietzsche's more critical views on resistance. Indeed, as we will see in Chapter 4, Nietzsche's critique of resistance disconnects active power from resistance altogether and leads him to advance forms of non-resistance.

3. The third line of the note [C] gives us the third and crucial meaning of resistance in Nietzsche's philosophy of conflict: resistance as *stimulant*. Here Nietzsche mobilizes the primacy of (the will to) pleasure over pain (the second line [B] of the note) against Schopenhauerian life-negation: against his use of pain and suffering as an argument against life, Nietzsche integrates pain *within* life, as part of its intrinsic dynamic of growth or intensification (*Steigerung*) of power and pleasure. Indeed, it is in the highest form of life-affirmation, 'the *tragic-Dionysian* state', that pain – pain of *every kind* – is intrinsic, as a 'means of intensification' (*Steigerung*). In other words, in this state, resistance and the concomitant pain of resistance do not reduce power, inhibit desire

or pleasure; they act as a means or *stimulant* for the intensification of power-pleasure. Hence, to affirm life as power-pleasure maximally also means to affirm the resistance-pain that acts as the stimulant of life.

A related, more tangible example of this is the sexual act, which Nietzsche describes as follows:

> There are even cases where a kind of pleasure is conditioned by a certain *rhythmic sequence* of small unpleasure-stimuli: a very rapid growth of the feeling of power, of pleasure is thereby reached. This is the case e.g. with tickling, also with sexual tickling in the act of coitus: we see in this form unpleasure acting as an ingredient of pleasure. It seems a small hindrance that is overcome and upon which again a small hindrance immediately follows, which is again overcome – this play of resistance and victory arouses that total-feeling of overflowing excessive power, which makes up the essence of pleasure, to the strongest degree. – (14[173] 13.358)[4]

The point of Nietzsche's account of coitus is to break with an oppositional model of pleasure-pain by showing how pain (resistance) can be an ingredient or stimulant of pleasure (empowerment). Resistance-pain, far from being opposed to the feeling of power-pleasure as the feeling of impotence or loss of power, acts as a 'condition' or 'ingredient' of sexual pleasure; indeed, as a *stimulant* that arouses the pleasure of 'overflowing power' to the maximum. The notion of resistance as stimulant is made explicit and generalized in the subsequent note (14[174] 13.360 ff.), where Nietzsche describes unpleasure – identified with the hindering (*Hemmung*) of power by resistance – as 'a normal fact [*Faktum*], the normal ingredient in every organic occurrence':

> It is so little the case that unpleasure necessarily has a *reduction of our feeling of power* as its consequence that, in average cases, it works precisely as a stimulus of the feeling of power, – the hindrance is the *stimulus* of this will to power. (14[174] 13.361)[5]

Nietzsche goes on to distinguish two forms of unpleasure, depending on the consequences for a given form of life of the hindrance or restriction (*Hemmniss*) of its power through the encounter with resistance. In one case, the unpleasure felt in the restriction of its power has an actual loss of power and a feeling of impotence as its

---

[4] 'Es giebt sogar Fälle, wo eine Art Lust bedingt ist durch eine gewisse r h y t h m i s c h e A b f o l g e kleiner Unlust-Reize: damit wird ein sehr schnelles Anwachsen des Machtgefühls, des Lustgefühls erreicht. Dies ist der Fall z.B. beim Kitzel, auch beim geschlechtlichen Kitzel im Akt des coitus: wir sehen dergestalt die Unlust als Ingredienz der Lust thätig. Es scheint, eine kleine Hemmung, die überwunden wird und der sofort wieder eine kleine Hemmung folgt, die wieder überwunden wird – dieses Spiel von Widerstand und Sieg regt jenes Gesammtgefühl von überschüssiger überflüssiger Macht am stärksten an, das das Wesen der Lust ausmacht. –'.
[5] 'Die Unlust hat also so wenig nothwendig eine V e r m i n d e r u n g u n s e r e s M a c h t g e f ü h l s zur Folge, daß, in durchschnittlichen Fällen, sie gerade als Reiz auf dieses Machtgefühl wirkt, – das Hemmniß ist der S t i m u l u s dieses Willens zur Macht.'

consequence; unable to resist the 'excessive stimulation' (*übermässige Reizung*) exerted by the resistance encountered, it squanders energy uselessly (*Vergeudung*) resulting in 'a deep reduction [*Verminderung*] and depression [*Herabstimmung*] of the will to power, a measurable loss of strength'. In this case, 'resistance' signifies *energetic loss* or *disempowerment*. In the other case, the unpleasure of restriction (*Hemmniss*) acts as a 'stimulus' ('Reiz', 'Reizmittel') for the intensification or strengthening (*Verstärkung*) of power. Resistance is therefore sought out and challenged (*Herausforderung des Widerstehenden*), for the intensification of power that comes from resisting and overcoming it:

> Every victory, every feeling of pleasure, every occurrence presupposes a resistance that has been overcome.
>
> [J]eder Sieg, jedes Lustgefühl, jedes Geschehen setzt einen überwundenen Widerstand voraus. (14[174] 13.360)

Here 'resistance' signifies, not disempowerment but a *source of power, a stimulant*. The psychologists, Nietzsche argues, have mistaken the first kind of unpleasure, that of 'exhaustion' (*Erschöpfung*), for *all* unpleasure and have neglected unpleasure as stimulant. But what, then, makes for these different kinds of unpleasure?

In the background of Nietzsche's distinction is a two-fold differential. (1) The first is a *power-differential*. Forms of life that lack the power to react and overcome the restriction of their power by an overwhelming or excessive resistance (Nietzsche writes of 'übermässige Reizung') experience and conceive resistance as loss of power, as disempowering. According to Nietzsche, this incapacity to resist (*Die Unfähigkeit zu Widerstand*) is a sign of exhaustion (*Erschöpfung*) and typical of décadence – the signature illness of modernity, as well as the congenital defect of philosophers and psychologists! On the other side are forms of life with the power or capacity to resist and overcome the resistance(s) they seek out, and for them resistance is empowering (i.e. the term 'resistance' signifies a source of power). (2) The second differential behind the distinct kinds of unpleasure is that between *active and reactive forms of life*. Where 'resistance' signifies *disempowerment*, it is described from the standpoint of one who has *reacted* to a prior overwhelming resistance, failed to resist it and suffered a loss of power. Where 'resistance' signifies a *source of power*, it is described from the standpoint of one who *will react* to a resistance, but it is a resistance that was *actively* sought out in the first place (precisely as a source of power). In this light, we can distinguish *active* from *reactive meanings* of 'resistance', depending on the position from which it is uttered: an *active position of strength or power* on one side (resistance = a source of power/empowering), or a *reactive position of weakness or lack of power* vis-à-vis the resistance (resistance = loss of power/disempowering).

Central to Nietzsche's active concept of resistance is the thought that *the actual hindrance (Hemmnis) of my power by a resistance and the pain it engenders can give me the feeling (not of obstruction or limitation, but) of power-pleasure*. The absence of this thought among psychologists expresses their *reactive* standpoint, which begins to think, not from excess and the activity of increasing power-pleasure, but from a lack of power and from unpleasure – a No! to the outside. From this standpoint it is impossible to break through the meaning of resistance as *disempowering* to its active meaning as a *source of power-pleasure*, as a stimulant. Once again, we are confronted with the question as to whether Kant's philosophy of conflict is reactive. Is Nietzsche right that pain has been systematically confused with one kind of the pain, the pain of impotence, to the neglect of resistance-pain as stimulant? Does this go for Kant? Does Kant think resistance from a *reactive* standpoint, from a lack of power and unpleasure – a No! to the outside? Or is he able to break through the meaning of resistance as *disempowering* to its active meaning as a *source of power-pleasure*? Does he, in other words, express the thought that the *actual hindrance* (*Hemmnis*) of my power by a resistance can give me the *feeling* (not of hindrance, but) *of power-pleasure*?

III Nietzsche vs. Kant on productive resistance

These questions can be put to a passage on health from the *Anthropology* (book II: Of sensible pleasure):

> Enjoyment is the feeling of the advancement of life; pain is that of a hindrance of life. But (animal) life, as physicians also have already noted, is a continuous play of *the antagonism of both*.
> Therefore pain must *always precede every enjoyment*; pain is always first. For what else would follow from a continuous advancement of the vital force, which cannot be intensified above a certain degree anyway, but a rapid death from joy?
> Also, *no enjoyment can immediately follow another*; rather, between one and another pain must occur. Small inhibitions of the vital force mixed in with advancements of it constitute the state of health that we erroneously consider to be a continuously felt well-being; when in fact it consists only of intermittent pleasant feelings that follow one another (with pain always intervening between them). Pain is the spur of activity, and in this, above all, we feel our life; without pain lifelessness would set in. (Anth VII:231)[6]

---

[6] 'Vergnügen ist das Gefühl der Beförderung; Schmerz das einer Hinderniß des Lebens. Leben aber (des Thiers) ist, wie auch schon die Ärzte angemerkt haben, ein continuirliches Spiel des A n t a g o n i s m u s   v o n   b e i d e n.
  Also muß v o r j e d e m V e r g n ü g e n d e r S c h m e r z v o r h e r g e h e n; der Schmerz ist immer das erste. Denn was würde aus einer continuirlichen Beförderung der Lebenskraft, die über einen gewissen Grad sich doch nicht steigern läßt, anders folgen als ein schneller Tod vor Freude?
  A u c h k a n n k e i n V e r g n ü g e n u n m i t t e l b a r a u f d a s a n d e r e f o l g e n; sondern zwischen einem und dem anderen muß sich der Schmerz einfinden. Es sind kleine Hemmungen der Lebenskraft mit dazwischen gemengten Beförderungen derselben, welche den Zustand der Gesundheit ausmachen, den wir irrigerweise für ein continuirlich gefühltes Wohlbefinden halten; da er doch nur aus ruckweise (mit immer dazwischen eintretendem Schmerz) einander folgenden angenehmen Gefühlen besteht. Der Schmerz ist der Stachel der Thätigkeit, und in dieser fühlen wir allererst unser Leben; ohne diesen würde Leblosigkeit eintreten.'

In the first line Kant draws on the basic meaning of 'resistance' (*Grundbedeutung*) in normal usage: as an obstacle, impediment, hindrance (*Hemmung, Hemmniss, Hindernis*). And by identifying pain with the feeling of hindrance (*Hindernis*), he appeals to the standard experience of resistance as an obstacle that *restricts, inhibits or disempowers* us. The last line, by contrast, identifies the pain of resistance as a *spur* (*Stachel*) to activity in which we first feel our life. Here, then, is the productive notion of resistance. It is crucial for Kant's account of health as the continual alternation of the feeling of power or the advancement of life (*Beförderung des Lebens*), and the feeling of resistance (*Hemmung*) or disempowerment; or as a continual antagonism between pleasure and pain. For in this account, Kant privileges pain over pleasure: pain must come first, since a continual enhancement (*Steigerung*) or advancement of life without a prior resistance to overcome would lead only to a rapid death out of joy (*Tod der Freude*)! Pain is the principle of life, not pleasure, since all activity begins with the pain of resistance, and without pain there would be lifelessness (*Leblosigkeit*).

Kant's 'continuous play of the *antagonism*' (*continuirliches Spiel des A n t a g o n i s m u s*) between the feeling of advancement (*Gefühl der Beförderung*) and the hindrance of life (*Hinderniß des Lebens*) brings to mind Nietzsche's 'play of resistance and victory' (*Spiel von Widerstand und Sieg*) in the passage on coitus considered above, when he writes:

> It seems a small hindrance that is overcome and upon which again a small hindrance immediately follows, which is again overcome – this play of resistance and victory arouses that total-feeling of overflowing excessive power, which makes up the essence of pleasure, to the strongest degree. – (14[173] 13.358)[7]

At first sight, these passages bear striking similarities. If we consider the identification of pain with the feeling of hindrance (*Hindernis*) in the first line, and the last line on pain as a spur (*Stachel*) to activity in which we feel our life, the passage seems to span the two meanings of 'resistance' we have seen in Nietzsche: resistance as disempowering, and productive resistance as a stimulant for the intensification of power-pleasure – and thereby to refute Nietzsche's claim about the philosophers congenital blindness to the empowering qualities of pain. In the same vein, where Kant says that 'pain must *always precede every enjoyment*', Nietzsche says that 'every feeling of pleasure, every occurrence presupposes a resistance that has been overcome' (14[174] 13.360). And finally, Kant's talk of the alternation of 'small hindrances [*Hemmungen*] of the vital force mixed in with advancements of it' is uncannily close to the 'small hindrance [*Hemmung*] that is overcome and upon which again a small hindrance immediately follows, which is again overcome' in Nietzsche's 'play of resistance and victory'. However, these affinities should not blind us to the profound differences between them.

Whereas Kant's alternation of hindrance and advancement (or pain-and-pleasure) serves to describe a state (*Zustand*) of health, Nietzsche's play of resistance and victory

---

[7] 'Es scheint, eine kleine Hemmung, die überwunden wird und der sofort wieder eine kleine Hemmung folgt, die wieder überwunden wird – dieses Spiel von Widerstand und Sieg regt jenes Gesammtgefühl von überschüssiger überflüssiger Macht am stärksten an, das das Wesen der Lust ausmacht. –.'

describes a process of intensification (*Steigerung*), culminating in an orgasmic explosion of pleasure-power. As we saw, Nietzsche's text breaks with an oppositional model of pleasure and pain by showing how pain (resistance) can be an ingredient or stimulant of pleasure (empowerment). In Kant's account, pleasure and pain are opposed from start, as the feeling of the advancement of life and the feeling of the hindrance of life, and this opposition seems unaffected by the closing remark: when pain is described as the spur of activity, the question of pleasure is passed over in silence. The Nietzschean thought that the *actual hindrance* (*Hemmnis*) of my power by a resistance and the pain it engenders can give me the *feeling* (not of hindrance, but) *of power-pleasure* is absent in Kant, where *pain* is simply equated with *the feeling of hindrance*. How Kant gets from this meaning of resistance-pain to productive resistance is unexplained in the text.

But the most striking difference between them concerns the notion of the intensification (*Steigerung*) of life or power. For Nietzsche, as we saw in the opening text (14[24] 13; p. 127), the dynamic of growth or intensification is intrinsic to life: the will to growth and pleasure is the primary principle of reality or life. For Kant, by contrast, pain must come first, both practically and logically; for a continual intensification (*Steigerung*) or advancement of life without a prior resistance to overcome and without intermittent feelings of pain would lead only to a rapid death from joy (*Tod der Freude*).[8] Pain, not pleasure, is the principle of life: 'Pain is the spur of activity (*Stachel der Tätigkeit*), and in this, above all, we feel our life; without pain lifelessness (*Leblosigkeit*) would set in.'

From Nietzsche's point of view this expresses a typically *reactive* standpoint, which begins to think, not from the activity of increasing power, but from a No! to the outside, a hindrance and unpleasure. In specific it is captive to a *reactive concept of power*, which is oriented towards self-preservation (i.e. *not* 'lifelessness', *not* 'death from joy') in the face of a prior threat from the outside, to which it reacts. Action is therefore reaction, since prior to resistance there is only inactivity, rather than activity (the activity of increasing power), which Nietzsche takes as his starting point. As a consequence, it is unable to break through the meaning of resistance as *disempowering* to the active meaning as a *source of power*. From Kant's point of view, on the other hand, it is logically and practically incoherent to start out from intensification and pleasure as does Nietzsche. But Kant's view, I want to suggest, rests on presuppositions that Nietzsche's concept of power throws into question.

Kant's account of enjoyment and pain in the context of health is actually one of three different explanations of pain and pleasure in §60 of the *Anthropologie*, which presents considerable interpretative difficulties. To begin with (VII.230), Kant takes up the notion of real opposition from NG, where, as we saw, pleasure and pain serve to exemplify the relation of real opposition with the claim that unpleasure (*Unlust*) is a positive feeling (*Empfindung*) which negates pleasure through privation, *Beraubung* or *Aufhebung* (*nihil privativum*), and is not the logical negation or mere absence (*nihil negativum*) of pleasure (see p. 27). Somewhat confusingly, this distinction between real

---

[8] What to us sounds like a joke is not for Kant or contemporaries such as Villaume or Zückert, who took death from excessive laughter seriously and refer to authors from antiquity such as Pliny and Gellius. See Brandt (1999 341).

and logical negation is blurred in Anth §60, when Kant writes that 'one is opposed to the other **not merely** as *opposite* [G e g e n t h e i l] *(contradictorie s. logice oppositum)*, but **also** as *counterpart* [W i d e r s p i e l] *(contrarie s. realiter oppositum)*' (**HS**).⁹ It's hard to see how unpleasure can be both the absence of pleasure (logical opposite) and a positive feeling that cancels pleasure (real opposite). In the second explanation (VII.231), Kant describes the relation of pleasure and pain from the subjective perspective of consciousness (*Bewußtsein, Gemüt*). Here, Kant argues, enjoyment cannot be a positive increase of pleasure (in anticipation of something agreeable); instead, 'enjoyment is nothing other than the ending of a pain and something negative'.¹⁰ In this case, pleasure is felt as the mere absence of pain, which comes first, as in the third explanation in the passage on health cited above (VII.231/27). In these cases, I suggest, Kant privileges pain because, in line with the tradition since Plato, he works with a negative concept of desire and pleasure: desire is the absence of what is desired, pleasure is the absence of pain (the pain of desire). Consequently the satisfaction of desire is nothing positive, but the end of desire, and pleasure is no more than the elimination of pain. This same logic drives the feeling of power or the advancement of life in Kant: it can only be understood as the absence of the feeling of hindrance or disempowerment. The continual *Steigerung* of the feeling of power, where this means: the absence of pain and impotence, is therefore unthinkable as a form of life, and can only signify the end of life: death or *Leblosigkeit*.

For Nietzsche, (the opening text, line [B]), pleasure is primary and positive, as the feeling that accompanies the will to power, and pain is secondary as a consequence of 'the will to pleasure (the will to Becoming, growth, form-giving, consequently to overpowering, to resistance, to war, to destruction)' (14[24] 13). Resistance, hindrance and pain are by no means absent; they are essential to *Steigerung*. As we saw, the succession of resistance and overcoming or advancement is the fastest route to the 'total-feeling of excessive overflowing power that makes up the essence of pleasure' (14[173] 13). Resistance and pain are presupposed for *Steigerung*, but they are not the presuppositions for negative concepts of pleasure and power. Against Kant and the philosophical tradition, Nietzsche works with excess as the principle of life and

---

⁹ 'V e r g n ü g e n ist eine Lust durch den Sinn, und was diesen belustigt, heißt a n g e n e h m. S c h m e r z ist die Unlust durch den Sinn, und was jenen hervorbringt, ist u n a n g e n e h m. – Sie sind einander nicht wie Erwerb und Mangel (+ und 0), sondern wie Erwerb und Verlust (+ und -), d.i. eines dem anderen nicht blos als G e g e n t h e i l (*contradictorie s. logice oppositum*), sondern auch als W i d e r s p i e l (*contrarie s. realiter oppositum*) entgegengesetzt.'
   'They are opposed to each other not as profit and lack of profit (+ and o), but as profit and loss.
¹⁰ 'Es frägt sich nun: ob das Bewußtsein des V e r l a s s e n s des gegenwärtigen Zustandes, oder ob der Prospect des E i n t r e t e n s in einen künftigen in uns die Empfindung des Vergnügens erwecke. Im ersten Fall ist das Vergnügen nichts anders als Aufhebung eines Schmerzes und etwas Negatives; im zweiten würde es Voremfindung einer Annehmlichkeit, also Vermehrung des Zustandes der Lust, mithin etwas Positives sein. Es läßt sich aber auch schon zum Voraus errathen, daß das erstere allein statt finden werde; denn die Zeit schleppt uns vom gegenwärtigen zum künftigen (nicht umgekehrt), und daß wir zuerst genöthigt werden aus dem gegenwärtigen herauszugehen, unbestimmt in welchen anderen wir treten werden, nur so daß er doch ein anderer ist, das kann allein die Ursache des angenehmen Gefühls sein' (Anth VII.231/13f.).

the presupposition of desire (*Rausch*, the Dionysian). But life, *as power*, can only be thought in relation to the resistance of other powers, as a seeking out of resistance with its concomitant pain. For Nietzsche, then, we can say: excess is the *ontological* presupposition for thinking life, desire, power; and pain is the *logical* presupposition for thinking life as power. In these terms it becomes possible, *pace* Kant, to think the ideal of health as continual *Steigerung*, not without pain, but in spite of pain or resistance. And in this process, the concept of resistance works not simply as a hindrance to (the feeling of) life and power, but as a stimulant for the advancement of life.

Ironically, it is the relation of real (and logical) opposition, at the heart of Kant's philosophy of conflict, that is the problem. From a Nietzschean perspective, the opposition between pleasure and pain is what prevents him from breaking through the reactive meaning of 'resistance' as disempowering, lack, pain to its active meaning as a stimulant or source of power, since this turns precisely on overcoming the oppositional relation in the thought that *the actual hindrance (Hemmnis) of my power by a resistance and the pain it engenders can give me the feeling (not of obstruction or impotence, but) of power-pleasure*. In note 14[174] 13, where Nietzsche distinguishes the two kinds of unpleasure in relation to resistance, he tells us something about the conditions that divide them. Where resistance-pain is conceived as disempowering, as it is by Kant, it is described from the standpoint of one who has reacted, but lacked the power to overcome an excessive resistance, thereby squandering energy uselessly, resulting in energetic loss (*Vergeudung*) and a depression (*Herabstimmung*) of the will to power. This is what Nietzsche calls the unpleasure of exhaustion (*Erschöpfung*), and it raises the question whether Kant's attempt to describe pain as a stimulant or 'spur' to activity, by fixing pain in a relation of opposition to negative pleasure, is not in the end an expression of pain as exhaustion.

One cannot help noticing how Kant's account of health is beset on both sides by death or lifelessness: without pain as the spur of activity, 'lifelessness would set in', and without painful episodes to punctuate the pleasures of advancing the life force, a 'rapid death of joy' would follow from continuous intensification. Kant does not, of course, advocate a death of joy or the lifelessness of inactivity; his concern is with health, understood within his philosophy of conflict as the 'play of the *antagonism*' (*continuirliches Spiel des A n t a g o n i s m u s*) between the feeling of advancement and the hindrance of the life force. But one cannot help wondering about the proximity of death to Kantian health. Health is predicated on *inactivity*, from which we are stirred by the 'spur' of pain. In Chapter 2 we encountered inactivity in his political-historical texts as hypothetical primordial state of passivity and indolence, from which we were awakened by conflict (pp. 84–6). Why has this now been radicalized from a state of indolence to lifelessness or death? In the political-historical texts, as we saw Kant rejects the longing for this state of indolence as a dream of false peace. But one cannot help wondering what a *positive* sense of pleasure would look like in his account of health, what he calls a 'presentiment' (*Vorgefühl*) or 'prospect' of joy to come (Anth VII. 231/12,18) – if not an end to the exhausting 'play of *antagonism*' between life-advancement and -hindrance. How different would this be from the idea of pleasure (*Lust*) Nietzsche associates with the condition of exhaustion: the pleasure of 'falling asleep' (*Einschlafen*), the wish for 'peace, limb-stretching, peace, tranquillity' typical of 'nihilistic religions and philosophies' (14[17413.361f.)?[11] The ambiguity of Kant's frictionless ideal of eternal peace was noted at the end of the previous chapter – as a nihilistic ideal that condemns life-as-conflict, or as an instrument for an expanding, life-enhancing league of states in limited conflict. This ambiguity is also alive in Kant's account of health.

The tremendous weight given to pain in Anth §60, as the condition for life and health, is subject to a further Nietzschean objection. In the *Nachlass* of early 1883, he takes up Kant's reference to the physiologist Pietro Verri (Anth VII.232) and writes:

> Kant says: I endorse with complete conviction these sentences
> by Count Verri (1781 sull'indole del piacere e del dolore)
>   il solo principio motore dell'uomo è il dolore. Il dolore
> precede ogni piacere
>   il piacere non è un essere positivo. (7[233] 10.314)[12]

So Nietzsche knew Kant's position on negative pleasure and his source in Pietro Verri, an economist and philosopher of the eighteenth century. Its similarity to Schopenhauer's view will not have escaped him. Nietzsche's source is a book (in his library) by Léon Dumont *Vergnügen und Schmerz. Zur Lehre von Gefühlen* (1876), which he excerpted in notes 7[233]–7[236] in this notebook.[13] The passage in Dumont, from which these excerpts were taken, includes the entire passage on health from the Anth §60 (partly quoted by Nietzsche in note 7[234] 10.314), so Nietzsche will have known it. We get no indications of Nietzsche's position on these views in the notebook, but the same passage in Dumont includes his view that the primacy of pain combined with the negative concept of pleasure can only lead to a life-negating attitude, so familiar to Nietzsche from Schopenhauer.[14] Perhaps this is one reason why, by early 1888, he rejects this concept of pain and pleasure unequivocally: '[…] one does *not* react to pain: unpleasure is not a "cause" of actions, pain itself is a

---

[11] 'Die Lust welche im Zustande der Erschöpfung allein noch empfunden wird, ist das Einschlafen; die Lust im anderen Fall ist der Sieg …

Die große Verwechslung der Psychologen bestand darin, daß sie diese beiden L u s t a r t e n die des E i n s c h l a f e n s und die des S i e g e s nicht auseinanderhielten

die Erschöpften wollen Ruhe, Gliederausstrecken, Frieden, Stille –
es ist das G l ü c k der nihilistischen Religionen und Philosophien […]' (14[174] 13.361 f.).

[12] 'Kant sagt: diese Sätze des Grafen Verri (1781 sull'indole del piacere e del dolore) unterschreibe ich mit voller Überzeugung
  il solo principio motore dell'uomo è il dolore. Il dolore
precede ogni piacere
  il piacere non è un essere positivo.'

[13] See Berti (1997 580).

[14] '[…] dass das Leben uns unter der hassenswerthesten Form erscheinen muss, und dass alle unsere Bemühungen dahin zielen müssten, es selbst zu unterdrücken' KGW VII 4/1.184.

reaction [...]' (14[173] 13.360).[15] With these words, Nietzsche directly contradicts the closing line of Kant's account of health on pain as the cause or 'spur of activity'. They are from the note in which Nietzsche takes issue with the false opposition between pleasure and pain (14[173] 13.358; p. 129)[16] by arguing that they are qualitatively distinct (different physiological processes) and can even converge – as in the act of coitus, when the pain of resistance is an ingredient in pleasure. This argument is part of a broader assault on Enlightenment moral psychology,[17] made explicit in the succeeding note (14[174] 13), in which pleasure and pain are displaced from the motivational or causal picture of agency and reduced to being mere 'consequences' (*Folgen*) or 'accompanying phenomena' (*Begleiterscheinungen*) of the will to power.[18] In Nietzsche's relational concept of powers, pleasure is the feeling of more-power-than ('a *plus-feeling* of power') and is normally accompanied by pain, as a feeling of hindrance, because power needs, and seeks out, resistance for the feeling of more-power-than. Pain is therefore *not* avoided, but 'a normal fact [*Faktum*], the normal ingredient in every organic occurrence'.[19] But nor is it the *cause* of any action or reaction (*Gegenbewegung*):

---

[15] 'Man reagirt, nochmals gesagt, n i c h t auf den Schmerz: die Unlust ist keine "Ursache" von Handlungen, der Schmerz selbst ist eine Reaktion, die Gegenbewegung ist eine andere und f r ü h e r e Reaktion [...]'.

[16] Note 14[173] 13.358 begins with the words: 'Pain is something other than pleasure, – I mean, it is *not* the opposite [of pleasure].' ('Der Schmerz ist etwas Anderes als die Lust, – ich will sagen, er ist n i c h t deren Gegentheil'). And further on: 'Pleasure and pain are, then, not the reverse of one another.' ('Lust und Schmerz sind eben nichts Umgekehrtes.') In the opening line, Nietzsche uses the same word as Kant in Anth §60, when he introduces the real opposition between pleasure and pain: Gegentheil (Kant: 'one is opposed to the other not merely *as opposite* [G e g e n t h e i l] (*contradictorie s. logice oppositum*), but also as *counterpart* [W i d e r s p i e l] (*contrarie s. realiter oppositum*)': see note 9 above). This leads Wahrig-Schmidt (1988 462) to suggest that they agree on the relation of real opposition between pleasure and pain, but I disagree with her, since (1) Kant's statement also allows for a logical relation between them, as argued above (p. 133f.), and (2) Nietzsche does not share Kant's negative concept of pleasure.

[17] See, e.g., 'what nature teaches us' in Descartes's Meditation VI: 'Further I was sensible that this body was placed amidst many others, from which it was capable of being affected in many different ways, beneficial and hurtful, and I remarked that a certain feeling of pleasure accompanied those that were beneficial, and pain those which were harmful [...] My nature, then, in this limited sense, does indeed teach me to avoid what induces a feeling of pain and to seek out what induces feelings of pleasure, and so on.' Cf. Kant's Anth VII.231: 'One can also explain these feelings by means of the effect that the sensation produces on our state of mind. What directly (through sense) urges me to *leave* my state (to go out of it) is *disagreeable* to me – it causes me pain; just as what drives me to *maintain* my state (to remain in it) is *agreeable* to me, I enjoy it.' As I understand it, Kant disregards this approach for his second explanation of pleasure and pain, dependent as it is on teleological reasoning, in favour of efficient causality, in which pain is the cause of negative pleasure, as the effect of leaving the state of pain, as we have seen above.

[18] 'The human being does *not* seek pleasure and does *not* avoid pain: one understands, which famous prejudice I hereby contradict. Pleasure and displeasure are mere consequences, mere accompanying phenomena – what the human wants, what every smallest part of a living organism wants, that is a plus of power.' ('Der Mensch sucht n i c h t die Lust und vermeidet n i c h t die Unlust: man versteht, welchem berühmten Vorurtheile ich hiermit widerspreche. Lust und Unlust sind bloße Folge, bloße Begleiterscheinung, – was der Mensch will, was jeder kleinste Theil eines lebenden Organismus will, das ist ein plus von Macht.') (14[174] 13.360).

[19] Quoted above, p. 129.

> That pain is the cause of reactions [or counter-movements: *Gegenbewegungen*] has appearances [*den Augenschein*] in its favour and the prejudice of the philosophers; but in sudden cases the reaction [*Gegenbewegung*] comes evidently earlier than the feeling of pain, if one observes closely. (14[173] 13.359)[20]

Unlike pleasure, Nietzsche argues, the feeling of pain is a belated reverberation (*Nachzittern*) in the cerebral nervous system of a breakdown of equilibrium following a shock (*choc*) to the organism, and it is projected belatedly (*nachher*) to a location on the body on the basis of an interpretation (*intellektueller Vorgang*) or judgement of the shock as 'harmful' (*das Urtheil 'schädlich'*), itself the result of accumulated evolutionary experience. When we trip over something, for instance, the reaction (*Gegenbewegung*) to avoid falling precedes the feeling of pain. This objection to pain as 'first' applies equally to the account of respect for the law in Kant's concept of freedom, to which I now turn.

IV Freedom, respect for the law and the physiology of agency

For both thinkers, the dynamic figure of hindrance-advancement/resistance-overcoming also plays a crucial role in their reflections on freedom and sovereignty. For Kant, the moral worth of actions requires that pure practical Reason be the sole and immediate motive for action; for only if the moral law determines the will immediately can the will be said to be free (free of influence by other sensible motives). In Chapter III of KpV: *Of the Motives (*Triebfeder*) of Pure Practical Reason*, he tackles the problem of how pure practical Reason can be a motive for action at all. In ZeF, as we know, Reason acknowledges its impotence in practice; since it cannot improve humans morally, it cannot count on 'inner morality' and looks instead to make use of the conflict of their hostile inclinations to secure its own end of eternal peace under the rule of law (ZeF II.366). In KpV, by contrast, he sets out to show that pure Reason *can* be practical by involving some kind of passionate element or feeling in the motivational story of moral action; for as the young Hegel noted against Kant, we all know that it is the passions or inclinations that move us to act. Only, it must be very peculiar kind of feeling or passion, one that plays into the motivation of moral action as a sensible *mobile without* impinging on or interfering in the immediate determination of the will by the moral law: a feeling that somehow 'promotes [*beförderlich ist*] the influence of the law on the will' (KpV V.75) *without* preceding the law, *without* tainting the purity of practical Reason or the freedom of the will with 'sensible feeling', *without* mediating the immediate relation between the law and the will. Kant's candidate for this task is 'respect for the law', *Achtung fürs Gesetz*, presented as the one and only motive

---

[20] 'Daß der Schmerz die Ursache ist zu Gegenbewegungen, hat zwar den Augenschein und sogar das Philosophen-Vorurtheil für sich; aber in plötzlichen Fällen kommt, wenn man genau beobachtet, die Gegenbewegung ersichtlich früher als die Schmerzempfindung.' See Wahrig-Schmidt (1988 462), who argues that Nietzsche here is opposing Féré, for whom pleasure and unpleasure are polar opposites (feeling of power/feeling of impotence), and against von Hartmann on pain.

(*Triebfeder*) for moral action. On the one hand, respect must be a real feeling if it is to serve as a credible motive for moral action; on the other, it cannot be a feeling like others with sources in our sensible, 'pathologically determinable self' (KpV V.74), lest it compromise the exclusive determination of the will by the moral law.

Since free will is intelligible and inaccessible to knowledge, Kant circumvents the question of causes altogether; instead, he assumes that the moral law *can* motivate our will and focuses his investigation on the *effect* produced by the moral law on our disposition (*Gemueth*), our faculty of desire or feelings (KpV V.72) in cases where it *conflicts* with our inclinations and sensible impulses (*sinnliche Antriebe*). Once again, we see Kant drawing on the notion of real opposition, this time in the dynamic confrontation or antagonism (*Gegensatz, Widerspiele*) between the moral law of Reason in us and our sensible desires and motives. This is not to say that they are always in opposition; our sensible impulses can concur (*einstimmen*) and co-operate (*mitwirken*) with the moral law. But the cases of conflict allow Kant to exhibit the freedom of the will in its determination by the moral law alone, despite the inaccessibility of 'the force of pure practical reason as a motive' to knowledge. And here Verri's account of the primacy of pain seems to have offered Kant a way to do this.[21] True to his principle that pain must come first, Kant's account of respect begins with the pain of frustrated desires in cases where the moral law motivates our will against our sensible inclinations. In cases where the determination of the will by the moral law requires rejecting (*Abweisung*) all sensible impulses, and 'breaking' or 'checking' (*Abbruch*) 'all inclinations so far as they might be opposed to that law' (KpV V.72), the very real effect on our feeling is negative: the pain of frustrated desires or inclinations. All feelings that precede the moral law are affected, whether natural (self-love: *Selbstliebe*) or not (self-conceit: *Eigendünkel*): self-love is broken or interrupted (*Abbruch*) by being limited (*eingeschraenkt*) to rational self-love (that is in agreement – *Einstimmung* – with the law); self-conceit is struck down (*niedergschlagen*) (KpV V.73).

> Since it is so far only a **negative** effect which, arising from the influence of pure practical reason, checks the activity of the subject, so far as it is determined by inclinations, and hence checks the opinion of his personal worth (which, in the absence of agreement with the moral law, is reduced to nothing); hence, the effect of this law on feeling is merely humiliation. We can, therefore, perceive [*einsehen*] this *a priori*, but cannot know by it the force of the pure practical law as a motive, but only the resistance to motives of the sensibility. (KpV V.78f.; **HS**)[22]

---

[21] See Brandt (1999 342ff.), who writes that the idea that pain precedes pleasure, which Kant gets from Verri, seems to have given him the possibility of conceiving respect (*Achtung*) as a moral motive.

[22] 'Da sie aber blos so fern eine n e g a t i v e Wirkung ist, die, als aus dem Einflusse einer reinen praktischen Vernunft entsprungen, vornehmlich der Thätigkeit des Subjects, so fern Neigungen die Bestimmungsgründe desselben sind, mithin der Meinung seines persönlichen Werths Abbruch thut (der ohne Einstimmung mit dem moralischen Gesetze auf nichts herabgesetzt wird), so ist die Wirkung dieses Gesetzes aufs Gefühl blos Demüthigung, welche wir also zwar *a priori* einsehen, aber an ihr nicht die Kraft des reinen praktischen Gesetzes als Triebfeder, sondern nur den Widerstand gegen Triebfedern der Sinnlichkeit erkennen können.'

The negative feeling of humiliation (*Demüthigung*) – when we identify our 'pathological self' with our entire self (KpV V.74) – or intellectual (self-)contempt (*intellektuelle Verachtung*), when we do not (KpV V.75), is then interpreted or judged by reason to be a sign that the moral law has overcome the resistance of our sensible inclinations and thereby advanced the causality of freedom:

> There is indeed no feeling for this law; but inasmuch as it removes the resistance out of the way, this removal of an obstacle is, *in the judgement of reason*, esteemed equivalent to a positive help to its causality. (KpV V.75; HS)[23]

The judgement of Reason that the pain of humiliation is a sign that the resistance of our inclinations has been overcome by the motivational activity of the moral law, thereby advancing the causality or activity of freedom, gives rise to a positive[24] feeling of elevation (*Erhebung*) in our esteem for the law on our intellectual side.

It is important for Kant's argument that 'respect for the moral law is a feeling which is produced by an 'intellectual cause' or 'ground'' (KpV V.73), so that we need not posit a moral feeling as the ground of respect, leaving the key principle intact that 'the moral law should immediately determine the will' (KpV V.71) for our action to be morally worthy. The precise argument seems to be that the intellectual source of respect or *Achtung* is reason's judgement that (1) the painful feeling of self-contempt or *Verachtung* is an effect of the motivational activity of the moral law on our will (against the 'resistance' or 'antagonism [*Widerspiele*]'[25] of our inclinations); (2) the success of the motivational activity of the moral law, signalled by *Verachtung*, is a sign that the moral law has *overcome the resistance* offered by our inclinations (our pathological self); and (3) the overcoming of this resistance or obstacle to the moral law as motive is equivalent to (*gleichgeschaetzt*) an advancement of the causality of freedom. Further on, Kant clarifies this third moment in Reason's judgement with reference to the quasi-mechanistic

---

[23] '[…] für welches Gesetz gar kein Gefühl stattfindet, sondern im Urtheile der Vernunft, indem es den Widerstand aus dem Wege schafft, die Wegräumung eines Hindernisses einer positiven Beförderung der Causalität gleichgeschätzt wird.'

[24] It is tempting to call it 'pleasurable' – for what else could 'positive feeling' mean? –, but Kant carefully avoids this term in his account, indeed denies and displaces it with the concept of interest: 'If this feeling of respect were pathological, and therefore were a feeling of *pleasure* based on the inner *sense*, it would be in vain to try to discover a connection of it with any idea a priori. But [it] is a feeling that applies merely to what is practical, and depends on the conception of a law, simply as to its form, not on account of any object, and therefore cannot be reckoned either as pleasure or pain, and yet produces an *interest* in obedience to the law, which we call the *moral* interest, just as the capacity of taking such an interest in the law (or respect for the moral law itself) is properly *the moral feeling*' (KpV V.80).

[25] 'But as this law is something positive in itself, namely, the form of an intellectual causality, that is, of freedom, it must be an object of respect; for, by opposing the subjective antagonism [*Widerspiele*] of the inclinations, it *weakens* self-conceit; and since it even *breaks down* [*niederschlägt*], that is, humiliates [*demüthigt*], this conceit, it is an object of the highest *respect* and, consequently, is the ground of a positive feeling which is not of empirical origin, but is known a priori. Therefore respect for the moral law is a feeling which is produced by an intellectual cause, and this feeling is the only one that we know quite a priori and the necessity of which we can perceive [*einsehen*]' (KpV V.73).

principle: 'Whatever reduces the obstacles to an activity advances this activity itself.'[26] This principle, Kant argues, occasions a juxtaposition or transformation – the text is not clear on this – of feelings: the painful humiliation (*Demüthigung*) or feeling of contempt (*Verachtung*) for our sensible side, when judged by Reason to be a sign that the resistance of our inclinations has been overcome by the motivational activity of the moral law (step 2), thereby advancing the causality or activity of freedom (step 3), gives rise to a positive feeling of elevation (*Erhebung*) in our esteem for the law on our intellectual side. This *Erhebung* is, in other words, *Achtung fürs Gesetz*.

∗∗∗∗

This equivalence between the overcoming of resistance and the feeling or consciousness of freedom is also central to Nietzsche's much-commented account of the sovereign individual in GM II 2: his 'pride' (*Stolz*) derives from the judgement that his promise, in determining the will when it is redeemed, has overpowered ('Macht über') resistances both within ('über sich': conflicting inclinations) and without ('das Geschick' or destiny), thereby advancing consciousness of his sovereignty or freedom. Nietzsche writes of

[t]he proud knowledge of the extraordinary privilege of *responsibility*, the consciousness of this rare freedom, this power over oneself and over destiny has dug itself into his lowest depths and has become instinct, his dominant instinct [...] (GM II 2 5.292)[27]

What is striking is the *connection or equivalence made by both between the overcoming of resistance, and the advancement of freedom*. However, when we turn to the *Nachlass* we find Nietzsche questioning this phenomenology of freedom. Thus, on one side we read:

[...] it is *the feeling of our **more** force*, which we designate with 'freedom of the will', the awareness that our force *compels* in relation to a force that is compelled. (34[250] 11.505f.)[28]

---

[26] 'Denn eine jede Verminderung der Hindernisse einer Thätigkeit ist Beförderung dieser Thätigkeit selbst' (KpV V.79).
[27] 'Das stolze Wissen um das ausserordentliche Privilegium der V e r a n t w o r t l i c h k e i t, das Bewusstsein dieser seltenen Freiheit, dieser Macht über sich und das Geschick hat sich bei ihm bis in seine unterste Tiefe hinabgesenkt und ist zum Instinkt geworden, zum dominirenden Instinkt [...]'.
[28] '[...] es ist das G e f ü h l u n s e r e s **Mehr** v o n K r a f t, welches wir mit "Freiheit des Willens" bezeichnen, das Bewußtsein davon, daß unsere Kraft z w i n g t im Verhältniß zu einer Kraft, welche gezwungen wird.'
The full note reads:
'Daß wir wirkende Wesen, Kräfte sind, ist unser Grundglaube.
Frei: heißt "nicht gestoßen und geschoben, ohne
Zwangsgefühl".
NB. Wo wir einem Widerstand begegnen und ihm nachgeben müssen, fühlen wir uns unfrei: wo wir ihm nicht nachgeben sondern ihn zwingen, uns nachzugeben, frei. D.h. e s i s t das G e f ü h l u n s e r e s **Mehr** v o n K r a f t, welches wir mit "Freiheit des Willens" bezeichnen, das Bewußtsein davon, daß unsere Kraft zwingt im Verhältniß zu einer Kraft, welche gezwungen wird.'

On the other side:

> the relation of tension of our muscular feeling: pleasure as the feeling of power: of resistance overcome – are these illusions? (14[81] 13.260)[29]

Or, more assertively:

> [...] what have we done? We mis*understood* a feeling of force, strain, resistance, a muscular feeling, which is already the beginning of the act as cause : or understood the will to do this and that as cause, because the action follows upon it [...] (14[98] 13.274)[30]

Over a period of seven to eight years (1880–8), we find Nietzsche attempting time and again to redescribe the physiology of agency in a way that explains this false phenomenology and the illusion of free will that it sustains. Nietzsche's critical target is not the dynamic figure of resistance-overcoming as such, but the false interpretation or judgement that it evinces the causal effectiveness of the will:

> 'Freedom of the will' – that is the word for the multi-faceted state of pleasure of the one willing, who commands and, at the same time, identifies himself with the one who executes [the act] – who as such shares the joy of the triumph over resistances, but judges to himself that it is his will alone that actually overcomes the resistances.

---

[29] 'das Spannungsverhältniß unseres Machtgefühls: die Lust als Gefühl der Macht: des überwundenen Widerstandes – sind das Illusionen?'
 The full note reads:
  'Kritik des Begriffs "Ursache"
  Psychologisch nachgerechnet: so ist der Begriff "Ursache" unser Machtgefühl vom sogenannten Wollen – unser Begriff "Wirkung" der Aberglaube, daß das Machtgefühl die Macht selbst ist, welche bewegt...
   ein Zustand, der ein Geschehen begleitet, und schon eine Wirkung des Geschehens ist, wird projicirt als "zureichender Grund" desselben
   das Spannungsverhältniß unseres Machtgefühls: die Lust als Gefühl der Macht: des überwundenen Widerstandes – sind das Illusionen?
   übersetzen wir den Begriff "Ursache" wieder zurück in die uns einzig bekannte Sphäre, woraus wir ihn genommen haben: so ist uns keine Veränderung vorstellbar, bei der es nicht einen Willen zur Macht giebt. Wir wissen eine Veränderung nicht abzuleiten, wenn nicht ein Übergreifen von Macht über andere Macht statt hat.
   Die Mechanik zeigt uns nur Folgen, und noch dazu im Bilde (Bewegung ist eine Bilderrede)'.

[30] '[...] was haben wir gemacht? wir haben ein Gefühl von Kraft, Anspannung, Widerstand, ein Muskelgefühl, das schon der Beginn der Handlung ist, als Ursache mißverstanden: oder den Willen, das und das zu thun, weil auf ihn die Aktion folgt, als Ursache verstanden [...].'

'Freiheit des Willens' – das ist das Wort für jenen vielfachen Lust-Zustand des Wollenden, der befiehlt und sich zugleich mit dem Ausführenden als Eins setzt, – der als solcher den Triumph über Widerstände mit geniesst, aber bei sich urtheilt, sein Wille selbst sei es, der eigentlich die Widerstände überwinde. (JGB 19)

In this connection, note 27[24] (11.281) from 1884 is worth commenting paragraph by paragraph:

> Freedom and feeling of power. The feeling of play in the overcoming of great difficulties, e.g. of the virtuoso; self-certainty that upon the will the precisely corresponding action follows – a kind of *affect of supremacy [hubris]* is there, highest sovereignty of *one who commands*. There must also be the feeling of resistance, pressure. – But with this goes a *deception* concerning the will: it is not the will that overcomes the resistance – we make a synthesis between 2 simultaneous states and place a unity therein. The will as condensation.
> 1) one believes that it itself moves (while it is only a stimulus, upon which a movement begins)
> 2) one believes that it overcomes resistances
> 3) one believes that it is free and sovereign, because its origin remains concealed from us and because the affect of commanding accompanies it
> 4) because in by far the most cases one only *wills* when success can be *expected*, the 'necessity' of success is ascribed to the will as *force*.[31]

---

[31] 'Freiheit und Machtgefühl. Das Gefühl des Spiels bei der Überwindung großer Schwierigkeiten, z.B. vom Virtuosen; Gewißheit seiner selber, daß auf den Willen die genau entsprechende Aktion folgt – eine Art A f f e k t d e s Ü b e r m u t h e s ist dabei, höchste Souveränität des B e f e h l e n d e n. Es muß das Gefühl des Widerstandes, Druckes dabei sein. – Dabei ist aber eine T ä u s c h u n g über den Willen: nicht der Wille überwindet den Widerstand – wir machen eine Synthese zwischen 2 gleichzeitigen Zuständen und legen eine *Einheit* hinein.
Der Wille als Erdichtung.
  1) man glaubt, daß er selber bewegt (während er nur ein Reiz ist, bei dessen Eintritt eine Bewegung beginnt)
  2) man glaubt, daß er Widerstände überwindet
  3) man glaubt, daß er frei und souverän ist, weil sein Ursprung uns verborgen bleibt und weil der Affekt des Befehlenden ihn begleitet
  4) weil man in den allermeisten Fällen nur w i l l, wenn der Erfolg e r w a r t e t werden kann, wird die 'Nothwendigkeit' des Erfolgs dem Willen als K r a f t zugerechnet' (27[24] 11.281f.).

Paragraph 1: The reference to sovereignty here and in the second paragraph ('Souveränität', 'souverän') in relation to the consciousness or feeling of power ('Machtgefühl'), of supremacy ('*Übermuth*') and a sense of control or command ('Befehlenden') connects clearly with Nietzsche's use of 'sovereign' in GM II 2. At the same time sovereignty in this text also connects with Kant's judgement of reason insofar as the consciousness of freedom and power is bound up with the overcoming of great difficulties ('Überwindung großer Schwierigkeiten') and the simultaneous feeling of resistance or pressure ('Gefühl des Widerstandes, Druckes'). However, Nietzsche goes on to call this a '*deception concerning the will*' ("T ä u s c h u n g über den Willen') and argues that the Kantian judgement of reason is a misinterpretation of actual power-relations, a misunderstanding of the physiology of agency. This argument instantiates an important feature of Nietzsche's philosophy of power, which is the need to distinguish actual relations of power from our interpretations/consciousness/ feelings of power. This distinction is needed for those cases, such as sovereignty, where there is a radical disjunction between them: for, as Patton, Saar and others have shown, the feeling of power is not always simply the consequence of greater power.[32] What, then, according to Nietzsche, is the nature of the misinterpretation or illusion at play in sovereignty? When he writes that we make a 'synthesis between 2 simultaneous states and place a unity therein', we can take him to mean that a state of power, play, supremacy, commanding (*Macht/Spiel/Uebermuth/Befehlen*) on one side, and a state of resistance, pressure, difficulty (*Schwierigkeiten/Widerstand/Druck*) on the other, are (falsely) synthesized into the unified concept of the will.

Paragraph 2 helps to fill out this picture: When the two stimuli or feelings, that of power and command and that of resistance or pressure, are accompanied by movement (the beginning of action), this is (mis)interpreted by us as the will overcoming resistance to cause our action, which in turn is (mis)interpreted by us as the sovereignty or freedom of our will to cause action. In this last step we can recognize clearly the equivalence drawn by Kant's judgement of reason between the overcoming of resistance and the advancement of the causality of freedom. Only it is judged by Nietzsche to be, not the effect of the moral law motivating the will, but a deception or illusion, a misinterpretation of the physiological processes he describes here and elsewhere.

Another note throws more light on these processes in a way that invokes and explains (away) the two key feelings linked by Kant's judgement of reason: painful humiliation or self-contempt (*Demütigung, Verachtung*) and elevation or respect (*Erhebung, Achtung*):

> All physiological processes are the same insofar as they
> are explosions of force, which, when they land in the sensorium
> commune, bring with them a certain heightening and strengthening:

---

[32] See the essays by P. Patton ('Nietzsche on Rights, Power and the Feeling of Power') and M. Saar ('Forces and Powers in Nietzsche's Genealogy of Morals') in Siemens and Roodt (2008).

these, measured against the oppressive, burdened states of
constraint, are interpreted as a feeling of 'freedom'.[33]

Here Kant's elevation or *Erhebung* is recast as a feeling of heightening and strengthening (*Erhöhung und Verstärkung*) that derives from all physiological processes, understood as discharges or explosions of force.[34] Whereas in Kant's account, *Erhebung* follows from Reason's judgement or interpretation that freedom is advanced, in Nietzsche's version, the feeling of *Erhebung* or *Erhöhung* comes *before* the judgement or feeling of freedom. The feeling of freedom is a result or rather interpretation of the feeling of *Erhöhung*, when it is measured against states of pressure, constraint, restriction. In Kant's terminology we might say: the painful feeling of humiliation that comes from the restriction of our inclinations, when juxtaposed with the feeling of *Erhebung* that accompanies all physiological processes, is (mis)interpreted by us as the-will-overcoming-resistance-of-the-inclinations, giving rise to the feeling of freedom. Here the juxtaposition of painful *Demütigung* and positive *Erhebung*, so central to Kant's account of *Achtung*, is redescribed physiologically in a way that makes nonsense of Reason's judgement.

In Kant's account, the feeling of painful humiliation is judged by Reason to be the effect of the law motivating the will against conflicting inclinations. In Nietzsche's account, the sources of the states of pressure, constraint, restriction are less clear, but we can assume they refer to the resistances intrinsic to all relations of power ('Resisting is the form of power': 11[303] 9.558). In the following note, these states of constraint are identified with what Nietzsche called the 'stimulus' (*Reiz*) or 'feeling of resistance and pressure' (*Widerstand, Druck*) in the first note above (27[24] 11.281f.). The present note makes it clear that the feeling of freedom is the result of a physiological process that begins when one drive stimulates a feeling of pressure or constraint on another, provoking that other into an activity of mastering the first:

> The human has, in opposition to animal, nurtured
> a wealth of *opposed* drives and impulses: by virtue of
> this synthesis he has become master of the earth. –
> moralities are the expression of locally confined *hierarchies*
> in this multi-faceted world of drives: so that the human does
> not go to ground because of its *contradictions*. So,

---

[33] 'Alle physiologischen Vorgänge sind darin gleich, daß sie Kraftauslösungen sind, welche, wenn sie in das sensorium commune gelangen, eine gewisse Erhöhung und Verstärkung mit sich führen: diese, gemessen an drückenden, lastenden Zuständen des Zwangs, werden als Gefühl der "Freiheit" ausgedeutet' (27[3], 11.275; 1884).

[34] The concept of *Auslösung* is taken from Robert Mayer. In 1867 Mayer published a collection of papers with the title *Mechanik der Wärme*, which contains, among others, his ground-breaking book *Bemerkungen über die Kräfte der unbelebten Natur* from 1842, as well as a new article *Über Auslösung*. For a discussion of Mayer's concept of discharge, see Mittasch (1952 114ff.) and Aydin (2003 157–63).

one drive as master, its counter-drive weakened, refined, as
an impulse, which gives the *stimulus* for the activity of the
main drive.
   The highest human would have the greatest multiplicity of drives,
and also in the relatively greatest strength that can be endured.
Indeed: where the plant human shows itself to be strong
one finds the instincts powerfully driving *against* one another
(e.g. Shakespeare) but contained [lit. tamed].[35]

In this text, we are squarely in the domain of Nietzsche's *homo natura* as a multiplicity of competing drives – and about as far as possible from Kant's ghostly *homo noumenon*. The unified concept of the will is dissolved, and the feeling of freedom is relativized to any drive that gains relative supremacy over others in an ongoing struggle of drives. The critical force of Nietzsche's physiological discourse is to expose the key Kantian concepts of will and (the causality of) freedom as errors, illusions that condense or hypostasize infinitely complex, multiple processes and tensions into unities.

> The usual errors: we credit the *will* with making numerous and complicated habituated movements possible. The commander confuses himself with his obedient instruments (and their wills). (27[65] 11.291)[36]

In order to gauge how Nietzsche responds to his physiological critique of the illusions subtending Kantian freedom, we need to bear three things in mind:

(1) Exposing Kant's 'judgement of reason' as a misunderstanding of the physiology of agency is *not* for Nietzsche to empty Kantian freedom of value. *Pace* those who accuse him of the genetic fallacy, Nietzsche is quite clear:

> Whoever has gained insight into the conditions under which a moral
> evaluation has arisen, has not thereby touched upon its value: there are many

---

[35] 'Der Mensch hat, im Gegensatz zum Thier, eine Fülle
g e g e n s ä t z l i c h e r Triebe und Impulse in sich groß gezüchtet:
vermöge dieser Synthesis ist er der Herr der Erde. –
Moralen sind der Ausdruck lokal beschränkter R a n g o r d n u n g e n
in dieser vielfachen Welt der Triebe: so daß an ihren
W i d e r s p r ü c h e n der Mensch nicht zu Grunde geht. Also
ein Trieb als Herr, sein Gegentrieb geschwächt, verfeinert, als
Impuls, der den R e i z für die Thätigkeit des Haupttriebes
abgiebt.
   Der höchste Mensch würde die größte Vielheit der Triebe
haben, und auch in der relativ größten Stärke, die sich noch
ertragen läßt. In der That: wo die Pflanze Mensch sich stark zeigt,
findet man die mächtig g e g e n einander treibenden Instinkte
(z.B. Shakespeare), aber gebändigt' (27[59] 11.289).
[36] 'Die gewöhnlichen Irrthümer: wir trauen dem W i l l e n zu, was zahlreiche und complicirte eingeübte Bewegungen ermöglichen. Der Befehlende verwechselt sich mit seinen gehorsamen Werkzeugen (und deren Willen).'

useful things, and also important insights that have been found in a faulty and unmethodical way; and every quality remains still unknown, even if one has understood under which conditions it arises.[37]

While Nietzsche's physiological discourse certainly undermines the transcendental-normative aims of Kant's moral philosophy, it does not collapse the normative question driving Kant's moral thought. As this note makes clear, it leaves the value, or more precisely: the *qualitative evaluation* ('Qualität') of his key moral concepts or values – freedom or sovereignty, the will – untouched. An indication of what Nietzsche means by 'quality' is given in note 27[59] 11 above (p. 146), which suggests that the quality of human life is greatest ('Der höchste Mensch') where the conflictual multiplicity of drives that is the hallmark of *homo natura* is maximized in a way that can still be synthesized ('Synthesis') or contained ('gebändigt') within the bounds of a unified existence. And if the normative question is focused on the quality or worth (for Kant: moral worth) of actions, Nietzsche's position is diametrically – not to say: polemically – opposed to Kant's. For Nietzsche locates the quality or value of actions, not in the universalizability of their maxims, but in their capacity to individuate, to actualize the radical particularity of their agents – where these are understood as unique multiplicities:

> The value of an action depends upon who performs it
> and whether it stems from their depths or from their surface:
> i.e. how deeply individual it is.[38]

As long as our moral values or concepts are bound up with such individuating actions – as their motives, or as part of the agent's self-understanding – they could be considered as 'useful' for qualitatively valuable agency and therefore as valuable – even if they falsify the physiology of action.

(2) Nietzsche also recognizes the need to work with the illusory concepts of morality like will and sovereignty, and the need to rework them from within, so to speak: what he calls the '*self-overcoming of morality*' ('die S e l b s t a u f h e b u n g d e r M o r a l': M Vorrede 4 3.16). While his thought is geared towards overcoming or 'transvaluating' all our values, it is also informed by a realism about the linguistic and conceptual constraints on such an undertaking, as when he writes:

---

[37] 'Wer die Bedingungen eingesehn hat, unter denen eine moralische
Schätzung entstanden ist, hat ihren Werth damit noch
nicht berührt: es sind viele nützliche Dinge, und ebenso wichtige
Einsichten auf fehlerhafte und unmethodische Weise gefunden
worden; und jede Qualität ist noch unbekannt, auch wenn man
begriffen hat, unter welchen Bedingungen sie entsteht' (27[5] 11.276).
[38] 'Der Werth einer Handlung hängt davon ab, wer sie thut
und ob sie aus seinem Grunde oder aus seiner Oberfläche stammt:
d.h. wie tief sie individuell ist' (27[32] 11.283).

> That a morality with such reversed goals could only be taught and cultivated in connection with the prevailing moral law and under its words and pomposities, so that many transitional and deceptive forms are to be invented [...] (34[176] 11.479)[39]

(3) And yet, Kant's moral law and his language of 'the will', 'freedom of the will' and 'the causality of freedom', being bound up with an illusory feeling of power, are not without their dangers. In a series of posthumous notes from 1880 (notebook 4, KSA 9), in which Nietzsche first reflects systematically on 'the feeling of power', the dangers of such illusory bubbles are very much in mind:[40]

> The bubble of imagined power bursts: this is the cardinal event in life. The human then withdraws angrily or falls apart or becomes stupid. Death of the most beloved, collapse of a dynasty, infidelity of the friend, untenability of a philosophy, a party, – One then wants *comfort*, i.e. a new bubble.[41]

If the 'untenability of a philosophy' evokes the extreme rigours of Kant's pure practical Reason, this goes equally for the 'extreme moralities' discussed in another note that deals with the dangers of those illusions of power that mask actual impotence:

> These wars, these religions, the extreme moralities, these fanatic arts, this party-hatred – that is the great melodrama of impotence that lies itself into a feeling of power and for once wants to signify strength – always with the relapse in pessimism and misery! What you lack is *power over yourselves*![42]

In these culture-critical comments, Nietzsche warns of the dangers of war-mongering and fanaticism pursued for the illusory feeling of power they create. But he also decries 'untenable philosophies' and 'extreme moralities', when they are used to create an illusion of power that masks an actual lack of power over oneself. No doubt Nietzsche

---

[39] 'Daß eine Moral mit solchen umgekehrten Absichten nur in Anknüpfung an das beherrschende Sittengesetz und unter dessen Worten und Prunkworten gelehrt werden könne und angepflanzt werden könne, daß also viele Übergangs- und Täuschungsformen zu erfinden sind [...]'.

[40] The following discussion owes much to the fascinating analysis of pride and vanity (*Stolz, Eitelkeit*) in Kant, Schopenhauer and Nietzsche by Wolfgang Müller-Lauter (1999a).

[41] 'Die Blase der eingebildeten Macht platzt: dies ist das Cardinalereigniß im Leben. Da zieht sich der Mensch böse zurück oder zerschmettert oder verdumnt. Tod der Geliebtesten, Sturz einer Dynastie, Untreue des Freundes, Unhaltbarkeit einer Philosophie, einer Partei. – Dann will man T r o s t d.h. eine neue Blase' (4[199] 9.149).

[42] 'Diese Kriege, diese Religionen, die extremen Moralen, diese fanatischen Künste, dieser Parteihaß – das ist die große Schauspielerei der Ohnmacht, die sich selber Machtgefühl anlügt und einmal Kraft bedeuten will – immer mit dem Rückfall in den Pessimismus und den Jammer! Es fehlt euch an M a c h t ü b e r e u c h !' (4[202] 9.150).

has Schopenhauer in mind, but these expressions apply even more to Kantian morality, built as it is around an illusory consciousness of freedom and power. The danger comes when the illusory bubble of power, masking an actual lack of power, bursts – with consequences in isolationism, pessimism, self-denial[43] or disintegration.

In view of these dangers, the question becomes: How to strip the feeling of power of its illusory character?, or as Nietzsche puts it:

> How can the feeling of power 1) be made ever more substantial
> and not illusory? 2) be stripped of its effects which
> injure, oppress, devalue etc.?[44]

One response attested in modern philosophy is to seek validation of one's feeling of power in values or actions that are recognized as valuable by others. Such values might be generally acknowledged virtues,[45] or Kantian moral law. This response is considered, but rejected by Nietzsche on the grounds that others are prey to the illusory feelings of power, no less than one is oneself:

> The cleverest thing to do is to restrict oneself to the things where we can acquire a feeling of power, [things] that are recognised [*anerkannt*] by others. But the lack of *knowledge* of themselves is so great: they are thrown by fear and reverence onto areas where they can *only* have a feeling of power *through* illusion [*Illusion*]. (4[195] 9.148 ff.)

To seek the feeling of power from the recognition of others can only break the illusion of power on the assumption that they have self-knowledge sufficient to see through their own illusions of power – which Nietzsche denies:

> The value of an action can be determined if the human being
> itself can be known: which in general will have to be denied. (27[33] 11.283)

For Nietzsche, the greatest danger comes when the feeling of power is sought in recognition 'from the outside' (*von außen her*), because it cannot be derived 'from

---

[43] 'Wenn die Don Quixoterie unseres Gefühls von Macht einmal uns zum Bewußtsein kommt und wir aufwachen – dann kriechen wir zu K r e u z e wie Don Quixote, – entsetzliches Ende! Die Menschheit ist immer bedroht von dieser schmählichen S i c h - s e l b s t - V e r l e u g n u n g am E n d e ihres Strebens' (4[222], 9.156).

[44] 'Wie kann das Gefühl von Macht 1) immer mehr substantiell
und nicht illusionär gemacht werden? 2) seiner Wirkungen,
welche schädigen, unterdrücken, geringschätzen usw. entkleidet
werden?' ([216], 9.154).

[45] See, e.g., 4[245], 9.160: 'Die großen Fürsten und Eroberer sprechen die pathetische Sprache der Tugend, zum Zeichen, daß diese vermöge des Gefühls von Macht, welches sie giebt, unter den Menschen anerkannt ist. Die Unehrlichkeit jeder Politik liegt darin, daß die großen Worte, welche jeder im Munde führen muß, um sich als im Besitz der M<acht> zu kennzeichnen, nicht sich mit den wahren Zuständen und Motiven decken k ö n n e n .

within' (*von innen her*) – that is to say: when the feeling of power is sought from a position of impotence, fear, subjection:[46]

> To have your power demonstrated from the outside, while you do not believe in it yourself – that is, through the fear of being subordinated under the judgement of the others – a detour for vain people. (4[196] 9.149)

In the end, the individual is thrown back on itself to 'substantiate' its feeling of power 'from within' through individuating actions that actualize its particularity (or unique multiplicity), a task that requires the virtually impossible self-knowledge that he calls 'die individuelle Wissenschaft':

> Knowledge of one's forces, the law of their order and discharge, the distribution [of forces] without using some too much, others too little, the sign of unpleasure as an unfailing hint that a mistake, an excess etc. has been committed – all with a view towards one goal: how difficult this individual science [*individuelle Wissenschaft*] is! And in its absence, one reaches out for the folk-superstition of morality: because here, the prescriptions are already prepared. But look at the results – we are the victims of this superstitious medicine; it is not the individual, but the community that was supposed to remain preserved through its prescriptions! (4[118] 9.130)

Nietzsche's physiological discourse is not intended to *replace* the prevailing language of morality or Kantian moral law, but to make them less illusory, to give them new naturalistic meanings through an 'ever more substantial' physiology of agency. Nor does it serve to collapse the normative questions of the value of our agency or the moral values that subtend it. But it does collapse the autonomy of the normative sphere onto the plane of immanence and transform the terms of these questions quite radically, as questions of 'quality' (*Qualität*: 7[5] 11.276), that is, the *qualitative* evaluation of our agency, our values and the forms of life they exhibit. Having examined Nietzsche's physiological destruction of Kantian freedom in this chapter, we will turn in the next to his constructive, 'more substantial' alternative: his socio-physiological reinterpretation or reconstruction of freedom. The individual has deeply social origins for Nietzsche, and in the early 1880s he develops a 'socio-physiology' to describe the formation of the individual through the internalization of social relations, mores and prohibitions, but also to outline a naturalistic ideal of sovereignty that hinges on our treatment of others.[47] The key to making the feeling of power 'ever more substantial' can only lie in ever better knowledge of our body and its energetic economy, the distribution, order and discharge of its forces, as well as those of others with whom we interact.

---

[46] The most detailed analysis of the quest for the feeling of power from a position of weakness, and the dangers it houses, is of course to be found in the account of the slave revolt of morality in GM I 7-10.
[47] On this, see Siemens (2015); and Siemens (2016).

4

Towards a new agonism?

Nietzsche's 'fine, well-planned, thoughtful egoism' *contra* Kant's 'unsociable sociability'

I Introduction

The question of productive resistance will be approached from a different angle in this chapter. It begins with an analysis of Kant's best-known treatment of productive resistance in the Fourth Proposition of the 1784 text *Idea for a Universal History with a Cosmopolitan Aim* (*Idee zu einer allgemeinen Geschichte in weltbürgerlicher Absicht*; henceforth IaG) under the rubric of *ungesellige Geselligkeit* or 'unsociable sociability'. The argument is that Kant's unsociability involves a very *limited* notion of egoism, derived from Hobbes, in which others are either *obstacles* or *means* to our own selfish ends. On this basis he tries to formulate a productive notion of resistance, as the engine of human – cultural and moral – development, but it remains captive to the reactive notion of power derived from Hobbes. In the end, Kant's unsociable unsociability describes a conflict or real opposition between a thin notion of egoism (pursuit of self-centred ends) and an under-determined notion of sociability (pursuit of common or other-centred ends), which remain *external* to one another.

This conflict resonates with Nietzsche's diagnosis of the malaise of individuals in modernity, but his response involves a far richer notion of egoism, one to which sociability is not external, but in which our treatment of others – specifically: acting for the sake of others' well-being – is central. It is what Nietzsche calls 'fine, well-planned, thoughtful egoism' *(feiner planmäßiger gedankenreicher Egoismus)* in the *Nachlass* of 1881 (notebook 11 = M III I in KSA 9). In this period he initiates his *turn to philosophical physiology*. Drawing on Wilhelm Roux, Robert Mayer among other scientists,[1] he develops a *socio-physiological prehistory of the individual* and the *emergence of the first individuals* modelled on his concept of the organism and organismic life-processes.[2]

---

[1] See Müller-Lauter (1978).
[2] In this regard, I view these notes as filling a gap in GM, where the emergence of the first individuals is not thematized until the 'sovereign individual' suddenly appears on stage in GM II (5.329), whom Nietzsche describes as a 'ripest fruit' of the long pre-history of the human race, the 'morality of mores' (*Sittlichkeit der Sitte*). It is with the breakdown of these first social units and 'the loosening of the bonds of society' that the first individuals emerge.

The notion of thoughtful egoism, in which this account culminates, brings a complexity to the question of our treatment of others, which is marked by *reciprocity* and *ambiguity* to the point of undermining Kant's sociability-unsociability opposition. But it also designates a *naturalistic ideal of autonomous self-regulation on the basis of physiological self-knowledge*, i.e. an intelligent, affirmative attention to our needs as unique living beings and the processes of self-regulation that we, and all living creatures, must perform if we are to meet our conditions of existence, thrive and grow. Nietzsche's main polemical targets in these notes are Spencer and Spinoza,[3] but his thoughtful egoism is also specifically opposed to Kant's morality. As noted in the last chapter, Nietzsche's commitment to life-affirmation and -enhancement leads him to locate the 'quality' or value of actions, not in the universalizability of their maxims, but in their capacity to individuate, to actualize the radical particularity of their agents, understood as unique multiplicities (p. 147). In this vein, thoughtful egoism involves *radically individual self-legislation* (as opposed to self-subjection to the universal law) on the part of a *radically socialized and plural subject* or *dividuum* (against the substantive, autonomous subject: *homo noumenon*). As such, it represents an attempt to reconstruct the moral ideal of freedom and the associated feeling of power in a way that is 'less illusory' by giving them a 'more substantial' physiological or socio-physiological interpretation.

As a naturalistic ideal of autonomy, Nietzsche's thoughtful egoism harbours resources not just for ethics but for a Nietzschean agonistic politics, which I adumbrate at the end of the chapter. I do not mean agonism in the senses we are familiar with in political theory – as a model for deliberation or an approach to questions of identity, authority, etc. – but as a mode of engagement with others. As J-F Drolet has remarked, Nietzsche's failure to address the political institutions, markets and bureaucracies governing late-modern societies has, as its other side, his conviction that 'any serious plan for an institutional transformation of the international [order] had to start with a radical transformation of the modalities of interaction between individuals and between individuals and their world' (Drolet 2013 39, 46). Having concentrated on Nietzsche's affirmative uses of 'resistance' in Chapter 3, these reflections take off from his critical uses of the term. In Nietzsche's work, there is a shift of emphasis from resistance and the capacity to resist, to *non*-resistance, or the capacity *not* to resist, which comes to light in his late critiques of mechanism, décadence and his epistemic ideal of 'learning to see'. The chapter closes with a sketch of what I think could be a promising basis for an agonistic disposition towards others, as a kind of *hostile calm* or *calm hostility*.

Nietzsche's account of thoughtful egoism falls within his sustained project to reorient philosophical reflection on moral values from the autonomous domain claimed by morality and moral philosophy – including Kant's transcendental-normative sphere – towards their socio-physiological conditions in the body (politic), in the effort to make morality 'more substantial'. For Nietzsche the physiology developed by contemporary

---

[3] Scholars have argued that Nietzsche most likely never knew Spinoza's work directly, and that his knowledge came from (the second 1865 edition of) Kuno Fischer's work *Geschichte der neuern Philosophie* (Scandella 2012 309), which he first read in 1881, the period of the notes we will examine in this chapter. For details on Nietzsche's acquaintance with Spinoza in the literature, see Ioan (2019 98ff.).

biologists like Roux afforded a 'manner of speaking' (*Sprechart*) that enabled him to develop his philosophy of conflict on the model of the (social) organism, and explore its implications for human existence and morality in ways that were in line with (or could be adapted to) the presuppositions of his ontology or counter-ontology of becoming: the emphasis on *processes* of self-regulation and self-organization that account for the formation of *derivative, living unities* or organisms out of the *struggle* of multiplicities at all levels: molecules, cells, tissues and organs. But in his preface to the *Anthropology*, Kant issues a challenge to this move when he excludes physiology – 'what *nature* makes of the human' – from his 'pragmatic' point of view and its focus on 'what he as a free-acting being, makes of himself, or can and ought to make of himself' (Anth VII.119). As Kant scholars tell us, Kant's statement is addressed to a number of physiologists of his time.[4] Yet it also poses a challenge to Nietzsche's physiology. For in support of his exclusion he levels two criticisms at his contemporary physiologists, which also bear on Nietzsche's turn to physiology. The physiologist, Kant argues, cannot influence human existence: he remains 'a mere observer' and 'must let nature do the acting', because (1.) his knowledge of physiology is insufficient, and (2.) he doesn't know how to make use of it (*Handhabung*) for his own ends (ibid.). The Kantian anthropologist, by contrast, aspires to influence human existence, not just 'to know the world' by understanding the game he observes (*das Spiel verstehen*), but to 'have the world' by playing the game (*mitspielen; Welt kennen/Welt haben*: Anth VII.120). And he can do so because 'from a pragmatic point of view', anthropology is knowledge of what the human, 'as a free-acting being, makes of himself', and is addressed to the human 'as a free-acting being' by an author who plays the same game as a free, purposive agent. To whom, then, is Nietzsche to address his partial knowledge of physiology, and what are they or 'we' to make of it? The challenge for Nietzschean physiology is to bridge the chasm Kant opens up between what nature makes of the human and what the human as a free-acting being can make of himself. For Nietzsche, I will argue, it is a matter of *translation* – from the language of reason and moral sentiment into the language of physiology, and from the latter back into the former; a practice through which our moral terms acquire new meanings and nuances, informed by our history and long prehistory as living beings. On the question of influence, Nietzsche urges us to use the insights won in this process to influence our affects, on which our self-regulation as human animals turns.

II Kant: *ungesellige Geselligkeit*

Kant's political-historical writings can be read as attempts to negotiate the disjunction between *Sein* and *Sollen*, between what is and what ought to be. 'For it may be', he writes in KrV (A550/B578), 'that all that *has happened* in the course of nature, and in accordance with empirical laws must have happened, *ought not to have happened*'.

---

[4] Louden (2008 516) and Sturm (2008 496) mention Ernst Platner, whose book *Anthropologie für Ärzte und Weltweise* was published in 1772, when Kant began his anthropology course. Others include Julien Offray La Mettrie (author of *L'homme machine*, 1747), Johann Gottlob Krüger, Charles Bonnet, Albrecht van Haller and Georges-Louise Leclerc de Buffon.

Or to put it differently: they serve to reconcile the absence of morality in reality,[5] the non-appearance of freedom, with the demand (indeed the *authority* of the demand) that morality and freedom be realized – to reconcile them by arguing that we have *reasonable hope* in the realization of 'a *moral* whole' (IaG 4) under cosmopolitan law. For there can be no doubt: the content of the moral law is directly opposed to the radical evil – the 'childish malice and mania for destruction' (IaG 1), 'the quarrelsomeness, the spiteful competitive vanity, the insatiable desire to possess or even to dominate' (IaG 4) – that human history so amply exhibits. The hope, Kant argues, is *grounded* in the claim that moral progress is inseparable from the evils of civilization, which spring from the very conditions in our own nature that make rational insight into the moral law possible (see Wood 2015 123). These conditions are what he calls 'unsociable sociability'.

Despite his call for eternal peace, Kant shares with Nietzsche (1.) the realist view that conflict is *irreducible*, or at least *deeply rooted* in human action and interaction, and (2.) the view that conflict can have *valuable constructive* or *productive qualities*. As we have seen, conflict plays an essential role for him, no less than for Nietzsche, across various domains of his thought. Concerning the particular form of conflict he calls 'unsociable sociability' Allen Wood (2015 115) writes: 'No interpretation of Kant's views on any aspect of human psychology, sociology or history will get matters right as long as it ignores the theme of unsociable sociability.'

The notion of 'ungesellige Geselligkeit' is to be found across wide range of Kant's writings,[6] but the expression itself occurs only once, in the Fourth Proposition of IaG. I shall therefore take my starting point and bearings from this text, which begins:

> *The means nature employs in order to bring about the development of all their predispositions is their* **antagonism** *in society, insofar as the latter is in the end the cause of their lawful order.* Here I understand by 'antagonism' the *unsociable sociability* of human beings, i.e. their propensity to enter into society, which, however, is combined with a thoroughgoing resistance that constantly threatens to tear this society apart. The predisposition for this obviously lies in human nature. The human being has an inclination to become socialized, since in such a condition he feels himself as more a human being, i.e. feels the development of his natural predispositions. But he also has a great propensity to *singularise* (isolate) himself, because he simultaneously encounters in himself the unsociable property of willing to direct everything according to his wishes alone, and hence expects resistance everywhere because he knows of himself that he is inclined on his side toward resistance against others. Now it is this resistance that awakens all the powers of the human being, brings him to overcome his propensity to indolence, and, driven by ambition, tyranny and greed, to obtain for himself a rank among his fellows, whom he cannot stand, but also cannot leave alone.

---

[5] As Nietzsche points out in note 11[303] 9.557: 'To glorify selflessness! and concede, as Kant does, that such a deed has probably never been done!'

[6] MA VIII.120–1; RH VIII.65; KU V.429–31; VA VII.324, 328.

Das Mittel, dessen sich die Natur bedient, die Entwickelung aller ihrer Anlagen zu Stande zu bringen, ist der **Antagonism** derselben in der Gesellschaft, so fern dieser doch am Ende die Ursache einer gesetzmäßigen Ordnung derselben wird. Ich verstehe hier unter dem Antagonism die u n g e s e l l i g e G e s e l l i g k e i t der Menschen, d.i. den Hang derselben in Gesellschaft zu treten, der doch mit einem durchgängigen Widerstande, welcher diese Gesellschaft beständig zu trennen droht, verbunden ist. Hiezu liegt die Anlage offenbar in der menschlichen Natur. Der Mensch hat eine Neigung sich zu v e r g e s e l l s c h a f t e n: weil er in einem solchen Zustande sich mehr als Mensch, d.i. die Entwickelung seiner Naturanlagen, fühlt. Er hat aber auch einen großen Hang sich zu v e r e i n z e l n e n (isoliren): weil er in sich zugleich die ungesellige Eigenschaft antrifft, alles bloß nach seinem Sinne richten zu wollen, und daher allerwärts Widerstand erwartet, so wie er von sich selbst weiß, daß er seinerseits zum Widerstande gegen andere geneigt ist. Dieser Widerstand ist es nun, welcher alle Kräfte des Menschen erweckt, ihn dahin bringt seinen Hang zur Faulheit zu überwinden und, getrieben durch Ehrsucht, Herrschsucht oder Habsucht, sich einen Rang unter seinen Mitgenossen zu verschaffen, die er nicht wohl *leiden*, von denen er aber auch nicht *lassen* kann. (IaG VIII.20f.)

II.1 Unsociability and resistance

How are we to understand the notion of 'unsociability'? Rooted in a predisposition (*Anlage*) of human nature, it is a great propensity to *singularize or isolate* ourselves that threatens to tear society apart. The propensity to isolate ourselves is no innate misanthropy, but the consequence of our wanting to direct everything according to our own wishes alone: *alles bloß nach seinem Sinne richten zu wollen*. The word 'bloß' (according to our wishes *alone*) is important, since it connects unsociability with what Kant calls 'moral egoism' in the *Anthropology*. The egoist 'limits all ends to himself, and sees no use in anything except that which is useful to himself' (*welcher alle Zwecke auf sich selbst einschränkt, der keinen Nutzen worin sieht, als in dem, was ihm nützt*) (Anth §2 VII.8-9). Unsociability is, then, wanting to direct everything according to one's wishes alone, in the sense that one's concerns are strictly limited to one's own selfish ends, to which everything else is subordinate as a means or not: as useful or not. But others are not just *means* (or not) for the egoist's ends. They are often unwilling to be used by the egoist, for they too have the unsociable propensity to pursue their own ends alone. More often than not, then, others are *obstacles* to our ends, just as we are obstacles their selfish ends. This is why we have the unsociable propensity to isolate ourselves, so as to avoid the obstacles others put up to our own ends. This brings us to the question of resistance.

The concept of resistance takes two forms in IaG 4. There is first the 'thoroughgoing resistance' that our unsociability puts up to our sociable tendency. As a 'resistance that constantly threatens to tear this society apart', it is directly opposed by Kant to the 'propensity to enter into society' in each and every subject. Then there is resistance *between* subjects: the resistance that I expect and encounter from others when single-mindedly pursuing my own ends, just as I (would) resist them in their single-minded pursuit of their own ends. It is here that Kant locates his notion *of productive resistance* with the claim that this resistance does not just obstruct us from getting our own way, but stimulates or stirs us to try to overcome it. On the presupposition of a primordial state of indolence or passivity, and true to the primacy of pain adopted in the *Anthropology*, resistance is what 'awakens all the powers [*Kräfte*] of the human being'. Given that, for our unsociable propensity to pursue our own ends alone, others are either *means* or *obstacles*, productive resistance means: turning an (expected) obstacle to my pursuit of my ends into a *means* that stimulates me to overcome it and attain my ends. So how does this work? How is an *obstacle* to my agency turned into a *means* that stimulates all my powers?

One clue is given by Kant's reference to the 'powers [*Kräfte*] of the human being'. My suggestion is that Kant's notion of unsociability is inspired and underpinned by the notion of power set out in Chapter 10 of Hobbes's *Leviathan*: Of Power, Worth, Dignity, Honour, and Worthinesse, and that his notion of productive resistance is an implication he draws from a close reading of that text. As is well known, Hobbes begins with a general or 'universal' definition of 'the power of man' as 'his present means, to obtain some future apparent Good'. This, I would say, matches Kant's unsociable propensity to have everything go as we wish (*alles nach seinem Sinne richten*), i.e. pursue one's own goods or ends, where power is any means to do so. Hobbes then goes on to modify this general notion of power significantly, when he writes:

> *Natural* power is the eminence of the faculties of body, or mind; as extraordinary strength, form, prudence, arts, eloquence, liberality, nobility. *Instrumental* are those powers which, acquired by these, or by fortune, are means and instruments to acquire more; as riches, reputation, friends, and the secret working of God, which men call good luck. For the nature of power is, in this point, like to fame, increasing as it proceeds; or like the motion of heavy bodies, which, the further they go, make still the more haste. (Hobbes's *Leviathan* 10)

Here power is redefined in terms of 'eminence' or 'extra-ordinary' power; that is to say it is redefined in relative or relational terms as 'more power than'. In these lines Hobbes breaks through to the essence of human, social power, which, unlike mechanistic force, cannot be fixed and quantified, because it is intrinsically comparative and relational: more power than … The question interpreters face is how Hobbes gets from his first general definition of power to this social concept of power. The answer, as MacPherson (1962 35–40) pointed out, lies in the concept of resistance: it is because others will use their means or power to resist my effort to obtain my future 'good' or end that I need more means or power than them, so as to overcome their resistance and get what I want.[7] This coincides precisely with Kant's concept of unsociability, who shares MacPherson's insight concerning resistance and social power, but also adds to it

---

[7] Or as Hobbes writes explicitly in *The Elements of Law*: 'because the power of one man resisteth and hindreth the effects of the power of another: power simply is no more, but the excess of the power of one above that of another' (Elements I, 8, 4).

another, not present in MacPherson or Hobbes: that the resistance offered by others can act not just as an *obstacle* to my capacity to obtain my ends, but also as a *means* that stimulates new capacities or powers in me that enable me to overcome it and attain my ends.

Instead, Hobbes's text comes to focus on *acquired* or *instrumental powers*, in a line of thought that can also be tracked in Kant's Fourth Proposition. Even if the resistance of others does not stimulate the development of new powers or capacities in me, it does stimulate me to look for other means. And since power is just 'more power than', and since we know not the nature or sources of future resistance to our power, Hobbes can posit 'for a generall inclination of all mankind, a perpetuall and restlesse desire for Power after power, that ceaseth onely in Death' (Lev. Ch. 11). Among instrumental powers he mentions riches, reputation and friends in the passage cited, and much of Chapter 10 is devoted to cataloguing the various forms that instrumental power can take. Instrumental power has the peculiarity that it is not a means to an end or 'good', but a means or instrument to acquire more power, i.e. *a means to more means in abstraction from a specific end or 'good'*. Hence the desire for power after power, or what Hobbes describes as a dynamic of acceleration intrinsic to instrumental power: 'the further they go, make still the more hast'. What is clear from Hobbes's account is that others figure as either obstacles or threats, or as means, as they do in Kant's concept of unsociability; and that instrumental power involves *using others (their power or means) as means*, so that we can speak with MacPherson (1962 37) of power as the *ability to command the services of other men*.

In Kant's text, Hobbes's instrumental power is at work in his attempt to explain the notion of resistance as stimulant, when he writes:

> Now it is this resistance that awakens all the powers of the human being, brings him to overcome his propensity to indolence, and, driven by ambition, tyranny and greed [*Ehrsucht, Herrschsucht, Habsucht*], to obtain for himself a rank among his fellows, whom he cannot *stand*, but also cannot *leave* alone.
>
> (IaG 4 VIII.21)

At first sight this looks like a sociable desire for recognition, but it is not. Ambition or the craving for honour (*Ehrsucht*) is not the love of honour (*Ehrliebe*), which is a legitimate demand that one be esteemed for one's 'inner (moral) worth' (Anth §85 VII.272). It is the striving for the reputation of honour, even where it is mere semblance.[8] Together with tyranny or the craving to rule (*Herrschsucht*) and greed or the craving for possessions (*Habsucht*), it is one of Kant's three cultural or acquired passions (*Leidenschaften*) (Anth §81 VII.268). For Kant, passions are intelligent and purposive; they are connected with reason, since they presuppose a maxim to act according to an end prescribed to us by our inclinations. They therefore pose the most serious threat to freedom – far greater than blind and momentary affects – and are

---

[8] This echoes the importance of illusion and reputation in Hobbes's account of instrumental of power, where the reputation for power *is* power, since (regardless of whether the reputation is warranted) it draws the adherence of others offering their power in exchange for protection.

without exception evil (Anth §81 VII.267). What is striking in Kant's account is their *instrumental* character akin to Hobbesian instrumental power. The three acquired passions – for honour, power and wealth – are referred by Kant to our desire to have influence over others. The direct objects or ends of these passions – honour, power and wealth – are in fact mere means to gain influence over others through their good opinion, their fear or their self-interest, which in turn is not an end in itself, but a means to use others as means for one's own ends, whatever they be. Kant can therefore write that if one possesses honour, power or money 'one can get to every human being and use him according to one's purposes, if not by means of one of these influences, then by means of another' (Anth §84 VII.271).

Clearly, we are in the realm of Hobbes's instrumental power: using others as means to our own ends through the capacity to command their services.[9] Unlike Hobbes, however, Kant claims that these unsociable passions have the unintended side-effect of developing new capacities and powers in us; or that resistance works (not just as an obstacle, but) as a means to 'awaken all the powers of the human being', making possible the transition from a brutish condition to culture and the social worth of humans. Indeed, our unsociability is essential for the establishment of a manner of thinking (*Denkungsart*) that can 'form society into a moral whole' under a legal order through insight into the principles of pure practical Reason (IaG 4 VII.21).[10] These are strong claims, but the Fourth Proposition has little to say by way of explaining and justifying them. We can suppose that our passions for ever more honour, power and wealth, being closely allied with purposive reasoning, develop our intellect to the point where it gains insight into the autonomy and demands of pure practical Reason; but this is not stated. Kant writes of the *odium figulinum* that first appears in Hesiod: the 'potter's hatred' that prompts one to toil, to which Kant adds a twist, leading back to a state of indolence: to toil so as to find means to relieve oneself of toil. He also tells us that 'the sources of unsociability and thoroughgoing resistance [...] drive human beings to a new exertion of their powers and hence to further development of their natural predispositions' (IaG VIII.22). But this describes, without explaining, how resistance can incite us to overcome it. We can still ask how an obstacle, instead of crushing, stopping or inhibiting us, can turn into a means to rise above it.

---

[9] Kant even hints at the peculiar acceleration when power, as a means to more means, gets cut off from its ends: 'It is true that here the human being becomes the dupe (the deceived) of his own inclinations, and in his use of such means he misses his final end' (Anth §84 VII.271). 'Possessing the means to whatever aims one chooses certainly extends much further than the inclination directed to one single inclination and its satisfaction' (Anth §82 VII.270). 'On the other hand, if the inclination is directed merely to the means and possession of the same toward satisfaction of all inclinations in general, therefore toward mere capacity, it can only be called a passion' (Anth §82 VII.269 [B version]).

[10] '[...] thus all talents come bit by bit to be developed, taste is formed, and even, through progress in enlightenment, a beginning is made toward the foundation of a mode of thought which can with time transform the rude natural predisposition to make moral distinctions into determinate practical principles and hence transform a pathologically compelled agreement to form a society finally into a moral whole.'

The overall tenor of the Fourth Proposition is that, absent unsociability, human nature is inclined to inactivity, indolence, maximal comfort with minimal effort. Indeed, the opening passage is the *locus classicus* for the state of indolence or passivity, posited by Kant as a longed-for primordial condition or slumber, from which we are awakened by unsociable resistance (see pp. 84–6). It is also fully in line with the notion of pain, adopted from Verri in the *Anthropology* and posited as the 'spur' of activity. Underpinning both is the essentially *reactive* concept of power that Kant takes from Hobbes, both here and in ZeF (see pp. 104, 107; cf. p. 133). As Paul Patton (2001 153) has shown, Hobbesian power is governed by the telos of self-preservation, because it presupposes an external threat; it is exercised from a position of weakness or lack (of security, of a future good) in relation to external power(s) and can only act by reacting to the latter. While Hobbes's relational-differential concept of power as more-power-than is shared by Nietzsche (power as 'a plus of power'), the presuppositions of Nietzsche's concept of power could not be further from Hobbes's. It is not reactive, but active and presupposes excess, rather than lack; power is defined with reference to process (expending energy) or activity (extending or increasing power), rather than goals (self-preservation). And the activity of increasing power can only be an *overpowering*, because power-as-activity can only act *in relation to* the resistance offered by other counter-powers, which it therefore seeks out.

II.2 Sociability and resistance

I turn now to what has so far been bracketed out of the discussion of the Fourth Proposition: the notion of sociability, and the first form of resistance mentioned there: the 'thoroughgoing resistance' that our unsociability puts up to our sociable tendency. How are we to understand the opposition between unsociability and the 'resistance that constantly threatens to tear this society apart', and our 'propensity to enter into society'?

Kant scholars typically refer to the passage on the original predisposition towards the good in human nature from Kant's *Religion* text (RGV VI.27) for guidance. Kant breaks our disposition towards the good down into three: our disposition towards animality, towards humanity and towards personality. Our disposition towards animality is named a 'merely mechanical self-love' and involves three pre-rational instincts: for self-preservation, reproduction and society with others. Our sociability is, then, located at the pre-rational or instinctual level.[11] Our disposition towards humanity, by contrast, depends upon reason: means-ends and comparative thinking on the part of purposive beings. It is placed under the heading of 'comparative self-love', and is our predisposition to pursue happiness, where happiness is judged only in comparison with others.

---

[11] This departs markedly from Rousseau. In the Preface to the *Discourse on the Origins of Inequality*, he identifies two principles prior to reason in the human soul, self-preservation and pity, and seeks to derive the 'rules of natural right' from a combination of these principles 'without the need for introducing that of sociability' (Rousseau 1987 35).

From this stems the inclination *to obtain a worth in the opinion of others*; indeed originally only the worth of *equality*: to allow no one superiority, bound up with a constant worry that that others would like to strive after that; from which eventually an unjust desire arises to gain superiority over others. (RGV VI.27)[12]

Note how even the desire to be recognized as equal has negative sources in Kant's reactive concept of power: in the desire not to allow others superiority over us and the worry that this is what they would like. Unsociability, in the form of jealousy, competitiveness and hostility, is just a rational development of these sources, described in terms that repeat the logic of Hobbes's second cause for war in Leviathan Chapter 13, the war for security out of diffidence:[13] They are

> [...] inclinations, in the face of the anxious endeavours of others at a hateful superiority over us, to procure it [superiority] over them as a preventative measure for the sake of security [...] (RGV VI.27)[14]

In this text, then, unsociability is focused on the conflictual striving for superior standing over others and concomitant anxieties. It is important for Kant that it is not simply a consequence of our animal instincts, but *socially conditioned*, and that it depends on *purposive reasoning*. To blame our instincts would be to exculpate us from responsibility for our unsociable behaviour and for curbing it. Only if we are freely choosing to act on a maxim to follow our inclinations can we be held morally responsible for our unsociability. Even if '[u]nsociable sociability is nature's way of developing our rational predisposition both to humanity and to personality' (Wood 2005 115),[15] unsociability is evil for Kant and ultimately we are obliged to curb it.

In consideration of these sources of unsociability in social relations and our rational predispositions, scholars view it as an *internal feature or modification* of our sociability.

---

[12] 'Von ihr rührt die Neigung her, s i c h i n d e r M e i n u n g A n d e r e r e i n e n W e r t h z u v e r - s c h a f f e n; und zwar ursprünglich bloß den der G l e i c h h e i t: keinem über sich Überlegenheit zu verstatten, mit einer beständigen Besorgniß verbunden, daß Andere darnach streben möchten; woraus nachgerade eine ungerechte Begierde entspringt, sie sich über Andere zu erwerben.'

[13] 'And from this diffidence of one another, there is no way for any man to secure himself so reasonable as anticipation; that is, by force, or wiles, to master the persons of all men he can so long till he see no other power great enough to endanger him: and this is no more than his own conservation requireth, and is generally allowed. Also, because there be some that, taking pleasure in contemplating their own power in the acts of conquest, which they pursue farther than their security requires, if others, that otherwise would be glad to be at ease within modest bounds, should not by invasion increase their power, they would not be able, long time, by standing only on their defence, to subsist. And by consequence, such augmentation of dominion over men being necessary to a man's conservation, it ought to be allowed him' (Hobbes's *Leviathan*, chapter 13).

[14] '[...] bei der besorgten Bewerbung Anderer zu einer uns verhaßten Überlegenheit über uns Neigungen sind, sich der Sicherheit halber diese über Andere als Vorbauungsmittel selbst zu verschaffen [...].'

[15] The predisposition to personality is the third predisposition to the good in human nature, encompassing reason and moral responsibility.

In a sense this is obvious. After all, unsociability is predicated of sociability. But there are a number of problems with this picture. Let me focus on two:[16]

1. In the Fourth Proposition, unsociability is not focused on self-worth and our striving for superior standing, but on our passions for honour, dominance and wealth. The latter are not means for gaining superior standing over others through their opinion, their fear or their self-interest.[17] As the *Anthropology* shows, the standing (*Rang*) we gain through honour, dominance and wealth is itself a means to gain influence over others, so as to be able to use them as means to our ends, whatever they may be. The focus on self-worth and superior standing misses Kant's focus on the thoroughly instrumental character of our passions and the moral problem it raises: using others as means to our own selfish ends, so that we can have it all our own way (*alles bloss nach seinem Sinne richten*).

2. It is, Kant argues in the Fourth Proposition, because others act as obstacles to our own ends that we have a 'great propensity to singularise ourselves (isolate ourselves)' so as to get what we want without their interference. This can hardly be viewed as an internal feature or modification of our sociability. It is anti-social through and through, and Kant opposes it quite explicitly to our 'propensity to enter into society'. It is because our unsociability puts up a 'thoroughgoing resistance' to our sociability that it 'constantly threatens to tear this society apart'.

In IaG, then, our unsociability is *external* to our sociability, and their relation is one of *antagonism* or *tension*. Readings that draw on Kant's *Religion* text get this wrong, because their relation in that text is significantly different. We do much better, I suggest, if we consider a passage from the 1766 text: *Dreams of a Spirit Seer illustrated by Dreams of Metaphysics*, when Kant writes:

> Among the forces that move the human heart, some of the most powerful seem to lie outside it [the heart], those namely which do not, as mere means relate to one's own self-interest and private needs as a goal that lies *within* the human being; but rather which make it that the tendencies of our impulses displace the focal point of their convergence *outside us* in other rational beings; from which a conflict of two forces arises, namely of singularity [ownness], which relates everything to itself, and of common interest, through which the soul is driven or drawn towards others outside itself [...]

---

[16] Two further considerations are:
3. There is no reason why unsociability cannot also be located at the level of our animal instincts (self-preservation, reproduction and sociability). It is clear that, being weak creatures, we join society out of fear for our self-preservation. But self-preservation can also override social goods, creating a tension or conflict between our instincts for self-preservation and for association with others.
4. Kant says little about our instinct for sociability, and scholars are hard pressed to mine his works for the little he says about love, sympathy and friendship. The account in the Fourth Proposition of IaG itself is vague and psychologically underdetermined: it is because in society we feel ourselves 'more as human beings, that is the development of our natural predispositions'. Whatever this means, it sounds more like a consequence of our predisposition to *humanity*, than a consequence of our animal instincts.

[17] See Wood (2015 118): 'Specifically, social passions represent to us the acquisition of honor, power, and wealth as means of gaining superiority over others, through (respectively) their opinion, their fear, or their interest (VA 7:271).' In my view, this correct of RGV, but not of IaG 4 or Anth.

> Unter den Kräften, die das menschliche Herz bewegen, scheinen einige der mächtigsten außerhalb demselben zu liegen, die also nicht etwa als bloße Mittel sich auf die Eigennützigkeit und Privatbedürfniß als auf ein Ziel, das i n n e r h a l b dem Menschen selbst liegt, beziehen, sondern welche machen, daß die Tendenzen unserer Regungen den Brennpunkt ihrer Vereinigung a u ß e r u n s in andere vernünftige Wesen versetzen; woraus ein Streit zweier Kräfte entspringt, nämlich der Eigenheit, die alles auf sich bezieht, und der Gemeinnützigkeit, dadurch das Gemüth gegen andere außer sich getrieben oder gezogen wird. [...] (TG II.334)[18]

This passage captures several features of unsociability in IaG 4. First, the means-end thinking that refers all utility to what is useful to oneself, treating others as mere means to ends that are limited to oneself and one's a-social or private needs. Secondly, as in IaG 4, sociability is *opposed* to sociability and *external* to it in the precise sense that it displaces the end or 'focus' of our (sociable) impulses 'outside us' in others and in the common good. And thirdly, TG describes the opposition between sociable and unsociable propensities in dynamic terms as a relation of tension or antagonism. Indeed, the expression used in this text – the 'Streit zweier Kräfte' or 'conflict of two forces' – is the same expression used three years earlier to describe the concept of real contradiction or 'Realrepugnanz' in *Negative Magnitudes* (1763).[19] Perhaps the most pertinent example of real opposition for us concerns impenetrability (see p. 25). The impenetrability of a body can only be explained if we presuppose an inner force of repulsion that resists the force attracting other bodies, so that a body occupies space by virtue of a balance between conflicting forces: a 'Conflictus zweier Kräfte, die einander entgegengesetzt sind' (NG II.179). Thus, repulsion, although a 'true force' of repulsion or *Zurückstoßung*, can also be called negative attraction: *negative Anziehung*, to indicate that it is a *positive* ground that resists the force of attraction.[20] It is by analogy with this example of real opposition that Kant presents unsociable sociability in the *Dreams*

---

[18] See also: 'Wenn wir äußere Dinge auf unser Bedürfniß beziehen, so können wir dieses nicht thun, ohne uns zugleich durch eine gewisse Empfindung gebunden und eingeschränkt zu fühlen, die uns merken läßt, daß in uns gleichsam ein fremder Wille wirksam sei, und unser eigen Belieben die Bedingung von äußerer Beistimmung nöthig habe. Eine geheime Macht nöthigt uns unsere Absicht zugleich auf anderer Wohl oder nach fremder Willkür zu richten, ob dieses gleich öfters ungern geschieht und der eigennützigen Neigung stark widerstreitet, und der Punkt, wohin die Richtungslinien unserer Triebe zusammenlaufen, ist also nicht bloß in uns, sondern es sind noch Kräfte, die uns bewegen, in dem Wollen anderer außer uns. Daher entspringen die sittlichen Antriebe, die uns oft wider den Dank des Eigennutzes fortreißen, das starke Gesetz der Schuldigkeit und das schwächere der Gütigkeit, deren jedes uns manche Aufopferung abdringt, und obgleich beide dann und wann durch eigennützige Neigungen überwogen werden, doch nirgend in der menschlichen Natur ermangeln, ihre Wirklichkeit zu äußern' (TG II.334–5).

[19] In NG Kant uses the expression 'Streit zweier einander aufhaltenden Bewegkräfte' (recalling the 'Streit zweier Kräfte' used for unsociable sociability in the *Dreams* essay) for the state of rest when it is a consequence of 'two effective causes, of which one which cancels [*aufhebt*] the consequence of the other [i.e., motion] through real opposition' (NG II.184).

[20] 'Die Ursache der Undurchdringlichkeit ist demnach eine wahre Kraft, denn sie thut dasselbe, was eine wahre Kraft thut. [...] so ist die Undurchdringlichkeit eine negative Anziehung. Dadurch wird alsdann angezeigt, daß sie ein eben so positiver Grund sei als eine jede andere Bewegkraft in der Natur [...]' (NG II.180).

essay with his talk of the conflict of two forces ('Streit zweier Kräfte'), that of singularity (ownness: *Eigenheit*), which relates everything to oneself, and that of common interest (*Gemeinnützigkeit*) which drives or attracts the soul towards others. This model gives a *dynamic* character to unsociable sociability: as a continuous and never-ending conflict between active forces in us that move us to use others (external forces) as means to our own good, and external forces in others that move (drive or attract) us to consider the good of others or the common good. It is only on this model, I submit, *the real opposition or conflict between a 'force' or concern for our own good, and a force or concern for the common interest*, that we can understand the 'thoroughgoing resistance' that our unsociability puts up towards our sociability in the Fourth Proposition of IaG.[21]

III Nietzsche on fine, well-planned, thoughtful egoism

With the conflict between an exclusive concern for one's own good and a concern for the common good, Kant's unsociable sociability makes contact with Nietzsche's thought. In this section, I concentrate on the *Nachlass* of 1881 (the period of M/FW), where Nietzsche inaugurates his turn to the body and the project of a philosophical physiology. In this context, he develops a *socio-physiological prehistory of the individual* and the *historical emergence of the first individuals*, modelled on his concept of the organism and organismic life-processes. It involves a speculative narrative of our long prehistory as organs of the social organism, which then undergo a difficult and painful transition into the self-regulating organisms that we take for individuals (11[182] 9). This narrative serves both critical and constructive ends: to generate a *critical diagnosis* of the malaise of modern individuals, as a condition of bondage, and *constructive guidelines* for overcoming this condition and realizing individual sovereignty. So, although this project is worked out in polemical opposition to Kant (as well as Spinoza and Spencer), we can say that, like Kant's historical-political writings, it is a response to the *non-appearance of freedom* in history and the *demand that freedom be realized*; a very different response, of course, in approach and normative orientation. As such it is the constructive pendant or counterpart to Nietzsche's physiological destruction of Kantian freedom set out in Chapter 3.

Nietzsche's socio-physiology is part of his sustained effort to naturalize morality. For Nietzsche this means *first* a *critical-theoretical* project to collapse the normative domain onto the plane of immanence by translating moral values from the language of reason and morality back into their 'natural "immorality"'[22] and the physiological language of life-processes and life-forms. But it also involves *secondly* the *practical-normative project* to reconstruct moral values and modes of practical engagement in terms that acknowledge (*Erkennen und Anerkennen*), affirm and enhance life or

---

[21] Saner (1967 20f.) takes the analogy all the way to the conflict of attractive and repulsive forces within and between monads in Kant's early metaphysics.

[22] '[M]y task is to translate the apparently emancipated moral values that have become *nature-less* back into their nature – i.e., into their natural "immorality"' ('[M]eine Aufgabe ist, die scheinbar emancipirten und n a t u r l o s gewordenen Moralwerthe in ihre Natur zurückzuübersetzen – d.h. in ihre natürliche "Immoralität"': 9[86] 12).

nature in its highest forms. In this sense Nietzsche's socio-physiology represents one articulation of his life-long commitment to life-affirmation and -enhancement. And it culminates in a naturalistic ideal of autonomous self-determination that revolves around a 'thoughtful egoism' informed by physiological self-knowledge and knowledge of others; that is, knowledge of one's needs as a living being and one's life-processes as a self-regulating organism, as well as those of others.

In these notes, Nietzsche works mainly with a model of the organism derived from the evolutionary biologist Wilhelm Roux.[23] On this view, any form of life must perform certain processes that enable it to regulate itself and so meet its conditions of existence. For Nietzsche, this does not mean self-preservation through the calculus of compensation for energetic loss, but a *non-teleological dynamic of over-compensation, accumulation, boundless growth and reproduction*. As the basic process in all organic life, Nietzsche takes assimilation, appropriation or incorporation (*Habsucht, Aneignungslust, Assimilation an sich, Einverleiben*) within a dynamic of overcompensation (*überreichlicher Ersatz*).[24] Other essential life-processes discussed by him include excretion or secretion, transformation, regeneration and metabolism.

The first phase of Nietzsche's story concerns our long prehistory as members of tightly knit social groups, what the GM calls 'those immense periods of the "morality of mores" [...] that precede "world history"', 'the real and decisive principal history, which fixed the character of humanity' (GM II 2). In this phase the organismic model is applied by Nietzsche not to individual humans or proto-humans, but to the social

---

[23] These notes attest to Nietzsche's first encounter with Roux's *Kampf der Theile im Organismus: Ein Beitrag zur Vervollständigung der mechanischen Zweckmässigkeitslehre* (1881), to which returned in 1883 and 1884. See Müller-Lauter (1999b 163) (also Müller-Lauter 1978) and Pearson (2018 306–42). Nietzsche was first drawn to Roux by two key moves he made: (1) to extend Darwinian evolutionary struggle *between* organisms to the relations *within* the organism; and (2) to displace teleological accounts of the inner purposiveness of organisms with non-teleological, mechanistic causation, as the explanans of organizational struggle or conflict at all levels: molecules, cells, tissues and organs. Over time, Nietzsche comes to criticize and reject Roux's account for relying on covert teleological principles: survival of the organism, the struggle for nutrition and overcompensation for energetic loss. In their place, Nietzsche develops the dynamic of power and overpowering, based on excess (rather than loss or lack) and an economy of expenditure (rather than compensation/overcompensation for loss). He also rejects Roux's mechanistic causation as insufficient to explain self-regulation as a function of power relations, in favour of commanding and obeying (Müller-Lauter 1978, 209ff.). But as Pearson (2018 318, 306–41) has shown, the processes assimilation or incorporation (*Einverleibung*) and excretion, first gleaned from his reading of Roux, remain central to the will to power, albeit on these different terms. In the 1881 notes to be discussed in this chapter, Nietzsche's criticisms do not appear yet, but he seems to appropriate Roux in ways that prefigure key elements of the will to power: accumulation, boundless growth through assimilation, the craving for power, commanding and expenditure.

[24] E.g. '[...] 2) overcompensation: in the form of *acquisitiveness* the pleasure of appropriation the craving for power/3) assimilation to oneself: in the form of praise reproach making others dependent on oneself, to that end deception cunning, learning, habituation, commanding incorporating [*Einverleiben*] judgements and experiences [...].'
'[...] 2) überreichlicher Ersatz: in der Form von H a b s u c h t
  Aneignungslust Machtgelüst
  3) Assimilation an sich: in der Form von Loben Tadeln
  Abhängigmachen Anderer von sich, dazu Verstellung
  List, Lernen, Gewöhnung, Befehlen Einverleiben von
  Urtheilen und Erfahrungen [...]' (11[182] 9.509).

group, so that humans are but organs of a larger, self-regulating social organism to which they belong ('society'/'the state'). As organs, their actions and impulses are determined by the needs and interests of the organism to which they belong: they feel the '*affects of society* towards [*gegen*] other societies and single beings [...] and *not* as individuals'; there are *only* public enemies. But as an organ, the human being also assimilates or incorporates the interests, needs, the 'experiences and judgements' of the organism, so that later 'when the ties of society break down', it can use them to reorganize itself into an independent, self-regulating organism.

The second phase begins with the emergence of the first experimental individuals or *Versuchs-Individuen*, as the bonds of society weaken. On Nietzsche's organismic model, the emergence of individuals requires that organs in the service of the social organism learn to become independent organisms. This means that the affects, experiences and judgements of the social organism they have incorporated as organs in its service must be re-oriented towards their own conditions of existence as independent organisms, rather than organs of a larger whole – a process described as a painful and difficult '*reordering, and assimilation and excretion of drives*'.

> The times when they emerge are those of de-moralization [*Entsittlichung*], of so-called corruption, that is, all drives now want to go it alone and, since they have not until now *adapted* to that personal utility [i.e. the vital interests of the individual – HS], they destroy the individual through excess [*Übermaaß*]. Or they lacerate it in their struggle [*Kampfe*] with one another. (11[182] 9.511f.)[25]

The destructive conflict of drives unleashed by the emancipation of the first individuals from bondage to the social organism has one of three likely results: (1) One drive gains absolute supremacy over the others and a unified individual is attained, but one that is dominated by one excessive drive and the interests of that drive, rather than the entire organism; the individual perishes. Alternatively (2) in the conflict of drives, those functions that have long-served the social organism gain ascendancy over others that serve the new emerging organism, with the result that it cannot meet its conditions of life as a new unity and perishes:

> In the one who wants to become free, those functions with which he (or his forefathers) served society inevitably predominate in strength: these pre-eminent functions guide and further or limit the rest – but he needs *all of them* in order to *live* as an organism himself, they are *conditions of life*! (11[182] 9.488)[26]

---

[25] 'Die Zeiten, wo sie entstehen, sind die der Entsittlichung, der sogenannten Corruption d.h. alle Triebe wollen sich jetzt persönlich versuchen und nicht bis dahin jenem persönlichen Nutzen a n g e p a ß t zerstören sie das Individuum durch Übermaaß. Oder sie zerfleischen es, in ihrem Kampfe mit einander'.
[26] 'Unvermeidlich überwiegen bei einem, der frei werden will, die Funktionen an Kraft, mit denen er (oder seine Vorfahren) der Gesellschaft gedient haben: diese hervorragenden Funktionen lenken und fördern oder beschränken die übrigen – aber a l l e hat er nöthig, um als Organism selber zu l e b e n, es sind L e b e n s b e d i n g u n g e n !'

Or (3) the conflict of drives remains unresolved and the organ fails to attain the unity of an individual organism altogether. The problem for the emerging individual is, then, *how to attain unity*, and on Nietzsche's organismic model this means: *the unity of a viable organism able to meet its conditions of life by means of self-regulation*, so that he can write:

> Self-regulation does not just happen of its own accord. Indeed, all in all, the human is a being that necessarily goes to ground, because it has not yet attained it. (11[130] 9)[27]

The conflict of the drives moves the first moral philosophers to save the individual by commending a reactionary path of bondage:

> The ethicists [*Ethiker*] then come forward and seek to show human beings how they can still live without suffering so from themselves – mostly by commending to them the *old conditioned way of life* under the yoke of society, only that in place of society it is [the yoke of] a concept – they are *reactionaries*. But they *preserve* many, even if they do so by recurring back to bondage [*Gebundheit*]. Their claim is that there is an *eternal moral law* [ewiges Sittengesetz]; they will not acknowledge the individual law [*das individuelle Gesetz*] and call the effort to attain it immoral and destructive. – (11[182] 9.512)[28]

The individual is hereby saved and saved from suffering, but *not* its sovereignty. The ethos of self-subjection to the concept of the moral law enables the nascent individual to impose measure and peace among its drives, but it does so at the cost of bondage and conformism. The achievement of the first moral philosophers or 'wise men' was to exploit the predominance of the social drives (2. above) and to teach the nascent individuals how to thrive as individuals in bondage to society and social goods ('to demonstrate the old morality as agreeable and useful *for the singular being* [d e n E i n z e l n e n]': 11[189] 9.516); that is, how to achieve viable unity, not as autonomous organisms, but as individual organs of society.

III.1 Nietzsche's critical diagnosis of the modern subject

According to Nietzsche, this reactionary strategy has had enormous consequences. It inaugurates the history of the 'herd-animals and social plants' (11[130] 9.488) that

---

[27] 'Die Selbstregulirung ist nicht mit Einem Male da. Ja, im Ganzen ist der Mensch ein Wesen, welches nothwendig zu Grunde geht, weil es sie noch nicht erreicht hat.'

[28] 'Die Ethiker treten dann auf und suchen dem Menschen zu zeigen, wie er doch leben könne, ohne so an sich zu leiden – meistens, indem sie ihm die a l t e b e d i n g t e L e b e n s w e i s e unter dem Joche der Gesellschaft anempfehlen, nur so daß an Stelle der Gesellschaft ein Begriff tritt – es sind R e a k t i o n ä r e. Aber sie e r h a l t e n Viele, wenn gleich durch Zurückführung in die Gebundenheit. Ihre Behauptung ist, es gebe ein e w i g e s S i t t e n g e s e t z; sie wollen das individuelle Gesetz nicht anerkennen und nennen das Streben dahin unsittlich und zerstörerisch. –.'

have come to dominate in modernity. Nietzsche's socio-physiological analysis allows him to draw three consequences for his diagnosis of the malaise of modern individuals:

1. The first consequence is the *continued predominance of social drives in their conflict with individual drives*. As modern individuals, we are more concerned with the well-being of our group or society than with our own being and well-being (11[130] 9.487 f.).[29] The predominance of what Nietzsche's variously calls our 'herd feelings', 'herd-drives', 'herd-forming affects' or 'function-feeling' ('Heerden-Gefühle', 'Heerdentriebe', 'heerdenbildenden Affekte' or 'Funktionsgefühl') derives from the sheer weight of time that we spent as organs of the social organism, and it serves Nietzsche to reinterpret some prevailing moral and social phenomena today and to explain their prevalence. These include:

* Our desire for recognition, encapsulated in the value of 'honour', unmasked by Nietzsche as vanity.

* The ease with which fall for patriotism, patriotic hatred and wars, and our willingness to sacrifice ourselves for family, church, political parties and other socio-political groupings.[30] What Nietzsche's analysis highlights is not our altruism, nor the freedoms of the modern subject, but the patterns of conformism, piety and self-subordination (on the model of the nascent individual's self-subordination to the moral law). Indeed, according to Nietzsche, one of modernity's discoveries is that the structure of self-subjection (for Foucault: subjectification) is so 'natural' or effective that political and social power need not be imposed by coercive means.[31]

2. The second consequence is that, due to the predominance of our social drives over individual drives, *egoism is very weak in modernity*; indeed, that *as modern individuals, we have yet to attain egoism*. The thesis in the notes on socio-physiology is that we are still governed by the group-oriented or social drives cultivated and fixed in the course of our prehistory and think of our selves as functions of a greater whole, rather than autonomous living beings.

---

[29] 'Our drives and passions have been cultivated over immense stretches of time in *social* and *family* groups (previously in ape-*troupes*): hence as social drives and passions, they are stronger than individual [drives and passions], even still day.' ('Unsere Triebe und Leidenschaften sind ungeheuere Zeiträume hindurch in G e s e l l s c h a f t s - und G e s c h l e c h t s v e r b ä n d e n gezüchtet worden (vorher wohl in Affen-H e e r d e n): so sind sie als sociale Triebe und Leidenschaften stärker als individuelle, auch jetzt noch.').

[30] 'Man h a ß t mehr, plötzlicher, u n s c h u l d i g e r (Unschuld ist den ältest vererbten Gefühlen zu eigen) als Patriot als als Individuum; man opfert schneller sich für die Familie als für sich: oder für eine Kirche, Partei. Ehre ist das stärkste Gefühl für Viele d.h. ihre Schätzung ihrer selber ordnet sich der Schätzung Anderer unter und begehrt von dort seine Sanktion. - Dieser nicht individuelle Egoismus ist das Ältere, Ursprünglichere; daher so viel Unterordnung, Pietät (wie bei den Chinesen) Gedankenlosigkeit über das eigene Wesen und Wohl, es liegt das Wohl der Gruppe uns mehr am Herzen. Daher die Leichtigkeit der Kriege: hier fällt der Mensch in sein älteres Wesen zurück.-' (11[130] 9).

[31] We see 'that the *propensity towards the herd* is so great that it always breaks through against all freedoms of thought! There *is* only *very rarely* an ego! The demand for the state, for social establishments, churches etc. has not diminished. vide the wars! And the "nations"!' ('[...] daß der H a n g z u r H e e r d e so groß ist, daß er immer wieder durchbricht, gegen alle Freiheiten des Gedankens! Es g i e b t eben noch s e h r s e l t e n ein ego! Das Verlangen nach Staat, socialen Gründungen, Kirchen usw. ist nicht schwächer geworden. vide die Kriege! Und die "Nationen"!' 11[185] 9).

> ***Egoism*** is *still* incredibly weak! The effects of *herd-forming affects* are so-called [egoistic] very inaccurately: one is greedy and amasses a fortune (family tribe drive), another is promiscuous, another vain (measuring oneself by the standard of the herd), one speaks of the egoism of the conqueror, the statesman etc. – they think only of themselves, but of their 'self' insofar as the ego has been developed by the herd-forming affects. Egoism of mothers, of teachers. (11[226] 9.528)[32]

Vices that we normally perceive and condemn as forms of egoism are unmasked by Nietzsche as multiple effects of our social drives or 'herd-forming affects': greed (as the wish to enrich our family or tribe); promiscuity (as the wish to propagate our family or tribe); and vanity (as the wish for recognition from family or group).

> – Even in the awakened individual the primordial legacy of herd feelings still predominates and is associated with good conscience. (11[185] 9.514)[33]

None of this is to deny that they represent a form of egoism. Rather, ever since the first moral philosophers, we know how to maintain a viable unity as individuals; only we act, not as autonomous beings, but as *individual organs or functions of our social group*, so that Nietzsche can write that statesmen and conquerors 'think only of themselves', but only because their 'selves' or egos have been thoroughly permeated by the 'herd-building affects'. Nietzsche distinguishes sharply between this *functional* or *non-individual egoism* (*nicht individuelle Egoismus*) and *individual egoism* concerned with the individual's being and well-being:

> – This non-individual egoism is the older, the more originary; hence so much subordination, piety (as with the Chinese) thoughtlessness about one's own being and well-being, the well-being of the group is closer to our hearts. (11[130] 9.488)[34]

Nowhere is this functional egoism (*Funktionsegoismus*) spelled out more clearly than in a note where Nietzsche describes it as a 'precursor' or 'preceding stage' (*Vorstufe*) to (real, individual) egoism:

> It is the *stage before* egoism, not opposed to it: the human being *is* really not yet [longer] individual and ego; he still feels *his* existence most and best justified as

---

[32] 'Der **E g o i s m u s** ist n o c h unendlich schwach! Man nennt so die Wirkungen der h e e r d e n b i l d e n d e n A f f e k t e, sehr ungenau: Einer ist habgierig und häuft Vermögen (Trieb der Familie des Stammes), ein Anderer ist ausschweifend in Venere, ein Anderer eitel (Taxation seiner selbst nach dem Maaßstabe der Heerde), man spricht vom Egoismus des Eroberers, des Staatsmanns usw. – sie denken nur an sich, aber an "sich", soweit das ego durch den heerdenbildenden Affekt entwickelt ist. Egoismus der Mütter, der Lehrer.'

[33] '– Auch im erwachten Individuum ist der Urbestand der Heerdengefühle noch übermächtig und mit dem guten Gewissen verknüpft.'

[34] '– Dieser nicht individuelle Egoismus ist das Ältere, Ursprünglichere; daher so viel Unterordnung, Pietät (wie bei den Chinesen) Gedankenlosigkeit über das eigene Wesen und Wohl, es liegt das Wohl der Gruppe uns mehr am Herzen.'

a function of the whole. That is why he allows himself to be ordered by parents teachers castes princes, so as to attain a kind of *self-respect* [...] Obedience duty appears to him as 'morality', that is, he *pays homage* to his herd-drives by setting them up as *onerous virtues*. – (11[185] 9.513)³⁵

Our ready compliance with the powers that be, which we dress up as moral duties and virtues, is unmasked by Nietzsche as a way for us to gain 'self-respect' by paying homage to the 'herd-drives' that dominate us as individual functions of a social whole. This is one of Nietzsche's key objections to Spinoza, another well-known advocate of egoism, whose notion of *conatus* is dismissed by Nietzsche as a primitive form of egoism or '*proto*-egoism':

[...] *My* counter-position: *proto*-egoism [V o r egoismus], herd-drives are older than 'wanting-to-preserve-oneself'. The human being is first *developed as a function* [F u n k t i o n]: later on the individual breaks loose from it insofar as it has, *as a function*, **come to know** and gradually *incorporated* [sich e i n v e r l e i b t] countless conditions for the *whole*, the organism. (11[193] 9.518)³⁶

The assumption that humans, like everything in nature, strive to preserve themselves ignores the predominance of our social drives, fixed in our prehistory, reinforced by ruling powers throughout history and justified by the philosophers, who have taught us to think of the self as a social function, not an autonomous living being (11[303] 9.557). What Nietzsche calls '*proto*-egoism' (V o r egoismus) is the 'prejudice' (*Vorurteil*) that we already know ourselves without the need for research:

The prejudice prevails, one knows the ego, it does not fail to assert itself continually: but hardly any work or intelligence is expended on it – as if we were exempted from research for self-knowledge through an intuition! (11[226] 9.528)³⁷

This criticism applies as much to Spencer and to contract theorists like Hobbes and Locke, for whom self-preservation is both a fact (an anthropological given) and a

---

³⁵ 'Der Egoism ist etwas Spätes und immer noch Seltenes: die Heerden-Gefühle sind mächtiger und älter. Z.B. noch immer s c h ä t z t sich der Mensch so hoch als die Anderen ihn schätzen (Eitelkeit) Er faßt sich gar nicht als etwas Neues in's Auge, sondern strebt sich die Meinungen der Herrschenden anzueignen, ebenfalls erzieht er Kinder dazu. Es ist die V o r s t u f e des Egoismus, kein Gegensatz dazu: der Mensch i s t wirklich noch nicht mehr individuum und ego; als Funktion des Ganzen fühlt er s e i n e Existenz noch am höchsten und am meisten gerechtfertigt. Deshalb läßt er über sich verfügen, durch Eltern Lehrer Kasten Fürsten, um zu einer Art **S e l b s t a c h t u n g** zu kommen [...] Gehorsam Pflicht erscheint ihm als "die Moral" d.h. er v e r h e r r l i c h t seine Heerdentriebe, indem er sie als s c h w e r e T u g e n d e n hinstellt. –.'
³⁶ 'Dagegen i c h: V o r egoismus, Heerdentrieb sind älter als das "Sich-selbst-erhalten-wollen". Erst wird der Mensch als F u n k t i o n e n t w i c k e l t: daraus löst sich später wieder das Individuum, indem es a l s F u n k t i o n unzählige Bedingungen des G a n z e n, des Organismus, **kennen gelernt** und allmählich sich e i n v e r l e i b t hat.' This is an excerpt from a long note on Spinoza containing several criticisms, which will be touched on in the course of this chapter.
³⁷ 'Es herrscht das Vorurtheil, man kenne das ego, es verfehle nicht, sich fortwährend zu regen: aber es wird fast gar keine Arbeit und Intelligenz darauf verwandt – als ob wir für die Selbsterkenntniß durch eine Intuition der Forschung überhoben wären!'

norm (Hobbes's Right to Everything; Locke's Law of Nature). We have not even begun to think in a fine, well-planned and thoughtful way about our selves.

3. In the third place, Nietzsche's socio-physiological history of the self *unmasks the prevailing morality of altruism*[38] *as a form or proto-form of egoism, where the ego or self is taken to be (not an autonomous being, but) a function of a social whole*. At stake in 'altruistic' or 'un-egoistic' actions, like all our actions, is our 'feeling of power' and continued existence as individuals. Under the continued influence of our pre-historical *Funktionsgefühl* we gain our individual feeling of power, whether as patriots, soldiers, princes or mothers, by putting others (the nation, the people, the child) before ourselves in our actions. In truth, 'altruistic' actions like these, far from being self-sacrificial, are the condition for us to continue existing as the patriots, princes or mothers that we are; that is, as individual functions.[39]

According to Nietzsche's socio-physiology, then, altruism is not opposed to egoism, but the dominant form of egoism in a social order where the ego is identified with a social function or role: altruistic actions are conditions of existence (*Existenzbedingungen*) for individuals who *are* their social role or function. We put dependents first, since their dependency is the condition for our continued existence as the function that we are; and we strive for our individual feeling of power by having our status as a function

---

[38] One of Nietzsche's main polemical targets in these notes is the prevailing morality of 'altruism', especially Spencer's variety, which he thinks promotes a *loss of individuality and diversity*, a levelling assimilation of all to all, by subordinating the individual to the 'Zwecke der Gattung' (11[46] 9; cf. 11[40] 9): the purposes or interest of the species. Against this, Nietzsche advances a '*new praxis*' (11[63] 9.464f.) that would make possible 'as many changing, diverse organisms as possible, which drop fruits that have come to their ripeness and decomposition [*möglichst viele wechselnde verschiedenartige Organismen, die zu ihrer Reife und Fäulniß gekommen ihr Frucht fallen lassen*]' (11[222] 9), or what he also calls 'the ever enduring dissimilarity and most possible sovereignty of the singular being [*die immer bleibende Unähnlichkeit und möglichste Souveränität des Einzelnen*]' (11[40] 9).

[39] 'Gehorsam Funktionsgefühl Schwächegefühl haben den Werth "des **Unegoistischen**" aufgebracht [...] Auch unsere Zustände wollen Sklaverei, und das Individuum soll gehemmt werden – daher Cultur des Altruismus. In Wahrheit handelt man "unegoistisch", weil es die Bedingung ist, unter der a l l e i n man noch f o r t e x i s t i r t d.h. man denkt an die Existenz des Anderen gewohnheitsmäßig eher als an die eigne (z.B. der Fürst an das Volk, die Mutter an das Kind) weil sonst der Fürst nicht als Fürst, die Mutter nicht als Mutter existiren könnte: sie wollen die Erhaltung i h r e s Machtgefühls, wenn es auch die beständige Aufmerksamkeit und zahllose Selbstopferung zu Gunsten der Abhängigen fordert: oder, in anderen Fällen, zu G u n s t e n d e r M ä c h t i g e n, wenn unsere Existenz (Wohlgefühl, z.B. im Dienste eines Genie's usw.) nur so behauptet wird' (11[199] 9.521).

At the limit, where altruistic action requires the sacrifice of one's life, the logic of this explanation breaks down. Here Nietzsche appeals to the priority of the species and its survival over the individual as an explanatory principle:

'Die sämmtlichen thierisch-menschlichen Triebe haben sich bewährt, seit unendlicher Zeit, sie würden, wenn sie der E r h a l t u n g d e r G a t t u n g schädlich wären, u n t e r g e g a n g e n sein: deshalb können sie immer noch dem Individuum schädlich und peinlich sein – aber die Gattung's-Zweckmäßigkeit ist das Princip der erhaltenden Kraft. Jene Triebe und Leidenschaften a u s r o t t e n ist erstens am Einzelnen u n m ö g l i c h – e r b e s t e h t aus ihnen, wie wahrscheinlich im Bau und in der Bewegung des Organismus dieselben Triebe arbeiten; und zweitens hieße es: Selbstmord der Gattung. Der Zwiespalt dieser Triebe ist ebensonothwendig wie aller Kampf: denn das Leiden kommt für die Erhaltung der Gattung so wenig in Betracht, wie der Untergang zahlloser Individuen. Es sind ja nicht die vernünftigsten und direktesten Mittel der Erhaltung, die denkbar sind, aber die e i n z i g w i r k l i c h e n. – [...]' (11[122] 9.484). But see also his critique of 'Gattungs-Zweckmässigkeit' as an abstraction that does not exist in 11[178] 9; see also 11[46] 9.

recognized by others. *Altruism is the self-assertion (Selbstbehauptung) of the individual qua organ through the exercise of its function and the desire for recognition as a function.*

III.2 Thoughtful egoism *contra* unsociable sociability

The effect of Nietzsche's socio-physiological narrative is to insert modern individuals in a long history and prehistory which cannot simply be ignored if we are to take seriously the problem of sovereignty or freedom in the present. As modern individuals, Nietzsche contends, we are still confronted with the same conflict faced by the first emergent individuals between the group-oriented or social drives, cultivated and fixed in the course of our prehistory, and self-oriented drives. As such, Nietzsche's socio-physiology recalls the conflict at the heart of Kant's unsociable sociability, between a concern for one's own good or well-being and a concern for the common good. Yet Nietzsche's account involves a very different analysis of this conflict and its consequences for sovereignty, as well as a different, if not an opposed, normative orientation.

For Nietzsche the conflict is not between an egoistic focus on ends located *within* the human being and *external* ends in other beings or the common good. From his naturalistic point of view, egoism is not a moral principle or choice (*Du sollst*), but a necessity (*Du mußt*),[40] since it refers to the processes of self-regulation that every living being must perform if it is to meet its conditions of life and survive. Every living being is necessarily egoistic, and the conflict is between what Nietzsche calls '*non-individual*' or '*functional egoism*' and '*individual egoism*'. In functional egoism, the self is identified with a non-unique social role, 'function' or 'organ' of a social whole, rather than a unique and autonomous living being. Altruistic actions are conditions of existence for individuals who *are* their social role and who demand recognition of their status as that role or function. The prevailing morality of altruism is therefore a misnomer for this form of egoism that has been dominant, largely [but not only] as a result of 'the primordial legacy of our herd-feelings' (11[185] 9.513). Indeed, it follows from Nietzsche's socio-physiological history that the opposition between altruism and egoism, understood as moral principles, collapses: both are thoughtless forms of functional egoism in the service of social wholes, divided by a veil of ignorance from each individual's needs and conditions as a unique form of life. In this regard, Nietzsche's objections to Spinoza and Spencer apply equally to Kant's unsociability or 'moral egoism' (Anth §2 VII.8–9): all are forms of '*proto*-egoism, herd-drive', *Voregoismus*, since we have not even begun to think in a fine, well-planned and thoughtful way about our selves. Nietzsche's objections apply equally to the instinct of self-preservation Kant appeals to in *Religion* (RGV VI.27). If it is part of our 'disposition towards animality', as Kant says, it is only because our animality is thoroughly socialized. Indeed, Nietzsche goes so far as to implicate Kant in the *political* reasons for the historical predominance of functional egoism:

---

[40] 'NB. Der Egoismus ist kein Moralprincip, kein "Du sollst!" denn es ist das einzige "Du mußt".' (7[182] 10.301).

> *Egoism* has been maligned by those who *exercised* it (communities princes party leaders founders of religion philosophers like Plato); they needed the opposed disposition in people who were to perform *functions* for them [...] To glorify selflessness! and concede, as Kant does, that such a deed has probably never been done! Thus, only in order to disparage the opposed principle, to reduce its value, to make people cold and contemptuous, consequently *thoughtless* towards egoism! – For until now it has been the *lack* of a fine well-planned thoughtful egoism that has kept human beings as a whole on so low a level! *Equality* counts as binding and worth striving for! (11[303] 9.557)[41]

What worries Nietzsche is both our unfreedom as individuals and the loss of human diversity that have resulted from the patterns of self-subjection, conformism and functional egoism uncovered by his socio-physiology. Since our self-subjection as functions of a greater whole has been the path of bondage and uniformity, the path to sovereignty requires the cultivation of difference and diversity among individuals through 'a fine well-planned thoughtful egoism'. If our self-subjection as equals to state law or the moral law (whether Socratic or Kantian) has confined us to the level of interchangeable functions, our *enhancement into autonomous individuals requires the cultivation of individual diversity through radically individual self-legislation.*

> Richness of individuals is richness of those who are no longer ashamed of what is their own and what in them is deviant. (ibid.)[42]

In response to his critical *Zeitdiagnose*, Nietzsche calls for the cultivation of our freedom of thought and our individual drives and passions, over our social drives and our 'propensity towards the herd' ('Hang zur Heerde': 11[186] 9.514); he calls on us to conceive ourselves 'as something new', not just as a 'function of a whole' ('Er faßt sich gar nicht als etwas Neues in's Auge': 11[185] 9.513) and for the liberation of our ego from 'herd-building affects' through the '*ascertainment of the ego* before ourselves': 'd i e F e s t s t e l l u n g d e s e g o vor uns selber' (11[226] 9.528).

---

[41] 'D e r E g o i s m ist verketzert worden, von denen die ihn ü b t e n (Gemeinden Fürsten Parteiführern Religionsstiftern Philosophen wie Plato); sie brauchten die entgegengesetzte Gesinnung bei den Menschen, die ihnen F u n k t i o n leisten sollten [...] die Selbstlosigkeit verherrlichen! und zugeben, wie Kant, daß wahrscheinlich nie eine That derselben gethan worden sei! Also nur, um das entgegengesetzte Princip herabzusetzen, seinen Werth zu drücken, die Menschen kalt und verächtlich, folglich g e d a n k e n f a u l gegen den Egoismus stimmen! – Denn bisher ist es der M a n g e l an feinem planmäßigen gedankenreichen Egoismus gewesen, was die Menschen im Ganzen auf einer so niedrigen Stufe erhält! G l e i c h h e i t gilt als verbindend und erstrebenswerth!' It may seem odd to associate Kant with altruism, but there are moments where something like this comes out – as an aspect of sociability under the sign of normative equality: 'The characteristic of sociability is not always putting yourself before another. Always putting oneself before another is weak. The idea of equality *regulates* everything' ('Das Merkmal der Geselligkeit ist sich nicht jederzeit einem andern vorzuziehen. Einen andern sich jederzeit vorziehen ist schwach. Die Idee der Gleichheit *regulirt* alles' (*Nachlass* 1764–68 XX.54). There could not be a stronger sign of the difference between Kant and Nietzsche on equality than these two texts: for Nietzsche it is what keeps human existence on a low level, for Kant it is what makes social life possible.

[42] 'Reichthum an Individuen ist Reichthum an solchen, die sich ihres Eigenen und Abweichenden nicht mehr schämen.'

If Kant calls on us to take moral responsibility for our unsociable propensity to subordinate everything as means to our own ends and to curb it for the sake of realizing the kingdom of ends, we would expect the opposite from Nietzsche's egoism: to promote unsociability – the assertion of the individual's well-being as a unique form of life – and the resistance it offers to our sociability. This is exactly what he seems to do when he writes that sovereignty is attainable only by those few who are able to assert their own interests as living beings *against* the interest of the species in social wholes *without going to ground*:

> The strongest individuals will be those who go against the laws of the species and do not go to ground in the process, the singular beings. (11[126] 9.486)[43]

But Nietzsche does not simply take the side of unsociability against sociability. Instead he argues that 'all of our animal-human drives' ('sämmtlichen thierisch-menschlichen Triebe') have only endured because they serve the survival of our species; they cannot be eliminated, even if they conflict with our needs and life-interests as individuals:

> To *eliminate* those drives and passions in the singular being is first of all *impossible* – he consists of them, and the same drives are probably at work in the architecture and in the movement of the organism [...] (11[122] 9.485)[44]

As the path to sovereignty, 'thoughtful egoism' must acknowledge the social drives in us that subordinate us as individuals to social wholes, while at the same time directing us towards our own conditions of existence (*Existenz-* or *Lebens-Bedingungen*) as singular beings. Nietzsche can therefore write that '[t]he discord [*Zwiespalt*] of these drives is just as necessary as all conflict [*Kampf*] [...]' (ibid.). Since the conflict between social and individual drives cannot be eliminated, it needs to be borne and regulated by every sovereign individual. Taking its normative bearings from necessary life-processes, 'thoughtful egoism' differs sharply from unsociable sociability on this point. From the standpoint of pure practical Reason, unsociability is morally blameworthy, and Kant's historical thought is teleologically oriented towards the elimination of conflict, competition and the other evils of unsociability in a frictionless kingdom of ends[45] – even if in reality it can only be approximated.

---

[43] 'Die stärksten Individuen werden die sein, welche den Gattungsgesetzen widerstreben und dabei nicht zu Grunde gehen, die Einzelnen.'

[44] 'Jene Triebe und Leidenschaften a u s r o t t e n ist erstens am Einzelnen u n m ö g l i c h – er besteht aus ihnen, wie wahrscheinlich im Bau und in der Bewegung des Organismus dieselben Triebe arbeiten [...]'.

[45] 'The idea of a realm of ends is essentially that of a system of collective human action that precludes any ultimate competition between ends, but involves the adoption by rational beings only of those ends that can be combined with those of all others in a mutually reinforcing system of purposive activity.' (Wood 2015 121). 'In effect, then, the moral law of reason of which we become aware through the development of our faculties, has a content directly opposed to the natural purposiveness of the process through which we become aware of it. For it is only through our unsociable competitiveness that our faculties are developed, but of these faculties, the chief one – our moral reason – makes us aware of an unconditional law commanding us to renounce all competitive relations with others of our kind and to pursue only those ends that can be shared by all in common as part of an ideal universal community of all rational beings' (Wood 2015 123).

The most profound difference with Kant concerns the relation between unsociability and sociability. As argued above, in IaG our unsociability is *external* to our sociability, and their relation is one of *antagonism* modelled on the real contradiction or 'conflict of two forces'. In a sense, this relation is mirrored in Nietzsche's conflict between social drives, oriented to the well-being of the social group, and individual drives oriented to individual well-being. Yet this relation is complicated by his socio-physiology, which builds social drives into 'the [very] architecture and movement' of the human beings as the consequence of their pre-historical labour of incorporating the interests, needs, 'experiences and judgements' of the social organism. In other words, sociability is *intrinsic* to thoughtful egoism, which, in addressing the well-being of the individual, must also acknowledge its social drives. Indeed, this is but one of several ways in which sociability is built into Nietzschean egoism. Let me indicate three more.

1. In translating the human being back into nature, Nietzsche's socio-physiology has the immediate consequence of replacing the substantive, autonomous subject (*homo noumenon*) as the centre of our self-relation with a *pluralized subject* or *dividuum* and a more complex synthetic of unity modelled on the self-organizing organism. Nietzsche warns repeatedly against conflating our *self-conscious sense of unity* – *Das Ich, Das ich-Bewusstsein, Einheits-Gefühl des Bewußtseins* – with our unity as organic living beings.[46] Socio-physiology *displaces* the concept of unity from consciousness to the body and *decenters* it from a substantial, ruling I towards a self-regulating plurality of functions or life-processes; what Nietzsche's calls 'the amoeba-unity of the individual' (11[189] 9) or 'the really inborn incorporated working unity of all functions' (11[316] 9.563). Nietzsche does not, however, seek to *reduce* the human individual to an amoeba or protoplasm,[47] and the main task of his *socio*-physiology is to show how deep the process of socialization has gone:

> The naive egoism of the animal has been completely altered by our *social integration*: we just can no longer feel a singularity [*Einzigkeit*] of the ego, *we are always among many*. We have split and continue to divide ourselves again and again. *The social*

---

[46] See 11[316] 9.563:
'Die **letzten** O r g a n i s m e n, deren Bildung wir sehen (Völker Staaten Gesellschaften), müssen zur Belehrung über die ersten Organismen benutzt werden. Das Ich-bewußtsein ist das letzte, was hinzukommt, wenn ein Organismus fertig fungirt, f a s t etwas Überflüssiges: das Bewußtsein der E i n h e i t, jedenfalls etwas höchst Unvollkommenes und Oft-Fehlgreifendes im Vergleich zu der wirklich eingeborenen eingeleibten arbeitenden Einheit aller Funktionen. Unbewußt ist die große Hauptthätigkeit. Das Bewußtsein e r s c h e i n t erst gewöhnlich, wenn das Ganze sich wieder einem h ö h e r e n   G a n z e n unterordnen will – als Bewußtsein zunächst dieses höheren Ganzen, des Außer-sich. Das Bewußtsein entsteht in Bezug auf das Wesen, d e m   w i r   F u n k t i o n   s e i n k ö n n t e n – es ist das Mittel, uns einzuverleiben. So lange es sich um Selbsterhaltung handelt, ist Bewußtsein des Ich unnöthig. – So wohl schon im niedersten Organismus. Das Fremde Größere Stärkere wird als solches zuerst v o r g e s t e l l t. – Unsere Urtheile über unser 'Ich' hinken nach, und werden nach Einleitung des Außer-uns, der über uns waltenden Macht vollzogen. Wir b e d e u t e n uns selber das, als was wir im **höheren** O r g a n i s m u s g e l t e n – allgemeines Gesetz. Die Empfindungen und die Affekte des Organischen sind alle längst fertig entwickelt, bevor das Einheits-gefühl des Bewußtseins entsteht.'

[47] 'Whoever hates or disdains foreign blood is not yet an individual, but a kind of human protoplasm' ('Wer das fremde Blut haßt oder verachtet, ist noch kein Individuum, sondern eine Art menschliches Protoplasma.') (11[296] 9.555). We will return to this text in Chapter 5.

drives (like enmity envy hatred) (which presuppose a plurality) have transformed us: we have displaced 'society' within ourselves, compressed it, and to retreat into oneself is not a flight from society, but often a discomforting *dreaming-on and interpreting* of the processes in us according to the scheme of earlier experiences. [...] (6[80] 9.215)[48]

'We are always among many': By incorporating the needs, values and judgements of the social organism in our prehistory, 'we have displaced "society" inside us' and relate to ourselves in thoroughly socialized terms. Not only do the norms, prohibitions and moral judgements of the social organism in-form our moral sentiments; our very self-relation is constituted by social drives and practices like friendship, enmity, hatred, revenge, envy. Even individuals, as singular beings (*Einzelne*) achieve sovereignty through thoughtful egoism, must treat themselves as a social unity or organism and relate to themselves through social practices.

2. At stake in 'thoughtful egoism' is our emancipation from the thoughtless domination of functional egoism, in which the self is identified with a (non-unique) social role or function, rather than a unique and autonomous living being. Our enhancement into autonomous individuals requires *the cultivation of individual diversity through radically individual self-legislation*. Nietzsche's organismic model of sovereignty takes its normative guidance from the processes that all living beings must perform, yet each form of life is unique and the task of 'thoughtful egoism' is to apply the 'work and intelligence' needed for genuine 'research' into the life-processes that best enable one to meet the conditions of existence unique to oneself and thrive as a singular being. Radically individual self-legislation revolves around *radically individual self-regulation*.

For Nietzsche, the defining characteristic of an organism, as distinct from a machine, is that all life-processes have evolved *from within* and are *determined from within* by the co-ordinated activity (*Selbsttätigkeit*) of its diverse organs or parts (Müller-Lauter 1999c 163–64). But self-regulation includes regulating its relations with its environment, and since the human organism is profoundly social for Nietzsche, his concept of sovereignty depends on the kinds of social relations we maintain with others. We can therefore say that Nietzschean sovereignty is *non-sovereign* in the sense that it depends on cultivating certain relations with others; it is deeply embedded and thoroughly relational in character. But it is *sovereign* in the sense that those relations are determined *from within* by the specific life-form ('organism') in search of the optimal

---

[48] '[...] Wir wenden alle guten und schlechten gewöhnten Triebe gegen uns: das Denken über uns, das Empfinden für und gegen uns, der Kampf in uns – nie behandeln wir uns als Individuum, sondern als Zwei- und Mehrheit; alle socialen Übungen (Freundschaft Rache Neid) üben wir redlich an uns. Der naive Egoismus des Thieres ist durch unsere s o c i a l e E i n ü b u n g ganz alterirt: wir können gar nicht mehr eine Einzigkeit des ego fühlen, w i r s i n d i m m e r u n t e r e i n e r M e h r h e i t. Wir haben uns zerspalten und spalten uns immer neu. Die s o c i a l e n T r i e b e (w i e F e i n d s c h a f t N e i d H a ß) (die eine Mehrheit voraussetzen) haben uns umgewandelt: wir haben "die Gesellschaft" in uns verlegt, verkleinert und sich auf sich zurückziehen ist keine Flucht aus der Gesellschaft, sondern oft ein peinliches F o r t t r ä u m e n u n d A u s d e u t e n unserer Vorgänge nach dem Schema der früheren Erlebnisse.[...]'. See also 11[7] 9.443: 'We treat ourselves as a multiplicity and bring to these "social relations" all the social habits which we have towards humans animals things.'

conditions of existence unique to it and by the kind of self-regulation this requires. The socio-physiological turn in Nietzsche's thought allows him to rethink sovereignty as self-determination in both *radically individual* and *relational* terms. So what kinds of social relations are required for Nietzschean sovereignty?

3. We would expect the 'thoughtful egoist' to use others as means for its own ends, in line with Kantian unsociability. This is confirmed by Nietzsche, who points out that this applies equally to altruistic individuals – read: functional egoists: 'even when they subjected themselves: they furthered their advantage through the power of that to which they subjected themselves' (11[63] 9.464). But his emphasis is on the complexity of our self-regulation as social organisms and the complexity of the *task* of thoughtful egoism – to translate these processes into our affective and practical relations to others. As I will try to indicate, thoughtful egoism issues in ways of treating others that are characterized by *reciprocity* and *ambiguity* to the point of undermining the Kantian opposition between sociability and unsociability. At the same time, the ways in which Nietzsche translates the language of physiology into the language of morality and back show us how he answers the Kantian challenge to physiology – how it can influence human existence in the world.

III.3 Thoughtful egoism and sovereignty: *contra* Spinoza

Nietzsche's ethos of thoughtful egoism and its consequences for sovereignty and the treatment of others rest on a number of presuppositions, worked out by him in polemical opposition to Spinoza. They concern (1) the necessity of conflict all the way down *contra* peace; (2) the economy of expenditure in nature *contra* utility; and (3) the limits of consciousness.

1) *On the necessity of conflict*: We have seen that Nietzsche draws the consequence from his socio-physiological history that the 'discord [*Zwiespalt*]' of drives 'is just as necessary as all struggle [*Kampf*]' (11[122] 9). Thinking with Roux and against him, he argues (with) that conflict and the struggle for scarce resources are intrinsic to the life of the organism at all levels (cells, tissues, organs), but (against) that struggle requires difference and diversity:

> Where there is life there is a formation of corporate bodies, where the constituents struggle for nutrition and space, where the weaker ones accommodate themselves, live shorter, have less progeny: diversity rules in the smallest things, sperm-animals eggs – Equality is a great delusion (11[132] 9.490).[49]

---

[49] 'Wo Leben ist, ist eine genossenschaftliche Bildung, wo die Genossen um die Nahrung den Raum kämpfen, wo die schwächeren sich anfügen, kürzer leben, weniger Nachkommen haben: Verschiedenheit herrscht in den kleinsten Dingen, Samenthierchen Eiern – die Gleichheit ist ein großer Wahn.' For Roux conflict is mostly confined to approximately equal entities at each level of organization (molecules, cells, etc.) (Pearson 2018 308–9). This is one of several instances where we already see Nietzsche breaking with key principles in Roux in ways that point forward to the will to power.

Life-processes consist of the formation of ever larger corporate unities and presuppose (1) the struggle for nutrition and space, and (2) diversity and differentiation among its constituent parts. In Roux's book *Der Kampf der Theile im Organismus* the idea of a productive struggle in the organism is ultimately grounded in Heraclitus's *polemos* ('Der Streit is der Vater der Dinge': Roux 1881 65), while for Nietzsche all struggle is ultimately grounded in his 'ontology' of power: 'Resisting is the form of power – in peace as in war': 11[303] 9.557). This point is made with Spinoza in mind, as when Nietzsche writes:

> How Spinoza fantasises about *reason!* A *fundamental error* is the belief in concord and the absence of struggle – this would really be death! (11[132] 9.490)[50]

Against Spinoza's concept of aggregation through processes of harmonization among 'those which agree entirely with our nature' (or between 'individuals of the same nature'), rejected by Nietzsche as non-life or death,[51] he insists that life consists of processes of aggregation that can only take place through *struggle* among '*different* powers': without power differentials there can be no struggle, and without struggle there can be no formation of larger unities: '*without* struggle and passion everything becomes *weak*, the human being and society' (11[193] 9.517).

2) *Expenditure contra utility*: Another fundamental objection to Spinoza's project to naturalize morality concerns his appeal to 'usefulness' or 'efficacy' as a naturalistic norm. According to Nietzsche this falsifies the reality of nature, which is uneconomical – extravagant, wasteful and destructive:

> On the extravagance of nature! Then the sun's warmth in Proctor! [...] Hence, no false 'utility as norm'! Extravagance [Expenditure] is of itself not a reproach: it is perhaps *necessary*. The *vehemence of the drives* also *belongs here*. (11[24] 9.451)[52]

---

[50] 'Wie phantasirt Spinoza über die V e r n u n f t! Ein G r u n d i r r t h u m ist der Glaube an die Eintracht und das Fehlen des Kampfes – dies wäre eben Tod!'

[51] Nietzsche has Ethics IV 18 Scholium in mind here, where Spinoza writes that nothing is more useful to us 'than those which agree entirely with our nature. For if two individuals of the same nature are joined with each other, they constitute an individual twice as powerful as either. Nothing therefore is more useful to man than man. I mean by this that men can ask for nothing that is more efficacious for the preservation of their being that that all men should agree in everything in such a way that the minds and bodies of all should constitute one mind and one body [...]' (Spinoza 2000 240). See Nietzsche's excerpts in 11[193] 9.517 and his conclusion: 'Unsere Vernunft ist unsere größte Macht. Sie ist unter allen Gütern die Einzige, das alle gleichmäßig erfreut, das keiner dem anderen beneidet, das jeder dem Anderen wünscht und um so mehr wünscht als er selbst davon hat. – Einig sind die Menschen nur in der Vernunft. Sie können nicht einiger sein als wenn sie vernunftgemäß leben. Sie können nicht mächtiger sein als wenn sie vollkommen übereinstimmen. – Wir leben im Zustande der Übereinstimmung mit Anderen und mit uns selbst jedenfalls mächtiger als in dem des Zwiespalts. Die Leidenschaften entzweien; sie bringen uns in Widerstreit mit den anderen Menschen und mit uns selbst, sie machen uns feindselig nach außen und schwankend nach innen. – **ego**: das Alles ist **Vorurtheil**. Es g i e b t gar keine Vernunft der Art, und o h n e Kampf und Leidenschaft wird alles s c h w a c h, Mensch und Gesellschaft.'

[52] 'Zur Verschwendung der Natur! Dann die Sonnenwärme bei Proctor! [...] Also keine falsche "Nützlichkeit als Norm"! Verschwendung ist ohne Weiteres kein Tadel: sie ist vielleicht n o t h w e n – d i g. Auch d i e H e f t i g k e i t d e r T r i e b e g e h ö r t h i e r h e r.'

This gives us the second important presupposition for Nietzsche's naturalistic model of sovereignty: against 'utility' or 'usefulness' as the norm for moral behaviour, Nietzsche's sovereign individuals will take their normative bearings from the necessity of expenditure. The immediate consequence is to displace the *telos* of 'self-preservation' (*contra* Spinoza and Roux) and the calculus of compensation for energetic loss with a non-teleological dynamic of over-compensation, accumulation, boundless growth and reproduction, so that Nietzsche can write:

> To extend the concept of nutrition; not interpret one's life falsely,
> as do those who only have an eye on their preservation.
>   We must not allow our life to slip through our fingers, on account of
> a 'goal' – but rather reap the fruits of *all* the seasons of our lives.

> Den Begriff der Ernährung erweitern; sein Leben nicht falsch
> anlegen, wie es die thun, welche bloß ihre Erhaltung im Auge
> haben.
>   Wir müssen unser Leben nicht uns durch die Hand schlüpfen
> lassen, durch ein 'Ziel' – sondern die Früchte a l l e r
> Jahreszeiten von uns einernten. (11[2] 9.441; cf. 11[132] 9)

3) *Consciousness*: According to Nietzsche, we have seen, Spinoza succumbs to the common prejudice that we know ourselves and the error of conflating the unitary I of consciousness with our 'the really inborn incorporated working unity of all functions' (11[316] 9.563). Consciousness is not only a late and highly fallible organ; it first arises in relation to a greater social whole as a means for us to subordinate and incorporate (*einverleiben*) ourselves within it as a function through the power of representation. To begin with consciousness is *consciousness of a greater whole outside us*:

> – Our judgements concerning our 'I' limp behind and are carried out following the lead of that which is outside us, of the prevailing power over us. *We signify to ourselves what we are considered to be in the* **higher organism** – general law. (11[316] 9.563)[53]

On the basis of this general law (functional egoism), Nietzsche argues, it is a mistake to rely on our (self-)conscious reasoning for normative guidance on how to regulate ourselves and sustain our unity as *autonomous* living beings.[54] Instead, our cognitive

---

[53] '– Unsere Urtheile über unser "Ich" hinken nach, und werden nach Einleitung des Außer-uns, der über uns waltenden Macht vollzogen. W i r b e d e u t e n u n s s e l b e r d a s, a l s w a s w i r i m **höheren** O r g a n i s m u s g e l t e n – allgemeines Gesetz.'

[54] 'Sonderbar: das worauf der Mensch am stolzesten ist, seine Selbstregulirung durch die Vernunft, wird ebenfalls von dem niedrigsten Organism geleistet, und besser, zuverlässiger! Das Handeln nach Zwecken ist aber thatsächlich nur der allergeringste Theil unserer Selbstregulirung: handelte die Menschheit wirklich nach ihrer Vernunft d.h. nach der Grundlage ihres M e i n e n s und W i s s e n s, so wäre sie längst zu Grunde gegangen. Die Vernunft ist ein langsam sich entwickelndes Hülfsorgan, was ungeheure Zeiten hindurch glücklicherweise wenig Kraft hat, den Menschen zu bestimmen, es arbeitet im D i e n s t e der organischen Triebe, und emancipirt sich langsam zur G l e i c h b e r e c h t i g u n g mit ihnen – so daß Vernunft (Meinung und Wissen) mit den Trieben kämpft, als ein eigener neuer Trieb – und spät, ganz spät z u m Ü b e r g e w i c h t' (11[243] 9.533).

capacities must be put to work 'in service of the organic drives' and the 'real inborn incorporated working unity of all our functions' by developing and refining our physiological self-understanding as self-regulating organisms. Instead of regulating ourselves through rational deliberation of purposive agency alone – 'acting according to purposes [*Zwecken*] is actually only the smallest part of our self-regulation' (11[243] 9.533) – we need to take our normative guidance from the processes that enable us to live.

Purposive consciousness and agency are, of course, the element or medium of Kantian anthropology (p. 153), and Nietzsche's objections to Spinoza can equally be turned against Kant as an initial riposte to the challenge he issued to physiology. *Pace* Kant, purposive consciousness is captive to the levelling social 'purposes' of functional egoism; it is not the *mobile* of agency, but a small part of physiological processes within a non-teleological economy of expenditure; the overestimation of reason is a phantasm, which advances life-negating ideals of concord – not to mention the inestimable damage it has done:

> – Whether reason has overall preserved more than it has destroyed until now, with its conceit of knowing everything, to know the body, to 'will' – ? Centralization is far from perfect – and the conceit of reason to **be** this centre is certainly the greatest deficit of this perfection. (11[132] 9.490)[55]

But what exactly is to be gained philosophically from Nietzsche's translations of the language of reason and morality into physiology and back? And how can this praxis aspire to *influence* human behaviour in a way that surpasses the limitations of Kantian anthropology?

Nietzsche's response to the question of influence turns on affects. From his sociophysiology we know that we are not just organisms on the level of animal life, but thoroughly socialized beings. And for Nietzsche it is clear that 'our affects are the means to maintain the movements and constructions of a *social* organism'; it is the affects 'which self-regulate, assimilate, excrete transform, regenerate here'.[56] This goes equally for the social organisms that we are each of us as individuals, as for the greater social organisms to which we belong. A 'fine well-planned thoughtful egoism' must therefore focus on *understanding and influencing our affects*, as the means by which we regulate ourselves as individual social organisms and regulate our relations to others in the larger social organism we inhabit. And since for Nietzsche, 'our affects presuppose

---

[55] '– Ob die Vernunft bisher im Ganzen mehr erhalten als zerstört hat, mit ihrer Einbildung, alles zu wissen, den Körper zu kennen, zu "wollen" – ? Die Centralisation ist gar keine so vollkommene – und die Einbildung der Vernunft, dies Centrum zu **sein** ist gewiß der größte Mangel dieser Vollkommenheit.'

[56] See 11[241] 9.532: 'Wenn unsere Affekte das Mittel sind, um die Bewegungen und Bildungen eines g e s e l l s c h a f t l i c h e n Organism zu unterhalten, so würde doch nichts fehlerhafter sein als nun zurückzuschließen, daß im niedrigsten Organism es eben auch die Affekte seien, welche hier selbstreguliren, assimiliren, exkretiren umwandeln, regeneriren – also Affekte auch da vorauszusetzen, Lust Unlust Willen Neigung Abneigung. [...] – Unsere Affekte setzen Gedanken und Geschmäcker voraus, diese ein Nervensystem usw'.

thoughts and tastes' (ibid.), *individual sovereignty can be achieved only by using our knowledge of organismic self-regulation to influence the 'thoughts and tastes' upon which our affects depend, so as to adapt them to our needs as singular autonomous organisms, rather than organs of a social whole.* This describes both the work each of us must do on themselves and the task Nietzsche sets himself in this notebook. So what exactly does this mean for our treatment of others?

III.4 Thoughtful egoism and our treatment of others

Nietzsche's 'thoughtful egoism' requires research into *both* the life-processes that regulate each of us as organisms *and* our affective relations to others through which these processes are realized. For preliminary orientation, Nietzsche lists a number of questions near the beginning of the notebook:

a. How much do I need in order to live in a way that is healthy and agreeable to me?
b. How do I acquire this in a way that the process of acquisition is healthy and agreeable and meets the requirements of my spirit, especially as recreation?
c. How do I have to think of others in order to think as well as possible of myself and to grow in the feeling of power?
d. How do I bring others to acknowledge my power? (11[11] 9.444f.)[57]

These questions suggest what we would expect from an egoistic ethos of any kind, namely that it *uses others for its own ends*. This is confirmed by Nietzsche when, under the heading 'n e u e P r a x i s', he asks how we are to treat others:

> – *Use* them as powers for our goals – how else? Just as people always did (even when they subjected themselves: they furthered their advantage through the power of that to which they *subjected* themselves) – Our intercourse with people must be geared towards *discovering* the available *powers*, those of peoples classes etc. – and then disposing over these powers to the advantage of our goals (including allowing them to destroy one another, if this is necessary). (11[63] 9.464)[58]

---

[57] 'a. Wie viel brauche ich, um gesund und angenehm für mich zu leben?
b. Wie erwerbe ich dies so, daß das Erwerben gesund und angenehm ist und meinem Geiste zu Statten kommt, zumal als Erholung?
c. Wie habe ich von den Anderen zu denken, um von mir möglichst gut zu denken und im Gefühle der Macht zu wachsen?
d. Wie bringe ich die Anderen zur Anerkennung meiner Macht?'
[58] '– Als Kräfte für unsere Ziele sie v e r w e n d e n – wie anders? So wie es die Menschen immer machten (auch wenn sie sich unterwarfen: sie förderten ihren Vortheil durch die Macht dessen, dem sie sich u n t e r w a r f e n) – Unser Verkehr mit Menschen muß darauf aus sein, die vorhandenen K r ä f t e z u e n t d e c k e n, der der Völker Stände usw. – dann diese Kräfte zum Vortheil unserer Ziele zu stellen (eventuell sie sich gegenseitig vernichten lassen, wenn dies noth tut).'

The importance of this instrumental perspective (and its possible implications in parentheses!) for Nietzsche's *'new praxis'* is undeniable. Yet it cannot be left at that. Our self-regulation as social organisms is enormously complex, as is the 'thoughtful egoism' that would translate these processes into affective relations to others. We get an indication of this complexity from an organismic model of sovereignty sketched by Nietzsche in this notebook, in which a list of physiological processes on the left-hand side is then filled out in the language of morality on the right:

A strong free human being feels *the qualities of the* **organism** towards [*gegen*] everything else
  1) self-regulation: in the form of *fear* of all alien incursions, in the *hatred* towards [*gegen*] the enemy, moderation, etc.
  2) overcompensation: in the form of *acquisitiveness* the pleasure of appropriation the craving for power
  3) assimilation to oneself: in the form of praise reproach making others dependent on oneself, to that end deception cunning, learning, habituation, commanding incorporating [*Einverleiben*] judgements and experiences
  4) secretion and excretion: in the form of revulsion contempt for the qualities in itself which are *no longer* of use to it; communicating [*mittheilen*] that which is superfluous goodwill
  5) metabolic power: temporary worship admiration making oneself dependent fitting in, almost dispensing with the exercise of the other organic functions, transforming oneself into an 'organ', being able to serve
  6) regeneration: in the form of sexual drive, pedagogic drive, etc. (11[182] 9.509f.).[59]

---

[59] 'Ein starker freier Mensch empfindet gegen alles Andere die E i g e n s c h a f t e n d e s **O r g a n i s m u s**
1) Selbstregulirung: in der Form von F u r c h t vor allen fremden Eingriffen, im H a ß gegen den Feind, im Maaßhalten usw.
2) überreichlicher Ersatz: in der Form von H a b s u c h t Aneignungslust Machtgelüst
3) Assimilation an sich: in der Form von Loben Tadeln Abhängigmachen Anderer von sich, dazu Verstellung List, Lernen, Gewöhnung, Befehlen Einverleiben von Urtheilen und Erfahrungen
4) Sekretion und Excretion: in der Form von Ekel Verachtung der Eigenschaften an sich, die ihm n i c h t m e h r nützen; das Überschüssige mittheilen Wohlwollen
5) metabolische Kraft: zeitweilig verehren bewundern sich abhängig machen einordnen, auf Ausübung der anderen organischen Eigenschaften fast verzichten, sich zum "Organe" umbilden, dienen-können
6) Regeneration: in der Form von Geschlechtstrieb, Lehrtrieb usw'.

In what follows I will illustrate the complexity of 'thoughtful egoism' by concentrating on the function of nutrition, set out under rubric 2) 'overcompensation' above, and its implications for our treatment of others.

Nutrition as the guiding thread for our treatment of others

The presupposition for all organic life, as we saw earlier, is over-compensation for energetic losses within a non-teleological dynamic of expenditure:

> If we translate the properties of the lowest living being into our 'reason', they become *moral* drives. Such a being assimilates what is nearest, turns it into its property (property is first nutrition and storage of nutrition), it seeks to incorporate as much as possible into itself, not just to *compensate* for loss – it is ***avaricious***. Only thus does it *grow* and in the end it becomes *reproductive* – it splits into 2 beings. Growth and generation follow the unlimited *drive to appropriate*. (11[134] 9.490)[60]

Property, appropriation, assimilation, incorporation are all referred to the function of nutrition and the accumulation of nutrition needed to overcompensate for energetic losses, grow and reproduce. Clearly this can translate into using others for our own ends, exploiting, tyrannizing, even destroying them (11[134] 9.490). But we need to expand and refine our understanding of nutrition, according to Nietzsche:

> To extend the concept of nutrition; not to interpret one's life falsely,
> as do those who only have an eye on their preservation [...]
>   We want to reach out to everything that is outside us as to our
> nutrition. Often they are the fruits that have ripened just for our
> age. – Must one always have only the egoism of the robber or the thief?
> Why not that of the gardner? Joy in caring for others, like that of a garden! (11[2] 9)[61]

---

[60] 'Wenn wir die Eigenschaften des niedersten belebten Wesens in unsere "Vernunft" übersetzen, so werden m o r a l i s c h e Triebe daraus. Ein solches Wesen assimilirt sich das Nächste, verwandelt es in sein Eigenthum (Eigenthum ist zuerst Nahrung und Aufspeicherung von Nahrung), es sucht möglichst viel sich einzuverleiben, nicht nur den Verlust zu c o m p e n s i r e n – es ist **habsüchtig**. So w ä c h s t es allein und endlich wird es so r e p r o d u k t i v – es theilt sich in 2 Wesen. Dem unbegrenzten A n e i g n u n g s t r i e b e folgt Wachsthum und Generation.'

[61] 'Den Begriff der Ernährung erweitern; sein Leben nicht falsch
anlegen, wie es die thun, welche bloß ihre Erhaltung im Auge
haben [...]
  Wir wollen nach den Andern, nach allem, was außer uns ist,
trachten als nach unserer Nahrung. Oft auch sind es die Früchte,
welche gerade für unser Jahr reif geworden sind. – Muß man
denn immer nur den Egoismus des Räubers oder Diebes haben?
Warum nicht den des Gärtners? Freude an der Pflege der
Andern, wie der eines Gartens!'

Using others need not mean robbing them of their power or autonomy. It can coincide with caring for them and their well-being in our actions towards them, for then we benefit from the fruits of their energetic expenditure: there is nothing as useful to man as man. This deeply Spinozistic thought (E III 18) – malgré Nietzsche – is *reciprocal* for Nietzsche when he describes, under the function of '4) secretion and excretion [...] sharing [*mittheilen*] that which is superfluous goodwill' (11[182] 9; p. 181):

> When he '*shares*' with others, is '*unselfish*' – this is perhaps only the excretion of his *useless faeces*, which he *must* get rid of in order not to suffer from them. He knows that this dung is of *use* to other fields and makes a *virtue* out of his 'generosity'. – (11[134] 9.492)[62]

The use we make of others by enjoying the fruits of their well-being is *reciprocated* by processes of fertilization and fructification of use to them.

If *goodwill* or friendliness (*Wohlwollen*) is placed under the rubric of secretion/excretion in one note, in others it too is placed under nutrition in the form of *appropriation* (*Besitzlust*):

> In *goodwill* there is refined possessiveness, refined sexuality, refined laxness in security etc.
> As soon as refinement is there, the *earlier* stage is felt to be not a stage, but opposed. It is *easier* to think oppositions than degrees. (11[115] 9.482)[63]

Here Nietzsche's appeal to us to refine and extend our understanding of nutrition is repeated for our understanding of possessiveness (*Besitzlust*). What appears to be the opposite of *Besitzlust*, goodwill, is in fact a refined form of *Besitzlust*. The term 'Verfeinerung' – also called sublimation ('sublimirten': 11[105] 9) – recurs in these notes to denote *changes in degree and form of expression wrought upon our organismic functions by the process of social evolution*; changes in which the same function is still performed (this does *not* change), but is transformed into social modes of engagement, or what Nietzsche calls 'moral drives', like goodwill, care, exploitation, etc.

We saw earlier that caring for others is not the opposite of using them, since others are more useful to us if we care for their own well-being. We now see that goodwill is not the opposite of possessiveness, but its refined expression. Under Nietzsche's

---

[62] 'Wenn er "m i t t h e i l t" an Andere, "u n e i g e n n ü t z i g" ist – so ist dies vielleicht nur die Ausscheidung seiner u n b r a u c h b a r e n **faeces**, die er aus sich wegschaffen m u ß, um nicht daran zu leiden. Er weiß, daß dieser Dünger dem fremden Felde n ü t z t und macht sich eine T u g e n d aus seiner "Freigebigkeit". –'.

[63] 'Im W o h l w o l l e n ist verfeinerte Besitzlust, verfeinerte Geschlechtslust, verfeinerte Ausgelassenheit des Sicheren usw.
  Sobald die Verfeinerung da ist, wird die f r ü h e r e Stufe nicht mehr als Stufe, sondern als Gegensatz gefühlt. Es ist l e i c h t e r, Gegensätze zu denken, als Grade.'

socio-physiological perspective, moral modes of behaviour are not opposed to natural functions, as morality would have it, but are those same natural functions performed in a different register. What appear to be opposites – virtuous, altruistic acts on one side, and basic organic functions on the other – turn out not be opposites at all. In this way, the concept of refinement or sublimation introduces an irreducible *ambivalence* into the grammar of moral agency and interaction, which is the subject of another note:

> In the most acclaimed acts and characters are murder
> theft cruelty deception as necessary elements of power. In
> the most censured acts and characters there is *love* (esteem
> and over-esteem of something one desires to possess) and
> *goodwill* (esteem of something one has in possession, which
> one wants to retain for oneself)
>   Love and cruelty not opposites: in the best and most solid
> natures they are always found with one another. (The Christian
> God – a person very wisely conceived and without moral prejudices!) (11[105] 9.478)[64]

Once again this text performs a naturalization of Christian/post-Christian values by grounding them in organismic processes of self-regulation: 'love' and 'goodwill' are exposed as different variations of *Besitzlust*, (depending on whether one does or does not yet have one's object of desire), itself an extension of nutrition, as we know. Our most valued actions are but sublimated forms of (necessary) self-regulatory processes, in which we ignore certain elements because they conflict with social norms and values we have incorporated.[65] What is new here is the *radical ambivalence* this analysis brings to all our actions. If love and goodwill are not opposed to possessiveness, but related to it as refinements or sublimations, so too are they related (not opposed) to other degrees or (less refined) expressions of possessiveness, such as cruelty, hatred, theft, etc. The effect of Nietzsche's socio-physiology here is to 'contaminate' our most valued actions with an admixture of their 'opposites', not as their opposites, but as less

---

[64] 'In den gelobtesten Handlungen und Charakteren sind Mord Diebstahl Grausamkeit Verstellung als nothwendige Elemente der Kraft. In der verworfensten Handlungen und Charakteren ist L i e b e (Schätzung und Überschätzung von etwas, dessen Besitz man begehrt) und W o h l w o l l e n (Schätzung von etwas, dessen Besitz man hat, das man sich erhalten will)
    Liebe und Grausamkeit nicht Gegensätze: sie finden sich bei den besten und festesten Naturen immer bei einander. (Der christliche Gott – eine sehr weise und ohne moralische Vorurtheile ausgedachte Person!)'

[65] See the end of note 11[105] 9.478:
'Die Menschen sehen die kleinen sublimirten Dosen nicht und leugnen sie: sie leugnen z.B. die Grausamkeit im Denker, die Liebe im Räuber. Oder sie haben gute Namen für a l l e s, was an einem Wesen hervortritt, das ihren G e s c h m a c k befriedigt. Das "Kind" zeigt alle Qualitäten schamlos, wie die Pflanze ihre Geschlechtsorgane – beide wissen nichts von Lob und Tadel. Erziehung ist Umtaufen-lernen oder Anders-fühlen lernen.'

refined expressions of one and the same organic function fulfilled by both; and equally, to elevate our most reprobate (censured) actions by disclosing within them our most valued moral sentiments like love and goodwill.

Our most cherished value-oppositions are undermined and discredited by this analysis, which directs our attention as 'thoughtful egoists' towards the entwinement of 'good' and 'evil', love and cruelty, in all our actions, especially our best acts. Once we learn to see through our evaluation of actions as good or evil as an internalization of social norms and prohibitions that falsifies the real character of those actions, we must then learn to *rename* our actions so as to sensitize ourselves to their natural complexity and alter our affective responses to them. The knowledge of ourselves and others required for Nietzsche's 'thoughtful egoism' is a matter of education, where 'education is learning to rename [*Umtaufen-lernen*] or learning to feel otherwise [*Anders-fühlen lernen*]' (ibid.).

If there is an admixture of good and evil, love and hate in every deed; if caring for others is not opposed to using them, since others are more useful to us if we care for their well-being, then the basic oppositions in Kant's concept of unsociable sociability are undermined. Nietzsche's socio-physiology brings a complexity to our understanding of unsociable sociability that completely revises their relation of external opposition or contradiction in Kant. And in taking its normative bearings from the necessity of expenditure and from the life-processes that regulate us as organisms, it confronts the authority of Kant's practical Reason and the universal moral law head on.

These notes also enable us to formulate a Nietzschean response to the Kantian objection to physiology, since they illustrate well the philosophical benefits to be gained from the kinds of translation they perform between the discourses of morality and socio-physiology. Drawing on the different senses of opposition or *Gegensatz* in Nietzsche's vocabulary from Chapter 1, we can say that the basic and recurrent operation in these texts is to overcome metaphysical value-oppositions (Ggz I) by translating them into Nietzsche's genealogical notion of opposition (Ggz II.1), in which the terms are related (*verwandt*), 'linked, bound up in an incriminating manner [...] perhaps even essentially the same' (JGB 2; see pp. 39–40). When our values are viewed as refinements, sublimations or later stages of their so-called 'opposites', their meaning, structure and value are radically altered. Nietzsche's socio-physiology brings insights into the historical and pre-historical sediments of our most cherished moral values and sentiments, exposing their entwinement with 'those bad, apparently opposed things' and impulses, and brings a degree of nuance and complexity to our understanding of morality that is not only absent in Kant, but unprecedented in the history of philosophy. And with its focus on our affective lives and relations, socio-physiology supplements the exclusive attention to purposive consciousness in Kantian anthropology, as the way to influence human existence, by using its insights to rename and influence our feelings and affective relations with others.

III.5 Translating morality into knowledge

Clearly, the question of knowledge is crucial for 'fine well-planned thoughtful egoism' and the claim that it involves a more 'substantial', less illusory interpretation of the moral ideal of sovereignty and associated feelings of power. At issue for thoughtful egoism in specific is *knowledge of affects*, our own and those of others, for affects are for Nietzsche the means whereby we regulate ourselves as both individual and collective social organisms (pp. 179–80). A 'fine well-planned thoughtful egoism' must therefore focus on *understanding and influencing affects*, our own and others'. Strictly speaking, 'knowledge' is a misnomer here, for as we learned from Nietzsche's 'epistemology' in Chapter 1 (pp. 75–7) 'the affects (struggles, etc.) are only intellectual interpretations in areas where the intellect knows absolutely nothing, and yet *believes* itself to know everything'.[66] So knowledge of one's own affective life and others' is at once necessary and impossible for thoughtful egoism. With this caveat in mind, the egoist can only *interpret* where he knows nothing, and the question is what makes for better and worse interpretations. What, then, is the best 'manner of speaking' or 'image-language' (*Sprechart, Bildsprache*) for our affective lives and relations?

So far, we have focused on his practice of 'translation' between the language of physiology and the language of morality. But Nietzsche takes this question one step further. In exploring the question of knowledge, he experiments with the thought of translating the moral language of persons into an amoral and impersonal language of cognition. In effect, the experiment is to exercise his insatiable acquisitive drive in the register of knowledge by using insights gained from his socio-physiology to treat and engage with others, not as moral persons, but as things to be known.

In Nietzsche's socio-physiology, the knowledge-drive is a refinement or sublimation of nutrition and its extension in the acquisitive drive:

> The acquisitive drive – continuation of the *nutritional* and hunting *drive*. Even
> The knowledge drive is a higher acquisitive drive. (11[47] 9.459)[67]

The first task for thoughtful egoism is to transform one's feeling of subjectivity – 'das Ichgefühl umschaffen' – in the light of a refined understanding of our acquisitive drive:

> [...] the principal progress of morality lies [...] in a sharper grasp of what is true in the other and in me and in nature, hence to emancipate the will to possess ever more from the semblance of possession, from imaginary possessions, thus to purify the I-feeling of self-deception. (11[21] 9.450)[68]

The same goes for understanding others, for how can we know how to treat another unless we understand him or her as the unique person who (s)he is?

> [...] *probity* forbids [us] to *misapprehend* him, and to treat him on the basis of presuppositions that are imaginary and superficial [...] Not to treat everyone as a

---

[66] 11[128] 9.487. See p. 76.
[67] 'Der Eigenthumstrieb – Fortsetzung des N a h r u n g s- und Jagd-T r i e b s. Auch der Erkenntnißtrieb ist ein höherer Eigenthumstrieb.'
[68] '[...] der Hauptfortschritt der Moral liegt [...] im schärfer-Fassen des Wahren im Anderen und in [...] mir und in der Natur, also das Besitzenwollen immer mehr vom Scheine des Besitzes, von erdichteten Besitzthümern zu befreien, das Ichgefühl also vom Selbstbetrüge zu reinigen.'

human being, but as a human being constituted in *such* and *such* a way: first point of view! As something that must be known before it is treated in such and such away. Morality with universal prescriptions does every individual an injustice. (11[63] 9.464)[69]

If universal norms necessarily do injustice to others by ignoring their singularity, what then does it take to do them justice? Nietzsche's response is quite radical: to treat them *not* as persons but as things, and to do justice to them as we endeavour to do justice to all objects of knowledge:

> To treat the other human being first as a thing, to look upon it as an object of knowledge, to which one must do justice […] (ibid.)[70]

Along this line of thought, the task is to *de-personify* others in our cognitive interactions with them:

> To weaken the personal tendency! To accustom the eye to the reality of things. *To disregard persons as far as possible for the time being*! What effects must this have! (11[21] 9.450)[71]

This prescription is not, however, limited to our treatment of others, but to all beings, including ourselves: '– Just as we deal with things in order to know them, so also with living beings, so with us' (11[63] 9.464).[72] So the thought-experiment in these notes is to translate the idiom of moral persons into an impersonal, amoral idiom that would do more justice to the affects governing organismic self-regulation in ourselves and others. But what can it mean in practical terms to treat others and oneself as things to be known, as individual objects of knowledge, rather than individual persons? A first indication comes when Nietzsche writes:

> Perhaps it will end in such a way that instead of the I we know the affinities and enmities among things, *multiplicities* and their laws: that we *seek to emancipate* ourselves from the *error* of the I (altruism has also hitherto been an error). Not 'the sake of the other', but 'to live for the sake of the true'! Not 'I and you'! How

---

[69] '[…] die R e d l i c h k e i t verbietet, ihn z u v e r k e n n e n, ja ihn unter irgend welchen Voraussetzungen zu behandeln, welche erdichtet und oberflächlich sind. […] Nicht Jeden als Menschen behandeln, sondern als s o und s o beschaffenen Menschen: erster Gesichtspunkt! Als etwas, das erkannt sein muß, bevor es so und so behandelt werden kann. Die Moral mit allgemeinen Vorschriften thut jedem Individuum Unrecht.'
[70] 'Den anderen Menschen zunächst wie ein Ding, einen Gegenstand der Erkenntniß ansehen, dem man Gerechtigkeit widerfahren lassen muß […]'.
[71] 'Den persönlichen Hang schwächen! An die Wirklichkeit der Dinge das Auge gewöhnen. V o n P e r s o n e n   s o v i e l   w i e   m ö g l i c h   v o r l ä u f i g   a b s e h e n! Welche Wirkungen muß dies haben!'
[72] '– Wie wir mit den Dingen verkehren, um sie zu erkennen, so auch mit den lebenden Wesen, so mit uns.'

could we be permitted to advance 'the other' (who is himself a *summation of delusions*!). (11[21] 9.450)[73]

At issue for Nietzsche, as these lines make clear, is once again the prevailing morality of altruism and the false (substantive/noumenal, asocial) concept of personhood upon which it rests. Thoughtful egoism displaces the altruistic imperative: "'for the sake of the other'" with the cognitive imperative: "'to live for the sake of the true'". But as these lines also make clear, the falsification of the subject applies as much to the 'ego' of egoism as it does to the 'tu' of altruism. At issue is, then, not just altruism, but the entire egoism-altruism opposition and our emancipation as knowers from the erroneous concept of the self or person upon which it rests. Whatever the exact status of the I or ego, we do know as 'thoughtful egoists' that our organismic function of nutrition must be performed and our acquisitive drive (*Besitztrieb*) achieve satisfaction. Nietzsche therefore prescribes cognitive mastery over things, as a sublimated alternative to the egoistic drive to acquire or possess persons:

> To seek to become master over *things* and thereby satisfy one's will to possess! Not to want to possess persons! (ibid.)[74]

And yet, as thoughtful egoists we also know that one and the same drive can take *seemingly opposed* forms in our practical engagements with the world, and that *reciprocity* is a key element in those engagements. This insight allows Nietzsche to displace altruism, as the desire to be possessed by other persons, with a cognitive alternative that satisfies the same acquisitive drive: to be possessed by *things*:

> To **allow ourselves to be possessed** by things (not by *persons*) and from as great a range of *true things* as possible! (11[21] 9.451)[75]

---

[73] 'Vielleicht endet es damit, daß statt des Ich wir die Verwandtschaften und F e i n d s c h a f t e n d e r D i n g e e r k e n n e n, V i e l h e i t e n also und deren Gesetze: daß wir vom I r r t h u m des Ich uns zu b e f r e i e n s u c h e n (der Altruismus ist auch bisher ein Irrthum). Nicht "um der Anderen willen", sondern "um des Wahren willen leben"! Nicht "ich und du!" Wie könnten wir "den Anderen" (der selber eine S u m m e v o n W a h n ist!) fördern dürfen!'

[74] 'Über die D i n g e Herr zu werden suchen und so sein Besitzen-wollen befriedigen! Nicht Menschen besitzen wollen!' On agonal mastery, see Siemens (2021 34f.). Mastery is taken to denote a complex combination of limited affirmation and limited negation of the other, best expressed in note 10[117] 12.523:
'I have declared war on the anaemic Christian ideal (including what is closely related to it), not with the intention of annihilating [*vernichten*] it, but only of putting an end to its *tyranny* and making place for new ideals, more *robust* ideals… The *continued existence* of the Christian ideal belongs to the most desirable things that there are: and just for the sake of the ideals that wish to assert themselves next to it and perhaps over it – they must have opponents, *strong* opponents in order to become *strong*. – Thus we immoralists need the *power of morality*: our drive for self-preservation wills that our *opponents* retain their strength – wills only to become *master over them*. –.'

[75] 'Uns von den Dingen **besitzen lassen** (nicht von P e r s o n e n) und von einem möglichst großen Umfange w a h r e r D i n g e!'

In these texts, then, Nietzsche calls on us to *de-personify* our relations to others, so as to know them better, not as abstract substantive subjects, but as a plurality of autonomous living beings with their own affects and needs, their own affinities and enmities with others and with us: 'Perhaps it will end in such a way that instead of the I we know the affinities and enmities among things, *multiplicities* and their law' (ibid.). Thoughtful egoism combines seemingly opposed practices – taking possession of objects of knowledge (to the point of mastery) and being possessed by them (to the greatest extent) – as different ways to satisfy the organismic function of nutrition/acquisition. This 'oppositional' practice – to possess and be possessed by others as things to be known – is designed to displace the egoism-altruism opposition – to possess *persons* (egoism) or be possessed by other *persons* (altruism) – which trades on a false metaphysical understanding of the subject as substance.

From the notes it is not entirely clear whether knowing others better through de-personification is the *prerequisite* for treating them better as persons (i.e. as a plurality of autonomous living beings), or whether thoughtful egoism displaces persons with things altogether. On the one hand, he describes de-personification as provisional (*vorläufig, zunächst*), on the other hand, as an end state ('Vielleicht endet es damit.') that makes any kind of egoism impossible. For in that case, the ultimate consequence of Nietzsche's cognitive practice is not just purification (*Reingung*) or transformation (*Umschaffung*) of the I, but its dissolution (*Abschaffung*), as he is well aware:

– But does this not also mean to weaken the individuals? Something new is to be created: not ego and not tu and not omnes! (11[21] 9.450)[76]

At certain moments, it looks like Nietzsche's efforts to construct a 'more substantial', organismic account of sovereignty culminate in an overcoming of self- or personhood altogether, and with it existing notions of sovereignty, in favour of creating new 'images of human existence' (*Bilder des Daseins*) beyond individuation – 'In the end a point appears where we want to go beyond the individual and idiosyncratic' ('Endlich erscheint ein Punkt, wo wir über das Individuelle und Idiosynkratische hinauswollen': 11[171] 9.507). At other times, he asks how a 'more substantial' knowledge of others as things can benefit and enhance our self-regulation as organisms:

To **allow ourselves to be possessed** by things (not by *persons*) and from as great a range of *true things* as possible! What will *grow* from that remains to be seen: we are *fruit fields* for things. *Images of existence* ought to grow from us: and we ought to be such as this fruitfulness requires us to be: our inclinations and disinclinations are those of the field that is to bring forth such fruits. (11[21] 9.451)[77]

---

[76] '– Aber heißt dies nicht auch, die Individuen schwächen? Es ist etwas Neues zu schaffen: nicht ego und nicht tu und nicht omnes!'
[77] 'Uns von den Dingen **besitzen lassen** (nicht von P e r s o n e n) und von einem möglichst großen Umfange w a h r e r D i n g e! Was daraus w ä c h s t, ist abzuwarten: wir sind A c k e r l a n d für die Dinge. Es sollen B i l d e r d e s D a s e i n s aus uns wachsen: und wir sollen so sein, wie diese Fruchtbarkeit uns nöthigt zu sein: unsere Neigungen Abneigungen sind die des Ackerlandes, das solche Früchte bringen soll.'

To nourish ourselves by allowing ourselves to be possessed by others as things to be known, Nietzsche supposes, will lead to over-compensation and growth in the register of knowledge. What forms this can take is unknown, but he supposes that it can lead to the creation of new 'images of existence', that is, possible forms of sovereign human existence, which we can strive to actualize, offer up to others and use to guide our relations with them. In this way, nourishing ourselves on others turns us into fruit fields (*Ackerland*), which others can use and appropriate to nourish themselves and grow. We see here again the pattern of *reciprocity* Nietzsche discerns in our relation to others when we take our normative bearings from the life-processes that regulate us as organisms. We saw earlier how promoting their well-being so as to benefit from the fruits of their existence is coupled with processes of fertilization or fructification (excretion) on our part from which they benefit. The *pattern of reciprocity* is perhaps most clearly inscribed in Nietzsche's organismic model of sovereignty (p. 181), in which 'commanding' is complemented by obeying ('being able to serve'), 'making others dependent' by 'making oneself dependent', 'hatred' by 'goodwill', taking by giving and 'learning' by 'the pedagogic drive'.

IV Hostile calm, calm hostility: Towards a new agonism?

In the final part of the chapter, I take Nietzsche's thought-experiment one step further and consider another cognitive ideal of his as a modality for our self-relation and relations with others. Nietzsche's socio-physiology and his translation-experiment from the language of persons into the language of cognition harbour a conjuncture of promising elements for an agonistic politics appropriate to our historical juncture, as I will try to indicate in the Epilogue. At this point, the argument concerns only one such element: *pluralism*. For Nietzsche, genuine pluralism requires an openness to each and every person that allows us to understand each one as a unique, living multiplicity with a complex affective life, which can only thrive under conditions unique to it. The greatest obstacle to genuine pluralism are moralities that confound this kind of attunement by operating with an abstract, substantive concept of personhood and demanding subordination to the interest of an extraneous social whole (functional egoism) or self-sacrifice to the unknown – be it 'utility', Kantian moral law or the greatest happiness for the greatest number:

> Individual morality: as the result of a random throw of the dice a being is there, which seeks *its* conditions of existence – let us take *this* seriously not be fools to *sacrifice for the unknown*! (11[46] 9.458)[78]

Radically individual morality depends on radically individual knowledge, what Nietzsche calls 'die individuelle Wissenschaft' (4[118] 9.130), where 'knowledge'

---

[78] 'Die individuelle Moral: in Folge eines zufälligen Wurfs im Würfelspiel ist ein Wesen da, welches s e i n e Existenzbedingungen sucht – nehmen wir d i e s ernst und seien wir nicht Narren, zu o p f e r n f ü r d a s U n b e k a n n t e!'

and 'science' stand for practices of interpretation that take seriously the difficulty of knowing *'true things'*. As described in note 11[21] above, this means circumventing the false hypostases and oppositions of morality and attending to our acquisitive drive through the 'contradictory' practice of possessing and 'being possessed by as great a range of *true things* as possible', so as to open our eyes to 'the affinities and enmities among things, *multiplicities* and their law' (11[21] 9.451).

Nietzsche's socio-physiological *episteme* of openness can be taken further by considering the critical turn in the late Nietzsche's late thought on question of resistance, in which the affirmation of resistance and the capacity to resist gives way to *non*-resistance, or the capacity *not* to resist. Examining how Nietzsche works out the *ideal of non-resistance* in the sphere of knowledge will give a more concrete, phenomenological turn to his socio-physiological *episteme* of openness, as well as a new and rather surprising twist to agonistic relations – into relations of non-resistance.

In Chapter 3 we saw that Nietzsche promotes the active power to resist, a seeking out of resistance out as a stimulant or source of power, over and against the reactive 'incapacity to resist' (*Die Unfähigkeit zu Widerstand*). In the late 1880s, however, the meaning of active resistance shifts from *the capacity to resist* to *resisting the impulse to resist* or the capacity to resist resisting, which Nietzsche describes as a kind of calm hostility or hostile openness. This shift coincides with an increasing preoccupation with the problem of décadence and a conceptual shift in his thought from the active-reactive dyad to the governing distinction between rapid reacting/hyper-sensitivity and slow or not reacting.[79] The concept of décadence will serve as a guiding thread for reconstructing Nietzsche's changing views on resistance in this period.

The incapacity to resist, at the heart of the reactive meaning *of resistance*, is often linked to the condition of décadence by Nietzsche. As mentioned in the last chapter, décadence, recurrently identified with exhaustion (*Erschöpfung*), is for Nietzsche the congenital defect of philosophers and psychologists, leading them to think resistance and pain from a reactive standpoint. But it is first and foremost the signature illness of modernity. Here it is important to see that décadence is a peculiar, second-order illness. For Nietzsche (following Claude Bernard) health and sickness are not essentially or qualitatively different or opposed.[80] To be sick is to deal with your sickness (*Krankheit*) in a sickly (*krankhaft*) manner. That is to say: to *be unable to resist* damaging, pathogenic influences, those influences that make you sick because they interfere with the conditions of your existence as the specific form of life that you are. Nietzsche can therefore write under the rubric of 'décadence':

---

[79] See Brusotti (2012).
[80] 'G e s u n d h e i t und K r a n k h e i t sind nichts wesentlich Verschiedenes, wie es die alten Mediziner und heute noch einige Praktiker glauben. Man muß nicht distinkte Principien, oder Entitäten daraus machen, die sich um den lebenden Organismus streiten und aus ihm ihren Kampfplatz machen. Das ist altes Zeug und Geschwätz, das zu nichts mehr taugt. Thatsächlich giebt es zwischen diesen beiden Arten des Daseins nur Gradunterschiede: die Übertreibung, die Disproportion, die Nicht-Harmonie der normalen Phänomene constituiren den krankhaften Zustand. Claude Bernard' (14[65] 13.250).

> What is inherited is not sickness, but *sickliness*:
> the impotence in the resistance against the danger of damaging
> incursions etc.; the broken power of resistance – in *moral* terms:
> resignation and humility before the enemy. (14[65] 13.250)[81]

As we might expect, health is not opposed to sickness, but is the sick person's second-order capacity to resist pathogenic influences:

> The *energy of health* in sick persons is betrayed
> by *brusque resistance* against *pathogenic* elements ... (14[211] 13.389)[82]

But Nietzsche takes his diagnosis of décadence one step further, and in doing so he suggests a form of practice that goes beyond the (second order) opposition between the 'broken capacity for resistance' and 'brusque resistance'. The incapacity to resist hostile forces is referred back to a prior *incapacity to resist stimuli überhaupt*, a hyper-sensitivity or irritability typical of modern décadence and the prevailing morality of altruism:

> [N]ot to be able to offer resistance when a stimulus is given,
> but to *have to* follow it: this extreme irritability of the decadents [...] (14[209] 13.388)[83]

>   Towards the history of *nihilism*.
> *Most general types of décadence:*
> [...]
> 2): one loses the *power of resistance* towards
> stimuli, – one is conditioned by fortuities: one
> coarsens and exaggerates experiences to a monstrous degree ...
> a 'depersonalization', a disgregation of the will –
> – that is where an entire kind of morality belongs, the altruistic [morality] [...]
>   (17[6] 13.527)[84]

---

[81] 'Was sich vererbt, das ist nicht die Krankheit, sondern die K r a n k h a f t i g k e i t: die Unkraft im Widerstande gegen die Gefahr schädlicher Einwanderungen usw.; die gebrochene Widerstandskraft – m o r a l i s c h ausgedrückt: die Resignation und Demuth vor dem Feinde.'

[82] 'Die E n e r g i e d e r G e s u n d h e i t verräth sich bei Kranken in dem b r ü s k e n W i d e r s t a n d e gegen die k r a n k m a c h e n d e n Elemente...'

[83] '[N]icht Widerstand leisten können, wo ein Reiz gegeben ist, sondern ihm folgen müssen: diese extreme Irritabilität der décadents [...].'

[84] 'Zur Geschichte des N i h i l i s m u s.
A l l g e m e i n s t e T y p e n d e r décadence:
[...]
2): man verliert die W i d e r s t a n d s - K r a f t gegen die Reize, – man wird bedingt durch die Zufälle: man vergröbert und vergrößert die Erlebnisse ins Ungeheure...
eine "Entpersönlichung", eine Disgregation des Willens –
– dahin gehört eine ganze Art Moral, d i e a l t r u i s t i s c h e [...].'

One might still expect Nietzsche to prescribe the capacity to offer brusque resistance, to-be-an-enemy (*Feind-sein-können*) against such forms of altruism. But what we find is that where décadence signifies the *incapacity to resist stimuli*, Nietzsche's prescribes *the capacity to resist stimuli*. And the capacity to resist stimuli need not translate into enmity, warfare or wanting-to-resist (*Feind-sein-wollen*), but can entail precisely: *the capacity to resist resisting*. Where the stimulus is one of external resistance, the capacity to resist this stimulus involves: not resisting it, not reacting, that is, the capacity to overlook and *not-resist resistance*. Precisely this capacity is identified with the philosopher as an '[a]*scending type*' (*Aufgangs-Typus*): 'Strength in calmness. In relative indifference and difficulty reacting.'[85]

Nietzsche's anti-decadent philosophical counter-praxis of calm and non-resistance is taken further in GD Deutschen. Here the 'objectivity' prized by modern science is referred back to a compulsion to react to everything, to an incapacity *not* to react, against which Nietzsche prescribes an *episteme* based on a kind of hostile calm or openness

> All unspirituality, all commonness rests on the incapacity to offer resistance to a stimulus – one *must* react, one follows every impulse. In many cases such a compulsion is already sickliness [morbidity], decline, a symptom of exhaustion, – almost everything that the unphilosophical crudity designates by the name 'vice' is merely that physiological incapacity *not* to react. (GD Deutschen 6 6.108)[86]

If reactive forms of knowing are rooted in the incapacity to resist stimuli, the counter-capacity to resist stimuli makes possible an active form of knowing or seeing:

> Learning to *see* – habituating the eye to calm, to patience, to letting things come to it; learning to defer judgement, to peruse and grasp the particular case from all sides. That is the *first* preliminary schooling in spirituality: *not* to react immediately to a stimulus, but to get a hold over the inhibiting, concluding instincts in hand. (GD Deutschen 6 6.108)[87]

The attitude or practice of openness, patience, calm made possible by the capacity to resist reacting could not be further from the pugnacious ideal of active agency we are

---

[85] 'Problem des P h i l o s o p h e n und des w i s s e n s c h a f t l i c h e n Menschen. Stärke in der Ruhe. In der relativen Gleichgültigkeit und Schwierigkeit, zu reagiren' (14[83] 13.262).

[86] 'Alle Ungeistigkeit, alle Gemeinheit beruht auf dem Unvermögen, einem Reize Widerstand zu leisten – man *muss* reagiren, man folgt jedem Impulse. In vielen Fällen ist ein solches Müssen bereits Krankhaftigkeit, Niedergang, Symptom der Erschöpfung, – fast Alles, was die unphilosophische Rohheit mit dem Namen "Laster" bezeichnet, ist bloss jenes physiologische Unvermögen, n i c h t zu reagiren.'

[87] 'S e h e n lernen – dem Auge die Ruhe, die Geduld, das An-sich-herankommen-lassen angewöhnen; das Urtheil hinausschieben, den Einzelfall von allen Seiten umgehn und umfassen lernen. Das ist die e r s t e Vorschulung zur Geistigkeit: auf einen Reiz n i c h t sofort reagiren, sondern die hemmenden, die abschliessenden Instinkte in die Hand bekommen.'

used to associate with Nietzsche as a philosopher of conflict. This is not, however, to strip Nietzsche's epistemic ideal of all hostility or resistance:

> [O]ne will have become slow, mistrustful, resistant as a *learner* in general. One will allow the alien, the *novel* of every kind to approach one with hostile calm at first, – one will draw one's hand back from it. (GD Deutschen 6 6.109)[88]

The capacity to resist stimuli makes possible a form of resistance that is *qualitatively distinct* from the forwards-grasping, coercive forms of agency usually associated with Nietzsche. Instead, it is a capacity to *resist resisting*, which makes possible a non-coercive openness, a resistance to conceptual closure that would allow us to acknowledge what is radically other (*Fremdes*) and particular in its otherness and particularity. When viewed as modality of our interactions with others, it gives a tangible form to Nietzsche's socio-physiology of openness – of 'being possessed by as great a range of *true things* as possible' – and opens the prospect of non-coercive, non-oppressive forms of power. These are, I believe, of importance for agonistic politics and its aspiration to be genuinely pluralistic. In the final chapter, I consider a further permutation of our affective relations to others to come out of Nietzsche's philosophy of conflict with potential for agonistic politics: agonal hatred.

---

[88] '[M]an wird als L e r n e n d e r überhaupt langsam, misstrauisch, widerstrebend geworden sein. Man wird Fremdes, N e u e s jeder Art zunächst mit feindseliger Ruhe herankommen lassen, – man wird seine Hand davor zurückziehn.'

5

Nietzsche's philosophy of hatred: Against and with Kant

I Introduction

If there is one affect, above all, that any philosophy of conflict must address, it is surely *hatred*. In this chapter I will examine Nietzsche's philosophy of hatred by taking up the two impulses ascribed to both Nietzsche and Kant in the Introduction: their realism and perfectionism. In response to these impulses, I argue, Nietzsche subjects the notion of hatred in the Christian-moral tradition to a radical *reinterpretation* and *transvaluation* (*Umdeutung, Umwertung*). For his part, Kant's views on hatred are marked by a tension and ambivalence. On one side, we find the Christian-moral condemnation of hatred in favour of love, reconciliation and peace. But Kant is also a philosopher of conflict, and in response to the perfectionist and realist impulses in his thought he takes certain positions and attitudes towards hatred that are surprisingly close to Nietzsche's. To a different degree and from very different perspectives, we can say of Kant that he too performs a reconceptualization and re-evaluation of hatred.

Even more surprising than these affinities, are the implications of Nietzsche's philosophy of hatred for the kind of affectivity and affective relations to others appropriate for agonistic politics. They concern two issues of importance for agonism. The first is the concept of *agonistic respect* to which agonists typically appeal as a source of measure or limits on antagonism that would exclude Nietzsche's *Vernichtungskampf* from democratic life. Nietzsche knows a form of hatred *inter pares*, what can be called *agonal hatred*, which avoids the epistemic problems he sees in recognition by others (see p. 149) and involves an affirmation of the other that eclipses anything respect can muster. This point will be taken up in the Epilogue. The second issue concerns the emancipatory potential of agonistic politics: the claim (or aspiration) advanced by some theorists that agonism can emancipate those living on the margins of political society under conditions of radical inequality. From a Nietzschean perspective, there are two problems here that must be confronted. The first is that agonal relations presuppose an approximate equality of power among antagonists, ruling out those of radically unequal power, whether it be superior or inferior power. Secondly, in the dominant 'slave' morality of European modernity, the template for the emancipation from conditions of radical inequality is the 'slave revolt of morality' described in GM I. The problem confronting emancipatory agonisms is, then, how to avoid replicating the 'slave revolt in morality' and the degradation of the other through the dynamics of hate and *ressentiment*. In the last part of the chapter, I trace elements of this problematic to Kant's writing and offer a comparative analysis of a Kantian and a Nietzschean proposal for overcoming the pathologies they associate with revenge and slavish attitudes.

Most of the chapter is devoted to examining and explicating Nietzsche's views on hatred, beginning (§II) with its place in his ontology of conflict. This analysis isolates the familiar, negative sense of hatred as a destructive force, but also unfamiliar senses that disconnect hatred from contempt (*Verachtung*), moral condemnation and subjection, releasing affirmative potentials. Nietzsche's distinctive claim is that hatred need not be a destructive force, but can take creative forms, and in subsequent sections I examine two very different forms of creative hatred: an active agonal hatred *inter pares* that allows for an affirmative pride in one's enemy (§II.2), and the reactive hatred of the 'spirit of revenge' that gives birth to slave morality (§IV). Thereafter (§V), Nietzsche's philosophical response to the problem of hatred is discussed. Kant's reflections on hatred, revenge and anger are discussed in §III, which I then draw on and develop in the final section (§VI). Here I return to the origins of slave morality for a comparative examination of hatred, revenge and anger, and how each thinker envisions a solution to the pathologies of revenge he diagnoses.

Let me begin by giving clearer contours to the main thesis of this chapter: that Nietzsche performs a radical *reinterpretation* and *transvaluation* of hatred in the Christian-moral tradition. For the Christian-moral tradition, we can do no better than take our cue from Kant's *Religion* text, where he cites the Gospel of St. Matthew on Jesus:

> First, he demands that not the observance of external civic or statutory church duties but only the pure moral attitude of the heart shall be able to make a human being pleasing to God (Matt. 5:20–48) [...] that, e.g., hating in one's heart shall be tantamount to killing (5:22) [...] – that the natural but evil propensity of the human heart ought to be reversed entirely, the sweet feeling of revenge must pass over into tolerance (5:39, 40) and the hatred of one's enemies into beneficence (5:44). (RGV VI.159-160)[1]

Here Kant subscribes to the view that

1. hatred is purely negative and destructive towards other: *so viel als tödten*;
2. hatred is opposed to beneficence (*Wohlthätigkeit*) or love; it stands in 'real opposition' to love, so that Kant can say in NG (II.182): 'hatred [is] a *negative love*' (*de[r] H a ß eine n e g a t i v e L i e b e*);

---

[1] 'Zuerst will er, daß nicht die Beobachtung äußerer bürgerlicher oder statutarischer Kirchenpflichten, sondern nur die reine moralische Herzensgesinnung den Menschen Gott wohlgefällig machen könne (Matt. V. 20–48) [...] daß z.B. im Herzen hassen so viel sei als tödten (V. 22) [...] – daß der natürliche, aber böse Hang des menschlichen Herzens ganz umgekehrt werden solle, das süße Gefühl der Rache in Duldsamkeit (V.39.40) und der Haß seiner Feinde in Wohlthätigkeit (V. 44) übergehen müsse.'

3. hatred of one's enemies can be and ought to be overcome in favour of charity or love and reconciliation, or as he puts it in the *Metaphysics of Morals*: 'V e r s ö h n- l i c h k e i t *(p l a c a b i l i t a s)* [ist] Menschenpflicht' (MS VI:461), '*Forgivingness* [or *placability*] is a human duty'.

The thesis to be advanced is that Nietzsche reinterprets and transvaluates hatred in this sense along the following lines:

1. hatred need not be purely negative and destructive towards other: it can be *productive* or *creative* and can involve a profound *affirmation* of the other;
2. hatred is not simply opposed to love: in physiological terms, erotic or acquisitive love is inseparable from hatred; in a moral terms, Christian agapic love is but a disguised expression of priestly hatred;
3. hatred cannot be overcome in favour of love or reconciliation insofar as hatred and antagonism are deeply embedded in human existence and interaction; or in Nietzsche's terms: a necessary – ineliminable – ingredient in total economy of (human) life.
4. As a consequence: hatred is not simply an evil that ought to be eliminated in favour of its opposite, love. Under certain circumstances (agonal hatred *inter pares*) it can be affirmed as a valuable, creative attitude that is profoundly affirmative of the other. Where Nietzsche does think about the overcoming of hatred – and he does – it is not in favour of love or any other virtue, but in favour of going beyond good and evil: on the one hand: to 'improve' or sublimate hatred by drawing on its idealizing powers for constructive ends; on the other hand, to use physiological self-knowledge to correct the errors intrinsic to hatred and cultivate an *episteme* beyond love and hate.

II Nietzsche's philosophy of hatred

As pointed out in the Introduction, Nietzsche's realism involves confronting hard, ugly truths, truths that he says *cannot be lived with*. If, as JGB 23 suggests, one of the ugly truths disclosed by Nietzsche's realism is that hatred is a necessary ingredient in the total economy of life, then the demand to enhance life seems to entail the sickening consequence that hatred be enhanced and intensified:

> But supposing someone takes the affects hatred, envy, covetousness, the lust for domination as life-conditioning affects, as something that must be present fundamentally and essentially in the total economy of life and consequently must be enhanced further if life is to be enhanced further, – he suffers from such a bent of judgement as from a seasickness.[2]

---

[2] 'Gesetzt aber, Jemand nimmt gar die Affekte Hass, Neid, Habsucht, Herrschsucht als lebenbedingende Affekte, als Etwas, das im Gesammt-Haushalte des Lebens grundsätzlich und grundwesentlich vorhanden sein muss, folglich noch gesteigert werden muss, falls das Leben noch gesteigert werden soll – der leidet an einer solchen Richtung seines Urtheils wie an einer Seekrankheit' (JGB 23).

Is this something that can be practised, or even lived with? Does Nietzsche embrace an ethos of hatred and cruelty, corroborating Bertrand Russell's remark that he 'is so full of fear and hatred' that he cannot conceive a spontaneous love for humankind?[3] Or is it rather a question of how he negotiates the conflict or tension between his realist acceptance of the necessity of hatred and his perfectionist impulse to extend the range of human capacities and imagine new possibilities of existence and co-existence. Nietzsche knows a great variety of 'hatreds', and his question is whether their destructive potential can be contained and their explosive power channelled in ways that can be lived with and enhance human existence.

It is the ancient Greeks, of course, who first provoke Nietzsche's philosophical reflections on hatred. In the *Nachlass* of 1871–2, we read of the 'endless freedom for personal attacks' in Greek comedy as a sign that they 'felt differently' about hatred,[4] and that justice is a far greater virtue among Greeks than us, because 'hatred and envy is far greater' among them.[5] In *Homer's Wettkampf*, Nietzsche dwells on the predilection of Homer and other Greek artists for gruesome war scenes with dismembered bodies, wracked with hatred, and explains the brutal treatment of the vanquished sanctioned by the Greek law of war with the claim that 'the Greek [individual] considered a complete outpouring of his hatred as a serious necessity'.[6] Perhaps the most intriguing Greek-inspired remark is one that begins: 'The gods make human beings even more evil; that is human nature', and ends on a programmatic note:

> This belongs to the sombre philosophy of hatred, which has not yet been written, because it is everywhere the pudendum that everyone feels.[7]

A philosophy of hatred can indeed be made out across Nietzsche's writings, one that is experimental, pointillist, prismatic, but no less rich and complex for that. Indeed, Nietzsche knows many different forms of hatred with diverse effects, from the Greeks' 'abysses of hatred' to the priests' 'most abyssal hatred (the hatred of impotence)' and

---

[3] Russell (2004 735).
[4] 16[29] 7.405:
'7. Unendliche Freiheit des persönlichen Angriffs in der Komödie.
Der Neid der Götter.
Zeichen daß die Griechen anders empfunden haben über Haß und Neid.'
[5] 16[32] 7.406:
'2. Weil der Haß und Neid viel größer ist, ist die Gerechtigkeit eine so unendlich viel größere Tugend. Es ist die Klippe, an der Haß und Neid zerschellt.'
[6] '[...] so sehen wir, in der Sanktion eines solchen Rechtes, daß der Grieche ein volles Ausströmenlassen seines Hasses als ernste Nothwendigkeit erachtete; in solchen Momenten erleichterte sich die zusammengedrängte und geschwollene Empfindung: der Tiger schnellte hervor, eine wollüstige Grausamkeit blickte aus seinem fürchterlichen Auge' (HW 1.784).
[7] 'Es gehört dies in die düstere Philosophie des Hasses, die noch nicht geschrieben ist, weil sie überall das pudendum ist, das jeder fühlt' (5[117] 8.71, 1875–6). Hatred remains an under-researched topic in philosophy. For an exception, see Kolnai (1935 147–87). This essay is also discussed in Brock (2015 198–9, note 302), who points out some apparent similarities between Kolnai's and Nietzsche's accounts of hatred.

their 'deeply buried', but also 'ideal-creating, value-transforming hatred'; he knows 'brothers in hatred', the 'book of hatred', the 'curse upon the senses and spirit in One hatred and breath' and the 'odium generis humani'; then there is what is 'hateworthy' and 'ugly', the Christian's 'world of the hateworthy and eternally-to-be-battled', and the 'hatred of a world that causes suffering' of the metaphysicians; 'the hatred of mediocrity', typical, but unworthy of the philosopher; and the 'hatred of what is manifold, insecure, hovering, intuiting, as well as what is short sharp pretty well-meaning' of classical taste; but also the hatred, cruelty and fear ascribed by Nietzsche to all forms of organic life – to name just a few.[8]

II.1 Hatred in Nietzsche's ontology of conflict

From the early 1880s, as argued throughout this book, Nietzsche develops his philosophy of power as an ontology of conflict, culminating in the will to power. He does so by drawing on a range of contemporary physiologists to formulate a 'manner of speaking' (*Sprechart*) in line with his anti-metaphysical presuppositions (the primacy of occurrence; originary plurality; the *Ineinanander* of entities without substance; and real contradiction or antagonism). Of cardinal importance in this project is the problem of change and the dynamic character of reality falsified by the metaphysics of being and substance ontology. But the problem of morality and its impact on human existence, its deformation and decline (décadence) and the prospects of its enhancement and perfectibility are never far from his mind; arguably, even his main concern. In this period, Nietzsche's perfectionist impulse is typically translated into onto-physiological terms as the dynamics of growth, expansion, extension, intensification, enhancement, elevation or self-overcoming. The importance of hatred as a realist ingredient in this project is well expressed in a *Nachlass* note, where he writes:

> This one says: the whole world is thought – will – war – love – hate: my brothers, I tell you: each of these on its own is false, all of this together is *true*.[9]

As argued in Chapter 1 (pp. 57ff., 75–7) and Chapter 4 (pp. 163f., 182, 185), Nietzsche's procedure is typically to translate the first-person language of reason, moral values, sentiments and principles into the amoral, impersonal language of onto-physiological processes (*de-moralization, de-anthropomorphization*) and/or to translate onto-physiological processes and concepts into familiar, anthropomorphic

---

[8] 'Abgründe des Hasses' (HW 1.784); 'abgründlichste[.] Hass[.] (de[r] Hass[.] der Ohnmacht)' (GM I 7 5.266); 'zurückgetretene', 'Ideale schaffende[.], Werthe umschaffend[.] Hass[.]' (GM I 8 5.268; GM I 10 5.271); 'Brüder im Hasse' (GM I 14 5.283); 'Buch des Hasses' (GM I 16 5.286); 'Fluch auf Sinne und Geist in Einem Hass und Athem' (GM III 3 5.342); 'odium generis humani' (6[47] 9.205); 'hassenswerth als 'häßlich'' (10[168] 12.555); 'Welt des Hassenswerthen, Ewig-zu-Bekämpfenden' (11[297] 13.124); 'Haß gegen eine Welt, die leiden macht' (8[2] 12.327); 'Der Haß gegen die Mittelmäßigkeit' (10[175] 12.559); 'Haß gegen das Vielfache, Unsichere, Schweifende, Ahnende so gut als gegen das Kurze Spitze Hübsche Gütige' (11[312] 13.132).
[9] 'Dieser sagt: alle Welt ist Gedanke – Wille – Krieg – Liebe – Haß: meine Brüder ich sage euch: alles dies einzeln ist falsch, alles dies zusammen ist w a h r' (4[179] 10.164(1883).

terms in order to elucidate or make sense (*verdeutlichen*) of their dynamic qualities (*re-anthropomorphization*). A good example of the first move is given in a note from 1883, in which Nietzsche sets out the basic terms or 'grammar' for translating our moral concepts and drives into the language of will to power. Four levels of translation are differentiated according to the temporal structure of our affective-moral dispositions: there are '*qualities of the will*' ('W i l l l e n s q u a l i t ä t e n') corresponding to character traits, what we call virtues and their opposed vices (e.g. envy-goodwill, cruelty-mercy); then there are '*states of the will*' ('Z u s t ä n d e d e s W i l l e n s') corresponding to what we call 'moods' ('"Stimmungen"'); then there are '*modifications*' of the 'feeling of life', corresponding to what we might call 'felt movements' ('"gefühlte Bewegungen"', e.g. joy, courage, hope, despair), and fourthly, there are '*double-movements*', corresponding to explosive affects such as 'anger' or 'rage'. Within this broad scale, hatred occurs twice: once, together with love, joy, hope, etc., as a sustained movement or modification of our 'feeling of life'; and once as part of the double-movement of anger or rage:

Double-movements
Wrath, rage (the will first runs backwards, concentrates itself (hatred), and then
    runs suddenly to the periphery, in order to destroy).[10]

Hatred is here identified as an energetic resource within a dynamic of destruction or *Zerstörungsdynamik* – the amoral, physiological analogue of Kant's biblical *im Herzen hassen so viel sei als tödten* (p. 196). To be precise, hatred is identified as the movement in which energy is stored up and concentrated prior to its explosive release in destructive acts of rage. Of course, Nietzsche still recurs to anthropomorphic concepts like 'will', and 'the feeling of life (equanimity)' (*re-anthropomorphization*), but his concern is with the problem of spontaneity, and his aim in this text is to describe in energetic and processual terms the dynamic sources of explosive affects – what the young Nietzsche called the 'complete outpouring' (*Ausströmenlassen*) of hatred sanctioned by the Greek law of war, or 'that pre-Homeric abyss of a gruesome wildness of hatred and the thirst for annihilation'.[11]

In an earlier note (11[134] 9) from Nietzsche's first encounter with Wilhelm Roux in 1881, we see both processes of translation clearly at work and the results he draws from their combination. To begin with, he proposes a reinterpretation of our moral

---

[10] 'D o p p e l b e w e g u n g e n
Zorn, Wuth (der Wille strömt erst zurück, concentrirt sich
(Haß), und strömt plötzlich dann nach der Peripherie, um zu
zerstören)' (7[136] 10.288). In this and related notes, Nietzsche is excerpting and elaborating his readings of the philosopher Philipp Mainländer: *Die Philosophie der Erlösung* (1879[4]) and the physician Ernst Heinrich Weber: *Untersuchungen über den Erregungsprozess im Muskel- und Nervensystem* (1870). See KGW VII 4/1.174, where the second line is rendered as 'Haß *über* concentrirt sich': 'Hatred *over* concentrates itself'.

[11] 'jenen vorhomerischen Abgrund einer grauenhaften Wildheit des Hasses und der Vernichtungslust' (HW 1.791).

categories and drives by translating them from the language of "'reason'" into the language of physiology, modelled on the organism. In this translation process moral categories, such as hatred, love, generosity, respect, etc., are demoralized by being referred to the 'properties of the lowliest living being', i.e. the functions or drives that must be exercised for it to live. As we saw in Chapter 4, in these notes Nietzsche takes nourishment (*Nahrung*), assimilation, appropriation (*Aneignung*) or incorporation (*Einverleibung*) as the primary drive in any living being. By 1884, Nietzsche will reject the primacy of nourishment and its basis in energetic loss or lack, in favour of the expansionist dynamic of the will to power based on excess, but many elements of the will to power are already at work in this, his first appropriation of Roux's *Kampf der Theile im Organismus*. Thus, the expansionist dynamic of the will to power can already be discerned in the principle of *over*-compensation for energetic loss, driving growth through the 'unlimited drive to appropriate':

> Growth and generation follow the unlimited *drive to appropriate*. – this drive brings it [the living being – HS] to the exploitation of the weaker, and to competition with those of similar strength, it [the appropriative drive – HS] *struggles i.e. it* **hates**, *fears, disguises itself*. Even assimilation is: to make something alien *like oneself*, to *tyrannise* – **cruelty**.[12]

Here hatred is referred (together with cruelty, fear, disguise) to the process of ingestion, assimilation, incorporation needed for the organism to grow. But why should we hate what nourishes and enables us to grow? In this text, hatred is inscribed in the logic of struggle and enmity (*Kampf, Feindschaft*) that governs relations both within and between living beings, understood as relations of power or action-and-resistance: to the extent that the other *resists* being assimilated by us, we must hate it in order to conquer and assimilate it for the sake of growth. These relations of hatred-in-assimilation can take two significantly different forms. Between those of more-or-less equal or 'similar strength', they take the form of agonal struggle or competition (*Wettstreit*) *inter pares*; we will return to this. Between those of unequal force, they take the form of exploitation (*Ausnützung*). This is clearly the normal case, for Nietzsche continues:

> – Whoever has the most force to degrade others into functions, rules – but those subjected in turn have their subjects – their continual struggles: whose maintenance at a certain level is the condition of life for the whole. The whole in turn seeks its advantage and finds enemies.[13]

---

[12] 'Dem unbegrenzten A n e i g n u n g s t r i e b e folgt Wachsthum und Generation. – Dieser Trieb bringt es in die Ausnützung des Schwächeren, und in Wettstreit mit ähnlich Starken, er k ä m-p f t d. h. e r h a ß t, f ü r c h t e t, v e r s t e l l t s i c h. Schon das Assimiliren ist: etwas Fremdes sich g l e i c h m a c h e n, t y r a n n i s i r e n – **Grausamkeit** [...]' (11[134] 9.491).

[13] '– Wer am meisten Kraft hat, andere zur Funktion zu erniedrigen, herrscht – die Unterworfenen aber haben wieder ihre Unterworfenen – ihre fortwährenden Kämpfe: deren Unterhaltung bis zu einem gewissen Maaße ist Bedingung des Lebens für das Ganze. Das Ganze wiederum sucht seinen Vortheil und findet Gegner – ' (11[134] 9.491).

Within the living whole, relations of power involve a seeking out of enemies in order to functionalize (subordinate, assimilate) them – a process that is repeated by the enemies (those subordinated) on others and goes on *ad infinitum*. This exercise of power must, however, involve considerable resistance on the part of the enemies (those subordinated), for the living whole is contingent on the maintenance of a certain degree of internal struggle and subordination.[14] Following the same logic of enmity, the living whole in turn seeks out external enemies in order to subordinate and assimilate them. And to the extent that the other resists being assimilated by us, we must hate it in order to conquer and assimilate it for the sake of growth.

In this text, then, 'hatred' names the resources needed to overcome the resistance of others to assimilation or incorporation within the energetic economy of overcompensation geared towards growth or expansion. It takes the familiar form of hostile, destructive energy needed to destroy or overpower an opponent with overwhelming force. This physiological model has corrective implications for our moral thought, which Nietzsche is quick to draw:

> If everybody wanted to stay neatly within the bounds of 'reason' and only wanted to expend as much strength and enmity as they need in order *to live* – the driving force in everything would be *missing*: the functions of similar degree struggle, one must be constantly on *guard*, any slackness is exploited, the opponent is *on the watch*.[15]

Against homeostatic models of unity geared towards stability or self-preservation, Nietzsche proposes his expansionist model of unity and expenditure as the principle of life, on the grounds that the former fails to address the dynamic character of life and specifically: the question of spontaneity or 'the driving force' (*treibende Kraft*).[16] On

---

[14] As the notion of resistance indicates, being-subordinated or obeying is not passive, as distinct from the activity of subordinating or commanding, much less a distinct quality or disposition of some, say, 'natural slaves' as distinct from those born to rule. On the contrary, all forms of life or wills to power share only the one quality of activity (subordination, integration, command); which ones rule or subordinate and which ones obey or are subordinated is not somehow given in advance, but is the contingent outcome of actual power-relations among complexes all bent on subordination or command.

[15] '– Wenn alle sich mit "Vernunft" an ihren Posten stellen wollten und nicht fortwährend so viel Kraft und Feindseligkeit äußern wollten, als sie brauchen, um zu l e b e n – so f e h l t e die treibende Kraft im Ganzen: die Funktionen ähnlichen Grades kämpfen, es muß fortwährend A c h t gegeben werden, jede Laßheit wird ausgenützt, der Gegner w a c h t.' (11[134] 9.491). In my translation, I have corrected the 'nicht' with 'nur' ('only') in the first line, since I believe this to be a reading error.

[16] In the above note, Nietzsche uses physiology to correct 'reason', i.e. rational moralities grounded on the principle of compensation. He sees them as complicit with Darwinistic self-preservation on the one hand, and values like altruism, equality and peace (the minimization of hostility) on the other. In other notes, he takes issue with Darwinistic biologists for allowing these values to distort their understanding of life:
> '[...] Principle of life
> *Fundamental errors* of biologists until now: [...]
> Life is *not* adaptation of inner conditions to outer [ones], but rather will to power, which subjects from within ever more of 'what is outside' to itself and incorporates it
> These biologists *perpetuate* moral evaluations (the

this physiological model, then, enmity and hatred are not a matter of moral choice, but a necessary quality of any living being, whether it be a protoplasm, a human being or a state. There is, it seems, no way of getting around an ethos of hatred, cruelty or a politics of tyranny and empire. Nietzsche's early remarks on the 'abysses of hatred' on the ground of Greek culture are, it seems, reinforced by his later physiology.

These conclusions may, however, be too hasty. For Nietzsche's physiology also involves a translation of familiar moral categories into rather unfamiliar terms, and in this text the concept of hatred acquires new and surprising connotations. In this regard, three remarks are in order:

1. In the opening part of the text (cited above), we saw Nietzsche distinguishing 'the exploitation [*Ausnützung*] of the weaker' from 'competition [*Wettstreit*] with those of similar strength'. If hatred denotes the resources needed to overcome the resistance of others to assimilation, then we can suppose that hatred grows with the degree of resistance to be overcome, so that hatred really comes into its own as an *agonal hatred inter pares*. Conversely, the role of hatred in *un*equal relations of exploitation or subordination towards weaker parties who offer less resistance is attenuated, if not dissolved. For Nietzsche, exploitation, domination and subjection are not driven by hatred – at least as he understands it. We will return to this important point.

2. Assimilation or nourishment is not the only process needed for a living being to grow, and Nietzsche goes on to describe the necessary counter-process: secreting or excreting those parts of what has been assimilated, which are of no use in the dynamics of growth:

> Every body continually *excludes*, separates that which is of *no* use to it in the assimilated being: that which human beings despise, that for which they have revulsion, what they call evil, are the *excrements*. But their unknowing 'reason' often designates for them as evil what causes them trouble, what is uncomfortable, the other, the enemy, they **confuse** that which is *useless* with that which is difficult to acquire, to conquer to incorporate.[17]

---

higher value of altruism, enmity towards the desire to rule, towards war, towards redundancy [lit. uselessness], towards the order of rank and classes) [...]' (7[9] 12.294f.).

'[...] Princip des Lebens
G r u n d i r r t h ü m e r der bisherigen Biologen: [...]
das Leben ist n i c h t Anpassung innerer Bedingungen an äußere, sondern Wille zur Macht, der von innen her immer mehr "Äußeres" sich unterwirft und einverleibt
diese Biologen s e t z e n die moralischen Werthschätzungen
f o r t (der an sich höhere Werth des Altruismus, die Feindschaft gegen die Herrschsucht, gegen den Krieg, gegen die Unnützlichkeit, gegen die Rang- und Ständeordnung).'

[17] 'Fortwährend s c h e i d e t jeder Körper a u s, er secernirt das ihm n i c h t Brauchbare an den assimilirten Wesen: das was der Mensch verachtet, wovor er Ekel hat, was er böse nennt, sind die E x c r e m e n t e. Aber seine unwissende "Vernunft" bezeichnet ihmoft als böse, was ihm Noth macht, unbequem ist, den Anderen, denFeind, er **verwechselt** das U n b r a u c h b a r e und das Schwerzuerwerbende Schwerzubesiegende Schwer-Einzuverleibende' (11[134] 9.491f.).

If hatred is felt towards that which is to be *assimilated*, to be conquered through struggle for the sake of growth, revulsion (*Ekel*) is felt towards that which is to be *excreted* as useless, separated off and rejected; it is what we call 'evil'. Of importance is how the moral designation 'evil' is here attached to a completely distinct process of revulsion-excretion. The same goes for the pathos of contempt (*Verachtung*). The physiological distinction between the process of assimilation associated with hatred on one side, and the counter-process of excretion associated with revulsion on the other, has the effect of *disconnecting* hatred from contempt and the moral designation of 'evil' or 'wicked' in a quite radical way. Hatred is thereby de-moralized and freed up from the gestures of contempt, rejection, and that means: freed up *towards* attitudes of affirmation and acceptance of the other. And in this context, Nietzsche warns against confusing the two processes, that is: what is hard to assimilate or conquer, with what is useless, what is hateworthy with what is revolting. To reject, despise or condemn as 'evil' the object of our hatred is to misunderstand our body, the typical error of our '"reason"' and its 'ignorance in physiologicis' (15[89] 13.458).

3. In line with this physiological distinction, hatred is not opposed to love, as can be seen from the closing line of the text: '"Love" is the feeling for property or for what we wish to make our property.'[18] Just as 'hatred' acquires new connotations in Nietzsche's physiology, so too does 'love'. Like hatred, it is aligned with the process of assimilation, as the feeling of attraction towards that which we wish or desire to appropriate. In this sense, it is clearly the Platonic *eros*, not Christian *agape*, that Nietzsche has in mind. One might even connect the presupposition of energetic *loss* in Nietzsche's physiological economy of overcompensation with the negativity of desire in Platonic eros, grounded in *lack* or *poverty* (*Penia*, the mother of *Eros*),[19] and the growth and reproduction driven by overcompensation with the procreative power of Plato's eros. Only, Nietzsche's physiology of love is governed, not by a logic of transcendence, but by the radically immanent logic of enmity. Indeed, insofar as love can be identified with the drive to assimilate and the need to overcome the other's resistance to assimilation, it is unthinkable without the pathos of hatred. Nietzsche's ontology of conflict inscribes hatred – as a necessary ingredient – in our loves and desires for others.

From this brief incursion into Nietzsche's physiology, we see that hatred is referred to the process of assimilation as the means for over-compensation within an expansionist model of activity 'from within', devised to address the 'driving force' of life (first move: *de-anthropomorphization*); at the same time, hatred is also used to clarify the dynamics of this process (as the resources needed to overcome resistance: second move of *re-anthropomorphization*), but in the process it acquires new connotations and associations. Next to the familiar association of hatred with fear, cruelty and tyranny reminiscent of Nietzsche's vision of the Greeks, his physiology also compels us to rethink hatred in new and unfamiliar ways – as a pathos of contention that is free of

---

[18] '"Liebe" ist Empfindung für das Eigenthum oder das, was wir zum Eigenthum wünschen' (11[134] 9.492).

[19] Plato *Symposium* 203b. On the differences between Platonic and Nietzschean desire, see Rethy (1988 26f.).

contempt and moral rejectionism and foreign to relations of exploitation or subjection; and as a necessary ingredient in affirmative attitudes of accepting, valuing, even loving others.

Yet hatred need not take the familiar form of hostile energy needed to destroy or overpower an opponent with overwhelming physical force. After all, it was the Greeks who were also able to bend that hatred into a supremely creative force by channelling it into the envy and ambition of the contest or *Wettkampf*. And in note 11[134], as we saw, hatred is also inscribed in relations of acceptance and love towards others. For Nietzsche, hatred can be a creative and affirmative force, and I will concentrate on two *productive* forms of hatred, the active hatred *inter pares* of the *Wettkampf* (§II.2), and thereafter (§IV) the reactive, deep-seated and most spiritual form of hatred, which gave birth to slave morality; the first praised and commended by Nietzsche, the other severely criticized. At stake in both is still the question of spontaneity, now focused on creative interaction: How can a force spontaneously act in a creative way upon another force? The different forms this can take carry very different normative implications, to which I will turn in the last section.

II.2 Agonal hatred *inter pares*

One of the most intriguing areas of Nietzsche's philosophy of hatred is his exploration of the etymological relation between hatred and ugliness, 'Hass' and 'das Hässliche'. The adjective 'hazlih' (ahd.: Old High German)/'haz-, hezzelich' (mhd.: Middle High German) is derived from 'Hass' (hatred) and means originally that which arouses hatred, the hateful, hateworthy or hateable ('Hass erregend'/'gehässig'). Its long-standing application to morality, as the morally hateworthy ('hässliche Worte/ Gesinnung') still holds today. While retaining the meaning of 'hateworthy', it comes to be reinterpreted in opposition to 'beautiful' ('schön') and enters into aesthetic usage in Early Modern High German.[20] Nietzsche's awareness of this etymology is attested in several texts that exploit the connection between 'hässlich' and 'Hass'. In broad terms, we can distinguish *three key meanings* of 'ugliness' in Nietzsche's writings that draw on this connection.

1. The first is the meaning of 'ugly' as: the hateable, hateworthy: *das Hassenwerte*. Several texts attest to Nietzsche's awareness of the long-standing connection between the ugly as the hateable/hateworthy and the *morally* hateworthy, in short: with *evil*, and with sin:

> Until now there have been those who glorified man and those who slandered him, both however from a *moral* standpoint. La Rochefoucauld and the Christians found the sight of man *ugly*: but this is a moral judgement and one *knew* no other [judgement]! We count him as part of nature, which is neither good nor evil and as

---

[20] From the *Nietzsche-Wörterbuch* draft-article 'Hässlich' by Gerd Schank, based on: F. Kluge's *Etymologisches Wörterbuch der deutschen Sprache* (1999[23]); and H. Paul's *Deutsches Wörterbuch* (1992[9]).

such we do not always find him ugly, where they abhorred him, nor do we always find him beautiful where they glorified him.[21]

This note illustrates the moral meaning of ugliness (ugly = hateworthy = evil). But it also indicates the direction in which Nietzsche will take this insight: through his philosophical physiology, he seeks to free the human animal from moral judgement by naturalizing it on the basis of a de-moralized conception of nature ('neither evil nor good …'). Once freed from the moral stain with which we have besmirched it, the human animal opens itself up to what Nietzsche calls 'the passion for knowledge' (*Leidenschaft der Erkennntnis*):

> It is an endless study, this animal! It is no stain on nature, that stain has been placed there by us. We have treated this 'dirt' too superficially. One needs Lowlander-eyes to uncover beauty even here.[22]

Once released from the vertical hierarchy of good and evil to the lowlands of naturalism, ugliness no longer provokes a response of negation or rejection, becoming instead a source of endless fascination and disclosing hitherto unknown beauties of existence and nature.

If this describes Nietzsche's *positive* programme of life-affirmation that culminates in the doctrine of *amor fati* ('not to wage war against the ugly': FW 270), his *critical* programme takes off from the diagnostic question: How is it that the world and existence come to be perceived as ugly (i.e. hateworthy because 'evil')? Under what conditions does moral pessimism arise? The answer, developed over several years, is summarized in a late note on the physiology of art, when Nietzsche writes:

> – the feeling of *power* utters the judgement "beautiful" even about things and states which the instinct of *powerlessness* can only assess as hateworthy as 'ugly'.[23]

It is, then, under conditions of weakness, from the feeling or 'instinct of powerlessness' that things are perceived as ugly, hateworthy, evil. For Nietzsche, then, 'the ugly' signifies the pessimistic perception of things as hateworthy or evil, born of impotence. The same thought recurs in the context of the second meaning he ascribes to 'the ugly'.

2. For Nietzsche, 'the ugly' can also signify the moral hatred expressed by those that are ugly. Here ugliness is the stigma of those who feel hatred, an attitude that

---

[21] 'Bisher gab es Verherrlicher des Menschen und Verunglimpfer desselben, beide aber vom m o r a l - i s c h e n Standpunkte aus. La Rochefoucauld und die Christen fanden den Anblick des Menschen h ä ß l i c h: dies ist aber ein moralisches Urtheil und ein anderes k a n n t e man nicht! Wir rechnen ihn zur Natur, die weder böse noch gut ist und finden ihn dort nicht immer häßlich, wo ihn jene verabscheuten, und da nicht immer schön, wo ihn jene verherrlichten' (6[382] 9.295f.).

[22] 'Es ist ein Studium ohne Ende, dieses Thier! Es ist kein Schmutzfleck in der Natur, das haben wir erst hinein gelegt. Wir haben diesen "Schmutz" zu oberflächlich behandelt. Es gehören Niederländer-Augen dazu, auch hier die Schönheit zu entdecken.' (6[382] 9.295f.).

[23] '– das M a c h t gefühl spricht das Urtheil "schön" noch über Dinge und Zustände aus, welche der Instinkt der O h n m a c h t nur als hassenswerth als "häßlich" abschätzen kann.' (10[168] 12.555f.).

Nietzsche consistently associates with pessimism, as when he contrasts Schopenhauer with Kant, whose work habits denied him the leisure needed to 'burn in the passion for knowledge'. Schopenhauer, by contrast, 'possesses at least a certain *powerful ugliness* of nature, in hatred, desire, vanity, mistrust, he is of a somewhat wilder disposition and had time and leisure for this wildness'.[24] Typically, this hatred is also born of a feeling of impotence or weakness in the face of overwhelming powers, although it disguises itself as 'virtue' and 'goodness'. Of those who claim to be good, Nietzsche writes:

> *The Good one and Improvers.*
> *The hatred towards those privileged* in body and soul:
> Revolt of the ugly botched souls against
> The beautiful proud well-disposed [...][25]

At stake here is of course the 'slave revolt of morality' performed by the Jewish priests in GM. We will return to this, after considering the third, the *affirmative* meaning Nietzsche ascribes to 'ugliness' in connection with hatred.

3. Next to his critique of the first meanings of 'ugliness', Nietzsche also attempts a transvaluation (*Umwertung*) of 'ugliness' on the basis of an active and affirmative notion of hatred. The locus classicus for Nietzsche's transvaluation of ugliness is a passage from *Zarathustra* I Of War and Warring Peoples, where Zarathustra addresses his warrior brothers with the words:

> You are ugly? Very well, my brothers! Take the sublime [1]
> mantle about you, the mantle of the ugly!
> And when your soul grows great it grows arrogant and [3]
> In your sublimity there is wickedness. I know you well.
> In wickedness the arrogant one meets with the weakling. [5]
> But they misunderstand one another. I know you well.
> You may only have enemies to hate, but not [7]
> Enemies to despise. You must be proud of your enemy: then
> The successes of your enemy will be your successes too.[26]

---

[24] 'er [Schopenhauer] besitzt wenigstens eine gewisse h e f t i g e H ä s s l i c h k e i t der Natur, in Hass, Begierde, Eitelkeit, Misstrauen, er ist etwas wilder angelegt und hatte Zeit und Musse für diese Wildheit' (M 481 3.286). Or again, of the 'ugliest man' from *Zarathustra*: 'The "ugliest man" as the ideal of world-negating ways of thinking' ('Der "häßlichste Mensch" als Ideal weltverneinender Denkweisen': 25[10] 11).
[25] 'D i e G u t e n u n d d i e V e r b e s s e r e r.
D e r H a ß g e g e n d i e Leiblich- und Seelisch-P r i v i l e g i r t e n:
Aufstand der häßlichen mißrathenen Seelen gegen
die schönen stolzen wohlgemuthen [...]' (8[4] 12.332).
[26] 'Ihr seid hässlich? Nun wohlan, meine Brüder! So nehmt das
Erhabne um euch, den Mantel des Hässlichen!
Und wenn eure Seele gross wird, so wird sie übermüthig, und
in eurer Erhabenheit ist Bosheit. Ich kenne euch.
In der Bosheit begegnet sich der Übermüthige mit dem Schwächlinge.
Aber sie missverstehen einander. Ich kenne euch.
Ihr dürft nur Feinde haben, die zu hassen sind, aber nicht
Feinde zum Verachten. Ihr müsst stolz auf euern Feind sein: dann
sind die Erfolge eures Feindes auch eure Erfolge' (Z I Krieg 4.59).

In these lines ugliness is perceived or judged from two distinct perspectives, perspectives that cross in the encounter between the arrogant one and weakling in line 5. By tracking the shift from one perspective to the other, we can see how Nietzsche performs his transvaluation of ugliness.

1st perspective: The opening question – You are ugly? – just raises the question: Who calls the warriors ugly? The clue lies in the 'wickedness' ascribed twice over to the warriors (lines 4 and 5). The warriors ugly in the (first) sense of hateworthy, morally hateworthy or wicked. But who calls them that? When Zarathustra locates the warriors' wickedness in their encounter with the weaklings (line 5), it is clear that the judgement of wickedness and the judgement of ugliness are made by the weakling – *from a position of weakness*.

2nd perspective: Zarathustra then goes on to reinterpret the warriors' ugliness from the warrior's own perspective, that is, *from a position of strength*. Here Nietzsche draws on the second meaning of ugliness, as expressing hatred, in order to ask: What form does hatred take when it is hatred, not from a position of weakness, but from a position of strength? Zarathustra's answer is that hatred, from a position of strength, takes the form of *pride in one's enemy and in the successes of one's enemy*. This hatred does not seek to degrade or reject its object but affirms, rejoices and shares in its object's power, thereby enhancing both its object's power and its own. To hate one's enemy from a position of strength does not mean to condemn him as evil or wicked, but to *rejoice* in his strength and achievements, to *stimulate* and enhance his power.

So how can this kind of hatred occur? Zarathustra's answer comes with the distinction between hatred and contempt, *Hass* and *Verachtung*, a distinction familiar from Nietzsche's physiology of hatred considered in II.1 above. There, hatred was associated with the process of assimilation and disconnected from contempt (*Verachtung*) and moral condemnation, which were associated with the distinct process of excretion. In the same text, Nietzsche also distinguished agonal relations of 'competition [*Wettstreit*] with those of similar strength', as the site of greatest hatred, from unequal relations of exploitation or subordination towards weaker parties. Zarathustra's speech prefigures this vital physiological distinction and its underlying conditions with the claim that hatred can only occur under conditions of *approximately equal power* among antagonists; it is an *agonal hatred inter pares*, sharply distinguished from the contempt (*Verachtung*), understood as the affective signature of relations of exploitation or subjection towards lesser powers. Under conditions of relative parity, Zarathustra says, the antagonists' ugliness takes on a sublime (*Erhabene*) aspect or 'mantle'. This is the third meaning of 'the ugly', which denotes the dynamic of reciprocal affirmation, stimulation and self-empowerment through the affirmative empowerment of the other. Where the experience of ugliness is driven by an *active agonal hatred inter pares*, it acts as a tonic or stimulant that unleashes a process of reciprocal affirmation and empowerment – even love. Mirroring Nietzsche's physiology of hatred, agonal hatred is a pathos of contention that has nothing to do with contempt, moral condemnation, degradation, subjection or exploitation, but is instead a necessary ingredient in affirmative gestures of accepting, valuing, even loving others in the face of their resistance. Drawing on the erotic aspect of Nietzsche's physiology of assimilation ('the feeling for property or for what we wish to make our property': 11[134] 9.491), we might situate agonal hatred in the *attraction* exerted on us by an opponent's deed or work for the spaces it opens up for us to extend ourselves; the desire we feel to take this on and assimilate it into our being – however hard this may be. And it *is* hard when the achievements and successes of my enemy, as *my* enemy, are successes over me, when empowering it also means power-over-me. The difficulty here is that of combining contention for the sake of mastery with a non-coercive openness to the other, an 'oppositional' practice akin to Nietzsche's epistemic ideal encountered in Chapter 4 – to possess and be possessed by others as things to be known (pp. 189–90). How much easier to mistake what is hard to take on with what is worthless, to degrade and reject it. It is, I believe, with these tensions and difficulties in mind that Nietzsche writes: 'Not that which hinders us from being loved, but that which hinders us from loving [i.e. assimilating – HS] completely, is what we hate the most'; and even '[t]here is also jealousy in hatred: we want to have our enemy all to ourselves'.[27]

The terminological distinction between hatred and contempt, it should be said, is not sustained across all of Nietzsche's writing – hardly surprising, since he makes no effort to develop a systematic or even consistent vocabulary of 'technical terms'. Nonetheless, the restriction of 'hatred' to relations of equality, while not unique to him,[28] is a recurrent theme – even in texts where he is critical of hatred. Thus in FW 379, where Nietzsche disavows hatred in favour of contempt, he writes: 'Hatred by contrast treats as equal, confronts, in hatred there is honour, and finally: in hatred there is fear, a great deal of fear'.[29] Again, the thought of equality is at issue when Nietzsche writes: 'The proud and independent one feels deeply embittered by compassion "better hated than pitied"'.[30] According to Nietzsche, compassion expresses not a sharing among equals, but the exercise of power over another, stinging the pride of the one who prefers to be hated among equals than degraded. And in JGB 173, Nietzsche writes most explicitly: 'One does not hate as long as one still holds in low esteem, but only when one esteems as equal or higher.'[31] Yet hatred is not restricted to relations of parity here. It extends also to relations where one values the other higher than oneself; that is, from a position of relative weakness in unequal relations of power. But here a distinction needs to be made that does not appear in aphorism 173 above. The hatred of impotence (*Hass der Ohnmacht*) that moralizes the world and demands compassion is a radically different form of hatred from Nietzsche's agonal hatred *inter pares*. If proud and independent

---

[27] 'Nicht was uns hindert, geliebt zu werden, sondern was uns hindert ganz zu lieben hassen wir am meisten' (2[17] 10.47); and: 'Auch im Hasse giebt es Eifersucht: wir wollen unseren Feind für uns allein haben' (3[1].127 10.68).
[28] See the following section on Kant.
[29] 'Der Hass dagegen stellt gleich, stellt gegenüber, im Hass ist Ehre, endlich: im Hass ist Furcht, ein grosser guter Theil Furcht' (FW 379).
[30] 'Der Stolze und Unabhängige fühlt sich tief erbittert beim Mitleiden "ieber gehaßt als bemitleidet" (7[186] 9.355).
[31] 'Man hasst nicht, so lange man noch gering schätzt, sondern erst, wenn man gleich oder höher schätzt' (JGB 173).

beings are embittered by acts of compassion towards them, those of lesser power are wounded by their lack of compassion and seek revenge by demanding that they suffer with them:

> *The hatred towards those without compassion is essentially revenge: hence equally the demand for compassion*, it is the necessarily aroused opposition of feeling to that hatred.[32]

The story of hatred-as-*ressentiment* and the 'spirit of revenge' is told in the *Genealogy of Morals*, to which I will turn after considering some of Kant's thoughts on hatred. To conclude this section, I propose that in Nietzsche's 'philosophy of hatred' we can distinguish (1) (genuine) hatred, conditioned by relations of *approximately equal power* among antagonists, from (2) contempt (*Verachtung*) from a position of strength or greater power towards those of unequal, inferior power, and from (3) *ressentiment* and the spirit of revenge from a position of weakness or lesser power towards those of unequal greater power and worth. In the first case of 'agonal hatred inter pares', hatred is released from the usual *Zerstörungsdynamik* and becomes a profoundly affirmative and creative force.

III Kant on hatred

Despite our religious and moral duty to overcome hatred in favour of love, forgivingness and beneficence, Kant shares Nietzsche's *realist* view that hatred and antagonism are not to be rooted out of human behaviour and interaction – just as we have a duty to strive for peace in the face of our incorrigible 'malice and destructiveness' (IaG 1). In Kant's historical-political texts, IaG and ZeF, hatred makes only one explicit appearance – as the tendency to mutual hatred and war provoked by the diversity of languages and religions (ZeF VIII.367f.) – but it is clearly one of our ineradicable hostile inclinations. And even if hatred is supremely destructive – *so viel as tödten* (RGV VI.159) – our hostile inclinations are also prodigiously productive, as we have seen throughout this book, the motor of the *perfectibility* of the species. Without them 'all the excellent natural predispositions in humanity would eternally slumber undeveloped'; they are what impel human beings 'to new exertion of their powers and hence to further development of their natural predispositions' (IaG 4 VIII.21-22), above all our reason, giving us reasonable hope that society can be transformed into a 'moral whole' (ibid.). Perhaps Kant comes closest to Nietzsche's productive notion of agonal hatred *inter pares* in associating peace under cosmopolitan law with the healthy hostility or 'salutary resistance' (*heilsame Widerstande*) of powers in equilibrium, in which 'the liveliest

---

[32] 'Der Haß gegen die Nicht-Mitleidigen ist wesentlich Rache: also die Forderung des Mitleidens ebenfalls, es ist der nothwendig hervorgerufene Gefühls-Gegensatz zu jenem Haß' (7[284] 9.377). See also 14[20] 9.629.

competition' is governed by a 'principle of *equality* between its reciprocal *effect and counter-effect*, so that they may not destroy each other' (IaG VIII.26; ZeF VIII.367).

None of this is to deny the profound differences between them, which I have also been at pains to highlight, especially at the level of conceptual operations and normative orientation. Of fundamental importance here, is not just Kant's heuristic use of teleological constructions, but his reliance on conceptual oppositions (and their problematic consequences): the opposition between war and peace (which is undermined by the violence of the law: *Zwangsgesetzen/gesetzliche Zwang*) needed for the transition from violent conflict to legal process (pp. 103–5); between *pain* and the negative concept of pleasure (which precludes a productive concept of resistance, where the pain of resistance engenders the feeling of power-pleasure) (pp. 133–8); and the opposition between sociability and unsociability (which precludes an intelligent form of egoism in which my well-being coincides with that of others) (pp. 161–3). The same goes for the opposition between hatred and love, which forecloses the possibility, opened by Nietzsche's recourse to physiology, of forms of hatred that are inseparable from love and include an affirmation of the other to mitigate the pathos contention, an openness to their successes and a willingness to take them on as a stimulant to extend ourselves towards 'new possibilities of existence'.

III.1 Hatred and ugliness

On the other hand, Kant is as attuned as Nietzsche to the etymological connections and resonances between *Hass* and *hässlich*, hatred and the ugly. Some examples open revealing comparative perspectives on the two thinkers of conflict. The most obvious example concerns misanthropy or hatred of humanity (*Menschenhaß*), when Kant writes: 'M e n s c h e n h a ß aber ist jederzeit h ä ß l i c h', '*misanthropy* is always *ugly*', a clear case of the second meaning of 'ugly' evinced by Nietzsche: *as the expression of hatred*, which Nietzsche tends to associate with pessimism (p. 206f.). But a fuller reading of the passage on misanthropy shows that Kant also, or primarily, has the long-standing meaning of 'ugly' as *the morally hateworthy* in mind, identified as the first meaning of 'ugly' in Nietzsche's writings (p. 205f.). The context is the section on the love of humanity (*Menschenliebe*) in MS, when Kant discusses the vices of misanthropy or *Menschenhaß*, which stand in opposition to our duties of love (*Liebespflichten*):

> But *to hate man* is always *ugly*, even when it consist in merely completely avoiding men (separatist misanthropy), without active hostility toward them. For benevolence always remains a duty, even toward a misanthropist, whom one cannot indeed love but to whom one can still do good. (MS VI.402)[33]

---

[33] 'M e n s c h e n h a ß aber ist jederzeit h ä ß l i c h, wenn er auch ohne thätige Anfeindung blos der gänzlichen Abkehrung von Menschen (der separatistischen Misanthropie) bestände. Denn das Wohlwollen bleibt immer Pflicht, selbst gegen den Menschenhasser, den man freilich nicht lieben, aber ihm doch Gutes erweisen kann.'

The vices of misanthropy – envy, ingratitude and *Schadenfreude* – are ugly not just because they express hatred, but because they are morally hateworthy. But they are not ugly in the sense that they openly exhibit the moral vice of hatred in deeds, for Kant also remarks:

> Here hatred is not open and violent, but secret and veiled, adding meanness to one's neglect of duty to one's neighbour, so that one also violates a duty to oneself. (MS VI.458)[34]

Perhaps a clue to what Kant means by the 'duty to oneself' here is given in the *Nachlass* to MS, when he writes that we should not poison ourselves with hatred:

> Willingness to forgive towards one that has injured you and indeed all duties towards others are indirectly duties towards oneself. It is a duty to oneself not to poison one's soul with hatred towards an enemy. (*Nachlass* to MS (1797–98) XXIII.403)[35]

It is, however, noteworthy that after stating that we should do good (*Gutes erweisen*) to misanthropists in the first-cited passage above, he writes about the hatred of vice – what it means to hate vice:

> But to hate vice in human beings is neither a duty nor contrary to duty; it is rather, a mere feeling of aversion to vice, without the will having any influence on it, or conversely this feeling having any influence on the will. (MS VI.402)[36]

This is a strange remark for two reasons. First, by making hatred of vice morally neutral, it suggests that we can exercise our duties of good will (*Wohlwollen*) and forgivingness (*Versöhnlichkeit*) towards others while hating their vices; for Nietzsche, this kind of moral hatred is ugly (in the second sense). It is also strange, because, as if to condone moral hatred, he disconnects it from our faculty of desire (*Begehrungsvermögen*) and thus from agency and attaches it to the different faculty of feeling instead. This flies in the face of his oft repeated position that hatred is a passion (*Leidenschaft*), not an affect (*Affekt*) and therefore belongs to our faculty of desire, not to feeling. We will return to this important point.

---

[34] 'Der Haß ist aber hier nicht offen und gewaltthätig, sondern geheim und verschleiert, welches zu der Pflichtvergessenheit gegen seinen Nächsten noch Niederträchtigkeit hinzuthut und so zugleich die Pflicht gegen sich selbst verletzt.'
[35] 'Die Versöhnlichkeit gegen einen Beleidiger u. überhaupt alle Pflichten gegen andere Menschen sind indirect Pflichten gegen sich selbst. Seine Seele nicht mit dem Haß gegen einen Feind zu verderben ist Pflicht gegen sich selbst.'
[36] 'Das Laster aber am Menschen zu hassen ist weder Pflicht noch pflichtwidrig, sondern ein bloßes Gefühl des Abscheues vor demselben, ohne daß der Wille darauf, oder umgekehrt dieses Gefühl auf den Willen einigen Einfluß hätte.'

III.2 Hatred and equality

A second, self-referential example of ugliness in the sense of morally hateworthy occasions reflections on the relation between hate and equality that bring Kant close to Nietzsche again:

> If there were a person by whom I was hated, it would trouble me. Not as if I would fear him, but because I would find it ugly to have something within me that could be a reason for hatred by others for I would suspect that another could not have formed an aversion entirely without any apparent occasion for it. (*Nachlass* to GSE XX.87)[37]

The worry expressed in the first-person self-ascription of ugliness is that the other might be right; in his hatred he might have picked up real moral failings or vices of mine. If, after appealing to his good will and allowing him to know me better, I were to fail to assuage his hatred, Kant cites the epigram (*Sinnspruch*): 'es ist besser daß ich gehasset als daß ich verachtet werde': 'it is better to be hated than despised'. He goes on to distinguish it sharply from the expression 'ich will lieber beneidet als bedauert seyn', 'I prefer to be envied than felt sorry for', on the grounds that the latter is grounded in self-interest. Hatred, by contrast, implies equality, while contempt (*Verachtung*) negates the equality of the other and is therefore worse than hatred:

> The hatred of my fellow citizens does not cancel their concept of equality but contempt makes me small in the eyes of others and always occasions an annoying delusion of inequality. But it is far more damaging to be despised than to be hated. (ibid.)[38]

We see here the sharp distinction between hatred and contempt (*Verachtung*), which we traced from Nietzsche's physiology to the agonal hatred *inter pares* in Z and other texts in Sections II.1 and II.2; the restriction of hatred to relations among equals; and

---

[37] 'Wenn sich ein Mensch fände von dem ich gehasset würde so würde es mich beunruhigen. Nicht als wenn ich mich vor ihm fürchtete sondern weil ich es häslich fände etwas an sich zu haben was andern ein Grund eines hasses werden könte denn ich würde vermuthen daß ein anderer nicht gantz ohne alle scheinbare Veranlassung einen Wiederwillen hätte fassen können.' On moral self-hatred, see also:
'Erkenne dich selbst moralisch erforsche dich selbst was du für ein Mensch nach deiner moralischen qvalität bist lege die Maske in der Theatervorstellung deines Characters ab und siehe ob du nicht vielleicht Ursache habest dich zu hassen ja wohl gar zu verachten. Es gehört zur Pflicht des Menschen gegen sich selbst sich selbst auch Wort zu halten ist das geschehen ohne ein Tagebuch darüber zu führen muß jeder Abend einen Abschlus deiner Rechnung enthalten.' (*Nachlass* to MS XXIII.403-4).

[38] The whole note reads: 'Sähe ich es aber als unvermeidlich an daß gemeine u. pobelhafte Vorurtheile ein elender Neid oder eine noch verächtlichere eifersüchtige Vanität es unmöglich machen allem Hasse gäntzlich auszuweichen wohlan so würde ich bey mir sagen es ist besser daß ich gehasset als daß ich verachtet werde. Dieser Sinnspruch beruhet auf einem gantz anderen Grunde als derjenige welchen nur der Eigennutz aushekt ich will lieber beneidet als bedauert seyn. Der Haß meiner Mitbürger hebt ihren Begrif von der Gleichheit nicht auf die Verachtung aber macht mich in den Augen anderer gring u. veranlaßet immer einen sehr verdrießenden Wahn der Ungleichheit. Es ist aber der viel schädlicher verachtet als gehasset zu seyn' (ibid.).

the view that contempt degrades and subjects the other as inferior. Next to Kant's 'it is better that I be hated than despised', the Nietzschean analogue is 'better hated than pitied' (7[186] 9.355; p. 209), since compassion (*Mitleid*), unlike hatred, degrades the other.

For Kant equality is clearly a normative notion concerning equal worth,[39] and it is striking that he sees this as compatible with relations of hatred.[40] For Nietzsche, by contrast, hatred is distinguished from contempt by being entirely free of moral judgement and bound up with erotic attraction or love. We might say that for Nietzsche, relations of approximately *equal power* are the condition for hatred to be productive, whereas for Kant hatred implies *normative equality*. But this contrast is too stark. From the Nietzsche texts surveyed in Section II.2 it is clear that he does connect hatred with a normative sense of equality – as a matter of 'esteem' ('when one esteems [*schätzt*] as equal or higher': JGB 173) or 'honour' (*Ehre*) (FW 379). And in a *Nachlass* note on the same topic, honour (*Ehre*), we see Kant for his part thematizing equality not in normative terms, but in Nietzschean terms of perceived degrees of power:

> That the drive for honour only issues from the idea of equality can be seen 1 because insofar as another is also stronger but seems only to allow no comparison, we fear him (from which esteem issues) but we do not hate him. 2. that the inclination to exhibit one's worth towards [OR against/in comparison with] those who are greater is noble towards [against/in comparison with] equals or those below one is hateworthy and that a person who does not value himself is despised [...] (*Nachlass* to GSE XX.106–7)[41]

Here again, hatred goes hand-in-hand with the 'idea of equality', this time in the sense of perceived equality of power; for if the other is perceived as so much stronger as to be *hors de concours*, we do not hate, but fear him and do not honour him, but look up to him. In a manner reminiscent of Nietzsche's affirmative, aspirational notion of

---

[39] Thus, to subordinate oneself is to ignore one's inalienable right to equality: 'Alles was kriecht ist zugleich falsch. Denn ein jeder Mensch ist sich des unverlierbaren Rechts der Gleichheit bewust' (*Nachlass* to MS XXIII.403-4).

[40] In the *Nachlass* to MS, Kant counts hatred, together with ingratitude, envy and *Schadenfreude*, as a vice opposed to our duties: of respect towards others (*Achtungspflichten*) as duties 'of distance from one another' (*des Abstandes von einander*) in accordance with 'the right of others', and with duties of love (*Liebespflichten*) as duties 'of convergence' (*der Annäherung*): 'Liebespflichten zum Zweck Anderer Zusammenzustimmen die Achtungspflichten. Diese sind solche dadurch wir von Andern Verbunden werden ohne sie zu verbinden. Also blos negativ nicht hochmüthig – Man könnte jene die der Annäherung diese des Abstandes von einander, die der Gleichheit der Wirkung und Gegenwirkung derselben die Freundschaft nennen: Die Laster die ihnen entgegengesetzt sind sind Haß Undankbarkeit Neid u. Schadenfreude. Liebe ist Zusammenstimmung mit dem Zweck Anderer Achtung mit dem Recht Anderer aber nicht dem objectiven sondern dem subjectiven sich nicht geringerschätzen zu dürfen als etc.' (*Nachlass* to MS XXIII.410-11).

[41] 'Daß der Trieb der Ehre nur aus der Idee der Gleichheit entspringe, siehet man daraus 1 weil so ferne ein anderer auch stärker ist aber nur scheint keine vergleichung anzustellen so fürchten wir ihn wohl (woraus eine Hochschatzung entspringt) aber wir hassen ihn nicht. 2. daß die Neigung gegen Größere seinen Werth zu zeigen edel gegen gleiche aber oder niedrige haßenswürdig ist u. daß ein Mensch der sich selbst nicht schätzet verachtet wird [...]'.

equality – 'to raise oneself' to equal standing with the outstanding one (WS 29; p. 120) – Kant also views it as 'noble' (*edel*) to overcome one's fear and exhibit one's value to (or in comparison with) those of higher standing. For Nietzsche, this aspiration is just another aspect of hatred, which can be directed towards those whom 'one esteems as equal or *higher*' (JGB 173; *HS*; pp. 210, 214). Nor does he distinguish fear from hatred or honour, as Kant does, when in FW 379 he criticizes hatred, precisely because 'in hatred there is fear, a great deal of fear' (p. 209).

Fear is also central in another note of Kant's, where he takes a completely different view of equality and hatred, one that dis-connects them and replaces hatred with fear as the affective signature of equality:

> Although man does not naturally hate any other man he does still fear him. Consequently he is wary and the equality that he thinks he will lose any moment brings him to arms. The class [status] of the warrior begins. Only, because it rests on a noble basis it engenders great affliction but not maliciousness. To dishonour human nature is less dangerous than a servile peace.*
>
> * Our current war is only about the acquisition of money and *luxury*. The old [wars] were about equality and predominance not wealth but power with which virtue can still exist (*Nachlass* to GSE XX:102–3).[42]

We have already come across the anxieties of equality in Kant's account of the desire for recognition, turning into the desire for superiority by the worry (*Besorgniß*) that this is what others want (RGV VI.27; p. 215). The anxieties of equality are also attested by Nietzsche in both physiological and cultural contexts.[43] In the above note, fear brings relations of equality in the vicinity of warfare, occasioning what is probably the closest Kant gets to an affirmation of the warrior caste (*Stand des Kriegers*): despite the horrors of war, it still allows for nobility (*edel*) and virtue (*tugend*), provided it is a war for 'equality or domination' of power, not a war for financial gain or luxury.

---

[42] 'Obzwar der Mensch von Natur keinen andern menschen haßt so fürchtet er ihn doch. Daher ist er auf seiner Hut u. die Gleichheit die er alle Augenblike denkt zu verlieren bringt ihn in Waffen. Der Stand des Kriegers fängt bald an. Allein weil er auf einem edlen Grunde beruht so bringt er wohl große Ubel aber nicht niederträchtigkeit hervor. Er ist weniger gefährlich die Menschliche Natur zu verunehren als ein knechtischer Friede*
*Unser jetziger Krieg geht nur auf den Erwerb des Geldes u. auf den *luxus* heraus. Der alten ihrer auf die gleichheit u. das Übergewicht nicht des Reichthums sondern der Macht hiemit kann noch tugend bestehen'

[43] On the presupposition that '[a]ll Greeks (fr. Gorgias in Plato) believed the possession of power as tyrant to be the most enviable happiness', Nietzsche writes: 'The equality [*Gleichheit*] of citizens is the means for avoiding tyranny, their reciprocal invigilation and restraint.' ('Die Gleichheit der Bürger ist das Mittel zur Verhinderung der Tyrannei, ihre gegenseitige Bewachung und Niederhaltung') (4[301] 9). In a similar vein, Nietzsche writes of the inner struggles of the organism: '[…] the functions of similar degree struggle, one must be constantly on *guard*, any slackness is exploited, the opponent is *on the watch*.' ('[…]die Funktionen ähnlichen Grades kämpfen, es muß fortwährend A c h t gegeben werden, jede Laßheit wird ausgenützt, der Gegner w a c h t.') (11[134] 9.491; see p. 202).

We are reminded of Nietzsche's warriors in Z Krieg, only their warfare is affirmed, not for virtue, but for the productive and affirmative qualities of their hatred for their equals. The closest Nietzsche gets to an affirmation of virtue in warfare is Zarathustra's affirmation of a *plurality of virtues in conflict,* all yearning for hatred, love and rage:

> It is distinguishing to have many virtues, but it is a hard lot. And many went into the desert and killed themselves because they were weary of being the battle and battlefield of virtues.
> My brother, are war and battle evil? But this evil is necessary, envy and mistrust and slander among your virtues are necessary.
> Look, how each of your virtues is desirous for the highest: it wants your entire spirit, to be *its* herald; it wants your entire strength in rage, hatred and love. (Z Freuden 4.42)[44]

III.3 Hatred, justice and revenge

If for Kant 'the idea of equality' is the source of 'the drive for honour' (*Nachlass* to GSE XX.106–7; cited above), the 'feeling of equality' is the source of the 'idea of justice', understood as reciprocal obligation or indebtedness (*Schuldigkeit*):

> From the idea of equality justice issues that required [of us] as well as that [we] require. The former is the obligation [indebtedness] towards others, the latter the perceived obligation [indebtedness] of others towards me. (*Nachlass* to GSE XX.35–6)[45]

Kant goes on to argue that, were someone to disregard their obligation to me and make me suffer an injustice, I would hate him as my enemy, for '[n]othing ever enrages us more than injustice all other afflictions which we endure are nothing in comparison [...] I will hate anyone who sees my floundering in a pit and passes by in cold blood'.[46]

---

[44] 'Auszeichnend ist es, viele Tugenden zu haben, aber ein schweres Loos; und Mancher gieng in die Wüste und tödtete sich, weil er müde war, Schlacht und Schlachtfeld von Tugenden zu sein. Mein Bruder, ist Krieg und Schlacht böse? Aber nothwendig ist diess Böse, nothwendig ist der Neid und das Misstrauen und die Verleumdung unter deinen Tugenden.
Siehe, wie jede deiner Tugenden begehrlich ist nach dem Höchsten: sie will deinen ganzen Geist, dass er i h r Herold sei, sie will deine ganze Kraft in Zorn, Hass und Liebe.'

[45] 'Aus dem Gefühle der gleichheit entspringt die Idee der Gerechtigkeit so wohl der genöthigten als der nöthigenden. Jene ist die Schuldigkeit gegen andere diese die empfundene Schuldigkeit anderer gegen mich.'

[46] 'Diese Schuldigkeit wird als so etwas erkannt deßen Ermanglung einen andern mich würde als meinen Feind ansehen lassen und machen daß ich ihn hassete. Niemals empört etwas mehr als Ungerechtigkeit alle andere Übel die wir ausstehen sind nichts dagegen. [...] Ich werde aber auch einen jeden hassen der mich in einer Grube zappeln sieht u. kaltsinnig vorüber geht [...]' (ibid.).

If this sounds like the perspective from which of Nietzsche's slave morality was born, it is even more so in Anth §83, where Kant takes up the hatred from perceived injustice and calls it the 'desire for revenge' (*Rachbegierde*):

> [...] hatred arising from an injustice we have suffered, that is, the *desire for revenge*, is a passion that follows irresistibly from the nature of the human being, and, malicious as it may be, maxims of reason are nevertheless interwoven with the inclination by virtue of the permissible *desire for justice*, whose analogue it is. This is why the desire for vengeance is one of the most violent and deeply rooted passions; even when it seems to have disappeared, a secret hatred, called *rancour* [G r o l l], is always left over, like a fire smouldering under the ashes. (Anth §83 VII.270)[47]

The desire for revenge, Kant says, is the analogue of the desire for justice, that is, the desire to enjoy 'relations with one's fellow human beings such that each can have the share that justice allots him' (ibid.). They are analogues by virtue of the idea of justice they share. The difference between them is that the desire for justice is 'no passion [*Leidenschaft*], but a determining ground of free will [*Willkür*] by practical reason', while revenge has its sources in self-love and self-interest. It is a 'sensate drive of hatred' directed, not at injustice, but at the *person*: the one who made you suffer injustice. Kant describes this as an 'inclination (to persecute and destroy)', which distorts the injustice into a personal injury, and thereby 'transforms the desire for justice against the offender into the passion for retaliation [*Wiedervergeltung*], which is often violent to the point of madness' (Anth §83 VII.271).[48] The desire for revenge, then, takes up the idea of justice/injustice from the desire for justice and which it stimulates or arouses ('E r r e g b a r k e i t') by appealing to one's self-interest. But vengeance distorts the injustice through a hatred that *personalizes* it into an injury to my person (self-love) by the person who injured me, whom I then persecute and seek to destroy, thereby *de*forming the desire for justice into a passion for retaliation or revenge. It is, Kant says, the intellectual element of this passion that makes it so insidious: it is because it takes the idea of justice from the desire for justice, and even its rational maxims, that it is so deeply rooted and cannot be requited, living on as a 'secret hatred, called *rancour* [G r o l l] [...] like a fire smouldering under the ashes'.

---

[47] '[...] so ist der Haß aus dem erlittenen Unrecht, d.i. die R a c h b e g i e r d e, eine Leidenschaft, welche aus der Natur des Menschen unwiderstehlich hervorgeht, und, so bösartig sie auch ist, doch die Maxime der Vernunft vermöge der erlaubten R e c h t s b e g i e r d e, deren Analogon jene ist, mit der Neigung verflochten und eben dadurch eine der heftigsten und am tiefsten sich einwurzelnden Leidenschaften; die, wenn sie erloschen zu sein scheint, doch immer noch ingeheim einen Haß, G r o l l genannt, als ein unter der Asche glimmendes Feuer überbleiben läßt.'

[48] 'Die B e g i e r d e, in einem Zustande mit seinen Mitmenschen und in Verhältniß zu ihnen zu sein, da jedem das zu Theil werden kann, was das R e c h t will, ist freilich keine Leidenschaft, sondern ein Bestimmungsgrund der freien Willkür durch reine praktische Vernunft. Aber die E r r e g b a r k e i t derselben durch bloße Selbstliebe, d.i. nur zu seinem Vortheil, nicht zum Behuf einer Gesetzgebung für jedermann, ist sinnlicher Antrieb des Hasses, nicht der Ungerechtigkeit, sondern des gegen uns U n g e r e c h t e n: welche Neigung (zu verfolgen und zu zerstören), da ihr eine Idee, obzwar freilich selbstsüchtig angewandt, zum Grund liegt, die Rechtsbegierde gegen den Beleidiger in Leidenschaft der Wiedervergeltung verwandelt, die oft bis zum Wahnsinn heftig ist [...]'.

What Kant calls 'rancour' or *Groll*, a hidden, slow-burning, backwards-looking hatred over past injuries, is what Nietzsche calls *ressentiment*, the motor of the 'slave revolt of morality' recounted in GM I. Indeed, with a little licence, Kant's account of hatred-as-revenge can be made to recount a story that complements and at times converges with the story of hatred-as-*ressentiment*: beginning with the perception of injustice suffered, leading to a demand for justice, which is deformed into a personalized hatred of the one who injured us, giving rise to a desire to persecute and destroy him, which, under conditions of powerlessness, can only take the intellectualized form of imaginary revenge that would destroy him, but can never be sated and continues to burn inside and fuels retaliation or – in Nietzsche's terms – a *transvaluation* (*Umwertung*) of the other's values. In turning in the next section to Nietzsche's account of the hatred in the slave revolt, we will have occasion to draw on Kant's views on hatred and revenge. The closing section offers a comparative analysis of their respective solutions to the problems engendered by the hatred of impotence.

IV The hatred of impotence and the spirit of revenge

In keeping with Nietzsche's ontology of conflict, his genealogies of morality trace multiple, intersecting lines of conflict, in which hatred is often a driving force. In Essay III on the ascetic ideal it is, of course, life that is in conflict with itself, and hatred recurs in different forms across its various manifestations: as the 'hatred […] of knowledge, spirit and sensibility', as 'a curse upon the senses and the spirit in One hatred and breath' (GM III 3 5.342); as 'hatred of the senses' (GM III 8 5.355); as 'self-contempt' and the hatred that does not admit itself to be hatred (*Hass nicht als Hass einzugestehn*: GM III 14 5.368f.);[49] and finally, in the closing lines, where Nietzsche delivers his final diagnosis of nihilism as willing-nothingness (*das Nichts wollen*):

> It is absolutely impossible for us to conceal what was actually expressed by that whole willing that derives its direction from the ascetic ideal: this hatred of the human, and even more of the animalistic, even more of the material, this horror of the senses, of reason itself, this fear of happiness and beauty, this longing to get away from semblance, transience, growth, death, wishing, longing itself – all that means, let us dare to grasp it, a *will to nothingness*, an aversion to life, a rebellion against the most fundamental prerequisites of life, but it is and remains a *will*! … And, to conclude by saying what I said at the beginning: the human still prefers to *will nothingness*, than *not* to will …[50]

---

[49] 'Hass […] auf Erkenntniss, Geist und Sinnlichkeit'; '[e]inen Fluch auf Sinne und Geist in Einem Hass und Athem' (GM III 3 5.342); 'Sinnenhass' (GM III 8 5.355); 'Selbstverachtung' (GM III 14 5.368).

[50] 'Man kann sich schlechterdings nicht verbergen, was eigentlich jenes ganze Wollen ausdrückt, das vom asketischen Ideale her seine Richtung bekommen hat: dieser Hass gegen das Menschliche, mehr noch gegen das Thierische, mehr noch gegen das Stoffliche, dieser Abscheu vor den Sinnen, vor der Vernunft selbst, diese Furcht vor dem Glück und der Schönheit, dieses Verlangen hinweg aus allem Schein, Wechsel, Werden, Tod, Wunsch, Verlangen selbst – das Alles bedeutet, wagen

But it is especially in Essay I of Nietzsche's polemic or 'Streitschrift' (KSA 5.245) that conflict looms large, where he recounts the 'slave revolt of morality' instigated by the Jewish priests not just as a 'war', but as the 'the most fundamental of all declarations of war' (*grundsätzlichste aller Kriegserklärungen*: GM I 7 5.266), which evolves into the 'great politics of revenge' (*grosse Politik der Rache*), in which the priests propagated slave values by crucifying their avatar, culminating in the 'struggle' that still dominates today: "'Rome against Judea, Judea against Rome'" (GM I 16 5.286). Nietzsche's account of the slave revolt deepens and extends the distinction made earlier between hatred-as-*ressentiment* from a position of weakness towards those of greater power, and contempt (*Verachtung*) of the powerful towards those of lesser power or standing. It also takes further Nietzsche's reflections on the relation between hatred and ugliness, and between hatred and love.

The hatred of the priests is the 'most abyssal hatred' (*abgründlichste Hass*) – more so than the pre-Homeric 'abyss of hatred' – because it is a hatred born of impotence (*Hass der Ohnmacht*) in the face of oppressive, overpowering others (*Überwältiger*): 'the nobles', 'the violent ones', 'the masters', 'the ones in power' (GM I 7 5.266). Priestly hatred is a desperate, bitter hatred, since, as Nietzsche points out, 'it is the impotence over and against humans, *not* the impotence over and against nature that engenders the most desperate bitterness towards existence'.[51] Out of this impotence, therefore,

> their hate swells into something monstrous and uncanny, into a most intellectual and poisonous form. The greatest haters in world history, and the most intelligent haters, have always been priests: – next to the intelligence of priestly revenge all other forms of intelligence hardly come into consideration. The history of humankind would be far too stupid a thing if it had not had the intellect of the powerless injected into it [...].[52]

---

wir es, dies zu begreifen, einen W i l l e n z u m N i c h t s, einen Widerwillen gegen das Leben, eine Auflehnung gegen die grundsätzlichsten Voraussetzungen des Lebens, aber es ist und bleibt ein W i l l e!... Und, um es noch zum Schluss zu sagen, was ich Anfangs sagte: lieber will noch der Mensch d a s N i c h t s w o l l e n, als n i c h t wollen...' (GM III 28 5.412).

[51] 'die Ohnmacht gegen Menschen, n i c h t die Ohnmacht gegen die Natur, erzeugt die desperateste Verbitterung gegen das Dasein' (5[71] 12.214).

[52] '[...] wächst bei ihnen der Hass in's Ungeheure und Unheimliche, in's Geistigste und Giftigste. Die ganz grossen Hasser in der Weltgeschichte sind immer Priester gewesen, auch die geistreichsten Hasser: – gegen den Geist der priesterlichen Rache kommt überhaupt aller übrige Geist kaum in Betracht. Die menschliche Geschichte wäre eine gar zu dumme Sache ohne den Geist, der von den Ohnmächtigen her in sie gekommen ist [...]' (GM I 7 5.266f.). In a *Nachlass* note of 1887 Nietzsche distinguishes three kinds of priestly hatred:
'der Haß gegen die Mächtigen der Erde und ein versteckter grundsätzlicher Wettkampf und Wettstreit – man will die Seele, man läßt ihnen den Leib –
der Haß gegen den Geist, den Stolz, den Muth, die Freiheit, Ausgelassenheit des Geistes
der Haß gegen die Sinne, gegen die Freuden der Sinne, gegen die Freude überhaupt und eine Todfeindschaft gegen die Sinnlichkeit und Geschlechtlichkeit' (8[3] 12.331).

So how are we to understand the linkage between hatred and revenge (*Rache*) in the 'spirit of priestly revenge'? The first thing to note is that the connection between hatred and revenge is by no means limited to the powerless. The fear and trembling before a threatening power, the intolerable feeling of pressure that issues in the desire for revenge is felt even more acutely by those with power:

> The *proud being* hates to tremble and takes revenge on that which has made him tremble: this is the reason for his cruelty. He takes the greatest of pleasures in seeing before himself the one before whom he no longer trembles, even if he now does the most humiliating and painful things to him. – The proud being does not acknowledge that which exerts pressure on him as long as he does not see the possibility of taking revenge for this pressure. His *hatred* shoots forth at the moment in which he glimpses this possibility.[53]

We can recognize here Nietzsche's physiological description of hatred as the concentration of energy – here a concentration that comes from outside pressure (*Druck*) – prior to its discharge in destructive acts of rage (see p. 200 above). The problem for the priest is that he is denied actual revenge by his actual powerlessness vis-à-vis the overwhelming pressure he feels from the 'proud' beings, so that his revenge must take a 'spiritual' or 'imaginary' form. How, then, does he satisfy his desire for revenge and release himself from the feeling of intolerable pressure, from the bitterness of his existence, and attain a sense of his own worth and power?

Like Kant, Nietzsche was struck by the profound intelligence (*geistreichste, Raffinement des Geistes*) of deep-seated, secret, slow-burning hatred of revenge; he speaks of 'a far-sighted, subterranean revenge, slowly clenching and calculating in advance' (*einer weitsichtigen, unterirdischen, langsam-greifenden und vorausrechnenden Rache*: GM I 9 5.269). For Kant this is why passions (*Leidenschaften*) like hatred pose such a threat to reason, much more so than self-consuming affects (*Affekten*) like rage.[54] In Nietzsche's genealogy, by contrast, hatred of the priestly type is not a threat

---

[53] 'Der S t o l z e haßt es zu zittern und nimmt Rache an dem, der ihn zittern gemacht hat: dies ist der Grund seiner Grausamkeit. Er hat die größte Lust, den vor sich zu sehen, vor dem er nun nicht mehr zittert, ob er ihm schon das Schmählichste und Schmerzhafteste anthut. – Der Stolze gesteht sich das nicht ein, was ihm drückend ist, so lange er nicht die Möglichkeit sieht, Rache für diesen Druck zu nehmen. Sein H a ß schießt im Augenblick hervor, wenn diese Möglichkeit ihm zu Gesichte kommt' (14[20] 9.629).

[54] See e.g. Kant's *Anthropologie* §74: 'Was der Affect des Zorns nicht in der Geschwindigkeit thut, das thut er gar nicht; und er vergißt leicht. Die Leidenschaft des Hasses aber nimmt sich Zeit, um sich tief einzuwurzeln und es seinem Gegner zu denken. [...] Die Leidenschaft hingegen (als zum Begehrungsvermögen gehörige Gemüthsstimmung) läßt sich Zeit und ist überlegend, so heftig sie auch sein mag, um ihren Zweck zu erreichen. – Der Affect wirkt wie ein Wasser, was den Damm durchbricht; die Leidenschaft wie ein Strom, der sich in seinem Bette immer tiefer eingräbt. Der Affect wirkt auf die Gesundheit wie ein Schlagfluß, die Leidenschaft wie eine Schwindsucht oder Abzehrung. – Er ist wie ein Rausch, den man ausschläft, obgleich Kopfweh darauf folgt, die Leidenschaft aber wie eine Krankheit aus verschlucktem Gift oder Verkrüppelung anzusehen, die einen innern oder äußern Seelenarzt bedarf, der doch mehrentheils keine radicale, sondern fast immer nur palliativ-heilende Mittel zu verschreiben weiß' (Anth VII.252f.).

to reason, it is the *creative source* of reason, at least in its Christian-Platonic version, and of its core values; without it, 'human history would be a far too stupid affair' (*eine gar zu dumme Sache*). And for Nietzsche, unlike Kant, the priest's deep-seated hatred is profoundly creative. It is an 'ideal-creating, value-transforming hatred' (*Ideale schaffenden, Werthe umschaffenden Hass*) that creates a new discourse of morality, one where hatred becomes 'love' (agape), where retribution (*Vergeltung)* becomes 'Justice' ('Gerechtigkeit'), where the object of hatred is not my enemy (*Feind*), but 'injustice' (das 'Unrecht'), and brotherhood in hatred (*Brüder im Hasse*) becomes 'brotherhood in love' ('Brüder in der Liebe') (GM I 14 5.283). Essential to Nietzsche's argument is the claim that (Christian) 'love' – and the virtues embodied by Jesus – is not opposed to (Jewish) hatred, since Christianity (Jesus) is not opposed to Judaism, but its 'crown', driven by the aims of priestly hatred: 'victory, prey, seduction' (GM I 8 5.268). The crucifixion, Nietzsche contends, was a ploy by the Jewish priests to seduce those opposed to Israel to the most seductive avatar of slave values, their apparent opponent Jesus; this was their 'great politics of revenge'. As a consequence of this genealogy, the opposition between hatred and love is once again broken by Nietzsche, this time in the register, not of *eros*, but of *agape*.

In Nietzsche's physio-ontology of will to power, hatred can be a sustained movement or modification of our 'feeling of life' (like love, joy, hope, etc.); or it can be part of '*double-movement*', concentrating the will in readiness for explosive affects such as 'anger' or 'rage' (7[136] 10.288; see p. 200). For Kant this is impossible; hatred is a passion (*Leidenschaft*), and passions are sharply distinguished from affects (*Affekten*) both regarding their seat in the soul and their character. The *differentia specifica* between them is that affects are matter of feeling (*Gefühl*) only, which is a separate part of the soul from the faculty of desire (*Begehrungsvermögen*), the source of agency, to which passions belong.[55] With this goes a completely different character and temporal signature. Affects are fast and explosive (as in Nietzsche's '*double-movement*'): what 'anger does not do with speed, it does not at all; and it forgets easily'; passions like hatred take their time (like Nietzsche's sustained movements), bury themselves deeply and are highly reflective, thoughtful and purposive, not blind and impulsive like affects. Affects are a 'rush' or rapture (*Rausch*), which can hinder (*hemmen*) the freedom of the mind, passions like an illness from poisoning, which can cancel (*aufheben*) freedom altogether, because they interfere with the determination of the will (*Bestimmbarkeit der Willkür*) by reason.[56] This is why passions pose more of a threat to reason than affects:

---

[55] But see MS VI.402 on hatred of vice (p. 212).
[56] 'Affecten sind von Leidenschaften specifisch unterschieden. Jene beziehen sich bloß auf das Gefühl; diese gehören dem Begehrungsvermögen an und sind Neigungen, welche alle Bestimmbarkeit der Willkür durch Grundsätze erschweren oder unmöglich machen. Jene sind stürmisch und unvorsätzlich, diese anhaltend und überlegt: so ist der Unwille als Zorn ein Affect; aber als Haß (Rachgier) eine Leidenschaft. Die letztere kann niemals und in keinem Verhältniß erhaben genannt werden: weil im Affect die Freiheit des Gemüths zwar gehemmt, in der Leidenschaft aber aufgehoben wird' (KU V.277 footnote).
Also important: Anth §74 (VII.252f.): 'Was der Affect des Zorns nicht in der Geschwindigkeit thut, das thut er gar nicht; und er vergißt leicht. Die Leidenschaft des Hasses aber nimmt sich Zeit, um sich tief einzuwurzeln und es seinem Gegner zu denken. [...] Die Leidenschaft hingegen (als zum Begehrungsvermögen gehörige Gemüthsstimmung) läßt sich Zeit und ist überlegen, so heftig sie

A propensity to affect (e.g. *anger*) does not enter into relation with vice so readily as does *passion*. Passion is a sensible *desire* that has become a lasting inclination (e.g., *hatred,* as opposed to anger). The calm with which one gives oneself up to it permits reflection and allows the mind to form principles upon it and so, if inclination lights upon something contrary to the law, to brood upon it, to get it rooted deeply, and so to take up what is evil (as something premeditated) into its maxim. (MS VI.408)[57]

Passions are therefore for Kant 'without exception, evil' (*ohne Ausnahme böse*) (Anth §80 VII.267). For Kant, of course, vice and evil violate the moral law with its sources in pure practical Reason. For Nietzsche, by contrast, only a morality of radically individual self-legislation informed by physiological self-knowledge can be life-affirmative and -enhancing (pp. 152, 172, 175). But Kant's view of passions – 'like an illness from poisoning' that co-opts the operations of reason – clearly resonates with 'the most intellectual and poisonous form' of hatred born of impotence ascribed by Nietzsche to the figure of the priest. This raises the question whether the slave morality, born of vengeful hatred, is not 'evil' from *both* a radically immanent Nietzschean standpoint in life and a Kantian standpoint in pure practical Reason. We shall return to this in the final part of the chapter, when we consider the slave revolt from Nietzschean and Kantian perspectives in more detail.

The relation between hatred and ugliness is key to Nietzsche's further analysis of priestly hatred. The creative hatred born of impotence instigates an 'inversion' of aristocratic (Roman) values, one that sanctifies the impotence and ugliness of the Jewish priests and people as goodness and devoutness, so as to condemn the nobles as 'evil'.[58]

[O]nly the wretched are the good, only the poor, the powerless, the lowly are the good, the suffering, deprived, sick, ugly are also the only ones who are pious, the only ones blessed by God, for them alone there is blessedness, – you, on the

---

auch sein mag, um ihren Zweck zu erreichen. – Der Affect wirkt wie ein Wasser, was den Damm durchbricht; die Leidenschaft wie ein Strom, der sich in seinem Bette immer tiefer eingräbt. Der Affect wirkt auf die Gesundheit wie ein Schlagfluß, die Leidenschaft wie eine Schwindsucht oder Abzehrung. – Er ist wie ein Rausch, den man ausschläft, obgleich Kopfweh darauf folgt, die Leidenschaft aber wie eine Krankheit aus verschlucktem Gift oder Verkrüppelung anzusehen, die einen innern oder äußern Seelenarzt bedarf, der doch mehrentheils keine radicale, sondern fast immer nur palliativ-heilende Mittel zu verschreiben weiß.'

[57] 'Ein Hang zum Affect (z.B. Z o r n) verschwistert sich daher nicht so sehr mit dem Laster, als die L e i d e n s c h a f t. Leidenschaft dagegen ist die zur bleibenden Neigung gewordene sinnliche B e g i e r d e (z.B. der H a ß im Gegensatz des Zorns). Die Ruhe, mit der ihr nachgehangen wird, läßt Überlegung zu und verstattet dem Gemüth sich darüber Grundsätze zu machen und so, wenn die Neigung auf das Gesetzwidrige fällt, über sie zu brüten, sie tief zu wurzeln und das Böse dadurch (als vorsätzlich) in seine Maxime aufzunehmen.'

[58] Nietzsche writes: 'seine That, seine Schöpfung: er hat "den bösen Feind" concipirt, "den Bösen", und zwar als Grundbegriff.'

other hand, you noble and violent ones, you are in all eternity the evil, the cruel, the lustful, the insatiable, the godless ones, you will also be in all eternity wretched cursed and damned ...!⁵⁹

The 'spiritual' or 'imaginary revenge' performed by the priestly caste works by distorting, deforming or uglifying (*verhässlichen*) its oppressors. The making-ugly or uglification of objects of hatred is an attitude consistently associated by Nietzsche with 'ugliness' in the second sense, i.e. where it expresses hatred born of impotence, such as the priests'. The sanctification of their own ugliness and hatred goes hand-in-hand with an uglification of the object of their hatred.⁶⁰

It would therefore be wrong to see the hatred of impotence as simply creative. Hatred is not divested of its destructive qualities; they are just translated onto the imaginary plane. At the heart of imaginary revenge is once again a *Zerstörungsdynamik*, very far from the affirmation-empowerment of the other in agonal hatred. Agonal hatred does not include the need to reduce or degrade others in order to assert one's power, since it can arise only among those approximately equal power, who posit their will as equal to others;⁶¹ hatred can therefore open itself up to the other, rejoice in its successes and incorporate them into its own creative initiatives. Priestly hatred, by contrast, is predicated on relations of radical *inequality* which it is powerless to change. But it *can* create a sense of ascendancy and worth *by degrading the other in the imagination*, turning it into a monster, the 'evil enemy' to be destroyed.⁶² Self-affirmation through the 'uglification' or degradation of the other in the imagination: this is the zero-sum

---

⁵⁹ '"die Elenden sind allein die Guten, die Armen, Ohnmächtigen, Niedrigen sind allein die Guten, die Leidenden, Entbehrenden, Kranken, Hässlichen sind auch die einzig Frommen, die einzig Gottseligen, für sie allein gibt es Seligkeit, – dagegen ihr, ihr Vornehmen und Gewaltigen, ihr seid in alle Ewigkeit die Bösen, die Grausamen, die Lüsternen, die Unersättlichen, die Gottlosen, ihr werdet auch ewig die Unseligen, Verfluchten und Verdammten sein!"...' (GM I 7 5.267).

⁶⁰ According to Nietzsche, the uglification of the human and the world is broadly characteristic of pessimism – 'ugly manners or a pessimistic outlook, an eye that *makes ugly* [v e r h ä s s l i c h t] –' (AC 57 6.242f.); of modern decadence, and of Christianity: 'The Christian resolve to find the world ugly and bad has made the world ugly and bad'. On the 'uglification' (*Verhässlichung*) of the human and the world as a consequence of world-negation at the hands of Platonism and Christianity, see: 5[164] 8.86; MA I 137 2.131; MA I 247 2.206. Also Heller (1972 91).

⁶¹ On Nietzsche's notion of approximately equal power, see pp. 119. See also the formulations in JGB 259: 'to posit one's will as equal to the other's' (*seinen Willen dem des Andern gleich setzen*) for normative equality, and 'actual similarity in amounts of strength' (*thatsächliche Ähnlichkeit in Kraftmengen*) for approximate equality of power: 'Sich gegenseitig der Verletzung, der Gewalt, der Ausbeutung enthalten, seinen Willen dem des Andern gleich setzen: dies kann in einem gewissen groben Sinne zwischen Individuen zur guten Sitte werden, wenn die Bedingungen dazu gegeben sind (nämlich deren thatsächliche Ähnlichkeit in Kraftmengen und Werthmaassen und ihre Zusammengehörigkeit innerhalb Eines Körpers).'

⁶² This insight can already be found in the *Nachlass* of MA from 1879: 'Die Rache des Niederen am Höheren geht immer auf das Äußerste aus, Vernichtung: weil so allein den Rückschlag beseitigen kann' (42[8] 8.597).

game of 'imaginary revenge'.[63] Hence Nietzsche's claim that the engrained hatred (*zurückgetretene Hass*) of the weak *must* falsify the other and turn it into 'a real caricature and monster' (*zum eigentlichen Zerrbild und Scheusal umzuwandeln*), in contrast with the contempt (*Verachtung*) of masters, which distorts the slave, if it does, through careless indifference.

At play in the thematic of uglification is the *personalization* of perceived injustice pinpointed by Kant in his analysis of the desire for revenge, and the logic of persecution: the 'evil enemy' to be destroyed. Indeed, the virtue of law for Nietzsche, when conceived actively (not reactively as a codification of revenge à la Dühring), is that it *depersonalizes* injury by referring it to the impersonal instance of the law, as an 'injustice' (GM II 11 5.311–13). At the same time, however, Nietzsche raises the suspicion that the moral language of 'justice' and 'injustice' (*Gerechtigkeit, das Unrecht*) is just a cover for a deeply personal need for retribution (*Vergeltung*) against a perceived enemy (*Feind*), born of the creative power of priestly hatred. What for Kant is a 'permissible desire for justice' deformed by hatred into a personal desire for revenge looks instead like the creative falsification of an inveterate, personal desire for revenge by the 'ideal-creating, value-transforming hatred' of the priest (GM I 14 5.283). But in his analysis of personalization and persecution, Nietzsche also takes the intellectual dimension of hatred, emphasized by Kant, much further and in a distinctly anti-Kantian direction. Behind the construction 'the evil enemy' is the creation of a neutral substrate or substance with free will, a subject who chooses to inflict suffering on the weak and can therefore be held responsible and blamed (GM I 13 5.279–80); in short, the *homo noumenon* of Kantian morality. If for Kant contempt (*Verachtung*) degrades the other (or myself: *macht mich in den Augen anderer gring*) by cancelling its equality, true degradation in Nietzsche's eyes is 'bottom-up': a necessary part of the creative economy of hatred from a position of weakness, which degrades the other by blaming a moral subject behind its deeds for choosing to be evil and unjust, instead of a good man.

For Nietzsche, however, it is the Christian ideal of 'the good man' that embodies the destructiveness of this hatred most clearly, even if paradoxically. In 'the good man', the actual revenge denied the priest by his lack of power becomes an ideal of *self-denial*, the refusal 'to wage war in deeds and weapons' (11[297] 13.124). Nietzsche views this ideal as an attempt 'to reduce the human being to half' by 'cutting off the possibility of enmity [*Feindschaft*], uprooting *ressentiment*' in favour of harmony or 'peace as the only approved inner state'. War is opposed to peace, as good to evil:

> But: one considers *war* to be *evil* – and yet wages war! … In other words: one does not at all now stop hating, saying No, doing No: the Christian e.g. hates sin (not the sinner: as they are kept apart by the cunning of piety) – And precisely through this

---

[63] See Heidegger (1985 71) on persecution in the context of revenge: 'Revenge is not, after all, simply intended to chase something, capture and take possession of it. Nor does it intend merely to destroy what it pursues. Avenging persecution opposes in advance that upon which it takes revenge. It opposes its object by degrading it so that, by contrasting the degraded object with its own superiority, it may restore its own validity, the only validity it considers decisive. For revenge is driven by the feeling of being vanquished and injured.'

false separation 'good' and 'evil' the world of the hateworthy, of ever-to-be-battled has grown to monstrous proportions.[64]

In the polemical use of reason from KrV and in ZeF discussed in Chapter 2, we saw that Kant was unable to sustain the opposition between lawless force and violence (in the state of nature) and eternal peace (as the rule of law excluding violence) because the violence of coercive law is needed to establish peace (see p. 105). In the present text, Nietzsche puts his finger on an analogous problem. Caught in the opposition between good and evil, the 'good man' cannot but oppose, i.e. hate and fight what he opposes: conflict and hatred, thereby repeating what he opposes and multiplying the opposition exponentially at once. In waging war on 'sin' and 'evil', the 'good man' only replicates the 'sin' of conflict and hatred, and expands the imaginary world of ugly (hateworthy) things to be fought. In this text, the futility of trying to eliminate conflict and hatred is the consequence of a 'deconstructive' critique of the ideal of the 'good man' that shows its reliance on its opposite. But we can also make out Nietzsche's underlying ontology of conflict: since hatred and conflict are necessary, dynamic features of life and human interaction, moral strategies of denial serve not to diminish their destructiveness, but only to exacerbate it. How, then are we to respond *constructively* to hatred and conflict, given their ineradicability? If denial is the worst way to deal with the problem of hatred, what alternatives, if any, does Nietzsche's philosophy of hatred have to offer?

V Nietzsche's responses to the problem of hatred

It is important, first of all, to recall that the ineluctable necessity of hatred *is* a problem for Nietzsche. In the case of 'agonal hatred inter pares' hatred is released from the usual *Zerstörungsdynamik* and becomes a profoundly affirmative and creative force. But this is an exception, depending on particular conditions, and his commitment to affirm life as it is and to intensify or enhance (*Steigerung*) life implies the sickening consequence that the destructive powers of hatred be enhanced (JGB 23), as we saw at the beginning of the chapter.

If the enhancement of life entails the enhancement or intensification of hatred as a 'life-conditioning' affect, Nietzsche's response is to contain and exploit the energetic resources of hatred by drawing on the *idealizing powers intrinsic to hatred*. For as he learned from his study of hatred in both the Greeks and the priest, '[p]rofound hatred is also an idealist: whether we thereby make of our opponent a god or a devil, in any case we do him too much honour.'[65] One can argue, as I have elsewhere, that Nietzsche's 'agonal' style of critique consists precisely in turning priestly hatred (devil-

---

[64] 'Aber: man hält den K r i e g für b ö s e – und führt doch Krieg! ... Mit anderen Worten: man hört jetzt erst recht nicht auf, zu hassen, Nein zu sagen, Nein zu thun: der Christ z.B. haßt die Sünde (nicht den Sünder: wie sie fromme List auseinanderhält) – Und gerade durch diese falsche Trennung "gut" und "böse" ist die Welt des Hassenswerthen, Ewig-zu-Bekämpfenden ungeheuer angewachsen' (11[297] 13.124).
[65] 'Der tiefe Haß ist auch ein Idealist: ob wir aus unserem Gegner dabei einen Gott oder einen Teufel bilden, jedenfalls thun wir ihm damit zu viel Ehre an' (3[1].126 10.68).

building) into agonal hatred *inter pares* (god-building).⁶⁶ Of importance in the present context are Nietzsche's reflections on the rationale behind such a strategy. The starting point is to acknowledge the necessity of hatred as a 'life-conditioning' affect against the standard view that it is a matter of moral choice and can be put aside:

> – Where people do not grasp the purpose of a drive as necessary for preservation, as [they do] with defecation and urination, intake of nutrients etc., they believe they can *remove* it as redundant e.g. the drive to envy, to hate, to fear. And they consider the inability to rid oneself of it as an injustice, at least a misfortune: whereas one does *not* think like this about hunger and thirst.⁶⁷

Those, by contrast, who acknowledge the necessity of hatred are faced with the task, not of eliminating it, but of mastering it so as to use its power for constructive ends. The text continues:

> It ought not to *control* us, but we want to understand it as necessary and to control its power for our use. For that it is necessary that we do *not* preserve it in its *entire full* force, like a stream that is to drive a mill. Whoever does not completely know it, he will be assaulted by it, just as a mountain stream comes crashing down after winter-time.⁶⁸

Here, the Spinozistic thought that the destructive energies of hatred are best contained by knowing it better is coupled with the realist concession that we constantly risk failure. But on its own, the desire to know hatred better is not enough; hatred must first be released from the stigma of the pudendum and be affirmed:

> How a drive is felt to be good or evil according to whether it is praised or censured, to be shown for *love* (in the Greeks, in ascetic Christians, in Christian wedlock etc.)
> All *idealization of a drive* begins *when* it is counted among the praiseworthy things. Hint for the future?? NB
> Therewith to improve envy, hatred. To observe how different compassion has become.⁶⁹

---

⁶⁶ See Siemens (2021 esp. Chapters 1 and 9); Siemens (1998); and Siemens (2001).
⁶⁷ '– Wo die Menschen nicht den Zweck eines Triebes als nothwendig zur Erhaltung mit Händen greifen, wie beim Koth- und Urinlassen, Nahrungnehmen usw., da glauben sie ihn als überflüssig b e s e i t i g e n zu können z.B. den Trieb zu neiden, zu hassen, zu fürchten. Und das Nicht-loswerden-können betrachten sie als ein Unrecht, mindestens Unglück: während man so bei Hunger und Durst n i c h t denkt' (6[398] 9.299f.).
⁶⁸ 'Er soll uns nicht b e h e r r s c h e n, aber wir wollen ihn als nothwendig begreifen und seine Kraft zu unserem Nutzen beherrschen. Dazu ist nöthig, daß wir ihn n i c h t in seiner g a n z e n v o l l e n Kraft erhalten, wie einen Bach, der Mühlen treiben soll. Wer ihn nicht ganz kennt, über den fällt er her, wie nach den Winterzeiten ein Gebirgsbach zerstörend herunterkommt' (6[398] 9.299).
⁶⁹   'Wie ein Trieb, je nachdem man ihn lobt und tadelt, als gut
oder böse empfunden wird, an der L i e b e zu zeigen (bei Griechen,
bei asketischen Christen, in der christlichen Ehe usw.)
    Alle I d e a l i s i r u n g e i n e s T r i e b e s beginnt damit,
d a ß man ihn unter die lobenswerthen Dinge rechnet. Wink für
die Zukunft?? NB
    Den Neid, den Haß, dabei zu verbessern. Zu beachten, wie
verschieden das Mitleid geworden ist.' (7[75] 9.332).

Nietzsche's response to the problem of hatred is, then, *to 'improve' hatred through a programme of constructive idealization based on the affirmative acknowledgement of its necessity.* There is, however, also a response of a completely different order in Nietzsche's writings, one that appears to flatly contradict this programme and vitiate the whole project of naturalization. The problem is best seen by comparing the following notes:

> A strong free human being feels *the qualities of the **organism** towards* [*gegen*] everything else
> 1) self-regulation: in the form of *fear* of all alien incursions, in the *hatred* towards [*gegen*] the enemy [...][70]

> Whoever hates or despises alien [foreign] blood is not yet
> an individual, but a kind of human protoplasm.[71]

In the first excerpt, we see Nietzsche developing his naturalistic concept of freedom modelled on organismic self-regulation (see p. 181) by translating the moral category of 'freedom' or 'sovereignty' (freedom and power) into the language of physiology and the processes needed for an organism to live. As in note 11[134] 9 (see II.1, pp. 200–1; cf. 182), hatred is bound up with appropriation or incorporation (*Habsucht, Aneignungslust, Assimilation an sich, Einverleiben*), as the primary drive within an overall economy of overcompensation (*überreichlicher Ersatz*).[72] However, the second note issues a caveat against precisely this manner of thinking: the translation of organismic drives into moral/human-social relations and more broadly, the appeal to physiology for normative guidance in naturalistic, life-affirmative terms. At issue specifically is hatred in the physiological sense of the resources needed to overcome resistance of others to assimilation. The thought that as human individuals we do *not* need to replicate the protoplasm's hatred of foreign bodies is taken up and reformulated in positive terms by Nietzsche in the context of knowledge and his ideal of 'polytropia':

> beyond love and hate, also [beyond] good and evil, a
> deceiver with a good conscience, cruel to the point of self-mutilation,

---

[70] 'Ein starker freier Mensch empfindet gegen alles Andere
die Eigenschaften des **Organismus**
1) Selbstregulirung: in der Form von F u r c h t vor
allen fremden Eingriffen, im H a ß gegen den Feind [...]' (11[182] 9.509).

[71] 'Wer das fremde Blut haßt oder verachtet, ist noch kein
Individuum, sondern eine Art menschliches Protoplasma.' (11[296] 9.555).

[72] '[...] 2) overcompensation: in the form of *acquisitiveness* the pleasure of appropriation the craving for power 3) assimilation to oneself: in the form of praise reproach making others dependent on oneself, to that end deception cunning, learning, habituation, commanding incorporating [*Einverleiben*] judgements and experiences [...]'
'[...] 2) überreichlicher Ersatz: in der Form von H a b s u c h t
Aneignungslust Machtgelüst
3) Assimilation an sich: in der Form von Loben Tadeln
Abhängigmachen Anderer von sich, dazu Verstellung
List, Lernen, Gewöhnung, Befehlen Einverleiben von
Urtheilen und Erfahrungen [...]' (11[182] 9.509).

uncovered [or undiscovered] and before all eyes, a tempter [attempter], who lives from alien [foreign] blood, who loves virtue as an experiment, like vice.[73]

Against the fear and hatred of foreign beings, proposed as a necessary part of the exercise of human freedom modelled on organismic self-regulation, Nietzsche now takes a position at the opposite extreme with an ideal of knowledge that is not only 'beyond love and hatred', but 'lives from foreign blood'. But how can he advocate both hating what is foreign and living from what is foreign? What are we to make of the two extremes occupied by Nietzsche? One response is to see Nietzsche as the idealist *malgré lui*, recoiling from the consequences of his philosophical physiology and capitulating to the metaphysical separation of the ideal from reality. Another response is to question the philosophical function of Nietzsche's physiology and specifically: its status as a source of normative guidance. Instead of these alternatives, I suggest that it is *as a consequence* of Nietzsche's physiological insights into hatred, and the errors performed by us in hatred, that he proposes the corrective of knowledge beyond love and hatred.

The hatred of impotence, as we have seen, has its special home in the imagination, which enables it to degrade, distort or 'uglify' the overpowering other into 'the evil enemy'. While this kind of imaginary revenge is specific to the hatred of impotence, there is, according to Nietzsche, an imaginary relation to the object or a relation to imaginary objects in almost *all* forms of hatred, as well as love:

The *imagined* world (we love and hate mostly
imaginations [imaginary things], not realities, humans).[74]

In order to understand this claim, we need to consider once more Nietzsche's physiology of hatred and love. In note 5[45] (9.191), Nietzsche takes issue with the deceptions of language from a physiological point of view. At issue are the words we use to name feelings (*Empfindungsworten*) like 'hating', 'loving', 'willing', 'desiring', etc., which he berates for misleading us into thinking that one such word designates one thing:

---

[73] 'jenseits von Liebe und Haß, auch von Gut und Böse, ein
Betrüger mit gutem Gewissen, grausam bis zur Selbstverstümmlung,
unentdeckt und vor aller Augen, ein Versucher, der vom
Blut fremder Seelen lebt, der die Tugend als ein Experiment liebt, wie das Laster.' (13[21] 9.622).
In nineteenth-century German 'entdecken' can mean 'to uncover, disclose' (the probable meaning here), as well as 'to discover' (the meaning in contemporary German). See also 26[101] 11.177 on 'polytropia' and 'experience in oppositions' ('Erfahrung in Gegensätzen'). See also 11[10] 9.443f. on philosophy as 'indifference' (*Gleichgültigkeit*) and the need to overcome self-love and self-hatred (*Selbsthaß*) for knowledge; also 11[141] 9.494f. on 'indifference' and 'looking into the world with as many eyes as possible' ('möglichst aus v i e l e n Augen in die Welt sehen'). The Greek word 'πολυτροπία' means versatility or multifariousness, both applicable to Nietzsche's epistemic ideal. The adjective 'πολύτροπος', used of Odysseus, means much-travelled, versatile of mind, wily; also various manifold (Liddell and Scott 1996 1444–5).
[74] 'Die e i n g e b i l d e t e Welt (wir lieben und hassen meist
Einbildungen, nicht Realitäten, Menschen)' (2[11] 9.36).

Language brings great prejudices with it and maintains them e.g. that what is signified with One word is also One process: Willing, desiring, drive – complicated things!⁷⁵

But Nietzsche's main concern here, as in the preceding text (2[11] 9.36), is with the objects of our feelings, or what he now calls 'object-accusatives' (*Objektaccusative*): the 'you' in expressions like 'I love you' or 'I hate you'. We think of these as single feelings evoked by a single person, but when translated into the language of physiology (or will to power), expressions of this kind designate highly complex, multifarious physiological processes that give rise to states of pain. When, as a result of habituation and association, I then make the judgement that only 'you' can relieve my pain, I *misplace* (*verlegen*) the pain from my body to you as the supposed source of my pain and say 'I love you' or 'I hate you':

> Willing, desiring, drive – complicated things! Pain in all three cases (as a consequence of a pressure state of need) is displaced into the process "whither?": it has absolutely nothing to do with the latter, it is a habitual error [born] of association. "I have a need for you" No! I have a need, and my opinion is that you can assuage it (a *belief* is inserted) "I love you" no! there is in me a state of being in love in me and my *opinion* is that you will relieve it. These object-accusatives! A belief is contained in all these words for feelings e.g. willing hating etc. A *pain* and an *opinion* concerning its relief – that is the fact of the matter. Just so when there is talk of goals. – An intense love is the *fanatic* stubborn *opinion* that only such and such a person can relieve my need, it is belief that makes [us feel] blessed or cursed, occasionally when we have it even strong enough against every disappointment i.e. truth.⁷⁶

To fixate on the object of our love or hate and our first-person feeling towards it, as we do, is to misunderstand our body. It is to *misplace* the pain we experience as a consequence of pressure (*Druck*) or lack (*Noth*) by creating an imaginary relation to an (imaginary) object understood as the source and object of our love or hatred. At the

---

⁷⁵ 'Die Sprache trägt große Vorurtheile in sich und unterhält sie z.B. daß, was mit Einem Wort bezeichnet wird, auch Ein Vorgang sei: Wollen, Begehren, Trieb – complicirte Dinge!' (5[45] 9.191).

⁷⁶ 'Wollen, Begehren, Trieb – complicirte Dinge! Der Schmerz bei allen Dreien (in Folge eines Druckes Nothstandes) wird in den Prozeß "wohin?" verlegt: damit hat er gar nichts zu thun, es ist ein gewohnter Irrthum aus Association. "Ich habe solches Bedürfniß nach dir" Nein! Ich habe eine Noth, und ich meine, du kannst sie stillen (ein G l a u b e n ist eingeschoben) "ich liebe dich" nein! es ist in mir ein verliebter Zustand und ich m e i n e, du werdest ihn lindern. Diese Objektaccusative! ein Glauben ist bei all diesen Empfindungsworten enthalten z.B. wollen hassen usw. Ein S c h m e r z und eine M e i n u n g in Betreff seiner Linderung – das ist die Thatsache. Ebenso wo von Zwecken geredet wird. – Eine heftige Liebe ist die f a n a t i s c h e hartnäckige M e i n u n g, daß nur die und die Person meine Noth lindern kann, es ist Glaube der selig und unselig macht, mitunter selbst im Besitze noch stark genug gegen jede Enttäuschung d.h. Wahrheit' (5[45] 9.191).

core of Nietzsche's analysis is the problematic character of pain, what he elsewhere calls the 'stupidity', the 'excessive filling of the imagination (exaggeration)' intrinsic to pain.[77] The interpretative (or 'intellectual') nature of pain is often emphasized by Nietzsche, such that the location (mostly *mis*location) of pain is the result of an interpretation that is crude ('the lowest level of intellect') and more often than not erroneous. And if we see through these errors by understanding better our bodies, we need not replicate them: as individuals, we need not replicate the protoplasm's 'hatred of alien blood', for as knowers, we can see through the stupidity of this hatred and substitute for it the intelligence of 'living from alien blood' beyond love and hatred.

We are left, then, with two responses to the problem of hatred in Nietzsche's 'philosophy of hatred': to acknowledge the necessity of hatred for life and seek ways to exploit its prodigious idealizing powers and turn them *against* its destructiveness for constructive (life-affirming and -enhancing) ends; and to see through the errors of hatred through physiological (self-)knowledge and cultivate a style of knowing that is 'beyond love and hate'. These two responses can certainly pull in different directions – towards an *episteme* of confrontation, driven by agonal hatred *inter pares*, and towards an *episteme* of indifference (*Gleichgültigkeit*)[78] beyond all hatred. But they need not. For one could argue that the only viable basis for an *episteme* of indifference is *to cultivate a hatred of the necessary hatred on the ground of all life*, so as to 'control its power for our use' (6[398] 9.299). This holds promise as a way of knowing that addresses both the realist and perfectionist impulses in Nietzsche's philosophy. His *episteme* of indifference also resonates with the *episteme* of openness encountered in Nietzsche's physiology and the hostile calm of GD, also a kind of 'polytropia', a many-sided attentiveness to things, not persons, achieved by turning (not hatred against hatred, but) the capacity to resist against the impulse to resist. This is precisely what Nietzsche commends as an exercise for an *episteme* of indifference:

> To increase indifference! And *for that*, *practice* in seeing with *other* eyes: practice in seeing without human relations, thus seeing *proficiently*! (11[10] 9.444)[79]

---

[77] 'Intellektuell gemessen, wie i r r t h u m v o l l ist Lust und Schmerz! Wie falsche wäre geurtheilt, wenn man nach dem G r a d e von Lust oder Schmerz auf den Werth für das Leben schließen wollte! Im S c h m e r z ist so viel Dummheit wie in den blinden Affekten, ja es ist Zorn Rache Flucht Ekel Haß Überfüllung der Phantasie (Übertreibung) selber, der Schmerz i s t die ungeschieden zusammengeflossene Masse von Affekten, o h n e I n t e l l e k t giebt es keinen Schmerz, aber die niedrigste Form des Intellekts tritt da zu Tage; der Intellekt, der "Materie", der "Atome". – Es giebt eine Art, von einer Verletzung ü b e r r a s c h t zu werden (wie jener der auf dem Kirschbaum sitzend eine Flintenkugel durch die Backe bekam), daß man gar nicht den S c h m e r z f ü h l t. Der Schmerz ist G e h i r n p r o d u k t' (11[319] 9.565).

[78] See note 73 above.

[79] 'Vermehrung der Gleichgültigkeit! Und d a z u Ü b u n g, mit a n d e r e n Augen sehen: Übung, ohne menschliche Beziehungen, also s a c h l i c h zu sehen!'

VI The slave revolt of morality and the problem of emancipation

To conclude the examination of hatred in this chapter, I would like to return to the slave revolt of morality and consider its implications for the emancipatory potential of agonistic politics. As noted in the introduction to the chapter, the two obstacles confronting emancipatory aspirations of agonistic theory from a Nietzschean perspective have yet to be confronted by its proponents. The first is that agonal relations and agonal hatred – the only kind of hatred that is both creative and affirmative – presuppose approximately equal power among the constituents. While Nietzsche's concept of approximately equal power includes qualitative diversity and *relative* differences of power (the 'weakest' can still make a claim on the 'strongest') (see p. 192), it is ruled out by *radical* inequalities – whether it be a towering instance to which none are equal, or those in a position of weakness without resources to challenge those in power. This raises the second concern. Nietzsche's account of the slave revolt of morality, as the primal scene of the values that still dominate European modernity, raises the question whether emancipation from a position of radical inequality can be achieved without replicating the dynamics of destructive hatred, degrading those with power through imaginary revenge and *ressentiment*.[80] So the key question is whether Nietzsche and Kant, as thinkers of conflict and hatred, offer any conceptual resources for rethinking the question of emancipation without slavish attitudes and the logic of revenge.

Nothing we have seen so far in Kant's views on hatred, revenge or anger bears on the condition of powerlessness vis-à-vis overpowering others at the centre of the slave revolt of morality. But it would be wrong to think that he has nothing to say about those in a position of weakness or slavish attitudes; as when he writes, for instance,

> Everything that grovels is at the same time false. For every human being is aware of the inalienable right of equality.[81]

If servility means to violate our duty to ourselves, Kant's sharpest criticisms, bringing him close to Nietzsche, concern slavish attitudes to the moral law:

> – I have always insisted on cultivating and maintaining virtue and even religion in a joyful disposition. The morose compliance with one's duty with head bowed

---

[80] The only contemporary philosopher I know who is sensitive to this problem is Howard Caygill. In his book *On Resistance*, he points repeatedly to the danger besetting acts of resistance that, in *merely reacting* to an overwhelming enemy, may end up reproducing the structures of the opponent, foreclosing any chance of overcoming it; or that they may get trapped in an escalating reciprocal movement of repression, or a self-defeating escalation of violence. See esp. Caygill (2013 34–46, 66, 98–9, 162–3).

[81] 'Alles was kriecht ist zugleich falsch. Denn ein jeder Mensch ist sich des unverlierbaren Rechts der Gleichheit bewust' (*Nachlass* to MS XXIII.403).

groaning like a Carthusian as if under a tyrannical yoke is not respect [for the law] but slavish fear and thereby hatred of the law. (*Nachlass* to RGV XXIII.99f.)[82]

In his critical response to Schiller's *Anmuth und Würde* in RGV he writes in a similar vein of a 'fearful-stooping' and 'dejected' attitude to the law as a 'slavish disposition', which 'can never take place without a hidden hatred of the law'.[83] We are reminded of Nietzsche's critique of the apostle Paul and his hatred of the law he could not fulfil (M 68), but also of anarchists, so-called free-thinkers and other contemporary avatars of the hatred that gave birth to slave morality – their 'misarchism' or hatred of rule (GM II 12 5.315) and slogans like 'submissiveness to arbitrary laws', the 'tyranny of arbitrary laws' (JGB 188), or 'Ni dieu, ni maître' (JGB 22).

We would expect Kant to criticize the hatred of the law behind slavish attitudes if only because hatred is a passion. The sharp distinction he makes between passions and affects allows him to give them very different moral signatures. Unlike passions, affects are not unreservedly evil, but 'unfortunate dispositions of the soul' (*unglückliche Gemüthsstimmungen*), 'pregnant with many ills' (*mit viel Übeln schwanger*) (Anth VII.267). But this does not prevent him from making surprisingly affirmative remarks about the moral and aesthetic qualities of affects. In KU he writes of *enthusiasm* as sublime in a way that is close to Nietzsche's description of the pathos of the master morality in GM:

> The idea of the good with affect is called *enthusiasm*. This state of mind appears to be sublime: so much so that there is a common saying that nothing great can be achieved without it [...] (KU V.271-2)

Even if it is, as an affect, blind to the claims of reason,

> [...] from an aesthetic point of view, enthusiasm is sublime, because it is a tensing [*Anspannung*] of one's powers by ideas which give to the mind a buoyancy [*Schwung*] of far stronger and more enduring efficacy than the stimulus afforded by sensible representations. (ibid.)

---

[82] '– Ich habe immer darauf gehalten Tugend und selbst religion in fröhlicher Gemüthsstimmung zu cultiviren und zu erhalten. Die mürrische Kopfhängende gleich als unter einem tyrannischen Joch ächzende cartheusermäßige Befolgung seiner Pflicht ist nicht Achtung sondern knechtische Furcht und dadurch Haß des Gesetzes.'

[83] 'Frägt man nun: welcherlei ist die ästhetische Beschaffenheit, gleichsam das Temperament der Tugend, muthig, mithin fröhlich, oder ängstlich-gebeugt und niedergeschlagen? so ist kaum eine Antwort nöthig. Die letztere sklavische Gemüthsstimmung kann nie ohne einen verborgenen Haß des Gesetzes statt finden, und das fröhliche Herz in Befolgung seiner Pflicht (nicht die Behaglichkeit in Anerkennung desselben) ist ein Zeichen der Ächtheit tugendhafter Gesinnung [...]' (Note to RGV VI.2-24). That hatred of the law occurs from a position of weakness for Kant is confirmed when he contrasts the contempt (*Verachtung*) for evil (that which violates the law) from a position of strength in reason from the combination of fear and hatred when we lack that feeling of superiority: 'Nur das Moralisch-Gesetzwidrige ist an sich selbst böse, schlechterdings verwerflich, und muß ausgerottet werden; die Vernunft aber, die das lehrt, noch mehr aber, wenn sie es auch ins Werk richtet, verdient allein den Namen der Weisheit, in Vergleichung mit welcher das Laster zwar auch Thorheit genannt werden kann, aber nur alsdann, wenn die Vernunft gnugsam Stärke in sich fühlt, um es (und alle Anreize dazu) zu verachten, und nicht bloß als ein zu fürchtendes Wesen zu hassen, und sich dagegen zu bewaffnen' (RGV VI.93).

The passage ends with an account of the kinds of affects Nietzsche associates with strong, noble types and the active power to overcome resistance:

> Every affect of the hearty [or active: *wacker*] type (such, that is, as excites the consciousness of our power of overcoming every resistance (*animi strenui*)) is aesthetically sublime, e.g. anger, even desperation (the *rage of forlorn hope* but not *faint-hearted* despair). (ibid.)

Enthusiasm, on this account, can easily be read as a description of the pathos of the nobles in Nietzsche's narrative of the slave revolt, and the unreflective, spontaneous self-affirmation that gave rise to the value 'good' in the master morality (GM I 2, 4, 10). The convergence is even more striking when it comes to Kant's attitude to the affect of anger (*Zorn*). In one *Nachlass* note to GSE he contrasts revenge (*Rache*), as social form of hatred, with anger as a natural affect, writing: 'But anger is a much needed and fitting quality for a man, provided it is no passion (which is different from the *affect*).'[84] Recall the stormy 'rush' (*Rausch*) of self-consuming affects for Kant; what 'anger does not do with speed, it does not at all; and it forgets easily', so that it does not bury itself deep in the hidden recesses of the soul 'like an illness from poisoning': this is what Nietzsche describes as the nobles' 'enthusiastic suddenness of anger, love, reverence, gratitude and revenge' ('schwärmerische Plötzlichkeit von Zorn, Liebe, Ehrfurcht, Dankbarkeit und Rache'), and the explosive character of their *ressentiment*:

> When *ressentiment* does occur in the noble man himself, it is consumed and exhausted in an immediate reaction, and therefore it does not *poison*, on the other hand, it does not occur at all in countless cases where it is unavoidable for all who are weak and powerless. To be unable to take his enemies, his misfortunes and even his *misdeeds* seriously for long – that is the sign of strong, rounded natures with a superabundance of a power which is flexible, formative, healing and can make one forget (a good example from the modern world is Mirabeau, who had no recall for the insults and slights directed at him and who could not forgive, simply because he – forgot). A man like this shakes from him, with one shrug, many worms which would have burrowed into another man [...] (GM I 10 5.273)[85]

---

[84] 'Weil die Rache voraussetzt daß Menschen die sich hassen einander nahe bleiben wiedrigenfals wenn man sich entfernen kann wie man will der Grund sich zu Rächen wegfallen würde so kan dieselbe nicht in der Natur seyn weil diese nicht voraussetzt daß Menschen neben einander eingesperret seyn. Allein der Zorn eine sehr nöthige u. einem Manne sehr geziemende Eigenschaft wenn sie nemlich keine Leidenschaft (welche vom *Affect* unterschieden ist) ist liegt gar sehr in der Natur' (*Nachlass* to GSE XX.34).

[85] 'Das Ressentiment des vornehmen Menschen selbst, wenn es an ihm auftritt, vollzieht und erschöpft sich nämlich in einer sofortigen Reaktion, es v e r g i f t e t darum nicht: andrerseits tritt es in unzähligen Fällen gar nicht auf, wo es bei allen Schwachen und Ohnmächtigen unvermeidlich ist. Seine Feinde, seine Unfälle, seine, U n t h a t e n selbst nicht lange ernst nehmen können – das ist das Zeichen starker voller Naturen, in denen ein Überschuss plastischer, nachbildender, ausheilender, auch vergessen machender Kraft ist (ein gutes Beispiel dafür aus der modernen Welt ist Mirabeau, welcher kein Gedächtniss für Insulte und Niederträchtigkeiten hatte, die man an ihm begiengen, und der nur deshalb nicht vergeben konnte, weil er – vergass). Ein solcher Mensch schüttelt eben viel Gewürm mit Einem Ruck von sich, das sich bei Anderen eingräbt [...].'

Even more remarkable, in my view, is what Kant has to say about anger in the case of those in a position of weakness, both priests and those susceptible to the slave morality propagated by them:

> Anger is a very benign feeling of the weak human being. An inclination to suppress it leads to irreconcilable hatred. Women, priests. One does not always hate the one about whom one is angry. Good nature [benignity] of the human beings who are angry in this sense. Feigned decency hides anger and makes false friends.

> Der Zorn ist eine sehr gutartige Empfindung des schwachen Menschen Eine Neigung ihn zu unterdrücken veranlaßet den unversohnlichen Haß. Frauenzimmer, Geistliche. Man hasset den nicht immer über den man zürnet. Gutartigkeit der Menschen die da zürnen. Verstellte Sittsamkeit verbirgt den Zorn u. macht falsche Freunde. (*Nachlass* to GSE XX.32)

So what would a Kantian solution to the problem of hatred-as-ressentiment look like? If the problem with the slave revolt is that it is driven by hatred, a passion (always evil for Kant) which cannot be sated and buries itself in the soul, then the solution could be to take on, to appropriate from the oppressors their affect of anger: to substitute explosive, self-consuming bursts of anger for the slow-burning, reflective passion of hatred-ressentiment. The suggestion is that affects are better than passions ('benign') as a source of moral values for those in a position of weakness (e.g. women, priests), and that anger houses emancipatory potentials which avoid the problems of revenge-hatred and the slave revolt. In order to compare this with Nietzsche's solution, I propose to recount the slave revolt, with some licence, in a way that draws on both thinkers.

For Kant, all passions are inclinations directed by human beings to human beings, and hatred arises when their ends conflict.[86] But '[n]othing enrages us more than injustice', and we hate those who make us suffer an injustice or pass by with indifference (see p. 216). For Nietzsche, thinking from perspective in power rather than morality, 'it is the impotence over and against humans, *not* the impotence over and against nature that engenders the most desperate bitterness towards existence.'[87] For Kant, things go wrong when those without power are *either* servile and end up hating the law (of the masters) *or* when their legitimate desire for justice is deformed into a personal hatred of those who make them suffer injustice and the desire for revenge. For Nietzsche, the hatred of the impotent is personal from the start, and the moral discourse of justice and injustice is part of a brilliant reversal born of the creative, idealizing power of the hatred, disguising its object, 'my enemy', as 'injustice' (GM I 14 5.282f.). The morality of the priest teaches the powerless to 'treat those in power, the

---

[86] '§83. Da Leidenschaften nur von Menschen auf Menschen gerichtete Neigungen sein können, so fern diese auf mit einander zusammenstimmende oder einander widerstreitende Zwecke gerichtet, d.i. Liebe oder Haß sind [...]' (Anth VII.270).

[87] 'die Ohnmacht gegen Menschen, n i c h t die Ohnmacht gegen die Natur, erzeugt die desperateste Verbitterung gegen das Dasein' (5[71] 12.214).

violent ones, the "masters" as enemies' and to hate what makes them powerful: the will to power. With the help of priestly morality, the powerless come to believe they 'have a right to their contempt of the will to power' and that they have a higher right, a higher moral standing. From this position, Kant tells us, the passion for retaliation engenders an 'inclination to persecute and destroy' the offender, which can never be sated, even when requited, and lives on as a secret, smouldering hatred. The intellectual element of hatred, emphasized by Kant, is used by Nietzsche to elaborate how, under conditions of impotence, the persecution of revenge works: through the invention of a 'person' – a blameworthy, responsible subject behind the deed – upon whose degradation as 'evil' the elevation of the powerless to a higher moral standing depends. The priestly craving for revenge reaches its zenith for Nietzsche in the 'radical transvaluation' (*radikale Umwerthung*) of the oppressors' values,[88] the 'most spiritual revenge' that gave the powerless moral superiority and dignity as 'the patient ones, the humble ones, the righteous' (*Geduldigen, Demüthigen, Gerechten*) (GM I 13 5.280): "'We good ones – we are the righteous'" ("'Wir Guten – wir sind die Gerechten'": GM I 14 5.282).

The Kantian solution proposed above is for those without power to take on the masters' anger, in place of the passion for revenge, and direct it against the masters, anger serving as an alternative source of moral values free from the pathologies of revenge. What, then, is Nietzsche's solution? For guidance, I draw on part 9 of a well-known *Nachlass* text on 'European Nihilism', the so-called 'Lenzer Heide' fragment from 1887 (5[71] 12.211–18), which contains a highly condensed version of the slave revolt:

> Now, *morality* protected life from despair and from the plunge into nothingness for those men and classes who were violated and oppressed by
> *men*: for powerlessness against men, *not* powerlessness against nature, is what engenders the most desperate bitterness against existence. Morality treated the despots, the men of violence, the 'masters' in general, as the enemies against whom the common man must be protected, i.e., *first of all encouraged, strengthened*. Consequently, morality taught the deepest *hatred* and *contempt* for what is the rulers' fundamental trait: *their will to power*. To abolish this morality, to deny it, corrode it: that would be to imbue the most hated drive with a *reversed* feeling and evaluation. If the suffering, oppressed human being *lost his belief* in having a *right* to despise the will to power, he would enter the phase of hopeless desperation. This would be the case if the masters' trait were essential to life, if it turned out that even the 'will to morality' is only disguised this 'will to power', that even this hating and despising is a power-will. The human oppressed would realise

---

[88] 'Alles, was auf Erden gegen "die Vornehmen", "die Gewaltigen", "die Herren", "die Machthaber" gethan worden ist, ist nicht der Rede werth im Vergleich mit,dem, was die Juden gegen sie gethan haben: die Juden, jenes priesterliche Volk, das sich an seinen Feinden und Überwältigern zuletzt nur durch eine radikale Umwerthung von deren Werthen, also durch einen Akt der geistigsten Rache Genugthuung zu schaffen wusste' (GM I 7 5.267).

that he stands *on the same ground* as the oppressors and that he has no *privilege*, no *higher rank* than them. (5[71] 12.214f.)[89]

In order to break the zero-sum logic of self-elevation through degradation of those in power at the heart of slave morality, Nietzsche proposes that the oppressed learn to love and value what they hate and despise the most in the powerful, their will to power; to do so *by acknowledging that they stand 'on the same ground'* (auf gleichem Boden). That expression means acknowledging not just that their will to morality, and the hatred and contempt behind it, is also a form of will to power; but also that they cannot claim to occupy the moral high ground, but have the same or equal moral standing as the masters. It is striking how, unexpectedly, Nietzsche appeals to a principle of equality (auf gleichem Boden) as a way to overcome imaginary revenge and open the prospect of emancipation free of the pathologies of the slave revolt. What Nietzsche does not say is that the will to power can take countless, multifarious forms and need not issue in domination, violence or oppression. From Nietzsche's physiology and Z, for instance, we know that hatred is inseparable from love, and that those of approximately equal power can be driven by agonal hatred, a creative form of hatred that trades on affirming the other's achievements and drawing on them in a dynamic of creative self-overcoming.

We are left, then, with two responses to the question of emancipation from conditions of radical inequality which avoid the problems besetting the slave revolt: to take on from those in power the affective power of anger and turn it against them, instead of nurturing a slow-burning, insatiable passion for revenge; and to subvert the morality that legitimates hatred of the powerful by learning to love and affirm their

---

[89] 'Nun hat die M o r a l das Leben vor der Verzweiflung und dem Sprung ins Nichts bei solchen Menschen und Ständen geschützt, welche von M e n s c h e n vergewaltthätigt und niedergedrückt wurden: denn die Ohnmacht gegen Menschen, n i c h t die Ohnmacht gegen die Natur, erzeugt die desperateste Verbitterung gegen das Dasein. Die Moral hat die Gewalthaber, die Gewaltthätigen, die 'Herren' überhaupt als die Feinde behandelt, gegen welche der gemeine Mann geschützt, d. h. z u n ä c h s t e r m u t h i g t, g e s t ä r k t werden muß. Die Moral hat folglich am tiefsten hassen und verachten gelehrt, was der Grundcharakterzug der Herrschenden ist: i h r e n W i l l e n z u r M a c h t. Diese Moral abschaffen, leugnen, zersetzen: das wäre den bestgehaßten Trieb mit einer u m g e k e h r t e n Empfindung und Werthung versehen. Wenn der Leidende, Unterdrückte d e n G l a u b e n v e r l ö r e, ein R e c h t zu seiner Verachtung des Willens zur Macht zu haben, so träte er in das Stadium der hoffnungslosen Desperation. Dies wäre der Fall, wenn dieser Zug dem Leben essentiell wäre, wenn sich ergäbe, daß selbst in jenem "Willen zur Moral" nur dieser 'Wille zur Macht' verkappt sei, daß auch jenes Hassen und Verachten noch ein Machtwille ist. Der Unterdrückte sähe ein, daß er mit dem Unterdrücker a u f g l e i c h e m B o d e n steht und daß er kein V o r r e c h t, keinen h ö h e r e n R a n g vor jenem habe.'

will to power; acknowledging that both weak and strong 'stand on the same ground' with equal standing as forms of life and will to power. Next to these responses are the two Nietzschean responses to the problem of hatred considered earlier: to exploit its idealizing powers of hatred and turn them *against* its destructive tendencies, in favour of life-affirming and -enhancing ideals; and to see through the errors of hatred through physiological (self-)knowledge and cultivate an *episteme* of indifference 'beyond love and hate'. And just as these might be combined by cultivating a hatred of the necessary hatred on the ground of all life as the basis for an *episteme* of indifference, so too the cultivation of an affirmative love of life as will to power could be coupled with anger as an affective resource for resisting forms of domination. Indeed, there seem to be ways in which all four responses could be drawn on for an ethos appropriate to agonistic politics. Is an episteme 'beyond love and hate' not needed to subvert slave morality and acknowledge all forms of life as will to power? And is the recognition that we are of equal standing as forms of life not the precondition for cultivating radically immanent life-affirming and -enhancing ideals? These are but two of the many questions raised by our survey of Nietzsche and Kant in the course of these pages, questions which promise to open new perspectives for agonistic politics informed by two of the most brilliant philosophies of conflict.

Epilogue

In the course of this study, there have been several moments, in which the philosophies of conflict of Nietzsche and Kant carried implications for agonistic politics today worth considering. In this Epilogue, I will bring them together and add some reflections in the hope that they open fruitful avenues for further research.

The main issues in agonistic politics relevant to the ground covered in the foregoing chapters are: the principle of equality; pluralism; freedom; the boundary between non-violent agonism and violent antagonism, between contestation and political violence (Nietzsche's *Wettkampf* and the *Vernichtungskampf*); and the concept of agonistic respect as a way to secure that boundary. To my knowledge, Nietzsche does not have anything concrete to contribute to the question of political institutions appropriate for agonistic democracy, but this should not be taken to mean that he is somehow against or indifferent to political institutions per se. That much is clear from his admiration for Rome, whose 'construction was calculated to prove itself over millennia' (AC 58 6.246). He certainly expresses scepticism that lasting institutions can be forged in modernity (FW 356), but on balance I concur with Bonnie Honig (1993 72) that he is committed 'to maintaining institutionally a measure of stability, a measured stability, while at the same time refraining from too thoroughly domesticating the contingent world and selves that condition these communities'. Where Nietzsche does have something constructive to contribute, I believe it concerns 'the modalities of interaction between individuals and between individuals and their world' (Drolet 2013 39, 46) appropriate to agonistic democracy. To begin with, three preliminary remarks are in order. They concern the question of productive conflict, the problem of change and the critique of metaphysics, all germane to agonistic politics.

With agonistic politics in mind, I have tried in the course of the book to address the question: How to delimit and think through *productive forms of conflict*, which break with the devastating and destructive forms we know all too well, and can be affirmed? In Nietzsche's case, I have taken my bearings throughout from his vocation to be a philosopher of life, to think from a radically immanent standpoint in life, and from his normative commitments to the affirmation of life in its brutality and innocence, and to the enhancement of human life towards new possibilities. Among other things, this means resisting and undermining the oppositions of metaphysics (Ggz I) and the other-worldly, 'anti-natural' values behind them; reinterpreting them genealogically as related (*verwandt*) and conditioned in ways that transform their meaning and value (Ggz II.1); and looking for ways to articulate and defend the oppositional or contradictory character of reality (Ggz II.2) against the claims of logic and metaphysics. Nietzsche's affirmative notions of opposition (Ggz II.1 and II.2) offer a manner of thinking that avoids metaphysical oppositions with their other-worldly orientation, in which conflict (Ggz II.2) is constitutive of dynamic relations without substance, and which allows for a nuanced, graduated understanding of phenomena and their historicity.

Kant's principal achievement as a philosopher of conflict was to introduce the notion of radical negativity (as *privatio, Beraubung, Aufhebung*) into philosophy with his concept of real opposition or *Realrepugnanz*. Nietzsche's debt to this initiative is perhaps to be seen in the dynamic of fixing or making-fast (*Festsetzen, Feststellen*) through which power is exercised: like negation-as-privation, *Festsetzen* has the effect of robbing the opposing instance of its effects or effectiveness. If Kantian *Aufhebung* robs (privation) the other of its power to act against us, Nietzschean *Festsetzen* arrests the other's power to overpower us. But Nietzsche's notion of real opposition has a dynamic, pluralistic and multi-layered structure opened by his turn to physiology, which exposes the shortcomings of Kant's dyadic model derived from mechanistic science. Even if *Realrepugnanz* makes conflict integral to reality at all levels, it subtends a series of oppositions that severely limit Kant's philosophy of conflict and prevent him from formulating a genuinely productive notion of conflict: attraction-repulsion, love-hate, pleasure-pain, sociability-unsociability, 'the feeling of advancement' and the 'hindrance of life'. The opposition between pain and Kant's negative concept of pleasure precludes a productive concept of resistance, in which resistance-pain coincides with power-pleasure (p. 133–138); the opposition between sociability and unsociability precludes an intelligent form of egoism, in which my well-being coincides with that of others (p. 161–163); and the opposition between hatred and love forecloses the possibility of forms of hatred bound up with love, in which I can affirm and take on the successes of the other (p. 28, 196, 211, 221). In the end, Kant is unable to come up with a genuinely productive notion of conflict in his historical-political texts. Despite his references to a the 'liveliest competition' of forces in equilibrium, analogous to Nietzsche's idea of peace, conflict must negate itself for the sake of a legal order that makes peace and freedom possible (p. 93, 100–01, 107–08). In Nietzsche's idiom, Kant remains attached to the *Vernichtungskampf* as the condition for moral and intellectual progress, and to the *Vernichtung* of *Vernichtung* as the condition for peace, thereby closing down the question of conflict. For Nietzsche, by contrast, conflict is ineradicable, and the question is how destructive forms (the *Vernichtungskampf*) can be made productive of new orders and possibilities of (co-)existence through limited forms of antagonism or agonism (the *Wettkampf*).

Change

At issue in the philosophy of conflict for both Nietzsche and Kant is the problem of change, and change is of vital importance for agonistic theory. Agonistic politics is processual and disruptive; no settlements are permanent, all are open to contestation and responsive to differences excluded by any settlement. Connolly (1991 xxviii f.;

2005 121–35) speaks of a disruptive 'politics of becoming', a periodic 'denaturalization of settled identities and conventions' needed to accommodate ever-changing identities in late modernity; Honig (1993 1–17, 66–8, 115–25, 200–12), of a disruptive 'politics of virtú' needed to address the remainders excluded by any settlement. For both thinkers, agonistic democracy must negotiate the tension between the politics of disruption and a stabilizing politics of governance and consolidation, a 'politics of being' (Connolly) or 'politics of virtue' (Honig). Both impulses are of vital importance for Nietzsche. With Kant, Nietzsche shares the insight into the relational sources of change in conflict (p. 54, 78). But for Nietzsche it is clear that all forms of life, individual or collective, also need a degree of stability,[1] and his reflections on both change and stability, grounded in his counter-ontology of becoming as *Festsetzen*, raise fundamental questions for agonistic theory: How to theorize the necessity of change in ways that can accommodate the need for stability? And what is the right measure (*Maass*) or degree (*Grad*) of stability and change needed for agonistic politics? In Kant's philosophy of conflict these questions are foreclosed by his opposition between the state of nature, as lawless war where only the outcome (*Ausschlag*) of violent conflict is decisive and the only decisive outcome is annihilation (*Vernichtung*), and the rule of (cosmopolitan) law, where violent conflict is displaced by due process, and violent outcome (*Ausschlag*) by adjudication and settlement (*Ausgleich*). In NG and his lectures on metaphysics, I suggested, Kant comes close to a relational ontology of becoming without substance by displacing the 'real ground' of change (and with it, the notion of force), from things or substances to the dynamic 'nexus' between different things (p. 34–36). But for Kant this is a problem, not resolved until KrV, and it is to Nietzsche that agonists must turn in order to think change without relying on metaphysical presuppositions. His critique of the metaphysics of being and substance ontology is what first opens the prospect of theorizing process, change and disruption without relying on unitary grounds, and with his dynamic counter-ontology of *Festsetzen* he offers a way to think both change and relative stability without substance. With these anti-metaphysical initiatives, Nietzsche provides the presuppositions for agonistic theory with its post-foundationalist insistence on the contingency and contestability of all foundations.

Equality

Nietzsche is known for his strident critique of the democratic value of equality for breeding an actual 'equalization' (*Gleichmachung*) or levelling of human beings to one type, the domesticated herd-animal, to the exclusion of difference and diversity: 'One like all, one for all' (*Einer wie Alle, Einer für Alle*: 3[89] 9.73). But his thought also opens two different ways to think about equality with potential for agonistic theory. Throughout the book, I have drawn on his notion of approximate equality and the dynamic, relational notion of equilibrium first elaborated in the context of the origins

---

[1] For Nietzsche's views on duration and stability (*Dauer, Dauerhaftigkeit*), not to be confused with preservation (*Erhaltung*), see Müller Lauter (1999d 7, 24, 44, 48, 64, 105, 111, 113, 116, 133f., 139, 146, 180, 188, 197, 200, 213, 220, 230f., 244, 247f., 251, 275, 288, 298, 301, 322, 350; also 1999c 372–8).

of law in MA and WS (p. 119). 'Approximate equality' signifies not a principle or right, nor a quantitative measure, but the result of social powers or factors perceiving, judging and evaluating themselves in relation to others. Unlike the principle of equality criticized by Nietzsche, it is *inclusive* of relative differences of power and the qualitative diversity that makes for the richness of human life-forms and identities. Nietzsche offers little in the way of the kinds of political settlements, institutions and legal frameworks that would make for an approximate equality of power among constituents. But this does not make it a-political. It was in his reflections on the emergence of political institutions in ancient Greek culture, and the possibility of equal participation (*eunomia* and *isonomia*), that he first encountered equality, not as an abstract, normative principle, but as an element of labile equilibria (Müller 2019 97). The challenge for agonistic theory is to make good this deficit in his thought and integrate a dynamic, concrete sense of equality into agonistic politics in ways that make it less fragile.

The second notion of equality that avoids Nietzsche's critique of democratic equalization is what I called 'aspirational equality' in connection with WS 29 in Chapter 2 (p. 120, 123; cf. 214f.). With this expression is meant the impulse 'to raise oneself' (*sich bis dorthin erheben*) to equal standing with one who has risen above the 'common measure' (*gemeinsame Maass*) and stands out. And it is coupled with a sensitivity to the injustice of those who fare worse or better than the standard of equality due to good or bad fortune. Here again, equality is not an abstract norm attached to human dignity or a right of possessive individuals, but is bound up with achievement and merit. But that does not make it the privilege of a few elite individuals, as Nietzsche makes clear in MA 300:

> *Two kinds of equality.* – The thirst for equality can express itself either as a
> desire to draw everyone down to oneself (through diminishing them, spying
> on them, tripping them up) or to raise oneself with everyone else
> up (through acknowledging them, helping them, rejoicing in the success of others).[2]

We can speak here of equality as 'levelling up', or with Conant (2001 228) of a 'noble and elusive ideal of equality' shared by Nietzsche and other perfectionist thinkers, but lost in the historical process of democratization; one which draws and helps others to raise themselves to new standards of equality and rejoices in their successes. In this regard it mirrors Nietzsche's notion of agonal hatred (discussed below).

With these dynamic, conflictual notions of equality in mind, I argued in Chapter 2 (p. 117–123) for a revised, Nietzschean interpretation of Kant's theory of peace in ZeF, where this is understood (the 'approximative' reading) as an expanding, voluntary league of nations teleologically directed towards a global federation or state of states

---

[2] 'D o p p e l t e A r t d e r G l e i c h h e i t. – Die Sucht nach Gleichheit kann sich so äussern, dass man entweder alle Anderen zu sich hinunterziehen möchte (durch Verkleinern, Secretiren, Beinstellen) oder sich mit Allen hinauf (durch Anerkennen, Helfen, Freude an fremdem Gelingen).'

with coercive powers, never to be attained. On the revised interpretation, limited conflict would be integral to the voluntary league of approximately equal nations, and Kant's ideal of eternal peace, even if it excludes conflict, would serve as a life-enhancing means for the league, understood as a power-complex, to extend itself by raising new constituents to its level of equality and assimilating them. On this account, however, the league would always stand in need of external resistance and difference, and Kant's dream of an all-inclusive cosmopolitan rule of law without remainders would have to be abandoned.

Pluralism

In agonistic theory pluralism is not just a fact, but an axiological principle to be affirmed and nurtured. Pluralism is viewed as inherently (or at least potentially) antagonistic and concerns not just the diversity of values, faiths and life-styles among individuals and communities; it penetrates into the very identity of individuals and the 'multidimensional' elements that make up our complex and changing identities in late modernity. All three points are clearly in line with the anti-metaphysical presuppositions of Nietzsche's relational counter-ontology: 'originary plurality' or the 'in-one-another' (*Ineinander*) of entities without substance in ever-changing relations of conflict. The same holds for the profoundly social character of the individual or dividuum in Nietzsche socio-physiology: 'We are always among many' (6[80] 9.215) and relate to ourselves through social practices like friendship, hatred, revenge and envy.

Agonists tend to draw instead in problematic ways on Foucault, Derrida or Schmitt for their antagonistic pluralism; or when they do draw on Nietzsche, in no less problematic ways.[3] But Nietzsche's socio-physiology, explored in Chapter 4, offers a number of valuable impulses and initiatives for agonistic pluralism. The first is the ethos of 'fine, well-planned, thoughtful egoism', attentive to both life-needs as living organisms, our own and others', and to the ways its form of expression has been transformed by our social evolution into *ways of treating others*. Socio-physiology draws attention to the complexity, ambiguities and tensions brought to our moral sentiments and comportments through historical and pre-historical sedimentation; precisely what is obscured by the rigid oppositions of moral discourse. When our values are viewed as refinements, sublimations or later stages of their so-called 'opposites', we gain insight into the entwinement of good and evil, the possessiveness and cruelty in goodwill, and the ways in which egoism can coincide with care for the well-being of others. But Nietzsche's principal concern, and his most important contribution to agonistic pluralism, concerns the epistemic challenges posed by pluralism for our treatment of others. Genuine pluralism requires that we understand each person as a unique, living multiplicity with a complex affective life, which can only thrive under conditions unique to it. And the greatest obstacles to this kind of attunement are precisely the

---

[3] On Mouffe's use of Derrida and Schmitt, see Siemens (2012a); Fritsch (2008); and Rummens (2009). On Connolly's and Hatab's use of Nietzsche, see Siemens (2012b).

moral discourses of (substantive/noumenal) personhood and conformity to universal virtues or norms. Nietzsche's provocative response is to bypass the moral discourse of persons altogether and to take the problem of knowledge seriously by treating others as things to be known, so as to open our eyes to 'the affinities and enmities among things, *multiplicities* and their law' (11[21] 9.451). In line with the complexity of our socialized physiological processes, this involves a 'contradictory' practice that combines antagonism or agonistic 'mastery' over the other, with openness; what Nietzsche describes as a practice of 'possessing' others as things to be known, and 'being possessed by as great a range of *true things* as possible' (ibid.). A further initiative in this direction is what Nietzsche calls 'learning to see': '– habituating the eye to calm, to patience, to letting things come to it; learning to defer judgement, to peruse and grasp the particular case from all sides' (GD Deutschen 6). This is an episteme of 'hostile calm', which involves the exercise of resistance and non-resistance: it is 'slow, mistrustful, resistant' towards the other ('hostile'), but also resists the impulse to resist, to react, thereby opening our eyes and letting the other come to it ('calm'). This figure of thought: turning the capacity to resist against the impulse to resist recurs in Nietzsche's reflections on hatred and the cultivation of a hatred towards the necessary hatred on the ground of all life, so as to 'control its power for our use' (6[398] 9.299). When viewed as modalities of our interactions with others, both open the prospect of non-coercive forms of power that allow us to acknowledge what is radically other (*Fremdes*) and particular in its otherness. In my view, Nietzsche reminds us that nothing is more needful for agonistic pluralism than an *agonistic episteme* equal to the challenge of 'learning to see' 'as great a range of *true things* as possible', their 'affinities and enmities', '*multiplicities* and their law'.

Freedom

Nietzsche's commitment to life-affirmation and -enhancement leads him to locate the 'quality' or value of actions, not in the universalizability of their maxims, but in their capacity to individuate, to actualize the radical particularity of their agents, understood as unique multiplicities (p. 147–152, 172–175). We see this in his socio-physiology and the naturalistic ideal of autonomous self-determination, understood as *radically individual self-legislation* (as opposed to self-subjection to the universal law) on the part of a *radically socialized and plural subject* or *dividuum* (against the substantive, autonomous subject: *homo noumenon*). But this should not be understood as a retreat from social life into a kind of self-absorption. Self-legislation demands an intelligent, affirmative attention to our needs as unique living beings and the processes of self-regulation needed for each of us to meet our own conditions of existence, thrive and grow (thoughtful egoism); radically individual self-legislation revolves around radically individual self-regulation. But self-regulation is inseparable from the regulation of our relations with others. The human organism is profoundly social for Nietzsche, and his naturalistic ideal of freedom or sovereignty depends on the kinds of social relations we maintain with others. For Kant, the value of our actions also turns on how we treat others, but it is determined by the subject's direct relation to the moral law in him or her. Nietzschean freedom, by contrast, is *non-sovereign* in the sense that our relations to others are not external to our self-relation, but part of our self-regulation, and freedom depends on how we regulate our relations with others; it is deeply embedded and thoroughly relational in character. But it is also *sovereign* in the sense that those relations are determined *from within* by the specific life-form in search of the optimal conditions of existence unique to it and by the kind of self-regulation this requires. The socio-physiological turn in Nietzsche's thought allows him to rethink sovereignty as self-determination in both *radically individual* and *relational* terms. The question is: What kinds of social relations are required for Nietzschean sovereignty?

In order to address this question, one further ingredient in Nietzsche's ideal of freedom is needed. On the assumption (contra substance ontology) of an originary plurality of feelings, impulses and drives in conflict, the Socratic and Kantian ideal of inner harmony or agreement with oneself is ruled out (6[58] 9.208; p. 112–114). The best one can do is to weaken one's feelings and so reduce their vehement discord with their opposites, what Nietzsche calls a living death ('euthanasia') that favours uniformity and the loss of human diversity. And in his socio-physiological narrative, Nietzsche recounts how the first ethicists save the emerging individuals from suffering by commending bondage to the social whole under the concept of the moral law (11[182] 9.512; p. 181). Both contexts indicate that Nietzsche favours inner conflict as the condition for freedom, and the vehement antagonism of drives, not their diminution into a lukewarm peace, as the key to a plurality of vibrant individuals/ dividua. This is made explicit when he writes:

> The freest human has the greatest *feeling of power* over itself, the greatest *knowledge* about itself, the greatest *order* in the necessary *struggle* of its powers, the relatively greatest *independence* of its single powers, the relatively greatest *struggle* within itself: it is the *most divided* being and the *most changeable* and the one *who lives longest* and the extravagantly desirous one, [extravagantly] self-nourishing, the one who *eliminates* the most and *regenerates* itself [the most]. (11[130] 9.488)[4]

We can recognize here the organismic processes disclosed by 'intelligent egoism': acquisitiveness, assimilation, excretion, regeneration (11[182] 9.509f.; p. 164, 181). All of these functions fall under self-regulation, or the achievement of 'the greatest *order*' and the resultant '*feeling of power*' over oneself. Inner order by means of effective self-regulation is, then, the key to Nietzsche's concept of sovereignty. But these lines bring to it an emphasis on the antagonism or struggle among one's forces. And just as the vehement antagonism of our feelings must be maximized for there to be a plurality of vibrant individuals (6[58] 9), so here the greatest sovereignty comes from maximizing the antagonism of forces and the feeling of power over oneself that comes from being

---

[4] '– Der freieste Mensch hat das größte M a c h t g e f ü h l über sich, das größte W i s s e n über sich, die größte O r d n u n g im nothwendigen K a m p f e seiner Kräfte, die verhältnißmäßig größte U n a b h ä n g i g k e i t seiner einzelnen Kräfte, den verhältnißmäßig größten K a m p f in sich: er ist das z w i e t r ä c h t i g s t e Wesen und das w e c h s e l r e i c h s t e und das l a n g l e b e n d s t e und das überreich begehrende, sich nährende, das am meisten von sich a u s s c h e i d e n d e und sich e r n e u e r n d e.' See also 27[59] 11.289, p. 146f.

able to order them. We can therefore say, sovereignty requires that we sustain the tension between maximal antagonism and maximal order among the plurality of forces or drives that constitute each of us.

In Nietzsche's socio-physiological narrative, it is only deviant, solitary individuals who have achieved sovereignty in this sense – when they did not perish from the antagonism of their powers.[5] Their trajectory is quite distinct from the path of bondage,[6] which becomes the history of the 'herd-animal'. But Nietzsche also insists that it is only 'in league with' society – and in 'opposition' with it – that individual sovereignty can be brought to life:

> [...] in order to live individually, society must first be highly advanced and continue to be advanced further and further – the opposition: in league with it [society] individuality first receives some strength.

> [...] um individuell leben zu können, muß erst die Gesellschaft hoch gefördert sein und fort und fort gefördert werden – der Gegensatz: im Bunde mit ihr bekommt das Individuelle zuerst einige Kraft.
> (11[171] 9.506f.; cf. 11[229] 9.529f.)

The question is: What is the right measure of opposition or antagonism in our relations with others? What is the nature and degree of social antagonism that would allow a plurality of sovereign individuals to thrive by sustaining the tension between maximal antagonism and maximal order among their forces or drives? And how is it to be institutionalized, or at least propitiated? These are the questions with which agonistic theory must grapple if it is to take on Nietzsche's reflections on the kind of freedom that attends to the life-needs, our own and others', as a plurality of political animals.

Respect

One approach to these questions, taken by several agonistic theorists, turns on the notions of agonistic respect and 'the worthy opponent'.[7] At issue is the boundary between non-violent agonism and violent antagonism, between antagonism within

---

[5] '– Solitary [*Einzeln lebend*] humans, if they do not go to ground, develop into societies, a number of domains of work is developed, and much struggle of the drives for nutrition space time as well.' (11[130] 9.488) ('– Einzeln lebende Menschen, wenn sie nicht zu Grunde gehen, entwickeln sich zu Gesellschaften, eine Menge von Arbeitsgebieten wird entwickelt, und viel Kampf der Triebe um Nahrung Raum Zeit ebenfalls.').

[6] '– The development of the herd-animals and social plants is an entirely other one to that of the solitary [or singular: *einzeln lebend*] beings' (11[130] 9.488) ('– Die Entwicklung der Heerden-Thiere und gesellschaftlichen Pflanzen ist eine ganz andere als die der einzeln lebenden').

[7] Connolly (1991 xix f., xxv–xxx, 33–55, 81, 165 f., 185); Connolly (2005 16, 25, 47, 123–47); Connolly (2007 142 f.); Hatab (1995 60, 68–70, 97–9, 107, 142, 189, 191, 220).

the bounds of democratic principles and political violence (Nietzsche's *Wettkampf* and the *Vernichtungskampf*). I am sceptical about respect as a source of measure and restraint, and have argued elsewhere for a medial concept of measure in the relations *between* agonal opponents.[8] In my closing remarks, I will take up the notion of agonal hatred and propose that Nietzsche's phenomenology of hatred, or rather hatred-love, can serve to transform our understanding of respect in ways that may be useful for agonistic theory.

The notion of agonal hatred examined in Chapter 5 brings a realism back into agonistic theory, where the antagonism is strangely absent or eclipsed by 'respect'. It opens the prospect of a nuanced phenomenology of agonism, where hatred is bound up with love and can includes an affirmative pride and joy in the other, just as friend and enemy are entwined in Nietzsche's thought. It is an *embodied* phenomenology that directs our attention to the bodily processes and dispositions involved in our relations to others, with important ethical implications: to accept what is hard to assimilate and not to confuse it with moralistic rejectionism. Nietzsche's philosophy of hatred, of ugliness, envy and pride, in short, his entire philosophy of enmity with its substrate in the conflictual ontology of will to power, can have a corrective and constructive influence on the notion of agonistic respect.

If there is something like respect in Nietzsche, we must first ask: respect for what? It cannot be respect for the other as a bearer of rights conferred by political authority or any external instance. For Nietzsche, rights should not be understood as given in any way; they are a privilege that must be claimed or won *against* the claims of others – by overcoming their resistance through hatred.[9] Nor can it be a matter of respect for the humanity of the other. For there is no humanity in the sense of a human essence or telos; our only essence as humans is to have no essence as the 'as-yet-unfixed [OR undetermined: *noch nicht festgestellte*] animal' (JGB 62). Nor can it be respect for human dignity (*Würde*). Nietzsche's starting point is always the Schopenhauerian position that human life of itself is without meaning and therefore bereft of value; if there is to be sense, value or worth in a human life, it must be created by us. And this gives us a starting point.

From Nietzsche's agonal perspective, the only thing that merits respect are superlative deeds, works, creations that open new possibilities of human existence, new opportunities for us to grow, new worlds for us to inhabit. Here, respect would mean the *attraction* exerted on us by a deed or work for the spaces it opens up for us to extend ourselves; the desire we feel to take this on and assimilate it into our being – however hard this may be. It is in short, the erotic moment Nietzsche

---

[8] Siemens (2021 esp. 59–63).
[9] 'The rights that I have conquered for myself I will not *give* to the other: rather, he ought to *rob* them for himself! like me – and [he] may take them and *wrest* them from me! To this extent there must be a law which emanates from me, as if it wanted to make all into my likeness [*zu meinem Ebenbild mache*]: so that the singular individual finds himself in contradiction with it and strengthens himself [...] Whoever *appropriates* a right will not *give* this right to the other – but will be an opponent to him *insofar as he appropriates it for himself*: the love of the father who clashes with his son. The great educator, like nature: he must pile up *obstacles*, so that they are *overcome*' (16[88] 10).

calls love and describes in a physiological register as 'the feeling for property or for what we wish to make our property' (11[134] 9.490f.). In Nietzsche's physiology, this erotic-acquisitive love is inseparable from hatred, the hatred – even cruelty – needed to overcome the other's resistance to being assimilated. At the same time, however, love and attraction entail an affirmation of the other, what Zarathustra calls a *pride* in one's enemy that affirms and empowers, shares and rejoices in its successes. This brings home the profound difficulty of exercising respect in this sense, for the achievements and successes of my enemy, as *my* enemy, are also successes over me, and empowering it includes power-over-me. The difficulty here is that of combining the desire to take on and possess the other's achievements (against the other's resistance) with a non-coercive openness, a willingness to be possessed and overpowered by the other; an 'oppositional' practice akin to the epistemic ideal in which Nietzsche's physiology culminates – to possess and be possessed by others as things to be known (p. 185ff.). Indeed the first question for Nietzsche is always *epistemic*. And the first challenge for agonistic respect is 'learning to see' the other in its particularity, but also to possess and be possessed by 'as great a range of *true things* as possible', their 'affinities and enmities', '*multiplicities* and their law'. How much easier to mistake what is hard to take on with what is worthless, to degrade and reject it. For Nietzsche, this is to confuse the physiology of assimilation, bound up with hatred, with the physiology of excretion, which finds expression as revulsion and moral rejectionism. Hence the importance of attending intelligently to physiological processes in ourselves and others, and to the complexities of their expression in our treatment of others.

For both Nietzsche and Kant, hatred implies equality, and for Nietzsche, equality or approximate equality is a presupposition for agonal relations. But from an agonal perspective, respect cannot just mean to assimilate, make one's own or share in the achievements of an approximately equal other. Certainly, Nietzsche's concept of 'aspirational equality' is about rising to, and matching the standard and achievements of others. But agonal agency is about *rising above* and *overcoming* the other's deeds or works, about doing even better and outshining them. So the question becomes: What is involved in overcoming the other, and what does this imply for the notion of agonal respect? The most nuanced account I know in Nietzsche's oeuvre concerns Plato's relation to Homer and the poets in *Homer's Wettkampf*. It is perhaps unsurprising that Nietzsche, born lover of words and trained philologist, should bring the greatest precision and intelligibility to the question of overcoming in thinking, not about organisms or power-relations, but about the relation between texts. The strength of Plato's jealous attacks on Homer, he argues, must be understood as a double-movement that affirms and incorporates the standard or rule of the other and at the same time limits by containing it within an attempt to set an entirely new standard or rule. To overcome the other is to incorporate its achievement within a radically new form (deed or work) that overcomes, transgresses, outshines it; to do better than other by the other's standards, but to do so in a way that overcomes and supersedes that standard through a radically new form. Thus, Plato (1) acknowledges and affirms

Homer's achievements by incorporating tracts of poetry or mythology into his works, but they are myths that aspire to be better than Homer's *by Homer's own standards*. Plato wants to take Homer's place, so that he can say: 'Look, I can also do what my great rivals can; what is more, I can do it better than them'.[10] Yet (2) Plato incorporates his Homer's achievements in a way that also overcomes and supersedes his standard, by establishing a radically *new standard of greatness* and a radically new form of education: dialectics, over poetry (and rhetoric). So he continues: 'No Protagoras ever created as beautiful myths as I, no dramatist ever composed a living and gripping whole like the Symposium, nor any rhetorician speeches like mine in the Gorgias – and now I reject it all together and condemn all mimetic art! Only the contest made me into a poet, a sophist, and rhetorician!'

Drawing on Nietzsche's account of Plato's agon with Homer, we can make out two key moments of Nietzschean agonistic respect: (1) erotic love, attraction, affirmation, acknowledgement of the other's deeds that would incorporate or take them on in a way that outshines them by their standards and takes their place, (2) overcoming the other's deeds by taking them on in a way that creates a radically new form (deed, work) and a radically new standard of evaluation. We might also add a third moment, missing from Nietzsche's Plato, but not from Nietzsche's own relation to Plato: (3) gratitude; a kind of retrospective agapic love that gives something back to one's antagonist, a gratitude towards what one has overcome in order to become what one now is.[11] Nietzschean

---

[10] 'That which is of particular artistic significance in Plato's dialogues, for instance, is mostly the result of a contest with the art of the speakers, the sophists, the dramatists of his time, devised with the purpose of being able to say: "Look, I can also do what my great rivals can; what is more, I can do it better than them. No Protagoras ever created as beautiful myths as I, no dramatist ever composed a living and gripping whole like the Symposium, nor any rhetorician speeches like mine in the Gorgias – and now I reject it all together and condemn all mimetic art! Only the contest made me into a poet, a sophist, and rhetorician!" What a problem opens itself to us when we question the relation of the agon to the conception of the work of art!' (HW 1.790f.). ('Das, was z. B. bei Plato von besonderer künstlerischer Bedeutung an seinen Dialogen ist, ist meistens das Resultat eines Wetteifers mit der Kunst der Redner, der Sophisten, der Dramatiker seiner Zeit, zu dem Zweck erfunden, daß er zuletzt sagen konnte: "Seht, ich kann das auch, was meine großen Nebenbuhler können; ja, ich kann es besser als sie. Kein Protagoras hat so schöne Mythen gedichtet wie ich, kein Dramatiker ein so belebtes und fesselndes Ganze, wie das Symposium, kein Redner solche Rede verfaßt, wie ich sie im Gorgias hinstelle – und nun verwerfe ich das alles zusammen und verurtheile alle nachbildende Kunst! Nur der Wettkampf machte mich zum Dichter, zum Sophisten, zum Redner!" Welches Problem erschließt sich uns da, wenn wir nach dem Verhältniß des Wettkampfes zur Conception des Kunstwerkes fragen! – .')

[11] For the moment of gratitude:
  'To win *for myself* the *immorality* of the artist with regard towards my material (humankind): this has been my work in recent years.
  To win for *myself* the *spiritual freedom* and *joy* of being able to create and not to be tyrannized by alien ideals. (At bottom it matters little *what* I had to liberate myself from: my favourite form of *liberation* was the artistic form: that is, I cast an *image* of that which had hitherto bound me: thus Schopenhauer, Wagner, the Greeks (genius, the saint, metaphysics, all ideals until now, the highest morality) – but also a *tribute of gratitude*' (16[10] 10.501).

respect, as I am proposing it, is a transformative impulse organized around a *prospective* assimilation of the other's achievements and standing, aimed at bettering them; an *actual* transvaluation of the other's standard of evaluation; and a *retrospective* tribute of gratitude to the other as a stimulant for one's own deed or achievement. The challenge for agonistic theory is to translate these three moments of Nietzschean respect from the register of philology and physiology into the register of political relations.

Bibliography

For Nietzsche's and Kant's writings, editions used, abbreviations, reference forms and manner of citation, see pp. xiii–xv. For translations used, see p. xvi.

Reference Works

A Greek-English Lexicon (1996[10]), H.G. Liddell, R. Scott et al.
Deutsches Wörterbuch (1992[9]), Paul, H., Tübingen: Niemeyer.
Etymologisches Wörterbuch der deutschen Sprache (1999[23]), F. Kluge, Berlin/New York: De Gruyter.
Historisches Wörterbuch der Philosophie (=HWPh) (1971 ff.), J. Ritter and K. Gründer (eds), Basel/Stuttgart: Schwabe & Co Verlag. Also available as CD ROM.
Nietzsche-Wörterbuch (2004 ff.), P. van Tongeren, G. Schank, H. Siemens and M. Brussotti (eds), Nietzsche Online. Berlin/Boston: De Gruyter, n.d. (http://www.degruyter.com/view/NO).

Literature

Abbt, T. (1761), *Vom Tode für das Vaterland*, Berlin: Nicolai.
Abel, G. (1998), *Nietzsche. Die Dynamik der Willen zur Macht und die ewige Wiederkehr*, 2nd ed., Berlin/ New York: De Gruyter.
Abel, G. (2001), 'Bewußtsein – Sprache – Natur. Nietzsches Philosophie des Geistes', *Nietzsche- Studien* 30: 1-43.
Acampora, C.D. (2013), *Contesting Nietzsche*, Chicago: University of Chicago Press.
Airaksinen, T., and Siitonen, A. (2004), 'Kant on Hobbes, Peace, and Obedience', *History of European Ideas* 30: 315-28.
Angehrn, E. (1971ff.) 'Widerspruch' in HWPh 50522 (= HWPh vol. 12, p. 688 ff.).
Arendt, H. (1990), 'Philosophy and Politics', *Social Research* 57 (1) (Spring 1990): 73-103.
Augustine (412-426), de civitate dei (https://en.wikipedia.org/wiki/Wikisource).
Aydin, C. (2003), *Zijn en Worden: Nietzsches omduiding van het substantiebegrip*, Maastricht: Shaker.
Aydin, C. (2004), 'Nietzsche over de werkelijkheid als een georganiseerde strijd van willen tot macht', *Tijdschrift voor Filosofie* 67: 207-43.
Aydin, C. (2007), 'Nietzsche on Reality as Will to Power: Toward an "Organization–Struggle" Model', *Journal of Nietzsche Studies*, 33 (1): 25-48.
Baumgarten, A.G. (2009), *Aesthetica/Ästhetik*, etik (= Aesth), 2 vols. etc, Latin-German, D. Mirbach (ed and transl), Hamburg: Felix Meiner Verlag.
Baumgarten, A.G. (2010), *Metaphysica/Metaphysik* (= Met,) Historisch-kritische Ausgabe, G. Gawlick and L. Kreimendahl (eds and transl), Stuttgart-Bad Cannstatt: frommann-holzboog Verlag.

Beierwaltes, W. and Menne, A. (1971ff.), 'Gegensatz', in HWPh 7623 (= HWPh vol. 3, p. 120 ff.).
Brandt, R. (1999), *Kritischer Kommentar zu Kants Anthropologie in pragmatischer Hinsicht (1798)*, Hamburg: Meiner.
Brobjer, T., Berti, M.C., and Viola, S. (1997), 'Beiträge zur Quellenforschung', *Nietzsche-Studien*, 26 (1): 574–82.
Brock, E. (2015), *Nietzsche und der Nihilismus*, Berlin/New York: De Gruyter.
Brusotti, M. (1992), 'Die "Selbstverkleinerung des Menschen" in der Moderne. Studie zu Nietzsches "Zur Genealogie der Moral"', *Nietzsche-Studien*, 21: 81–136.
Brusotti, M. (2012), 'Reagieren, Schwer Reagieren, Nicht Reagieren. Zu Philosophie und Physiologie beim letzten Nietzsche', *Nietzsche-Studien* 41: 104–26.
Busch, T. (1989), *Die Affirmation des Chaos*, St. Ottilien: EOS Verlag.
Campioni, G., D'Iorio, P., Fornari, M.C., Fronterotta, F., and Orsucci, A. (2003), *Nietzsches persönliche Bibliothek*, Berlin/ New York: De Gruyter.
Caygill, H. (2013), *On Resistance. A Philosophy of Defiance*, London: Bloomsbury.
Conant, J. (2001), 'Nietzsche's Perfectionism', in *Nietzsche's Postmoralism*, 181–257, R. Schacht (ed), Cambridge: Cambridge University Press.
Connolly, W.E. (1991), *Identity\Difference: Democratic Negotiations of Political Paradox*, expanded ed., Minneapolis MI: University of Minnesota Press.
Connolly, W.E. (2005), *Pluralism*, Durham and London: Duke University Press.
Connolly, W.E. (2007), *Democracy, Pluralism, and Political Theory*, S. Chambers, T. Carver (eds), London, New York: Routledge.
Crawford, C. (1988), *The Beginnings of Nietzsche's Theory of Language*, Berlin/New York: De Gruyter.
de Saint-pierre, Abbé (1713), *Projet pour rendre la paix perpétuelle en Europe*.
Descartes, R. (1996), *Meditations on First Philosophy*, J. Cottingham (ed), Cambridge: Cambridge University Press.
Dodson, K. (1993), 'Kant's Perpetual Peace: Universal Civil Society or League of States?', *Southwest Philosophical Studies* 15: 1–9.
Dohmen, J. (2000), 'Nietzsche over het leven als kunstwerk', in *Links Nietzscheanisme*, 165–89, M. Van den Bossche and M. Weyembergh (eds), Budel: Damon.
Dohmen, J. (2008), *Het leven als kunstwerk*, Zutphen: Leminiscaat.
Drolet, J.-F. (2013), 'Nietzsche, Kant, the Democratic State, and War', Review of International Studies 39: 25–47.
Drolet, J.-F. (2021), *Beyond Tragedy and Eternal Peace: Politics and International Relations in the Thought of Friedrich Nietzsche*, Montreal: McGill-Queen's University Press.
Dumont, L. (1876), *Vergnügen und Schmerz. Zur Lehre von Gefühlen*, Leipzig: F. A. Brockhaus.
Fischer, K. (1854), *Geschichte der neuern Philosophie I. Das classische Zeitalter der dogmatischen Philosophie*, Mannheim: Friedrich Bassermann (*Geschichte der neuern Philosophie I, 2. Descartes' Schule – Geulinx, Malebranche, Baruch Spinoza* (1865), zweite völligumgearbeitete Aufl., Heidelberg; *Geschichte der neuern Philosophie I, 2, Fortbildung der Lehre Descartes'. Spinoza* (1880), dritte neu bearbeitete Aufl., München.)
Foucault, M. (2003), *Society Must Be Defended*, Lectures at the Collège de France 1975–76, D. Macey (transl), London: Penguin.
Foucault, M. (2011), *The Government of Self and Others: Lectures at the Collège des France 1982–1983*, Houndmills: Palgrave MacMillan.

Frautschi, S.C. (2007), *The Mechanical Universe: Mechanics and Heat*, Advanced ed., Cambridge: Cambridge University Press.
Friedman, M. (2013), *Kant's Construction of Nature: A Reading of the Metaphysical Foundations of Natural Science*, Cambridge: Cambridge University Press.
Fritsch, M. (2008), 'Antagonism and Democratic Citizenship (Schmitt, Mouffe, Derrida)', *Research in Phenomenology*, 38 (2): 174–97.
Gardner, S. (1999), *Routledge Philosophy GuideBook to Kant and the Critique of Pure Reason*, London: Routledge.
Gerhardt, V. (1983), 'Das "Princip des Gleichgewichts". Zum Verhältnis von Recht und Macht bei Nietzsche', *Nietzsche-Studien*, 12 (1): 111–33.
Gerhardt, V. (1988), 'Die kopernikanische Wende bei Kant und Nietzsche', in *Kant und Nietzsche – Vorspiel einer künftigen Weltauslegung ?*, 157–82, V. Gerhardt (ed), Wiesbaden: Freie Akademie von Jörg Albertz.
Gerhardt, V. (1995), *Immanuel Kants Entwurf 'Zum ewigen Frieden': eine Theorie der Politik*, Darmstadt: Wissenschaftliche Buchgesellschaft.
Gerhardt, V. (1996), *Vom Willen zur Macht: Anthropologie und Metaphysik der Macht am exemplarischen Fall Friedrich Nietzsche*, Berlin/New York: De Gruyter.
Gerhardt, V. (2005), 'Leben bei Kant und Nietzsche', in *Kant und Nietzsche im Widerstreit*, 295–311, B. Himmelmann (ed), Berlin/ New York: De Gruyter.
Habermas, J. (1997), 'Kant's Idea of Perpetual Peace with the Benefit of Two Hundred Years' Hindsight', in *Perpetual Peace: Essays on Kant's Cosmopolitan Ideal*, 113–53, J. Bohman and M. Lutz-Bachmann (eds), Cambridge, MA: MIT Press.
Hatab, L. (1995), *A Nietzschean Defence of Democracy: An Experiment in Postmodern Politics*, Chicago, IL: Open Court.
Heidegger, M. (1985), 'Who is Nietzsche's Zarathustra?', in *The New Nietzsche: Contemporary Styles of Interpretation*, 64–79, D. Allison (ed), Cambridge, MA: MIT Press.
Heller, P. (1972), *Von den ersten und letzten Dingen. Studien und Kommentar zu einer Aphorismenreihe von Friedrich Nietzsche*, Berlin/New York: De Gruyter.
Hershbell, J., and Nimis, S. (1979), 'Nietzsche and Heraclitus', *Nietzsche Studien*, 8 (1): 17–38.
Hobbes, T. (1991), *Leviathan*, R. Tuck (ed), Cambridge: Cambridge University Press.
Hobbes, T. (2020) *The Elements of Law, Natural and Politic*, F. Tönnies (ed), London: Routledge.
Höffe, O. (1995), 'Völkerbund oder Weltrepublik?', in *Immanuel Kant: Zum ewigen Frieden*, 109–32, O. Höffe (ed), Berlin: Akademie Verlag.
Höffe, O. (1998), 'Some Kantian Reflections on a World Republic', *Kantian Review* 2: 51–71.
Hölscher, U. (1977), 'Nietzsche's Debt to Heraclitus', in *Classical Influences on European Culture Vol III: 1650–1870*, 339–48, R. Bolgar (ed), Cambridge: Cambridge University Press.
Honig, B. (1993), *Political Theory and the Displacement of Politics*, Ithaca: Cornell University Press.
Ioan, R. (2019), *The Body in Spinoza and Nietzsche*, London: Palgrave Macmillan.
Kleingeld, P. (2004), 'Approaching Perpetual Peace: Kant's Defence of a League of States and His Ideal of a World Federation', *European Journal of Philosophy*, 12 (3): 304–25.
Kleingeld, P. (2006), 'Kant's Theory of Peace', in *The Cambridge Companion to Kant and Modern Philosophy*, 477–504, P. Guyer (ed), Cambridge: Cambridge University Press.

Kleingeld, P., Waldron, J., Doyle, M.w., and Wood, A. (eds) (2006), *Toward Perpetual Peace and Other Writings on Politics, Peace, and History*, New Haven: Yale University Press.
Knebel, S.K. (1971ff.), 'Repugnanz', in HWPh 32802 9 (= HWPh vol. 8, p. 879 ff.).
Kolnai, A. (1935), 'Versuch über den Hass', *Philosophisches Jahrbuch der Görres-Gesellschaft*, 48 (2/3): 147–87.
Kuijlen, W. van der, (2009), *An Unused but Highly Needful Concept: The Notion of Realrepugnanz in Kant's Early Philosophy and Kritik der reinen Vernunft*, Enschede: Ipskamp.
Kuijlen, W. van der, (2017), 'Inevitable Antagonism' [Het onvermijdelijke Antagonisme], *Tijdschrift voor Filosofie* 79: 775–800.
Lange, F.A. (1866), *Geschichte des Materialismus und Kritik seiner Bedeutung in der Gegenwart*, Iserlohn: Baedeker.
Lange, F.A. (1873–75), *Geschichte des Materialismus und Kritik seiner Bedeutung in der Gegenwart*, 2nd expanded ed., 2 vols, Iserlohn: Baedeker.
Leibniz, G.W. (2004), 'Codex Juris Gentium Diplomaticus' (Hannover: 1693) in *Sämtliche Schriften und Briefe, Vierte Reihe, Politische Schriften*, vol. 5, Berlin: Berlin-Brandenburgischen Akademie der Wissenschaften und der Akademie der Wissenschaften in Göttingen, Akademie Verlag.
Louden, R. (2008), 'Anthropology from a Kantian Point of View: Toward a Cosmopolitan Conception of Human Nature', *Studies in the History of the Philosophy of Science* 39: 515–22.
Lupo, L. (2006), *Le colombe dello scettico. Rifl essioni di Nietzsche sulla coscienza negli anni 1880–1888*, Pisa: ETS.
MacPherson, C.B. (1962), *The Political Theory of Possessive Individualism: Hobbes to Locke*, New York: Oxford University Press.
Mainländer, P. (1879[4]), *Die Philosophie der Erlösung*, Berlin: Grieben.
Marchart, O. (2018), *Thinking Antagonism: Political Ontology after Laclau*, Edinburgh: Edinburgh University Press.
Mattioli, W. (2017), 'The Thought of Becoming and the Place of Philosophy: Some Aspects of Nietzsche's Reception and Criticism of Transcendental Idealism via Afrikan Spir', in *Nietzsche's Engagements with Kant and the Kantian Legacy*, M. Brussotti, H. Siemens, J. Constâncio, and T. Bailey (eds), vol. I, *Nietzsche, Kant and the Problem of Metaphysics*, 71–102, M. Brusotti and H. Siemens (eds), London and New York: Bloomsbury.
Mayer, J.R. (1845), *Die organische Bewegung in ihrem Zusammenhange mit dem Stoffwechsel. Ein Beitrag zur Naturkunde*, Heilbronn: Drechsler.
Mayer, R. (1867), *Mechanik der Wärme*, Stuttgart: Cotta.
Meyer, K. (1998), *Ästhetik der Historie*, Würzburg: Königshausen & Neumann.
Mittasch, A. (1952), *Friedrich Nietzsche als Naturphilosoph*, Stuttgart: Kröner Verlag.
Müller, E. (2019), 'Competitive Ethos and Cultural Dynamic: The Principle of Agonism in Jacob Burckhardt and Friedrich Nietzsche', in *Conflict and Contest in Nietzsche's Philosophy*, 89–104, H. Siemens and J. Pearson (eds), New York and London: Bloomsbury.
Müller-Lauter, W. (1971), *Nietzsche: Seine Philosophie der Gegensätze und die Gegensätze seiner Philosophie*, Berlin/New York: De Gruyter.
Müller-Lauter, W. (1978), 'Der Organismus als innerer Kampf. Der Einfluß von Wilhelm Roux auf Friedrich Nietzsche', *Nietzsche-Studien*, 7: 189–235.
Müller-Lauter, W. (1999a), 'Über Stolz und Eitelkeit bei Kant, Schopenhauer und Nietzsche', in *Nietzsche-Interpretationen I Über Werden und Wille zur Macht*, 141–72, Berlin/New York: De Gruyter.

Müller-Lauter, W. (1999b), 'Der Organismus als innerer Kampf. Der Einfluß von Wilhelm Roux auf Friedrich Nietzsche', in *Nietzsche-InterpretationenI Über Werden und Wille zur Macht*, 97–140, Berlin/New York: De Gruyter.
Müller-Lauter, W. (1999c), 'Über "Das Ganze" und über "Ganzheiten" in Nietzsches Philosophie: Exkurse', in *Nietzsche-Interpretationen II Über Freiheit und Chaos*, 114–30, Berlin/New York: De Gruyter.
Müller-Lauter, W. (1999d), *Nietzsche-InterpretationenI ber Werden und Wille zur Macht*, Berlin/New York: De Gruyter.
Muthu, S. (2014), 'Productive Resistance in Kant's Political Thought: Domination, Counter-Domination, and Global Unsocial Sociability', in *Kant and Colonialism*, 68–98, K. Flikschuh and L. Ypi (eds), Oxford: Oxford University Press.
Patton, P. (2001), 'Nietzsche and Hobbes', *International Studies in Philosophy* 33 (3): 99–116.
Patton, P. (2008), 'Nietzsche on Rights, Power and the Feeling of Power', in Nietzsche, Power and Politics. *Rethinking Nietzsche's Legacy for Political Thought*, 471–88, H.W. Siemens and V. Roodt (eds), Berlin/New York: De Gruyter.
Pearson, J.S. (2018), 'Nietzsche's Philosophy of Conflict and the Logic of Organisational Struggle', PhD thesis, Leiden University.
Pearson J.S. (2022), *Nietzsche on Conflict, Struggle and War*, Cambridge: Cambridge University Press.
Piepmeier, R. (1972), 'Empfindung I', HWPh 2: 456–64.
Platner, E. (1772), *Anthropologie für Ärzte und Weltweise*, Leipzig: Dyck.
Plato, *Gorgias* (https://standardebooks.org/ebooks/plato).
Plato, *Phaedo* (https://standardebooks.org/ebooks/plato).
Plato, *Symposium* (https://standardebooks.org/ebooks/plato).
Pogge, T.W. (1988), 'Kant's Theory of Justice', *Kant-Studien* 79: 407–33.
Rethy, R. (1988), 'The Tragic Affirmation of the Birth of Tragedy', *Nietzsche-Studien* 17: 1–44.
Rethy, R. (1991), 'Schein in Nietzsche's Philosophy', in *Nietzsche and Modern German Thought*, 59–87, K. Ansell Pearson (ed), London/ New York: Routledge.
Rousseau, J.-J. (1987), 'Discourse on the Origin of Inequality', in *Basic Political Writings*, 83–100, Indianapolis: Hackett.
Roux, W. (1881), *Der Kampf der Th eile im Organismus. Ein Beitrag zur Vervollständigung der mechanischen Zweckmäßigkeitslehre*, Leipzig: W. Engelmann.
Rummens, S. (2009), 'Democracy as Non-Hegemonic Struggle: Disambiguating Chantal Mouffe's Agonistic Model of Politics', *Constellations* 16 (3), 377–91.
Russell, B. (2004), *History of Western Philosophy*, London: Routledge.
Saar, M. (2008), 'Forces and Powers in Nietzsche's "Genealogy of Morals" in Nietzsche, Power and Politics', in *Rethinking Nietzsche's Legacy for Political Thought*, 453–70, H.W. Siemens and V. Roodt (eds), Berlin/New York: De Gruyter.
Saner, H. (1967), *Kants Weg vom Krieg zum Frieden*, München: Piper Verlag.
Scandella, M. (2012), 'Did Nietzsche Read Spinoza?', *Nietzsche-Studien* 41 (1): 308–32.
Scandella, M. (2014), 'Zur Entstehung einiger Verweise auf Spinoza in Nietzsches Schriften anhand der Quellen und des Heftes M II 1', *Nietzsche-Studien* 43: 173–83.
Schank, G. (1993), *'Dionysos gegen den Gekreuzigten': Eine philologische und philosophische Studie zu Nietzsches Ecce homo*, Bern: Peter Lang.
Schlechta, K. and Anders, A. (1962), *Friedrich Nietzsche. Von den verborgenen Anfängen seines Philosophierens*, Stuttgart-Bad Cannstatt: Frommann.
Schlimgen, E. (1999), *Nietzsches Theorie des Bewußtseins*, Berlin/New York: De Gruyter.

Schmid, W. (2010), 'Uns Selbst Gestalten – Zur Philosophie der Lebenskunst bei Nietzsche', *Nietzsche-Studien* 21: 50–62.

Schneewind, J.B. (2015), 'Good out of Evil: Kant and the Idea of Unsocial Sociability', in *Kant's Idea for a Universal History with a Cosmopolitan Aim: A Critical Guide*, 94–111, A. Oksenberg Rorty and J. Schmidt (eds), Cambridge: Cambridge University Press.

Schnepf, R. (2001), 'Metaphysik oder Metaphysikkritik? Das Kausalitätsproblem in Kants Abhandlung Über die negative Größen', *Archiv für die Philosophie* 83: 130–59.

Schönfeld, M. (2000), *The Philosophy of the Young Kant. The Precritical Project*, Oxford: Oxford University Press.

Siemens, H.W. (1998), 'Nietzsche's Hammer: Philosophy, Destruction, or the Art of Limited Warfare', *Tijdschrift voor Filosofie*, 60 (2): 321–47.

Siemens, H.W. (2001), 'Nietzsche's Agon with Ressentiment: Towards a Therapeutic Reading of Critical Transvaluation', *Continental Philosophy Review* 34: 69–93.

Siemens, H.W. (2002), 'Agonal Communities of Taste: Law and Community in Nietzsche's Philosophy of Transvaluation', *Journal of Nietzsche Studies* 24: 83–112.

Siemens, H.W. (2009a), 'Nietzsche's Critique of Democracy (1870–1886)', *Journal of Nietzsche Studies* 38: 20–37.

Siemens, H.W. (2009b), 'Nietzsche contra Liberalism on Freedom', in *A Companion to Nietzsche*, 437–54, K. Ansell-Pearson (ed), Chichester, West Sussex: Wiley-Blackwell.

Siemens, H.W. (2011), 'Das Nietzsche-Woerterbuch Projekt: Darstellung des Konzepts und einiger Resultate am Beispiel des Wortes, in: "Groesse"', *Nietzsche - Macht – Größe Nietzsche – Philosoph der Größe der Macht oder der Macht der Größe*, Ed. by Caysa, Volker / Schwarzwald, Konstanze, De Gruyter.

Siemens, H.W. (2012a), 'The Rise of Political Agonism and Its Relation to Deconstruction', in *Beyond Deconstruction: Rethinking Myth, Reconstructing Reason*, 213–33, A. Martinengo (ed), Berlin/New York: De Gruyter.

Siemens, H.W., (2012b), 'Nietzsche's "post-Nietzschean" Political "Wirkung": The Rise of Agonistic Democratic Theory', in *'Einige werden posthum geboren': Friedrich Nietzsches Wirkungen*, 393–406, R. Reschke and M. Brusotti (ed), Berlin/New York: De Gruyter.

Siemens, H.W. (2013), 'Reassessing Radical Democratic Theory in Light of Nietzsche's Ontology of Conflict', in *Nietzsche and Political Thought*, 83–106, K. Ansell-Pearson (ed), London and New York: Bloomsbury.

Siemens, H.W. (2014), 'Nietzsche's Concept of 'Necessity' and Its Relation to Laws of Nature', in *Nietzsche and The Becoming of Life*, 82–102, V. Lemm (ed.), Fordham University Press.

Siemens, H.W. (2015), 'Nietzsche's Socio-Physiology of the Self', in *Nietzsche and the Problem of Subjectivity*, 629–53, J., Constâncio, M. Branco, and B. Ryan (eds), Berlin/New York: De Gruyter.

Siemens, H.W. (2016), 'Nietzsches Sozio-Physiologie des Selbst und das Problem der Souveränität', in *Nietzsche: Denker der Kritik und der Transformation*, 167–82, H. Heit and S. Thorgeirsdottir (eds), Berlin/New York: De Gruyter.

Siemens, H.W. (2017), 'Kant's "Respect for the Law" as "Feeling of Power": On (the Illusion of) Sovereignty', in *Nietzsche's Engagements with Kant and the Kantian Legacy*, M. Brussotti, H. Siemens, J. Constâncio, and T. Bailey (eds), vol. II, *Nietzsche and Kantian Ethics*, 109–36, J. Constâncio and T. Bailey (eds), London and New York: Bloomsbury.

Siemens, H.W. (2019a), 'On Productive Resistance', in *Conflict and Contest in Nietzsche's Philosophy*, 23–43, H. Siemens and J. Pearson (eds), New York & London: Bloomsbury.

Siemens, H.W. (2021), *Agonal Perspectives on Nietzsche's Philosophy of Critical Transvaluation*, Berlin/New York: De Gruyter (published with open access at www.degruyter.com).

Siemens, H.W., and Pearson, J.S. (eds), (2019b), *Conflict and Contest in Nietzsche's Philosophy*, New York and London: Bloomsbury.

Siemens, H.W., and van Tongeren, P. (2012), 'Das Nietzsche- Wörterbuch: Anatomy of a"großes Projekt"', in *Nietzsche – Macht – Größe*, 451–66, V. Caysa and K. Schwarzwald (eds), Berlin/New York: De Gruyter.

Siemens, H.W., van Tongeren, P., and Schank, G. (2000/2001), 'A Nietzsche Dictionary', *New Nietzsche Studies* 4 (3/4): 177–82.

Small, R. (1994), 'Nietzsche, Spir, and Time', *Journal of the History of Philosophy*, 32 (1): 85–102.

Small, R. (2010), *Time and Becoming in Nietzsche's Thought*, London/New York: Continuum.

Spinoza, B. (2000), *Ethics*, G.H.R. Parkinson (ed and transl), Oxford: Oxford University Press.

Spir, A. (1873/1877), *Denken und Wirklichkeit. Versuch einer Erneuerung der kritischen Philosophie*, 2 Bände, Leipzig: J. G. Findel.

Stack, G.J. (1983), *Lange and Nietzsche*, Berlin/ New York: De Gruyter.

Stegmaier, W. (2004), '"Philosophischer Idealismus" und die "Musik des Lebens". Zu Nietzsches Umgang mit Paradoxien. Eine kontextuelle Interpretation des Aphorismus Nr. 372 der Fröhlichen Wissenschaft', *Nietzsche-Studien* 33: 90–128.

Stegmaier, W. (2008), 'Schicksal Nietzsche? Zu Nietzsches Selbsteinschätzung als Schicksal der Philosophie und der Menschheit (Ecce Homo, Warum ich ein Schicksal bin 1)', *Nietzsche-Studien* 37: 62–114.

Sturm, T. (2008), 'Why Did Kant Reject Physiological Explanations in His Anthropology?', *Studies in the History of the Philosophy of Science* 39: 495–505.

van Tongeren, P. (2000), *Reinterpreting Modern Culture. An Introduction to Friedrich Nietzsche's Philosophy*, West Lafayette: Purdue University Press.

van Tongeren, P. (2012), *Leven is een kunst. Over morele ervaring, deugdethiek en levenskunst*, Zoetermeer/Antwerpen: Klement/Pelckmans.

Visser, G.T.M. (1989), *Nietzsche en Heidegger. Een confrontatie*, Nijmegen: SUN.

von Raumer, K. (ed) (1953), *Ewiger Friede: Friedensrufe und Friedenspläne seit der Renaissance*, Freiburg: Karl Alber Verlag.

Wahrig-Schmidt, B. (1988), '"Irgendwie-jedenfalls physiologisch": Friedrich Nietzsche, Alexandre Herzen (fils) und Charles Féré 1888', *Nietzsche-Studien* 17: 434–64.

Weber, E.H. (1870), *Untersuchungen über den Erregungsprozess im Muskel- und Nervensystem*, Leipzig.

Wolff, M. (2017), *Der Begriff des Widerspruchs. Eine Studie zur Dialektik Kants und Hegels*, Berlin: Eule von Minerva Verlag.

Wood, A. (2015), 'Kant's Fourth Proposition: The Unsociable Sociability of Human Nature', in *Kant's Idea for a Universal History with a Cosmopolitan Aim: A Critical Guide*, 112–28, A. Oksenberg Rorty and J. Schmidt (eds), Cambridge: Cambridge University Press.

Zinkin, M. (2012), 'Kant on Negative Magnitudes', *Kant-Studien* 103: 397–414.

Name Index

Anaximander 20
Anaximenes 20
Aquinas, Thomas 22
Arendt, Hannah 112
Aristotle 20, 21, 50
Augustine 89

Baumgarten, Alexander 18, 22, 30–31, 35, 65
Bismarck 113
Boethius 20

Cicero 21
Crusius, Christian 19, 22, 35

Darwin, Charles 59, 90, 164, 202
Derrida, Jacques 243
Descartes, René 137, 252
Dühring, Eugen 224

Empedocles 20
Erasmus 81
Euripides 112

Féré, Charles 138
Fischer, Kuno 152
Foucault, Michel 4, 83, 167, 243

Gerhardt, Volker 10, 45, 79, 81, 82, 119
Gersdorff, Carl von 55
Goethe, Johann Wolfgang von 113

Heidegger, Martin 75, 224
Heraclitus 6, 20, 41, 90, 177
Herder, Johann Gottfried 19, 34
Hesiod 90
Hobbes, Thomas 7, 13, 82–83, 93, 98–100, 102–7, 109, 115, 117, 151, 156–60, 169–70
Homer 90–91, 198, 248–49

Jaspers, Karl 9

Kästner, Abraham 23

Lange, Friedrich Albert 55
Leibniz, Gottfried Wilhelm 18, 25–27, 32–36, 61, 85, 87, 113

Mainländer, Philipp 200
Marx, Karl 20
Mayer, Robert 75, 145, 151
Mirabeau, Comte de 233
Müller-Lauter, Wolfgang 39, 42, 52, 58, 78, 113, 151, 164, 175

Newton, Isaac 19, 22–23, 25, 26, 28, 33, 35–36, 54, 56, 57

Parmenides 20
Pascal, Blaise 22
Plato 89, 112, 118, 134, 172, 204, 215, 223, 248–49
Proctor 177
Protagoras 249
Pythagoras 20

Rochefoucauld, François de la 205, 206
Rolph, William 59, 63
Rousseau, Jean-Jacques 105, 159
Roux, Wilhelm 13, 59, 62, 75, 119, 151, 153, 164, 176–78, 200–1
Russell, Bertrand 198

Saint-pierre, Abbé de 81
Saner, Hans 3, 9, 22, 28, 35, 38, 94, 108, 163
Schiller, Friedrich 232
Schopenhauer, Arthur 8, 55, 59, 90, 128, 136, 148, 149, 207, 247, 249
Shakespeare, William 146

Socrates 89, 112–14, 172, 245
Spencer, Herbert 152, 163, 169, 171
Spinoza, Baruch 18, 72, 73, 152, 163, 169, 171, 176–79, 183, 226
Spir, Afrikan 42, 46, 55
Sulzer, Johann Georg 96

Verri, Pietro 136, 139, 159
Virgil 106

Wagner, Richard 249
Weber, Ernst Heinrich 200
Wolff, Christian 18, 21, 32, 34, 36

Subject Index

A

Absolutsetzen, Sich 12, 85, 92, 99, 102
Abstraction 30, 31, 39, 64, 65, 157, 170
Achtung 13, 126, 138–41, 144, 145, 214, 232
    See also respect
acknowledgement 102, 227, 249
acquisitiveness 63, 164, 181, 227, 245
action-and-resistance 201
action-reaction 45
active 12, 14, 36, 60, 78, 85, 96, 125, 128, 130, 131, 133, 135, 159, 163, 191, 193, 196, 205, 207, 208, 211, 233
active-reactive 191
adequatio 50
adjudication 102, 241
affects, affectivity 43, 63, 64, 70, 74–76, 153, 157, 165, 167, 168, 172, 179, 180, 186, 187, 189, 195, 197, 200, 220, 221, 232–34
Affekt(en) / Affect(en) 64, 76, 143, 167, 168, 179, 195, 197, 212, 220–22, 225, 226, 230, 232–34
affirmation 5, 7, 17, 62, 109, 110, 127, 188, 191, 195, 197, 204, 208, 211, 215, 216, 239, 248, 249
affirmation-empowerment 223
affirmative 2, 3, 8, 12–15, 22, 85, 91–93, 109, 113–15, 120, 127, 152, 196, 197, 205, 207, 208, 210, 214, 216, 225, 227, 231, 232, 237, 240, 244, 247
agape, agapic 197, 204, 221, 249
agency 12, 13, 67, 69, 70, 82–84, 93, 100, 101, 107, 126, 127, 137, 138, 142, 144, 146, 147, 150, 156, 179, 184, 193, 194, 212, 221, 248
aggression, *Aggressiv-Mittel* 109, 123
agon, agonal 1, 2, 8, 14, 15, 90, 91, 112, 119, 120, 188, 194–97, 201, 203, 205, 208–10, 213, 223, 225, 226, 230, 231, 236, 242, 247, 248, 249
    See also Wettkampf, Wettstreit
agonism, agonistic 1, 14, 15, 151, 152, 190, 191, 194, 195, 231, 237, 239–44, 246–50
agreement 94, 112, 114, 139, 158, 245
altruism, altruistic, *Altruismus, altruistisch* 76, 112, 167, 170–72, 176, 187–89, 192, 193, 202, 203
amor fati 206
Aneignung, Aneignungslust, Aneignungstriebe 61, 63, 201, 164, 181, 182, 201, 210, 227
    See also appropriation
anger 14, 15, 76, 196, 200, 221, 222, 231, 233–37
    See also Zorn
annihilation 24, 87, 89–91, 103, 107, 108, 110, 111, 115, 122, 188, 200, 241
    See also Vernichtung
antagonism, antagonist, antagonistic 3, 4, 7, 11, 13, 15, 22, 42, 45, 49, 51, 52, 55, 57, 58, 68, 72, 75–78, 82, 83, 90–91, 95, 101, 102, 109, 111, 113, 114, 117, 118, 120–23, 126, 131, 132, 135, 139, 140, 154, 155, 161, 162, 174, 195, 197, 199, 208, 210, 239, 240, 244–47, 249
Antagonismi, lex 27
Antagonismus, Antagonisme(n) 3, 109, 118, 122, 131, 132, 135
anthropomorphization 69, 71
anti-metaphysical 8, 61, 199, 241, 243
Anziehen, Anziehung 25, 27, 69, 70, 162
    See also attraction
appearance(s) 35, 43, 44, 69, 78, 138
appropriation, appropriate 14, 15, 61–63, 164, 181–83, 190, 195, 201, 204, 227, 234, 237, 239, 247
    See also Aneignung
arcadian 84, 86
arche 11, 43

Subject Index

aspirational equality *See* equality
assassination 87, 106
assimilation, *assimiliren* 14, 47, 59, 62, 63, 74, 78, 114, 164, 165, 170, 179, 181, 182, 201–4, 208, 209, 227, 245, 247–48, 250
attraction, attractive 10, 14, 20, 22, 25, 26, 35, 57–62, 69, 70, 75, 77, 162, 204, 209, 214, 247–49
  See also Anziehung
attraction-repulsion 2, 58, 69, 76, 83, 109, 240
Aufhebung, aufheben 10, 18, 23, 24, 29–33, 78, 79, 133, 134, 162, 221, 240
  See also cancellation
Ausgleich, Ausgleichung 47, 55, 105, 119, 241
ausrotten, Ausrottungskrieg 87, 90, 91, 97, 101, 107, 112, 170, 173
  See also exterminate
Ausscheidung, ausscheiden 61, 63, 64, 74, 183, 245
  See also excretion
Ausschlag See outcome
autonomous, autonomy 5, 6, 12–14, 54, 84, 93, 101–2, 120–22, 152, 158, 164, 166–72, 174, 175, 178, 180, 183, 189, 244

B
beautiful 46, 87, 92, 121, 205–7, 249
beauty, beauties 28, 121, 206, 218
becoming 11, 37, 41–43, 45, 47, 61, 65, 72, 76, 77, 79, 110, 127, 128, 134, 153, 206, 241
  See also Werden
befehlen 60, 67, 143–44, 146, 164, 181, 227
  See also commanding
Begehrungsvermögen 212, 220, 221
  See also desire
being 8, 11, 18, 20, 27, 35, 36, 38, 40, 42, 43, 45, 47, 51, 53, 61, 74, 76, 83, 85, 110, 113, 115, 127, 199, 241
beneficence 196, 210
benevolence 211
Beraubung 10, 24, 30, 79, 133, 240
  See also privation
Besitz, Besitzenwollen See possession

bewegen, Bewegung(en), 27, 30, 45, 54, 69, 71, 76, 77, 110, 142, 143, 146, 162, 170, 173, 179, 200
  See also motion
Bewegkraft 25, 30, 54, 162
Bewusstsein, Bewußtsein 31, 47, 63, 134, 141, 149, 174
  See also consciousness
Bilderrede, image-language 11, 76, 77, 142, 186
biologism 8, 75
blame, blameworthy 28, 173, 224, 235
body 6, 13, 23–25, 30, 32, 50, 52–56, 58, 63, 66–68, 70, 77, 89, 126, 137, 138, 150, 152, 156, 162, 163, 174, 177, 179, 203, 204, 207, 229
  See also Leib
bondage 163, 165, 166, 172, 217, 245, 246
böse, bösartig 41, 103, 104, 107, 112, 148, 196, 203, 206, 216, 217, 222, 225, 226, 228, 232
  See also evil
boundary 15, 107, 239, 246

C
calm 14, 99, 100, 102, 111, 152, 190, 191, 193, 194, 222, 230, 244
cancellation, cancel 10, 18, 21, 23, 24, 28, 29, 30–35, 45, 57, 61, 65, 78, 79, 108, 134, 162, 213, 221, 224
  See also Aufhebung, aufheben
care, caring 182, 183, 185, 243
causality, causation, causal, *Causalismus, Causalität/ Kausalität* 13, 26, 29, 32–36, 45, 54, 56, 64, 68–76, 78, 110, 126, 137, 140–42, 144, 146, 148
  nexus 34, 35, 241
  See also Ursache
cause-and-effect 66
ceasefire(s), *Waffenstillstände* 84, 86, 99, 103, 116–17
change 8, 10, 11, 18, 20, 25, 26, 28, 29, 32–37, 42, 43, 45–47, 54, 57, 58, 61, 68–78, 85, 93, 127, 199, 223, 239–41
  See also Wechsel
chaos 43, 62
Christian, Christianity, *Christen, christlich* 6, 14, 22, 40, 81, 84, 125, 184, 188, 195–97, 199, 204–6, 221, 223, 224, 226

Christian-Platonic 6, 7, 221
circularity 76
citizen, citizenship 70, 88, 94, 108, 116, 213, 215
civilization 84, 85, 154
coercion, coercive 74, 88, 98, 102, 105–8, 115–17, 167, 194, 225, 243
　See also Zwang
coitus 13, 126, 129, 132, 137
combat(ive), combatants 60, 87, 91, 94, 95
commanding 60, 62, 67, 68, 77–79, 142–44, 164, 173, 181, 190, 202, 227
　See also befehlen
commanding-obeying 2, 60, 83, 109
commerce 9, 11, 79, 82
communicate, communication 32, 67, 68, 79, 181
compassion 209, 210, 214, 226
competition, compete, competitive, *Concurrenz* 2, 8, 47, 83, 88, 90, 91, 117, 119, 123, 146, 154, 160, 173, 201, 203, 208, 211, 240
complementary, *complementäre* 41, 92, 102–3
complexity 33, 51–54, 67, 68, 92, 176, 181, 182, 185, 243, 244, 248
conatus 169
conceit 140, 179
concord 1, 82, 84, 109, 117, 118, 123, 125, 177, 179
concordia discors 3
conflictus 2
Conflictus zweier Kräfte 3, 18, 25–27, 57, 60, 62, 77, 162
conformism, conformity 166, 167, 172, 144
consciousness, conscious 13, 31, 32, 55, 56, 63, 67, 68, 71, 73, 74, 126, 134, 141, 144, 149, 174, 176, 178, 179, 185, 233
　See also Bewusstsein
consensus 1, 83, 94, 108
contempt 14, 140, 141, 181, 196, 204, 205, 208–10, 213, 214, 219, 224, 232, 235, 236
　See also Verachtung
contest 8, 9, 90, 91, 119, 125, 205, 249
　See also agon, Wettkampf
contestation 2, 239, 240–41

contradict, contradiction(s), contradictio, contradictorie 2–6, 10, 11, 17–23, 28, 34, 36–39, 41, 43, 45, 46, 49, 50, 52–55, 57, 65, 72, 74, 77–80, 113, 134, 137, 145, 162, 174, 185, 199, 227, 247
　See also logical opposition
contradictory 4, 5, 9–11, 17, 20, 21, 23, 27, 36, 42, 77, 79, 80, 191, 240, 244
contrary 20, 21
cosmopolitan, *weltbürgerlich* 88, 91, 106, 111, 115, 117, 123, 151, 154, 210, 241, 243
courage 123, 200
creative, creativity 2, 3, 8, 11, 12, 14, 42, 60, 61, 65, 91–93, 113–15, 125, 196, 197, 205, 210, 221–25, 231, 234, 236
cruelty, cruel 36–37, 109, 184, 185, 198, 199, 200, 201, 203, 204, 220, 223, 227, 243, 248
　See also grausam
culture, cultural, *Cultur/Kultur* 2, 3, 7, 8, 13, 55, 81, 82, 91, 107, 108, 110, 112, 151, 157, 158, 170, 203, 215, 242

D

Dauer, dauerhaft 48, 51, 122, 241
de-anthropomorphization 46, 76, 78, 199, 204
　See also re-anthropomorphization
death 6, 83, 87–90, 11, 122, 131–35, 148, 157, 177, 218, 245
décadence 6, 130, 152, 191–93, 199, 223
deconstruction 225
deed 61, 91, 119, 154, 172, 185, 209, 235, 247–50
　See also Thun
defectus 10, 18, 23, 24
　See also lack
degrade, degradation 15, 196, 201, 208–9, 214, 223–24, 228, 231, 235–36, 248
degree(s) 11, 29, 31, 37, 40, 45, 51, 52, 78, 83, 90, 92, 110, 114, 123, 128, 129, 131, 132, 183–85, 192, 195, 202, 203, 214–15, 241, 246
　See also grades
deliberation 152, 179

democracy, democratic 1, 2, 9–10, 15, 118–20, 122, 195, 239, 241–42
de-moralization 76, 78, 165, 199, 201, 204, 206
Demüthigung, demüthigen 139–41, 144–45, 235
  See also humiliation
depersonalization, *Entpersönlichung* 192, 224
de-personification 187, 189
desire(s) 8, 28, 30, 31, 51, 59, 74, 89, 119–20, 128, 134, 135, 139, 154, 157, 158, 160, 167, 171, 184, 188, 203, 204, 207, 209, 212, 215, 217, 218, 220–22, 224, 226, 234, 242, 247, 248
  See also Begehrungsvermögen
despise 112, 203, 204, 207, 213–14, 227, 235, 236
  See also verachten
despotism 88, 116, 117, 235
destroy, destructive, destruction 1–2, 8, 12, 14, 15, 33–34, 81–83, 85, 87–88, 90–92, 100–1, 103, 106–9, 113, 115, 117, 127, 128, 134, 150, 154, 163, 165, 177, 179–80, 182, 196–98, 200, 202, 205, 210–11, 220, 217, 218, 223–26, 231, 235–37, 239–40
difference 19, 21, 43, 45, 46, 48, 51, 59, 60, 78, 110, 111, 118, 119, 172, 176, 241, 243
Differenz 59
Dionysian 12, 125, 135
discord 102, 107, 111, 173, 176, 245
discordia 3
disempowerment 13, 90, 130–35
Disput, disputiren 3, 108
dispute(s) 3, 93, 95, 97, 100, 101
diversity, diverse 43, 49, 64, 66, 77, 78, 88, 107, 108, 111, 113, 115, 118, 119, 123, 170, 172, 175–77, 198, 210, 231, 241–43, 245
  See also Verschiedenheit
dividuum, dividua 14, 66, 113, 114, 152, 174, 243, 244–45
domestication 84, 241
dominance 161
domination 60, 109, 113–15, 175, 197, 203, 215, 236, 237

drive(s) 6–7, 20, 33, 38, 43, 46, 52–54, 56–61, 63, 74, 81, 90, 113, 114, 116, 134, 145–47, 158, 163, 165–69, 171–77, 181–83, 186, 188, 190–91, 200–1, 204, 214, 216–17, 226–27, 229, 235, 245–46
  See also Trieb
dynamic, dynamics, *Dynamik* 2, 3, 6, 9, 11, 19, 20, 22, 26, 27, 34–36, 42, 44, 45, 47, 53, 56, 59–61, 63, 66, 77, 79, 90, 91, 108, 111, 114, 115, 119, 120, 128, 133, 138, 139, 142, 157, 162–64, 178, 182, 196, 199–204, 208, 225, 231, 236, 240–42
dynamic-antagonistic 22
dynamic-mechanical 26
dynamic-relational 128

E
effect, *Wirkung See* effect 28, 33, 35, 52–53, 57, 66, 69–73, 75, 79, 91, 118, 137, 139, 140, 141, 144, 145, 149, 168, 187, 211, 214, 240
  See also causality
effort 30, 31, 73
ego 167–70, 172, 174, 175, 177, 188, 189
egoism, *Egoismus* 13, 14, 40, 76, 118, 151, 152, 155, 163, 164, 167–76, 171, 172, 175, 176, 178–82, 185, 186, 188–90, 211, 240, 243–45
  fine, well-planned, thoughtful egoism 13, 151, 170–72, 179, 185, 186, 243
  functional egoism, *Funktionsegoismus* 168, 171, 172, 175, 176, 178, 179, 190
egoism-altruism 188, 189
Eigendünkel 139
Eigenthum, Eigenthumstrieb 182, 186, 204
Einheit, Einheits-gefühl 56, 59, 63, 64, 74, 108, 143, 174
  See also unity
Eintracht 108, 109, 118, 177
einverleiben, Einverleibung 56, 60, 164, 169, 174, 178, 181, 201, 203, 227
  See also incorporation
Eitelkeit 148, 169, 207, 213
  See also vanity
Ekel 181, 203, 204, 230
  See also revulsion

elevation, *Erhöhung* 13, 126, 140, 141, 144, 145, 199, 235
  See also Erhebung
emancipate(d), emancipation, *emancipirt* 6, 15, 163, 165, 175, 178, 186–88, 195, 231, 234, 236
empfinden, Empfindung 27, 30, 38, 47, 51, 53, 55, 63, 71, 74, 75, 133, 134, 136, 162, 174–75, 181, 198, 204, 216, 226–27, 234, 236
  See also feeling, sensation
Empfindungsworten 228–29
empire 88, 90, 203
empirical, *Empirie* 47, 51, 62, 77, 86, 116, 140, 153
empower(ment) 12–13, 85, 90–91, 109, 118, 125–26, 129–30, 132–33, 208–9, 248
endogenous 25, 29, 36, 61, 78, 85
enemy, enemies 14, 70, 73, 87, 96, 106, 165, 181, 192, 196–97, 201–3, 207–9, 212, 216, 221, 223, 224, 227, 228, 231, 233–35, 247, 248
  See also Feind, enmity
energy, *Energie*, energetic 2, 31, 82, 130, 135, 150, 159, 164, 178, 182, 183, 192, 200–2, 204–5, 220, 225–26
enhance, enhancement 5–7, 13, 15, 109, 111, 114, 115, 121, 122, 132, 152, 164, 172, 175, 197, 199, 208, 222, 225, 230, 237, 239, 244
  See also Steigerung
enlightenment 94, 95, 100, 137, 158
enmity, enmities 84, 114, 175, 187, 189, 191, 193, 201–4, 224, 247–48
  See also enemy, *Feind*
Entgegensetzung, entgegengesetzt 17, 24–25, 27, 30, 31, 33, 37, 40, 43, 44, 49, 52, 53–54, 118, 134, 162, 172, 214
  See also Gegensatz, opposed, opposition
enthusiasm 232, 233
Entnaturalisirung 121
envy, enviable 84, 120, 175, 197, 198, 200, 205, 212–16, 226, 243, 247
  See also Neid
episteme 14, 15, 191, 193, 197, 230, 237, 244

epistemic, epistemology 15, 21, 30, 42, 73, 75, 152, 186, 194, 195, 209, 228, 243, 248
equal, equality 3, 14, 15, 24, 28–30, 54, 57, 61, 70, 73, 78–79, 88, 91, 111–15, 117–20, 123, 160, 172, 176, 195, 201–2, 208–11, 213–16, 223, 224, 231, 236, 237, 239, 241–43, 248
  aspirational equality 120, 123, 214, 242, 248
  more-or-less equal 91, 114, 115, 118, 119, 123, 201
  See also gleich
equalization 11, 47, 62, 241, 242
equals 172, 209, 213, 214, 216
equilibrium, aequilibrium, *Gleichgewicht* 3, 10, 27, 28, 32, 34, 61, 78, 79, 88, 91, 113–15, 117–20, 123, 138, 210, 240, 241–42
Erhaltung 66, 170, 178, 182, 226, 241
  See also preservation
erheben, Erhebung 120, 140, 141, 144, 145, 242
  See also elevation
Eris 90, 120
eros, erotic 197, 204, 209, 214, 221, 248–49
  See also love, *Liebe*
error(s), *Irrthum* 15, 18, 70, 72, 90, 94, 146, 101, 177, 178, 187, 197, 202, 204, 229–30, 237
Erschöpfung 6, 130, 135, 136, 191, 193
  See also exhaustion
essence 11, 21, 42, 44, 45, 59, 61, 72, 77, 129, 132, 134, 156, 247
  See also Wesen
ethical 6, 7, 247
ethicists, *Ethiker* 166, 245
ethics, *Ethik* 2, 3, 27, 112, 152
ethos 111, 166, 176, 180, 198, 203, 237, 243
Europe, European 4, 6, 18, 19, 22, 81, 84–85, 122, 195, 231, 235
euthanasia 112, 113, 245
evil, evils 3, 7–9, 18, 24, 27, 40, 41, 46, 76, 83, 90, 92, 94, 103, 107–9, 112, 121, 122, 154, 158, 160, 185, 196–98, 203–6, 208, 216, 222–28, 232, 234, 235, 243
  See also böse

Subject Index

excess 41, 59, 90, 111, 115, 131, 134, 135, 150, 156, 159, 164, 165, 201
  See also Übermaass
exclusion, exclusionary 58, 61–62, 90, 92, 100–3, 108, 110, 115, 153, 203, 241
excretion, excrement, *Excremente, exkretiren* 14, 62–64, 74, 78, 164, 165, 179, 181, 183, 190, 203–4, 208, 245, 248
  See also Ausscheidung
exhaustion 6, 130, 135, 191, 193
  See also Erschöpfung
exogenous 25, 29, 54, 61, 72, 75
expansion, expansionist 2, 106, 85, 111, 114–15, 122–23, 136, 199, 201–2, 204, 242
expenditure 164, 176–79, 159, 182, 183, 185, 202
experiment, experimental 1, 7–8, 36, 83, 165, 186, 198, 228
exploitation 111, 182–83, 201, 203, 205, 208
exterminate, extermination 12, 19, 85, 87, 90, 92, 93, 97, 101, 103–4, 106–8, 112
  See also ausrotten

F
facticity 5, 53, 80
faeces 183
fear 82, 89, 149, 150, 158, 161, 181, 198, 199, 201, 204, 209, 213–15, 218, 220, 226–28, 232
  See also Furcht
federation, *Föderalism* 105, 116, 242
feeling(s) 12–14, 27, 43, 52, 53, 55, 56, 63, 70, 71, 73, 74, 111, 114, 120, 125, 126, 129–35, 137–46, 148–50, 152, 167, 168, 170, 180, 185–86, 196, 200, 204, 206, 207, 209–12, 216, 220, 221, 224, 228–29, 232, 234, 235, 240, 245, 248
  See also Empfindung, Gefühl
Feind, Feindschaft 71, 84, 87, 96, 105, 175, 181, 188, 192, 196, 201, 203, 205, 207, 209, 212, 216, 221, 222–24, 227, 235–36
  See also enemy, enmity
Feind-sein-können 193
Feind-sein-wollen 193

feindselig, Feindseligkeit 104, 106, 110, 177, 194, 202
fest-locker 51
Festmachen, Fest-machen, Festsetzen, Festsetzen, Feststellen 11, 29, 45, 47, 48, 52, 55, 63–64, 68, 77–79, 110, 113, 127, 240–41, 243
  See also fixing, making fast
fiction, fictional 29, 39, 69, 77, 102
fixing, fixation 11, 29, 39, 42, 45, 47–48, 52, 60–62, 77–79, 92, 110, 111, 121, 127, 135, 156, 164, 167, 169, 171, 240
  See also Festmachen, making fast
flux, *flüssig* 43, 44
force-atom 60
force-quanta 78
force(s) 2, 3, 10, 11, 14, 18, 20, 22–30, 32–36, 42, 43, 45, 54, 57–61, 64–66, 69–75, 77–79, 81–83, 85, 88, 91, 99–102, 105, 107–11, 114–15, 117–19, 122–23, 125, 127–28, 131, 132, 135, 139, 141–46, 150, 156, 160–63, 174, 192, 196, 201, 202, 204, 205, 210, 218, 225, 226, 240–41, 245, 246
  See also Kraft
foreign 174, 227, 228
  See also Fremdes
forgivingness (placabilitas), *Versöhnlichkeit,* forgive 197, 210, 212, 233
freedom 1–3, 7, 12–15, 82, 83, 86–88, 90, 91, 94, 97, 98, 100, 102, 106, 107, 117, 125, 126, 138–50, 152, 154, 157, 163, 167, 171, 172, 198, 221, 227, 228, 239, 240, 244–46, 249
Freiheit, frei 71, 88, 91, 97, 98, 104–5, 106, 108, 113, 141, 143, 145, 165, 167, 181, 198, 217, 219, 221, 227, 245
Fremdes, fremd 162, 181, 183, 194, 201, 227–28, 242, 244
  See also foreign
Freundschaft, Freund 109, 118, 148, 175, 214
  See also friend
Friede, Friedenszustand 81, 84, 86–88, 97, 98, 103, 104, 107–9, 117–18, 125, 128, 136, 215
  See also peace
Friedensrufe 81

Friedensschluß 103, 117
friedlich, friedfertig 88, 105
friendliness 183
friendship, friend(s) 109, 118, 123, 148,
　　156–57, 161, 175, 234, 243, 247
　　See also Freund
function-feeling, *Funktionsgefühl* 167, 170
function(s) *Funktion(en)* 47, 56, 63, 66, 74,
　　118, 165, 167–72, 174–75, 178–79,
　　201, 202, 215
Furcht, fürchten 112, 181, 201, 209,
　　213–15, 218, 226–27, 232, 214, 226
　　See also fear

G
gardner 182
Gefahr 106, 192
Gefühl(e), gefühlt 40, 52, 66, 71, 125, 131,
　　132, 134, 136, 139–45, 149, 167,
　　180, 183, 196, 200, 212, 216, 221
　　See also feeling, *Empfindung*
Gefühls-Gegensatz 210
Gegeneinander 45, 77, 78
Gegensatz, Gegensätze 5, 11, 20, 37–41,
　　43–45, 51–53, 57, 62, 77, 78, 92,
　　102, 113, 121–23, 139, 146, 169,
　　183–85, 222, 228, 246
　　See also Entgegensetzung, opposition
Gegner, Gegnerschaft 60, 90, 96, 118, 201,
　　202, 215, 220, 221, 225
　　See also opponent
genealogy 6, 11, 38–42, 46, 74, 84, 102, 144,
　　185, 201–2, 210, 215, 218, 220, 221, 239
Gerechtigkeit 187, 198, 216, 221, 224
　　See also justice
Geschehen 45, 51, 55, 63, 65, 69, 70, 72, 73,
　　75, 76, 110, 117, 128, 130, 142, 213
　　See also occurrence
Gesetz(e) 13, 27, 46, 69, 79, 91, 103–4,
　　126, 138–41, 162, 166, 174, 178,
　　188, 232
　　See also law
Gesetzgebung 79, 98, 101, 105, 217
　　See also legislation
gesetzlich 98, 100, 102, 105, 211
gesetzlos 104–6
Gesundheit 131, 191, 192, 220, 222
Gewalt, Gewaltthätigkeit 87, 91, 98, 105,
　　212, 223, 235–36
　　See also violence

Gezänk 3
gleich, Gleichheit 34, 46, 51, 54, 61, 112,
　　118–20, 160, 172, 176, 201, 209,
　　213–216, 231, 236, 242
　　See also equal, same
Gleichgewicht See equilibrium
Gleichgültigkeit See indifference
Gleichmachen 11, 47, 48, 55, 62–64, 68,
　　119, 241
god 6, 34, 43, 95, 96, 121, 123, 156, 184,
　　196, 222, 225
good, goodness 18, 20, 27, 39–41, 46, 76,
　　82–84, 86, 90, 92, 97, 98, 102, 104,
　　108, 109, 112, 117, 120–23, 156,
　　157, 159, 160, 162, 163, 171, 185,
　　197, 205–7, 211–13, 222, 224–27,
　　232–35, 243
　　See also gut
goodwill 40, 181, 183–85, 190, 243
grades, *Grad* 11, 37, 45, 110, 128, 131, 202,
　　215, 241
　　See also degree
grausam, Grausamkeit 37, 40, 184, 198,
　　201, 220, 223, 228
　　See also cruelty
graveyard of freedom 88, 90, 117
　　See also peace of the graveyard
Greeks, *Griechen* 7, 8, 198, 204, 205, 215,
　　225, 226, 249
Groll 217, 218
grow, growth 13, 43, 55, 59, 60, 63, 66–68,
　　78, 95, 109, 118, 123, 125, 127–29,
　　133–34, 152, 164, 178, 180, 182,
　　190, 199, 201–4, 218, 244, 247
　　See also wachsen
guarantee(s) 86–87, 104, 106–7
gut, Guten 40–41, 112, 206–7, 223, 225,
　　226, 228, 235
　　See also good

H
harmony 4, 11, 18, 27, 43, 83, 108, 111–13,
　　177, 213, 224, 245
Hass / Haß, hassen 51, 76, 88, 112, 167,
　　174–75, 181, 196, 198–200, 205,
　　207–10, 211–22, 224–30, 232–34,
　　236
　　See also hate
hassenswerth, haßenswürdig 136, 199,
　　205–6, 214, 225

Subject Index

hässlich /häßlich / häslich 121–22, 199, 205–6, 207, 211, 213, 223
  See also ugly
hate, hatred 2, 7, 10, 14, 15, 28, 76, 88, 107–9, 112, 120, 158, 167, 174–75, 181, 184–85, 190, 194–237, 240–244, 247, 248
  hatred-as-ressentiment 210, 218, 219, 234
  hatred-as-revenge 218
  hatred-in-assimilation 201
  hatred-love / love-hate 240, 247
  hatred-ressentiment 234
hateful 160, 205
hateworthy, hateable 199, 204–6, 208, 211–14, 225
health, healthy 3, 13, 126, 131–37, 180, 191, 192
Heerde 167, 168, 172
  See also herd
heerdenbildend 167, 168
Heerdengefühle, Heerden-Gefühle 167–69
Heerden-Thiere 246
Heerdentrieb(e) 167, 169
hemmen, Hemmnis(s) / Hemmniß, Hemmung 12, 71, 125, 126, 129, 130, 131–33, 135, 193, 221
  See also obstacle
herd 84, 118, 120, 122, 167, 168, 172
  See also Heerde
herd-animal(s) 84, 85, 113, 166, 241, 246
herd-building, herd-forming 167, 168, 172
herd-drive(s) 167, 169, 171
herd-feelings 171
Herrschen 43, 66, 236
Herrschsucht 7, 155, 157, 197, 203
hierarchy 61, 118, 120, 206
  See also Rangordnung
Hindernis / Hinderiß 12, 126, 131–32, 140–41
  See also obstacle
hindrance(s) 12, 13, 73, 125, 126, 129–35, 137–38, 240
hostile, hostility, hostilities 7, 9, 14, 82–83, 89, 91, 103–8, 115, 138, 152, 160, 190–94, 202, 205, 210–11, 230, 244
humanity, humankind, *Menschheit* 3, 7, 87, 89, 91, 107, 149, 159–61, 164, 178, 198, 210, 211, 219, 247, 249

humiliation 139–41, 144, 145, 220
  See also Demüthigung
hypersensitivity 191–92

I

Ich-bewusstsein / -bewußtsein 56, 174
Ichgefühl 56, 186
ideal 12–14, 82–86, 89, 91–93, 109–18, 120–23, 135, 136, 150, 152, 164, 173, 186, 188, 190, 191, 193, 194, 207, 209, 218, 224, 225, 227, 228, 242–45, 248
idealism, *Idealismus* 92, 121
identity, identities, (self-)identical (with itself) 11, 18, 19, 34–37, 39, 42–3, 46–48, 51, 55, 58, 64, 66, 152, 241–43
  See also sich-selber-gleich
image-language *See Bilderrede*
immanent, immanence 6, 7, 78, 109, 111, 122, 150, 163, 204, 222, 237, 239
immorality, *Immoralität*, immoralists 6, 163, 188, 249
imperative 5, 50, 81, 188
impotence 129, 131, 134, 135, 148, 150, 192, 198, 206, 207, 209, 218, 219, 222, 223, 228, 234, 235
  See also Ohnmacht, powerlessness
inactivity 31, 84, 85, 133, 135, 159
inclination(s) 3, 7, 13, 82, 88, 103, 105–8, 112, 115, 126, 138–41, 145, 154, 157, 158, 160, 189, 210, 214, 217, 222, 234, 235
  See also Neigung
incorporate, incorporation 56, 60–62, 65, 67–68, 78, 113, 123, 164–65, 169, 174–75, 178–79, 181–82, 184, 201–3, 223, 227, 248, 249
  See also Einverleibung
indifference, *Gleichgültigkeit* 15, 27, 28, 193, 224, 228, 230, 234, 237
indolence 84–86, 135, 154, 156–59
inequality 15, 78, 120, 159, 195, 213, 223, 231, 236
  See also unequal
inertia 28, 30, 36, 54, 85
inertiae, vis 36, 84, 85
injure, injury, injuries 104, 111, 149, 212, 217, 218, 224
injustice 98, 100, 120, 123, 187, 216–18, 221, 224, 226, 234, 242

inorganic 42, 58, 60, 66, 73–75, 78
instinct(s), *Instinkt(e)* 41, 50, 51–52, 141, 146, 159–61, 171, 193, 206
instrumental 107, 111, 157, 158, 161, 181
intelligence, *Intelligenz*, intelligent 13, 67, 78–79, 82, 152, 157, 169, 175, 211, 219, 220, 230, 240, 244, 245
intensification, intensify 6, 90, 121, 127–30, 131–32, 133, 135, 197, 199, 225
   See also Steigerung

J
jealousy 160, 209, 248
joy 131–33, 135, 142, 182, 200, 221, 247, 249
justice 104, 119, 123, 198, 216–18, 221, 224, 234
   See also Gerechtigkeit

K
Kampf, Kämpfe, kämpfen 2, 3, 39, 43, 45, 52, 60, 66, 68, 76, 78, 91, 110, 112, 119, 164–65, 170, 173, 175–78, 201–2, 215, 245, 246
   See also struggle
Kampfplatz 3, 191
Kirchhof See graveyard
knowledge, know 4, 14, 15, 19, 21, 30, 31, 39, 40, 44, 46, 48, 50, 76–77, 86, 89, 90, 100, 121, 122, 139, 141, 149, 150, 152, 153, 164, 169, 179, 180, 183, 185–87, 188–91, 206, 207, 218, 226–27, 228, 230, 237, 244, 245
knowledge-drive 186
Konflikt 2
Kontroverse 3
Kraft, Kräfte 2, 18, 25–27, 30, 31, 35, 43, 45, 52, 57, 59, 60, 62, 68–75, 77, 88, 90, 103, 107, 109–10, 118, 119, 123, 128, 139, 141–43, 145, 148, 155, 156, 162–63, 165, 170, 178, 180–81, 184, 201, 202, 216, 223, 226, 233, 245–46
   See also force
Kraftauslösungen 145
Kraftfeststellungen 60
Kraftgefühl 71, 73

Krankhaftigkeit See sickly
Krankheit See sick
Krieg 2, 9, 37, 45, 77, 78, 81, 84, 86, 88, 98, 103–7, 110, 118, 125, 127–28, 148, 167, 199, 203, 207, 215, 216, 219, 225
   See also war
Kultur See culture
Kunst(werk), künstlerisch 61, 65, 66, 249

L
lack 10, 18, 23–25, 27, 30–31, 50, 56, 58–59, 104, 111, 130–31, 134–35, 148–49, 159, 164, 201, 204, 224, 229, 232
law(s), lawful 3, 5, 7, 9, 12–14, 19, 25, 27, 28, 33, 35, 37, 43, 46, 54, 57, 65, 69, 75, 79, 82, 83, 87, 88, 90, 91, 93, 97–102, 104–9, 111, 112, 115–17, 119, 123, 126, 138–41, 144, 145, 148–50, 152, 154, 156, 166, 167, 170, 172, 173, 178, 153, 173, 185, 187, 189–91, 198, 200, 210, 211, 222, 224, 225, 231, 232, 234, 241–45, 247, 248
   See also Gesetz
lawless(ness) 87, 100, 102, 104–7, 109–11, 115, 116, 225, 241
league 105, 106, 109, 116–18, 122, 123, 136, 242, 243, 246
Leben, lebend, lebendig 7, 25, 27, 39, 48, 56, 60, 65–68, 84, 104, 113, 122, 131, 132, 136–37, 148, 165, 166, 176–78, 180, 182, 187–88, 191, 197, 202–2, 203, 219, 230, 236, 246
   See also life
Lebensbedingungen 165, 173, 197
Lebenskraft 131
Leblosigkeit 131–34
legal(ity) 99–102, 105, 111, 115, 117, 123, 158, 211, 240, 242
legislation 79, 88, 98–101
   See also Gesetzgebung
Leib See body 50, 207, 219
Leidenschaft(en) 108, 157, 167, 170, 173, 177, 206, 212, 217, 220–22, 233–34
   See also passion

Liebe, lieben 40, 63, 76, 81, 184, 196, 199, 204, 209, 211, 214, 216, 221, 226, 228, 229, 233, 234
  See also eros, love
life 2, 3, 5–8, 10, 13, 18, 27–30, 34, 39–43, 48, 51, 53–56, 58–61, 65–67, 72–75, 77, 83–85, 89, 90, 100, 109–13, 115, 119–23, 126, 128–36, 147, 148, 150, 163–66, 170–73, 175–79, 182, 186, 190, 191, 195, 197, 199–202, 204, 218, 221, 222, 225, 230, 235, 237, 239–41, 243, 244, 246, 247
  See also life
life-affirmation 6, 13, 15, 83, 89, 90, 91, 109, 111, 114, 115, 123, 128, 136, 152, 164, 206, 222, 227, 230, 237, 244
life-conditioning, life-enabling 11, 39, 47, 61, 62, 66, 72, 77, 79, 197, 225, 226
life-enhancing 91, 114, 123, 136, 243
life-form(s) 2, 6, 7, 33, 118, 119, 163, 175, 242, 245
lifelessness 131–33, 135
life-needs 48–50, 55, 56, 243, 246
life-negating, life-negation 6–8, 12, 85, 89, 93, 115, 117, 118, 120, 122, 128, 136, 179
life-processes 13, 56, 77, 151, 163, 164, 173–75, 177, 180, 185, 190
living 2, 12, 43, 48, 58, 60, 61, 63, 66–68, 74, 77, 81, 83, 85, 88, 90, 93, 109, 113, 114, 117, 137, 152, 153, 164, 167, 169, 171, 173–75, 178, 182, 187, 189, 190, 195, 201–3, 217, 228, 230, 243–45, 249
living being(s), living whole, organism(s) 13, 48, 63, 66–7, 137, 152, 153, 164, 167, 169, 171, 173–75, 167, 182, 187, 189, 201–3, 203, 243–44
living peace *See* peace
logic, *Logik* 2, 10, 11, 17–19, 21, 23, 34, 37, 38, 39, 46–49, 51
logical, *logisch* 2, 4, 5, 10, 11, 17–24, 27, 32, 33, 34, 37–39, 42, 44, 46–54, 56, 57, 61, 64–66, 72, 77, 79, 80, 93, 102, 133–35, 137
  logical opposition, logice oppositum 2, 4, 22–24, 38, 39, 51–52, 77, 93, 134–45, 137
    See also contradiction

logicize(d), *Logisirung, logisirt* 39, 48, 49, 56, 61
love 14, 15, 28, 40, 63, 76, 81, 84, 90, 125, 157, 161, 184, 185, 195–201, 204, 205, 208–11, 214, 216, 219, 221, 226–30, 233, 236, 237, 240, 247–49
  See also eros, *Liebe*
love-hate / hate-love 240, 247
Lust 51, 127–30, 132, 134–37, 142–3, 179, 220, 230
  See also pleasure

M
Maass, Maaß mässig / mäßig 51, 90, 91, 96, 119–20, 181, 201, 241, 242
  See also measure
Macht 43, 60, 69, 70, 81, 125, 129, 132, 137, 141, 142, 144, 148, 149, 162, 174, 177, 178, 180, 215
  See also power
Machtgefühl 129, 142–44, 148, 170, 206, 245
Machtgelüst 164, 181, 227
mächtig 48, 162, 169–70, 177, 219
making(-)fast 29, 45, 47–48, 78, 79, 110, 240
  See also Festmachen, fixing
making-the-same 47, 55
  See also Gleichsetzen
Mangel 10, 23–25, 30, 31, 118, 134, 172, 179
  See also lack
masters, *Herren* 219, 224, 234–36
mastery 43, 91, 145, 188, 189, 209, 226, 244
mathematics, *Mathematik* 22, 32, 36, 48, 72
measure 83, 90, 112–14, 119, 120, 166, 195, 239, 241, 242, 246, 247
measured 1, 8, 90, 91, 145, 239
  See also Maass
mechanics *Mechanik*, mechanism 10, 11, 19, 25–28, 32, 46, 55, 57–62, 66–70, 72, 75–77, 142, 145, 152, 156, 159, 164, 240
Menschheit See humanity
metabolism 74, 164, 181
metaphysics, metaphysica 2, 3, 8–11, 19, 22, 25–27, 32, 34–36, 38–49, 68, 72, 77–79, 94–96, 101, 110, 127, 161, 163, 197, 199, 239–41, 249
  metaphysics of being *See Seinsmetaphysik*

Subject Index

misanthropy, *Misanthropie, Menschenhaß* 155, 211, 212
modernity 4, 18, 38, 84–85, 90, 113, 119, 121, 122, 130, 149, 151, 163, 166–67, 171, 191–93, 195, 205, 223, 231, 233, 239, 241, 243
monad, monadology 9, 25–26, 33, 35–36, 60–61, 84, 163
monarchy 88, 90
moral(s), morality, *Moralen, moralisch* 3, 6, 7, 9, 13–15, 27, 40–41, 66–68, 82–85, 88, 92, 103, 108, 112, 113, 116–18, 121–23, 126, 137–41, 144, 146–55, 157, 158, 160, 161, 163–64, 166–73, 175–79, 181–88, 190–92, 195–97, 199–206, 208, 210–14, 217–19, 221–22, 224–27, 231–37, 240, 243–45, 248–49
more-or-less equal *See* equal
motion, movement(s) 20, 23–26, 28, 30, 42, 69–71, 42, 43, 45, 54, 61, 70–71, 76, 78, 91, 110, 143, 144, 146, 156, 162–63, 173, 174, 179, 200, 221, 231
  See also Bewegung
motive force 23, 24, 30, 54
motive (for action), motivate (the will) 3, 70–71, 126, 137–41, 144–45, 147, 149
  See also Triebfeder
multiplicity, multiplicities 14, 37, 43, 45, 55, 58, 63–64, 66–68, 77–78, 113, 114, 116, 123, 146, 147, 150, 152, 153, 175, 187, 189–91, 243–44, 248
  See also Vielheit

N

Nahrung 59, 63, 97, 176, 182, 186, 201, 226, 245–46
  See also nourishment
nation(s), *Nationen* 106, 116, 167, 170, 242–43
naturalism 6, 7, 13, 15, 75, 126, 150, 152, 163–4, 171, 177, 178, 184, 206, 227, 244
Naturstand(e) / Naturzustande 104–5
negation(s), negate 2, 4, 9–12, 17, 18, 22–25, 27–31, 37, 42–44, 48–50, 53, 72, 77, 83, 85, 90, 92–97, 100–1, 103–4, 106–9, 111, 113, 115, 117, 133–34, 188, 206, 213, 240

negative, negativity, negativum 4, 10, 14, 17, 18–19, 21–29, 31–34, 36, 43, 49, 53, 57, 59, 100, 106, 116, 118, 122, 134–37, 139, 140, 160, 162, 196, 197, 204, 211, 214, 240
Neid 84, 175, 197, 198, 213, 214, 216, 226
  See also envy
Neigung(en) 3, 103, 106, 112, 139, 155, 160, 162, 179, 214, 217, 221–22, 234
  See also inclination
nexus *See* causality
nihilism, nihilistic 6, 12, 85, 90, 109, 113, 117, 136, 192, 218, 235
nobility, noble 107, 120, 156, 215, 223, 233, 242
nobles 219, 222, 233
non-contradiction, principle of 4, 5, 11, 17, 19, 21, 37, 39, 42, 48–51, 53, 72, 77, 80
normative, norms 3, 5, 6, 86, 99–102, 116, 147, 150, 163, 171–73, 175, 178, 179, 184–85, 187, 190, 205, 211, 214, 223, 227, 228, 239, 242, 244
noumenon, noumenal 14, 146, 152, 174, 188, 224, 244
nourishment, nutrition 43, 59, 60, 63, 66, 74, 97, 119, 164, 176–78, 182–84, 186, 188, 189–90, 201, 203, 246
  See also Nahrung

O

obeying 43, 60, 62, 66–68, 77–79, 164, 190, 202
obstacle(s) 13, 70, 91, 126, 132, 140–41, 151, 155–58, 161, 190, 243, 247
  See also Hindernis, hindrance
occurrence 1, 11, 29, 31–33, 37, 43, 45, 49, 51, 55, 57, 58, 65, 66, 68–70, 72, 73, 76, 79, 110, 127–30, 131–32, 137, 199
  See also Geschehen
Ohnmacht, Ohnmächtigen 148, 199, 206, 209, 219, 223, 233–34, 236
  See also Ohnmacht, powerless
ontology, ontological 1, 2–4, 8, 10–12, 14, 17–19, 21, 25–26, 29, 30, 32–36, 38, 41–45, 48, 49, 53–55, 58, 65, 72, 76, 77–78, 83, 109, 110, 114–15, 125–27, 135, 153, 177, 196, 199, 204, 218, 225, 241, 245, 247

Subject Index 271

opponent(s) 60, 78, 87, 94, 95–97, 99, 117, 123, 188, 202, 205, 209, 215, 221, 225, 231, 246, 247
  See also Gegner
opposite(s) 10, 11, 25, 27–29, 32, 40, 41, 44, 46, 49, 52, 57, 62, 81, 92, 94, 111, 114, 122, 123, 134, 137–38, 173, 183–85, 197, 225, 228, 243, 245
opposition(s), oppositional, opposed 2–5, 9–14, 17–30, 31–34, 36–46, 49–54, 57–58, 60–62, 65, 66, 68, 73, 75–79, 81–83, 85, 92–4, 99–100, 102–3, 105–7, 108–10, 112–13, 115, 121, 122, 126–27, 129, 133–35, 137, 139, 145, 147, 151–52, 154–55, 159, 162–63, 170–73, 176, 183–85, 188–89, 191–92, 196–97, 200, 204–5, 209–11, 214, 221–22, 224–45, 228, 239–40, 241, 243–44, 246, 248
  See also Gegensatz, logical opposition, contradiction, real opposition, Realrepugnanz
oppositum 20, 134, 137
oppress, oppression 1, 2, 126, 145, 149, 219, 223, 234–36
organ, Organe 67, 68, 76, 165, 166, 171, 178, 181
organic, organisch 42, 58–61, 63–66, 74, 129, 137, 164, 174, 178–89, 181, 182, 184, 185, 199
organism(s), Organismus, organismic 13, 46–47, 51, 55, 58, 61–66, 74, 76–78, 119, 137–38, 151, 153, 163–67, 169–70, 173–81, 183–91, 201, 215, 227–28, 243–45, 248
outcome, Ausschlag 56, 87, 95, 105, 241
overcoming 12, 6, 13, 45, 73, 77–78, 110, 126, 130, 134, 135, 140, 141–43, 144, 147, 163, 189, 196, 197, 231, 233, 247–49
  See also Überwindung
overcompensation, überreichlicher Ersatz 164, 178, 181–82, 190, 201–2, 204, 227
overpower(ing) 11, 12, 45, 59, 62, 69, 72, 74, 76–79, 114, 141, 127–28, 134, 159, 164, 202, 205, 219, 228, 231, 240, 248

P
pain(ful) 12, 13, 59, 63, 125–41, 144–45, 156, 159, 163, 165, 191, 211, 220, 229, 230, 240
  See also Schmerz
paradox 5, 17, 20, 224
pares, parity 14, 15, 119, 195–97, 201, 203, 205, 208–10, 213, 225, 226, 230
particularity 14, 147, 150, 152, 194, 244, 248
passion(s) 6, 7, 15, 74, 83, 138, 157–58, 161, 167, 172–73, 177, 206, 207, 212, 217, 220–22, 232, 232–36
  See also Leidenschaft
passivity 60, 84–86, 135, 156, 159, 202
pathos 204, 208, 211, 232, 233
peace, pax, paix, pacific, peaceful 1–2, 3, 7, 12, 14, 81–90, 92–94, 96–118, 120, 122, 123, 125, 128, 135, 136, 138, 154, 166, 176, 177, 195, 202, 210, 211, 215, 224, 225, 240, 242, 243, 245
  living peace 2, 12, 81, 85, 88, 90, 93, 117
  peace of the graveyard 2, 12, 85–89, 109, 115, 117
  perpetual peace, paix perpétuelle, eternal peace 2, 3, 7, 12, 81–83, 85–87, 89, 90, 92–94, 96–101, 103, 106–9, 111, 115–18, 122, 123, 125, 136, 138, 154, 202, 225, 243, 252
  See also Friede
people(s) 3, 19, 88, 104, 105–08, 116, 117–18, 117, 170, 207, 222
  See also Volk
perfectibility, perfectionism 7, 8, 14, 195, 198–99, 210, 230, 242
perfection 10, 18, 26, 27, 34, 179
  See also Vollkommenheit
persecution 217–18, 224, 235
person(s), personhood, Personen 14, 55, 104, 108, 122, 186–90, 230, 235, 243–44
pessimism, pessimistic 8, 89–90, 103, 148–49, 206, 207, 211, 223
Pflicht(en) 88, 117, 169, 211–13, 232
Phänomenalismus 74
Phänomenal-Welt 43, 62

phenomena(l) 20, 25, 26, 30, 35–36, 44, 47, 62, 77, 137, 240
phenomenology 127, 141, 142, 191, 247
physics, physicists 6, 27, 35, 36, 69
physiology, physiological 6, 8, 11, 13–15, 19, 32–33, 46, 55–58, 60–62, 64–66, 70, 74–77, 119, 122, 126–27, 136–38, 142, 144–47, 150–53, 163–64, 176, 179, 181, 185, 186, 193, 197, 199–204, 206, 208–9, 211, 213, 215, 220, 222, 227–30, 236–37, 244, 248, 250
physio-ontology / onto-physiology 8, 10, 11, 199, 221
play 3, 13, 31, 60, 91, 126, 129, 131, 132, 135, 143, 144, 153
pleasurable 140
pleasure(s) 13, 27, 33, 34, 40, 51, 89, 126–40, 140, 142, 152, 160, 164, 181, 211, 227, 240, 244
See also Lust
pleasure-pain 129, 240
pleasure-power 12, 133
plural, plurality 2, 8, 11, 14, 17, 22, 41–43, 45, 49, 52, 53, 55–58, 61, 74, 76–78, 91, 110, 115, 119, 152, 174, 175, 189, 199, 216, 243–46, 248
See also Vielheit
pluralism 10–11, 15, 44–45, 49, 57, 110–13, 113, 115, 117, 190, 194, 239–40, 243, 244
pluralization 45, 60, 65, 82, 88, 107, 110, 127, 174
poison(ous) 87, 212, 219, 221–22, 233
polemic(al) 12, 93–96, 100, 102, 106, 108, 120, 125, 152, 163, 170, 176, 219, 225
Polemik 3
political, *Politik* 1, 6, 7, 9, 15, 28, 60, 66, 82, 83, 86–88, 107, 112, 114–18, 122, 149, 152, 167, 171, 195, 219, 239, 242, 246, 247, 250
politician(s) 7, 86, 89
polytropia 227, 228, 230
possess 14, 154, 184, 186, 188, 189, 191, 209, 244, 248
possessed, to be 188–91, 194, 209, 244, 248

possession(s), *Besitz* 157–58, 184, 186, 188, 189, 215, 224
possessiveness 40, 183, 184, 243
power(s) 1, 2, 5–6, 8–15, 19, 26, 29, 33, 34, 41–46, 50, 52, 55, 57–62, 66, 67, 69, 70, 72, 73, 76–79, 81, 82, 84, 90–93, 104–11, 113–21, 123, 125–35, 137, 138, 141–45, 148–52, 154, 156–61, 164, 167, 169–70, 176–78, 180, 181, 183, 184, 186, 188, 191, 192, 194, 195, 197–202, 204, 206, 207–10, 214, 215, 219–21, 223–27, 229–37, 240, 242–47
See also Macht, Wile zur Macht, will to power
power-as-activity 45, 159
power-complex(es) 2, 33, 45, 52, 59, 61, 77–78, 109, 111, 114–15, 121–22, 123, 243
power-differential(s) 60, 61, 130
powerful 15, 48, 148, 219, 235, 236
powerless(ness) 206, 218–20, 222, 223, 231, 233–35
power-pleasure 12, 126, 129–33, 135, 211, 240
power-relations 126, 144, 202, 248
preservation 36, 43, 47, 59, 66, 166, 169, 177, 178, 182, 226, 241
self-preservation 59, 104, 122, 133, 159, 161, 164, 169, 171, 178, 188, 202
See also Erhaltung
pressure 68, 69, 107, 114, 143–45, 220, 229
priest(s), priestly 197–98, 219–25, 235
privation, privation, privative 10, 18, 20, 24–25, 27, 30, 37, 49, 78–79, 133, 240
See also Beraubung
process(es), *Prozeß, Prozesse,* processual 6, 11, 13–14, 20, 43, 46–47, 48, 53, 55–68, 70, 71, 74, 76–79, 84, 97–101, 105, 110, 126, 133, 135, 137, 144–53, 159, 164–65, 171, 173, 174–77, 179–81, 183–84, 190, 199–204, 208, 211, 227, 229, 240–42, 245, 247, 248
productive 2, 3, 6–8, 12, 13, 83, 85, 93, 107–9, 113–15, 118, 119, 123, 125, 126, 131–33, 151, 154–56, 177, 197, 205, 210, 211, 214, 216, 239, 240

Subject Index

psychology, psychological 11, 19, 21, 27, 50, 55, 58, 69, 70, 72, 73, 76, 7, 137, 154
purpose(s) 69, 70, 72, 158, 170
See also Zweck
purposive(ness) 69, 70, 72, 74, 76–78, 153, 157–60, 164, 173, 179, 185, 221

Q
quality, *Qualität*, qualitative 7, 13, 30, 64, 76, 119, 147, 150, 152, 231, 242, 244
quanta, quantitative 8, 11, 42, 43, 45, 64, 77–78, 119, 242
quarrel, quarrelsomeness 94, 97, 100, 154

R
Rache 175, 196, 210, 219, 220, 223, 230, 233, 235
See also revenge, vengeance
Rachgier, Rachbegierde 217, 221
radically individual self-legislation 14, 152, 172, 175, 176, 190, 222, 244
radically individual self-regulation 175, 244
rage 200, 216, 220, 221, 233
rancour 217, 218
Rangordnung 61, 118, 120, 146
See also hierarchy
rank 154, 157, 203, 236
rapture, *Rausch* 135, 220–22, 233
reactive, reactivity 12–14, 85, 104, 107, 130, 131, 133, 135, 151, 159, 160, 191, 193, 196, 205, 224
real opposition 3, 5, 9–11, 13, 17–21, 23–30, 32–34, 37–39, 42, 45, 49, 51–54, 57, 58, 60–62, 65, 66, 73, 75, 77–79, 92–93, 108, 126, 133, 137, 139, 151, 162, 163, 196, 240
See also opposition
realism 7, 8, 83, 89, 103–5, 107, 116, 154, 195, 197, 199, 210, 226, 230, 247
Realrepugnanz 3–5, 10, 11, 17, 22–25, 27, 28, 45, 162, 240, 254
re-anthropomorphization 68–69, 76, 200, 204
See also de-anthropomorphization
Recht, Rechte, rechtlich 96, 103, 105, 109, 117–18, 123, 198, 214, 231
See also law, justice, *Gerechtigkeit*

Rechtsbegierde 217
reciprocal, reciprocity 13, 28, 29, 33, 45, 52, 78, 88, 91, 95, 111, 115, 119, 152, 176, 183, 208, 188, 190, 211, 215, 216, 231
recognition 149, 157, 160, 167, 168, 171, 195, 215, 237
reconciliation 14, 195, 197
re-evaluation 1–2, 14, 195
refinement 11, 40–41, 102, 183–86, 243
See also Verfeinerung
regulate, *regulieren* 39, 47, 61, 62, 88, 164, 173, 175, 178–80, 185, 186, 190, 244–45
Reiz, reizen 12, 74, 61, 91, 119, 125, 129, 130, 143, 145, 146, 192, 193
See also stimulant
relational 1, 10, 20, 25, 29, 34–36, 43, 45, 54, 57, 78, 83, 109, 110, 119, 126–28, 137, 156, 159, 175, 176, 241, 243, 245
Relationscharakter des Geschehens 110
religion 88, 107–9, 118, 121, 123, 136, 148, 172, 210, 231, 232
republic, republican 88, 105, 106–8, 115–16
Repugnanz, *repugnantia*, *repugnans* 4, 10, 21–24
repulsion 10, 20, 22, 23, 25, 26–28, 35, 57–62, 64, 69, 70, 75, 77, 162–63
See also Zurückstoßung
repulsiva, vis 26, 59, 62, 64, 67
resistance, resist 2, 7, 9–10, 12–14, 22, 24, 25, 43, 45, 52, 59–60, 62, 67, 78, 91, 94–96, 109, 114–15, 118, 123, 125–35, 137, 139–45, 151–52, 154–59, 161–63, 173, 177, 191–94, 201–4, 209–11, 227, 230–31, 233, 237, 239–40, 243–44, 247, 248
See also Widerstand
resistance-overcoming 138, 142
resistance-pain 129, 131, 133, 135, 240
respect 13, 15, 21, 82, 126, 138–40, 144, 195, 201, 214, 232, 239, 246–50
See also Achtung
responsibility 141, 160, 173, 224, 235
ressentiment 15, 120, 196, 210, 218, 224, 231, 233

revenge 14, 15, 175, 196, 210, 216–21, 223, 224, 228, 231, 233–36, 243
 See also Rache
reverence 149, 233
revulsion 14, 181, 203, 204, 248
 See also Ekel
right, rightness, rights 46, 70, 82, 87, 88, 90, 94, 96–107, 109, 114, 116, 118, 123, 144, 159, 170, 214, 231, 235, 242, 247

S
Schadenfreude 212, 214
Schein See semblance
Schmerz 63, 127, 131, 134, 136–38, 229, 230
 See also pain
schön 205, 207, 249
 See also beautiful
science 8–9, 27, 56, 64, 70, 71, 75–76, 100, 150, 191, 193, 240
 See also Wissenschaft
secretion, *Secretiren* 62–63, 78, 164, 183, 203, 242
security, *Sicherheit* 40, 91, 104–7, 116, 120, 159, 160, 183
Seele(n) 31, 65, 84, 112, 207, 212, 219, 228
 See also soul
Seinsmetaphysik, metaphysics of being 8, 35–36, 38, 42–43, 45, 58, 76, 127, 199, 241
Selbstregulirung See self-regulation
self 15, 56, 63, 68, 122, 139, 140, 168–71, 175, 178, 188, 189, 230, 237
self-affirmation 223, 233
self-annihilation 108, 115
self-assertion 90, 92, 94, 99, 102, 171
self-conceit 96, 139, 140
self-contempt 140, 144, 218
self-contradictory 4
self-determination 164, 176, 244, 245
self-hatred 213, 228
self-identical 11, 39, 43, 47–49, 52, 79, 92
self-interest 82, 158, 161, 213, 217
self-knowledge 13, 93, 149, 150, 152, 164, 169, 197, 222
self-legislation *See* radically individual self-legislation
self-love 139, 159, 217, 228

self-organization 58, 66–68, 77, 153
self-organizing 55, 68, 174
self-overcoming 2, 147, 199, 236
self-preservation *See* preservation
self-regulation, *Selbstregulirung* 13, 56, 58, 61, 63, 66, 74, 152, 153, 163–66, 166, 171, 174–76, 178–81, 184, 187, 189, 227, 228, 244, 245
self-relation 174, 175, 190, 245
self-respect 169
self-subjection 14, 152, 166, 167, 172, 244
semblance, *Schein* 44, 48, 53, 127, 157, 186, 218
sensation(s) 32, 47, 50–51, 53–55, 58, 62–63, 74–75, 137
 See also Empfindung
Sensationen-Chaos 43, 62
sensibility 13, 126, 131, 137–41, 218, 222, 232
 See also sinnlich
sentiment(s) 84, 153, 175, 185, 199, 243
sexual 12, 40, 125, 129, 181, 183
Sicherheit See security 104, 105, 120, 160
sich-selber-gleich, sich-selbst-identisch 39, 44, 48, 66
 See also identity
sich-widersprechend 4, 43
sick, sickness, *Krankheit* 191–92, 220, 222–23
sickliness, sickly, *Krankhaftigkeit* 191–92, 193
Sieg 98, 105, 129, 130, 132, 136
 See also victory
similar, *ähnlich* 46, 114, 201–3, 208
simplification, *simplificatio* 11, 49, 51, 52, 55–56, 61–62, 64–65, 68
singular, singularity 20, 28, 161, 163, 166, 170, 173–75, 180, 187, 246–47
sinnlich, Sinnlichkeit 51, 139, 217–19, 222
 See also sensibility
Sittengesetz 148, 166
slave, slavish 14, 15, 84, 195, 196, 202, 205, 217–19, 221, 222, 224, 231–37
 slave revolt of morality 15, 150, 195, 196, 207, 218, 219, 222, 231, 233–36
sociability 1, 3, 9, 10, 13, 151, 154–55, 157, 159–63, 171–74, 176, 185, 211, 240
 See also unsociability
sociability-unsociability 13, 152, 240

social 1–3, 6, 28, 55, 100, 112, 114, 119, 120, 150, 151, 153, 156, 158, 160, 161, 163–76, 178–81, 183–86, 190, 233, 242–46
socio-physiology 6, 13, 14–15, 126, 150–52, 163–64, 167, 170–72, 174, 176, 179, 184–86, 190–91, 194, 243–46
soul 26, 28, 30–34, 84, 89, 95, 96, 101, 113, 159, 161, 163, 207, 212, 221, 232–34
    See also Seele
sovereignty, *Souveränität*, sovereign 6, 13, 15, 100, 105, 111, 115–16, 125, 126, 138, 141, 143, 144, 147, 150, 163, 166, 170–73, 175, 176, 178, 180, 181, 186, 189, 190, 227, 244–46
    sovereign individual 13, 126, 141, 151, 173
Spannung 45, 113, 142
    See also tension
spontaneity 8, 11, 42–43, 58, 61, 76, 85, 198, 200, 202, 205, 233
Sprechart 8, 11, 44, 76, 77, 153, 186, 199
stages 11, 40, 41, 185, 243
Stärke 59, 110, 112, 113, 146, 174, 193, 232
    See also strength
Steigerung 90, 122, 127, 128, 132–35, 225
    See also intensification, enhancement
stimulant, stimulus, stimulate 2, 3, 12, 52, 61, 62, 74, 81, 91, 115, 119, 119–20, 125, 128–33, 135, 144–45, 156–57, 191–94, 208, 211, 217, 232, 250
    See also Reiz
Stolz 118, 141, 148, 178, 207, 209, 219–20
    See also pride
Streit, Streitigkeit, streiten 2, 3, 27, 45, 86, 89, 93, 98, 105, 108, 162, 163, 177, 191, 219 (*Streitschrift*)
strength, strengthen, strong 12, 15, 22, 52, 59, 90, 109, 112–14, 117–18, 123, 130, 144–46, 156, 165, 181, 188, 193, 201–3, 208, 210, 216, 223, 227, 232–33, 237, 246, 248
    See also *Stärke*
struggle 2, 3, 9, 10, 14, 43, 45, 47, 51, 52, 56, 58, 59, 61, 63, 68, 76–78, 87, 90, 91, 110, 111, 115, 119, 123, 146, 153, 164, 165, 176, 177, 186, 201, 202, 204, 215, 219, 245, 246
    See also *Kampf*

subject, *Subjekt*, subjective, subjectivity 4, 14, 19, 32, 33, 37, 39, 44, 47, 50–52, 62, 134, 139–40, 152, 155, 166, 167, 174, 186, 188–89, 214, 224, 235, 244
subjectification 167
sublimation, *sublimirt* 11, 40–41, 102, 111, 183–86, 188, 197, 243
sublime 7, 82, 207, 208, 232, 233
subordination 168, 190, 202, 203, 208
substance(s), *Substanz* 2, 8–9, 11, 19, 21, 25, 26, 34–36, 42–49, 52–55, 57–58, 61, 66, 68, 72, 74, 76–79, 83, 109–10, 127, 189, 199, 224, 240, 241, 243, 245
substance-accident 21
substance ontology 8, 11, 19, 35–36, 42–43, 45, 48–49, 53–55, 58, 72, 76–77, 110, 127, 199, 241, 245
substantive, *substantiell* 14, 46–47, 149, 152, 174, 188–90, 244
suffer(ing) 111, 113, 128, 166, 183, 199, 210, 216, 217, 222, 224, 234–35, 245
superiority 160, 161, 215, 224, 232, 235
surrogate, *Surrogat* 66, 105–6, 143, 116
synthesis *Synthese*, synthetic 55, 64, 66, 67, 110, 143–47, 174

T

taste 3, 108, 122, 123, 158, 199
teleological 137, 164, 211, 242
tensing 232
tension(s) 2, 13, 22, 28, 41, 45, 83, 112–15, 118, 120, 126, 142, 246, 161, 162, 232, 246
    See also *Spannung*
thing(s) 11, 14, 20, 21, 23, 24, 26, 28, 29, 32, 33, 35, 38, 40, 42–44, 46–51, 53, 62, 68, 70, 71, 121, 175, 176, 185–91, 193, 194, 209, 230, 241, 244, 248
threat 84, 86, 89, 94, 95, 104, 106, 107, 133, 157, 159, 220, 221
Thun 31, 71, 229
    See also deed
Todfeindschaft 219
Todkrieg 12, 85, 87, 90, 92, 94, 97, 106
tödten 196, 200, 210, 216
tragic-Dionysian 127, 128

transformation 2, 7, 11, 12, 20, 22, 40, 43–45, 61–62, 69, 77, 82–83, 91, 92, 100–1, 104, 109, 115, 123, 141, 152, 158, 164, 175, 179, 181, 183, 186, 189, 210, 217, 239, 243, 250
translation, translate 6, 43, 53, 58, 61–62, 68–69, 72–73, 77, 153, 163, 174, 176, 179, 181–82, 185–87, 190, 199–201, 203, 223, 227, 229, 250
transvaluation 2, 7, 14, 41, 125, 147, 195–97, 207, 208, 218, 235, 250
   See also Umwertung
Trieb 38, 43, 52, 53, 57, 58, 60, 61, 63, 74, 146, 162, 165, 167–68, 170, 173, 175, 177–78, 182, 201, 214, 226, 229, 236, 246
   See also drive
Triebfeder 3, 138, 139
   See also motive
truth(s) 4, 7, 18, 21, 39, 44, 50, 72, 73, 79, 90, 121, 127, 197, 229
   See also Wahrheit, will to truth
truth-claims 43, 50, 72, 73, 77
Tugend 3, 81, 149, 183, 198, 215, 228, 232
   See also virtue
tyranny, *Tyrannei,* tyrannical 7, 8, 154, 109, 157, 182, 188, 201, 203, 204, 215, 232

U
Übermaass / Übermaaß 90, 130, 165
   See also excess
Übermuth 143–44, 207
Übertragung 38, 51, 71, 73, 91
Überwältigung, Überwältiger 79, 127, 219, 235
Überwindung 143, 125, 129, 130, 132, 142–44, 155
   See also overcoming
uglification, *Verhässlichung* 223, 224, 228
ugly, ugliness 7, 28, 205–8, 211, 213, 219, 222, 223, 247
   See also hässlich
Umschaffung 48, 186, 189, 199, 221
Umwertung/ Umwerthung 2, 7, 14, 125, 195, 207, 218, 235
   See also transvaluation

unequal, *ungleich* 60, 61, 67, 78, 95, 195, 201, 203, 208–10, 213
   See also inequality
ungesellige Geselligkeit *See* unsociable sociability
unicity 64, 68, 76
unique 13, 14, 147, 150, 152, 171, 173, 175, 176, 186, 190, 243–45
unitary 13, 43, 54, 55, 57, 58, 60, 68, 74, 77, 126, 178, 241
unity, unities 9, 41, 42, 55, 56, 58–64, 66–68, 74, 76–78, 94, 111, 114, 143, 144, 146, 153, 165, 166, 168, 174, 175, 177–79, 202
   See also Einheit
universalizability 14, 147, 152, 244
unjust 56, 87, 160, 224
unpleasure, *Unlust* 10, 27, 28, 51, 129–31, 133–38, 150, 179
Unrecht 98, 187, 217, 221, 224, 226
unsociability 13, 83, 151, 154–63, 171, 173, 174, 176, 211, 240
   ungesellige Geselligkeit 3, 13, 28, 151, 153–55
   unsociable sociability 1, 3, 9, 10, 13, 151, 154, 162, 163, 171, 173, 185, 257
unthinkable 10, 23, 50, 134, 204
Ursache 25, 35, 66, 70–72, 75, 134, 137, 138, 142, 162, 213
   See also causality
Urtheil, urtheilen 31, 35, 39, 47, 52, 61, 66, 105, 108, 138, 140, 143, 164, 174, 178, 181, 193, 197, 206, 227

V
valeurs 11, 37
value(s), valued 6, 7, 11, 13, 38–41, 46–48, 66, 68, 72, 73, 78, 82–84, 90, 92, 100, 102, 103, 107, 111, 118–22, 146, 147, 149, 150, 152, 163, 167, 172, 175, 184–85, 199, 202–3, 205, 208, 214, 215, 218–19, 221, 222, 231, 233–36, 239–41, 243–44, 247
   See also Werth
value-oppositions 92, 122, 185
value-transforming 199, 221, 224
vanity 120, 148, 154, 167–68, 207
vanquish 60, 87, 88, 198, 224
vehement 111, 114, 117, 245

Subject Index

vengeance, vengeful 217, 222
    See also Rache
Verachtung, verachten, verächtlich 14, 112, 118, 140, 141, 144, 172, 174, 181, 196, 203–4, 207–8, 210, 213–14, 219, 224, 227, 232, 236
    See also contempt, despise
verdeutlichen 76, 77, 200
verdict 98, 99, 101
Verfeinerung 40, 66, 102, 146, 183
    See also refinement
Verhässlichung See uglification
Vernichtung, Vernichtigung, vernichten 12, 24, 33, 85, 90, 92–93, 97, 101, 103, 106–8, 115, 180, 188, 223, 240, 241
    See also annihilation
Vernichtungskampf 12, 85, 87, 88, 90–92, 94, 95, 99, 195, 239, 240, 247
Vernichtungskrieg 87, 103, 110
Vernichtungslust 200
Vernunft, Vernünftigkeit, vernünftig 11, 40, 79, 88–89, 93, 94, 96, 98, 103, 105, 106, 112, 139, 140, 162, 177–79, 182, 202, 203, 217, 218, 232
Vernunftglaube 96
Verschiedenheit, verschieden 32, 43, 46, 49, 51, 60, 88, 118, 170, 176
    See also diversity
Versöhnlichkeit See forgivingness
verwandt, Verwandtschaft 11, 40, 92, 102, 169, 185, 188, 239
vice(s) 112, 168, 193, 200, 211–14, 221, 222, 228
victory, victor 13, 69, 87–91, 94, 95, 97, 99, 100, 105, 110, 117, 119, 122, 123, 126, 129, 130, 132, 221
    See also Sieg
Vielheit(en) 37, 43, 45, 64, 66, 77, 146, 188
    See also multiplicity
violence 15, 22, 82, 87, 97–102, 109, 111, 211–12, 217, 219, 223, 225, 231, 235, 236, 239, 241, 246–47
    See also Gewalt
virtue(s) 3, 25, 35, 36, 42, 81, 88, 123, 145, 149, 162, 169, 183–84, 197, 198, 200, 207, 215–17, 221, 224, 228, 231, 241, 244
    See also Tugend

vis 25–27, 36, 54, 59, 61, 62, 64, 67, 84–85
    vis viva, vis activa 25–27, 36, 54, 61, 85
    vis inertiae 36, 84–85
Volk, Völker 103–7, 118, 170, 174, 180, 235
    See also people
Völkerbund (league of nations) 116
Völkerrecht (international law) 105–6
Völkerstaat (state of peoples) 105–6, 116
Vollkommenheit 18, 26, 27, 179
    See also perfection
voluntary league of states 116, 117, 123, 242, 243
Vorstellung 31, 70–72, 75

W
wachsen, Wachstum 59, 60, 63, 66–68, 106, 113, 118, 125, 127, 128, 180, 182, 189, 201, 219
    See also growth
Waffenstillstände See ceasefire
Wahrheit(en), wahr 25, 37, 43–44, 47, 50–51, 62, 73, 79, 109, 118, 127, 162, 170, 186, 188, 229
    See also truth
war, warfare 1, 2, 9, 12, 18–19, 31, 34, 37, 45, 78, 81–93, 97, 99–111, 115, 118, 122, 123, 125, 127, 128, 134, 148, 160, 167, 177, 188, 198–200, 203, 206, 207, 210, 211, 215–16, 219, 224, 225, 241
    See also Krieg
warrior 207–8, 215–16
weakness, weak 12, 15, 22, 43, 58–59, 62, 66, 82, 104, 108, 111, 119, 122, 130, 150, 159, 161, 167, 172, 176–77, 201, 203, 206–10, 219, 224, 231, 232–34, 237
weapons 19, 96, 97, 224
Wechsel, wechseln 37, 45, 77, 127, 170, 218, 245
    See also change
wechselseitig 88, 91, 108
well-being 13, 131, 151, 167–68, 171, 173, 174, 183, 185, 190, 211, 240, 243
Welt 27, 33, 34, 37, 39, 43, 44, 47, 48, 52, 55, 56, 58, 61, 62, 70, 74, 89, 146, 153, 199, 225, 228, 233
    See also world

weltbürgerlich See cosmopolitan
Weltrepublik (world republic) 106, 116
Werden 37, 43, 45, 65, 110, 127, 128, 218
 See also becoming
Werth(e), Werthbegriff 38, 40–41, 68, 92, 102, 110, 118, 121, 139, 147, 160, 170, 172, 199, 203, 214, 221, 223, 230, 235–36
 See also value
Wesen 44, 58, 59, 61, 141
 See also essence
Wetteifer 88, 90, 91, 249
Wettkampf 2, 90, 91, 93, 198, 205, 219, 239, 240, 247–49
 See also agon, contest
Wettspiel 2, 91, 119
Wettstreit 2, 201, 203, 208, 219
whole 7, 26, 61, 62, 66, 67, 83, 112, 117, 122, 154, 158, 165, 167, 169–73, 178, 180, 190, 199, 201, 202, 210, 213, 245
Widerspruch, Widersprüchen 2, 20, 21, 37, 38, 43, 45, 49, 78, 105, 113, 146
 See also contradiction, logical opposition
Widerstand, widerstehen 12, 52, 91, 96, 108, 125–30, 132, 139–45, 155, 191–93, 210
 See also resistance
Widerstreit 33, 82, 103, 162, 177, 234
will, *Wille, wollen* 2, 6, 10, 11, 13, 15, 19, 22, 29, 34, 40–44, 46, 55–57, 59, 63, 64, 67–75, 76, 78–79, 82, 85, 90, 102, 108, 111, 116, 121, 126–30, 133–35, 137–49, 154, 162, 164, 179, 186, 188, 192, 199–203, 212–13, 217–19, 221, 223, 224, 228–29, 233, 235–37
will to pleasure 127–28, 134
will(s) to power, *Wille zur Macht* 1–2, 8, 8, 10–11, 15, 19, 29, 33, 41–44, 46, 55, 57, 59, 62, 69–70, 72, 76, 78, 82, 111, 121, 126, 129–30, 134, 135, 137, 143, 162, 164, 176, 199–203, 212, 219, 221, 229, 236–37, 247
will to truth, *Wille zur Wahrheit* 73, 79, 127
Willensakt 68, 72, 75
Willenskraft, will-power 72, 74, 75, 77, 78
Willkür 71, 162, 217, 221
Wirkung See effect
Wissenschaft 9, 70, 71, 112, 150, 190
 See also science
world 4, 11, 12, 18–20, 26, 28, 30, 32–34, 36, 37, 39, 43, 44, 47–50, 55–58, 61, 62, 65, 70, 74, 75, 77, 79, 89, 93, 94, 105, 106, 112, 116, 122, 145, 152, 153, 164, 176, 188, 199, 206, 209, 219, 223, 225, 228, 233, 239
 See also Welt
world-negation 207, 223
world republic *See Weltrepublik*
worldly 7, 86, 89, 103
worth 29, 84, 117, 138, 139, 147, 157, 158, 160, 210, 214, 220, 223, 247

Z

zero 22, 24, 28, 31, 34, 39, 48, 85
zero-sum game 15, 223, 236
zerstören, Zerstörung 9, 91, 127, 165–66, 179, 200, 217, 226
Zerstörungsdynamik 200, 210, 223, 225
Zorn 200, 216, 220–22, 230, 233, 234
 See also anger
Zurückstoßung 25, 58, 69, 162
 See also repulsion
Zwang 71, 74, 98, 102, 104, 105, 107, 141, 145, 211
 See also coercion
Zwangsgesetze 103, 105, 106, 211
Zweck(e) 103, 155, 170, 178–79, 214, 220, 222, 226, 229, 234, 249
 See also purpose
Zwiespalt 2, 170, 173, 176–77
Zwietracht 2, 108, 245
Zwist 2

www.ingramcontent.com/pod-product-compliance
Lightning Source LLC
Chambersburg PA
CBHW071808300426
44116CB00009B/1239